BARON LAHONTAN'S MYSTERIOUS QUEST

A Reappraisal of the 1688 Long/Platte River Inland Passage Expedition

Louis-Armand, Baron de Lahontan was a French artistocrat, writer, and explorer who served in the French military in Canada.

BARON LAHONTAN'S MYSTERIOUS QUEST

A Reappraisal of the 1688 Long/Platte River Inland Passage Expedition

Steven G. Baker, W. Raymond Wood, George W. Gill,
and Claude J. Fouillade, Translator

Edited with a Foreword by Rick Hendricks

Sunstone books may be purchased for educational, business, or sales promotional use.
For information please write: Special Markets Department, Sunstone Press,
P.O. Box 2321, Santa Fe, New Mexico 87504-2321.
Printed on acid-free paper

Library of Congress Cataloging-in-Publication Data

Names: Baker, Steven G. author | Wood, W. Raymond author | Gill, George W. author | Fouillade, Claude J. translator | Hendricks, Rick, 1956- editor

Title: Baron Lahontan's mysterious quest : a reappraisal of the 1688 Long/Platte River inland passage expedition / Steven G. Baker, W. Raymond Wood, George W. Gill, and Claude J. Fouillade, translator ; edited with a new forward by Rick Hendricks.
Description: Santa Fe, NM : Sunstone Press, 2025. | Includes bibliographical references and index. | Summary: "Baron Lahontan's mysterious 1688 Long/Platte River inland passage quest reappraised"-- Provided by publisher.
Identifiers: LCCN 2025003544 | ISBN 9781632937131 paperback
Subjects: LCSH: Lahontan, baron de, 1666-1716 | Platte River (Neb.)--Discovery and exploration
Classification: LCC F672.P6 B35 2025 | DDC 978.2--dc23/eng/20250403

LC record available at https://lccn.loc.gov/2025003544

WWW.SUNSTONEPRESS.COM
SUNSTONE PRESS / POST OFFICE BOX 2321 / SANTA FE, NM 87504-2321 /USA
(505) 988-4418

DEDICATION

Dedicated to the memory of you "Darce" (Louis Armand, le Baron de Lahontan et Heslèche, a French aristocrat, writer, and explorer who served in the French military in Canada) and all of the other ancient adventurers who bravely explored unknown regions of the New World; and particularly, to those who left no records of their accomplishments; or those who did, and may have had them diminished by those who had not, unlike you claimed so long ago, had the privilege of beholding or even imagining what existed out in the still pristine human and geographical landscapes of an unspoiled continent.

And to those who were called from the team way too early: W. Raymond Wood, PhD (1931–2020), Emeritus Professor of Anthropology, University of Missouri and Claude Jean Fouillade, PhD (1946–2020), Emeritus Professor of French, New Mexico State University

—From Steven G. Baker and George W. Gill

CONTENTS

• FOREWORD •

In 1688 and 1689, Louis-Armand de Lahontan d'Arce, the Baron de Lahontan, embarked on an intrepid search for an inland waterway through the North American heartland, a passage to the Pacific Ocean, which would open a route to Asia. He departed from Michilimackinac on Lake Huron to the Platte River, penetrating the Great Plains almost as far as the Rockies. In so doing, Lahontan likely became the first European to explore that vast region. That, at least that is what Steven Baker, George W. Gill, and W. Raymond Wood set out to prove in this extraordinary example of scholarly revisionism. Historical revisionism is defined as "the reinterpretation of a historical account or narrative based on actual facts and authenticated evidence." This definition is perfectly applicable more broadly to other disciplines, and in the case of Lahontan's Mysterious 1688 Long/Platte River Inland Passage Quest, the authors have applied a revisionist lens to anthropology, archaeology, ethnohistory, physical geography, and translations from the French to name only some of the scholarly fields involved in this extensive reexamination of Lahontan's narrative. They have ferreted out the actual facts and authenticated evidence to a fare-the-well.

As will become apparent as one reads this book, Lahontan's narrative has never really been given any credence, a point the authors demonstrate with numerous examples. The rather complete dismissal of his account as mere fiction or even a lie derives from two main sources: his maps and narrative are one problem, and a second problem is a very incomplete understanding of the many cultural groups Lahontan encountered in his travels, a sort of anthropological ignorance that characterized most of his earliest critics, many of whom were otherwise towering figures in North American scholarship in the nineteenth century.

Although the authors go to exhaustive lengths to explain the errors in his maps and the misreading of parts of his narrative—and some of the rich details are quite delicious—the essence of their defense of Lahontan is fairly simple. He intentionally misled would-be readers of his work in order to keep anyone else from claiming the reward and renown that would redound to the benefit of discoverer of the inland passage.

The other main source of condemnation of Lahontan and his work was also fairly simple. Knowledge of Native cultures, particularly of Mississippian, Plains, and of the peoples of the mountain west was in its infancy in the nineteenth century. In subsequent decades a wealth of information has been developed. The authors of this book apply this new information to great effect in annotating Lahontan's narrative. They rightly point out that his work is truly pioneering anthropology and ethnohistory.

From the standpoint of Southwestern history, which is my area of specialization, this book makes two very significant contributions. First, it demonstrates the way in which Lahontan transmitted knowledge to the French of the people and places he encountered on his way to the Platte and beyond, quite literally blazing the way for further French penetration into the upper Midwest, which posed an existential threat to Spanish imperial defense and its colonies, particularly New Mexico. Second, Lahontan corroborates the existence of bearded Indians in the region of the Great Salt Lake. Discovering the nature of these people was something of an obsession for Spanish authorities because their existence suggested the possibility that they were somehow related to the presence of rival Europeans in Spanish territories. This is a topic Baker has explored in our earlier collaboration on the journals of the expeditions of Juan Rivera in 1765.

The work of Baker, Gill, and Wood deserves to be widely read as a major re-envisioning of the history of North America in the late seventeenth century. Acceptance may be slow in coming given the enormous number of negative views of Lahontan that have been expressed over the years when he has not been summarily dismissed and forgotten. If, however, acceptance does come, then Lahontan may take his rightful place in the pantheon of great explorers of North America, and the authors will receive due credit for making his achievements known and appreciated.

—Rick Hendricks, Santa Fe, New Mexico

• PREFACE •

It was simple serendipity that provided me and my co-authors this opportunity to solve a still important three-hundred-year-old major and mysterious "cold case" in the history of North American discovery. Because of the availability of very newly discovered Spanish historical documentation, this study is offered as resolution of the long-standing mystery of one such very exceptional, and generally discredited and overlooked account of New World exploration and descriptions of its Native peoples. That account is of the French Baron Lahontan's claimed exploration of the "Long River" which, we believe we have credibly demonstrated to have been Nebraska's Platte as well as the lower Missouri Rivers.[1] Because the account was written by a genius who was so far ahead of the general thinking of his pre-Enlightenment era regarding the American Native, it has long been discounted by scholars and not included in bibliographies and literature of these peoples. Because Lahontan's account, as the first of the Platte River and its then seemingly improbable Mississippian Native cultures, is an extremely rare one among the vast literature of the American Natives, it is still highly pertinent to today's scholarly understandings of what were then still literally "Stone Age" people and the very terminus of Great Plains prehistory. Lahontan was both the first and the last European to observe and write about them. This reappraisal is the only place where, to date, one can learn where Lahontan traveled and who the strangely named Natives that he met were in relation to today's historically better-known tribes and nations.

At more than 2,500 miles by canoe, Lahontan's monumental attempt to find an inland passage to the Pacific Ocean was a most major voyage. It ranks very high among others involving searches for that mythical passage, including the so well-memorialized travels of Lewis and Clark, Mackay and Evans, and the early French efforts of Father Marquette and his companion, Jolliet, as well as the famed La Salle and his company in their early explorations of the Mississippi River.[2]

As recounted herein, Lahontan's early inland search, which has never been understood or credited by historians for its positive contributions, was carried out in 1688–1689. In 1703 Lahontan, by then only a former young officer in France's Ministry of the Marine, published a book in which he described how he had in those years canoed southwest from the Great Lakes in Canada and far up a mysterious "Long River."This was in the remote then unexplored regions far west beyond the "Father of Waters" as the Mississippi River has at times been known.[3]

Lahontan left what by modern standards of ethnological knowledge, appears to have been a highly credible narrative of his observations made during his early remarkable travels among some Native peoples of North America's central Great Plains. That account has, unfortunately, probably to date been the most controversial and doubted one in the entire history of inland North American discovery.[4] Unfortunately, due to strong, long-lasting, uninformed, racist and critical early denouncements that it was likely only a fictitious journey, the baron's narrative has remained shrouded in mystery. This has precluded him from being acknowledged, as he seemingly should have been, as one of the truly great explorers of the New World. The present accounting of the baron's trip pulls the shrouds from the mystery surrounding it and robustly demonstrates its veracity. Important historians, such as Rueben Gold Thwaites and Stephen Butler Leacock have opined that Lahontan's thinking was far ahead of his peers and that it was well advanced beyond the norms of the "play book" for travel accounts of his period.[5] This, together with their lack of the supporting Spanish documentation, has persisted to this day and precluded other scholars from resolving the puzzle of Lahontan's account.

The denouncements of the baron's Long River narrative, but not his multitude of other observations about the colony of New France, have been so wide-spread and long-lasting that the notion that he lied about it has essentially come to be perceived as historical "fact" among students of history.[6] This makes the baron's account much different than a newly discovered travel narrative which would have no or little history of near universal condemnation traveling through time with it. This situation demanded that all the old negative, though near entirely unfounded, criticisms that led to formation of that so-called "fact" be exposed. There are just so many of them published that there is no way that many readers can readily judge this interpretation of the Long River narrative as authentic until they have closely read this reappraisal and come to understand how badly Lahontan's critics erred in most of their widely disseminated criticisms. These major criticisms are, therefore, discussed herein as individual case studies along with the authors' explications of the narrative itself. The intent is to demonstrate just how wrong his critics were and to free the baron from those that made him out to be a liar as a "fact" of history. This in turn deepens the time frame of ethnological knowledge regarding the Natives he met, including the Pawnee, Plains Apache, and the heavily bearded presumably Numic speakers from the vicinity of the Great Salt Lake.

There are three major stories involved in Lahontan's Long River narrative. The first is the actual narrative which, as presented herein, speaks for itself when allowed to with informed anthropological interpretation and without negative prejudgment. The second is the great underlying historiographic "backstory" of how historians over time have been so barren in their own anthropological knowledge and racist philosophical mindsets that they have not been able to comprehend the narrative and then diminished the baron's contributions. This has led to his being cast as one of the greatest of all world history's "travel liars."[7] The reality of this judgement threads through all aspects of the present study. It is an excellent example for teaching how historiography has evolved and has so soundly been influenced by culture, racism, and the climate of popular opinions of various past times, particularly of the much earlier ones such as those which involved critiques of Lahontan.[8] The third is how and why he so cunningly used a great deception to mislead his readers relative to the location of the Long River. That was foremost what led his critics to denounce him and added to the mystery of his narrative.

To present all these stories, this study introduces the baron and establishes the context for this new interpretation of his Long River narrative. It then presents a direct transcription of the baron's narrative and directly associated information on where he traveled and what he witnessed. The erroneous interpretations which led to the near wholesale denouncement of the narrative are discussed individually. A case study of the great deception or feint regarding the river's location which the baron implemented in his narrative is explained in the final chapter.

Lewis and Clark's famed search (1803 to 1806) for an inland water passage to the Pacific Ocean is one of the most deeply enshrined stories in the popular history of North American exploration and discovery.[9] Despite their intrepid travels, which took them all the way across the Great Plains to the Rocky Mountain headwaters of the Missouri River and on westward to the Pacific, these Americans never found that so heartily sought, yet non-existent, shortcut route toward Asia. Theirs was probably the longest, primarily water-borne, expedition of discovery ever completed in the lower forty-eight states and seemingly one of the only ones which surpassed that of the young Baron Lahontan. There are, however, numerous other true and important accounts of much earlier and classic attempts to locate such an important passage. These were most notably by the Spanish, such as with the voyages of Christopher Columbus and, surprisingly, even Coronado's overland travels in the early sixteenth century; as well as by the French from New France on multiple occasions.[10]

The major issues concerning the baron's expedition are reappraised herein and readily verify his Long River narrative. These include extremely critical ones that have never been mentioned, let alone explained, by his many detractors. These issues pose questions: 1) what river did he really explore and describe; or 2) did he make the trip and explore a river; 3) and, if so, why and how did he so inaccurately map its geographic position; and 4) finally, were the Natives he said he encountered as strange, exotic, and unbelievable in their behaviors as his critics have for so long charged? We, the authors, believe we have found the answers to all these enduring questions.

Since its inception this study has had two primary goals. The first was to answer the above questions and to test the past major criticisms of Lahontan's narrative to see if they have any veracity and, thereby, judge them to see if scholars should let them remain unchallenged. The second has been dependent on the outcome of the first one. If the baron's narrative were found to be as fraudulent, as his critics have for so long emphasized, then those opinions could be reinforced from modern scholarly perspectives. If, on the other hand, the old negative critiques proved to be suspect and without merit, as they are believed to have been, then the narrative could be recast as a major, authentic, and very early ethnographic study of American Natives. Such a positive conclusion should certainly lead, as it is believed to do, to Lahontan's elevation to the status of one of the truly important explorers of the New World.

As written by Lahontan, most of his narrative descriptions, but not his locational mapping and the text directly supporting it, demonstrate that the trip he claimed to have made involved canoe travel deep into the wild *tierra incognita* of the central Great Plains.[11] Only recently discovered and absolutely impeccable Spanish colonial documents and other ethnographic information have proven that much of what the baron observed about seemingly exotic Natives was true. This includes critical descriptions that were the butt of much criticism by nineteenth-century scholars that were uninformed about late prehistoric Native societies as well as the geography of the regions Lahontan explored.[12] They also help to demonstrate that the regions he described included the lower Missouri River and especially the Platte River in what is now Nebraska.

In the 1980s I began, in collaboration with Professor Emeritus, Donald C. Cutter, of the Department of History at the University of New Mexico, interpreting and writing on Juan Rivera's northward travels of 1765 from New Mexico toward the Land of *Teguayo* and its mysterious heavily bearded Natives who were said to look like Europeans. Such strange-looking Natives were finally encountered and described by Fathers Domínguez and Vélez de Escalante in 1776 from near the Great Salt Lake. This was in exactly the same general region that Lahontan had described as their home when he much earlier encountered some of these same peoples' presumed ancestors.[13] From the time many years ago when I first read the account of these Spanish Franciscans, I had pondered on who these people could have been as they fit no descriptions of America's Natives I was familiar with as a North American archaeologist. While doing the trail study with Professor Cutter I accidentally became familiar with Lahontan's Long River narrative and his description of the bearded men from near the Great Salt Lake whom the fathers finally met.

I quickly recognized that the newly discovered Spanish documents I was dealing with, along with those of the fathers, were also relevant to Lahontan's narrative. They indicated that they might confirm the veracity of his long and vehemently discredited account, including his travel route and destination. It was apparent that I had accidentally found keys that might unlock the so long-held secrets of his potentially very important Long River narrative so that its veracity might be judged anew. I recognized how they might make it possible to bury for good the old and, what I initially suspected to be, unjustified criticisms of it. I knew that it might be possible to help to establish his reputation as a very intelligent and reliable ethnographic observer, just as he was otherwise known to have been, rather than just a fabricator regarding only the Long River.

Following my purely chance discovery, I delivered a few professional papers on the subject.[14] Although by then I knew the baron's narrative indicated he had ended his trip on the Platte River, I had not yet published that information or worked out or tested most of the other key details of his travels and observations. In 2005 I invited Dr. W. Raymond Wood of the University of Missouri to Montrose, Colorado, to speak to our local archaeological society. During his stay with Nancy and me, I was visiting with him about my then pending volume on Juan Rivera. I mentioned the information that I had discovered relative to the baron's Long River narrative and how I believed it involved the Platte River.

Taking on a distinctly senior professorial tone, Wood set down his glass of bourbon, straightened up in his chair, looked me square in the eye, and emphatically admonished me "to forget it!" He was adamant that one could not rely on anything that the baron claimed he observed on that supposed trip and that all Plains archaeologists and ethnohistorians considered his narrative to have been fabricated, just as the historians had long believed.[15]

I then showed him my confirming evidence from the Spanish sources and his thinking on the matter abruptly changed! Though he was unsure of just where it might lead us, one of America's senior Great Plains and renowned archaeologists and ethnohistorians was convinced that I was on to something of exceptional importance and was willing to work with me to better understand it and publish about it.[16] He stressed, however, that his participation would be predicated on my assumption of the role of principal investigator and taking responsibility for the bulk of the research and writing. To ensure his participation, I of course agreed to do so.

Wood and I readily agreed that Lahontan had either witnessed what he said he did nearly one-hundred years prior to the creation of the confirming Spanish documents or else had obtained extraordinarily good, essentially unbelievably/impossibly accurate, detailed intelligence from another educated source(s). We thought that, even if we had no clue where he could have obtained it from another source in the descriptive form of educated and advanced natural history writing it was cast in at that early time.

Wood and I were in total agreement that the baron was describing the Platte in Nebraska and that the kinds of information he recorded could certainly not have originated with Natives or uneducated *Coureur de Bois*. Lahontan's descriptions fit the Platte entirely too well and there were simply no other possible choices for rivers that even remotely did so. The Platte and it's so-historically prominent valley was a region known to us both, as children of the central Plains, and one where there had been no known or even likely European penetration, even by Coureur de Bois, prior to the time Lahontan claimed to have arrived there in the winter of 1688.[17] Passages in the baron's narrative describing the Natives' surprised reactions to the French company's sudden appearance among them support this view. The Mississippi River was even then still only barely becoming known while no European was known to have even traveled any significant distance up the Missouri.[18]

Wood and I agreed to undertake this study which would reappraise the veracity of the entire narrative of the baron's Long River expedition. We also agreed that we would take a completely different vantage point than his past reviewers by not forejudging the question about his having made the trip or not. Until we found sound reasons to believe otherwise, we would accord the baron credibility and work from the presumption that his account was authentic. We simply had to figure out the nature of its mystery! While we would work to bring all our professional skills to understand the involved issues from such a perspective, we would proceed cautiously with the highest possible levels of scholarly diligence and unbiased testing.

Wood and I subsequently presented a two-part symposium on the baron's travels at the Plains Anthropological Conference in Topeka, Kansas, in 2006.[19] Wood's emphasis there was only on a re-examination of the baron's mapping, the most damning and justified of the past criticisms of his narrative. Wood's paper was, however, prepared long before I had completed my analysis of the entire narrative and all the key evidence discussed herein. Although he, as the senior scholar, read and approved our joint writings on the ethnography and archaeology, he never did delve any deeper into the matter prior to his decline and death in 2020.

Notable among these latter findings was my determination and agreement with most other writers that the baron was seeking an inland passage. Further, I came to realize that he intentionally mislocated the Long River on his maps and via his relative supporting text in order to deceive his readers, and possible competitors who might also seek it, into believing that it was not the Missouri but some other river. At that 2006 Topeka meeting I, however, only spoke about the comparative evidence on the Caucasian-looking bearded men of Teguayo and Mozeemlek from Utah and how it demonstrated that the baron had accurately described a real but highly unusual population as well as seemingly ended his claimed trip on the Platte.

Following our joint 2006 presentation I continued to speak about the baron and his Long River via regional professional venues.[20] I was so deeply absorbed in completing the substantive project on the highly relevant Rivera expeditions toward the Land of Teguayo, however, that I could not meaningfully follow up on our collaboration until 2016.[21] In the meantime, Wood had published a slightly revised version of his Plains Conference paper on the web.[22] Although he was then stepping more fully into retirement, Wood wanted to stay on the project and continued to read what I was writing and to advise and discuss it with me. Portions of his original online paper were folded into chapter 15 and his thoughts dealing with archaeology and ethnohistory on which we further collaborated are woven throughout this volume.

Wood entered an assisted living facility in 2020 and was no longer able to participate with me. He died in September of that year. This deprived our project of his further great wisdom and experience in Plains and Missouri River studies. As the primary writer of this collaborative volume, I am thus left responsible for most of the outcome(s). Claude Fouillade handled most of the translation issues, while George Gill took primary responsibility for dealing with the biological anthropology and the bearded, presumably Ute-speaking, men of Teguayo and Mozeemlek. Wood had closely followed my earlier work on that subject and was most interested in and approving of the treatment given it herein.

Although I believe that Lahontan made the trip, from the time that he published his on-line study until his death, because of the baron's mapping of the location of the Long River, Wood, in his exact words to me, considered it only a "most likely probability." He encouraged me to continue testing to try to prove it and I have done so. We always agreed that the baron was accurately describing the Platte as well as the Pawnees and Plains Apaches who lived along it.

Wood's latent hesitancy was only because the baron's mapping was not remotely accurate for any river known to exist in the location he showed.[23] Wood was a trusting man; he simply could not imagine that any explorer would not attempt to accurately map his travels or would overtly attempt to mislead anyone as to where he had traveled. It appears that he never considered the possibility that the baron might have been worried about competitors also in search of the inland passage and relied on an intentional deception as an ages-old means of leading them away from his own target and trail. Once we had established the fact that the baron had ended up on the Platte, however, the patterning in this complex feint became obvious. Once the baron's intentionally inaccurate location of the Long River is understood, there is simply no sound evidence within which a denial can reasonably be rooted. As emphasized herein, the fact that Lahontan simply had to have intentionally mislocated the Long River, does not demonstrate that he did not make the trip as some have claimed. These are two entirely separate matters and must always be treated as such.

At the start of the project, I was convinced that we needed to know just how good the baron's original English translation had been. Could a poorly rendered translation of 1703 have been the source of some of the questions raised by the critics? I thus enlisted the assistance of Dr. Claude J. Fouillade, Emeritus Professor of French, from the Department of Languages and Linguistics at New Mexico State University. He prepared a new English translation of the baron's original 1703 French narrative for comparison and testing against the first English translation.[24]

Just as I was beginning to finalize this manuscript in 2020, Fouillade died following extended illness before we could discuss many remaining issues relative to the emerging interpretations.[25] Due to his inability to speak for and finalize his own work, I felt I could not publish his new translation and fell back on that of the baron. In order to help us, Dr. John P. Wilson, an anthropologist and historian from Las Cruces, New Mexico, independently completed another translation of some of the baron's narrative for further comparison with the original 1703 translation and with Fouillade's.[26] Both of the new translations demonstrated that the original one had been quite competently done, particularly for someone who was probably English and had likely never even visited North America.

Dr. George W. Gill, Emeritus Professor of anthropology from the University of Wyoming, was also invited to join the project. Gill is a noted physical anthropologist who has worked extensively with ancient skeletons of American Natives which, like the highly publicized Kennewick Man, are thought to exhibit Caucasian-looking physiognomic (facial skeletal) traits that are unlike those more typically found in other presumed and more stereotypical American Native populations.[27] As detailed in chapter 11, Gill and some of his colleagues, namely those who are yet even familiar with them, believe that the bearded men of both the Rivera and Lahontan accounts, as well as those of Fathers Domínguez and Vélez de Escalante and others, may well descend from these or similar ancient populations.[28]

Completion of this project thus primarily involved me with assistance from only the small team working quietly for some years on a subject that has not been thoughtfully revisited in "modern times," and apparently never in-depth by ethnohistorians and archaeologists who know the central Plains and their Native ethnography.[29] Since it has been so long since the baron's narrative was starting to be denounced, and the fact that the documents confirming portions of it were only very recently recognized, few of this author's other contemporaries have, despite its importance, bothered to study it afresh and have never challenged the old criticisms and assumptions about it. For these reasons individuals who were truly knowledgeable about the baron's narrative, New France, the Natives, and geography of the Platte River and could effectively collaborate with us have been in notably short supply. Additionally, except for this tome and the recent publication of *Juan Rivera's Colorado:1765...*, I appear to have remained the only one who has seen, or at least recognized and attempted to tie together, all the Spanish evidence that confirmed so much of what Lahontan had to say.

I am hopeful that my colleagues in the study of the past, whether anthropologists, historians, historical cartographers, or students of French literature, will take the time to thoughtfully reconsider Lahontan's Long River narrative in the light of the evidence presented herein and, if they believe it, help in the promotion of his reputation. That will obviously take a great many years since a lone revisionist account will take much time to swim the oceans and seep into all the nooks and crannies of scholarship into which the negativism has so deeply settled over the past centuries.

I believe the entire Lahontan team is honored that "old mother serendipity" has seen fit to provide the opportunity to help in casting a new and hopefully more positive light on Lahontan's reputation and adding an informative, new, and important chapter to the early history of discovery and ethnography of the United States and Canada and their ancient peoples, including those hardy colonials of early New France.

Steven G. Baker. BA, MA
The Centuries Study Group
Centuries Research, Inc.
Montrose, Colorado
January 19, 2024

Notes:

1. Lahontan, *New Voyages*, 166-215.

2. Marquette, *Father Marquette's Journal*, *Voyages of Marquette*; Parkman, *France and England*; Norall, *Bourgmont*. e.g. Crouse, *In Quest of.* Lavender, *Way to the Western Sea*. Moulton, *Journals of Lewis and Clark.* Nastir and Ronda, *Before Lewis and Clark.* Wood, *Prologue to Lewis and Clark.*

3. Though they provide no reference for it, it has been said that the Mississippi River was once seemingly known to Algonquian-speaking Native Americans as the "Father of Waters." Shaffer and Tigges, *Mississippi River,* 1. In his thoughtful consideration of Lahontan's narrative, the famous Canadian writer, Stephen Leacock, also referred to the Mississippi River as the "Father of Waters" but he also gave no reference for the term. Leacock, *Lahontan in Minnesota*, 367. E.g. du Pratz, *History of Louisana.* Klinkenberg, *American Icon.*

4. Lahontan, *Nouveaux Voyages*. *New Voyages*.

5. Thwaites, "Introduction," xlvii. Leacock, "Lahontan in Minnesota."

6. Leacock.

7. e.g. Adams, *Travelers and Travel Liars*.

8. e.g. Skotheim, *The Historian and the Climate...;* Freed, *Anthropology.*

9. e.g. Crouse, *In Quest of.* Lavender, *Way to the Western Sea*. Moulton, *Journals of Lewis and Clark.* Nastir and Ronda, *Before Lewis and Clark.* Wood, *Prologue to Lewis and Clark.*

10. e.g. Flint and Flint, *The Coronado Expedition*; Crouse, *In Quest*. Heindenreich, *Early French Explorartion.* Norall, *Bourgmont.*

11. Lahontan, *New Voyages* original English edition of 1703. Lahontan, *New Voyages*, 1905 English reprint.

12. Baker, et al., *Juan Rivera's Colorado*. Chávez and Warner, *The Domínguez and Escalante Expedition*. Bolton, *Pageant*.

13. Baker, et al., *Juan Rivera's Colorado.* Chávez and Warner, *The Domínguez and Escalante Expedition*. Bolton, *Pageant*.

14. Baker, "Ethnographic Evidence of a Di-Hybrid;" "The Bearded Utes." "Spanish Documentary." "The Baron Lahontan's."

15. Raymond Wood personally explained to Steven Baker how the noted ethnohistorian and archaeologist, Mildred Mott Wedel (1912–1995), who specialized in Great Plains studies (*http://plaza.las.iastate.edu/directory/mildred-mott-wedel/* accessed March 29, 2022), had early in her career looked into the baron's Long River narrative and considered it a complete falsehood. Although he could not recall that she had ever published on that view, he respected her opinion and this led him to for a time to accept a very negative view of the narrative. Baker was further informed via a personal communication in December 2020 from Richard Krause, another noted Plains archaeologist and close friend and colleague of Wood, that this information was conveyed in informal remarks made by Wedel following a paper regarding historical method which Wood read before the Plains Anthropological Conference in 1961. Wood, *A White Bearded*, 307. Wood, however, recovered from his initial opinion and cast that view away once shown the Spanish documentation that so well demonstrated that the baron was accurate in his most critical and commonly denounced descriptions of Native Americans and particularly for those from the lands of Mozeemlek and Tahuglauk near the Great Salt Lake. Although it has not been possible to find anything she published on the subject, Mildred Wedel was an influential voice in Plains archaeology and ethnology for decades and was likely the source behind so many of her colleagues' negative views of the Lahontan's narrative.

16. Wood, *A White Bearded*. *Columbia Daily Tribune*, "W. Raymond Wood."

17. Raymond Wood was raised in Nebraska. Steven Baker grew up in northeastern Kansas not too far from the Platte River and began his professional archaeological career on the central Plains. Thus, after initial readings of the baron's narrative, it was readily apparent to both Wood and Baker that he was either on or writing about the Platte. In combination with the Spanish information in the 2015 Juan Rivera accounting, Baker et al., *Juan Rivera's Colorado...,* both the ethnography and geography described in the baron's account made it relatively easy to understand that point. Although that much was clear, it was difficult to come to understand how he arrived there because of the deception he built into his account regarding the direction that he traveled after arriving on the Mississippi.

18. Lahontan, *New Voyages*, 166-215.e.g. Wood, "Ethno-History and...".

19. Baker and Wood, "Reconsidering the Authenticity. Parts 1 & 2." " Baker, "Spanish Documentary Confirmation." Wood, "A Review of Past Criticisms."

20. Baker, "The Baron Lahontan's 1688–1689," "Ethnographic Evidence of a Di-Hybrid;" "The Bearded Utes." "Spanish Documentary." "The Baron Lahontan's."

21. Baker et. al., *Juan Rivera's Colorado,* 13-34.

22. Wood, "A Review of Past Criticisms."

23. Wood, "A Review of Past Criticisms."

24. Fouillade, "A New English Translation."

25. *Las Cruces Sun News*, "Claude Jean Fouillade."

26. Wilson, "A New English Translation."

27. Owsley and Jantz, *Kennewick Man*.

28. Baker et al., *Juan Rivera's Colorado*. Bolton, *Pageant*. Chávez and Warner, *The Domínguez-Escalante Journal.* Baker, "Ethnographic Evidence." "Spanish Documentary." "Evidence of a Di-Hybrid." "The Bearded Utes." "The Baron Lahontan's."

29. Examples include: Adams. Towle and George A. Rawlyk.

• ACKNOWLEDGEMENTS •

I am grateful to my co-authors for bringing their critical skills to assist in this admittedly difficult and obviously extremely revisionist study. It is my aspiration that our joint efforts, as well as those of Lahontan himself, may bring us all great pride. I thank my friend and occasional assistant, Dorothy Causey and my longtime artist, Gail Carroll Sargent, who completed a bit of the key artwork herein. Nancy Lamm completed the computer-generated maps while. Rod Rasmussen again assisted me with my computer issues. Others who assisted the project were: Marcel Mousette and Réal Ouellet of Laval University in Montreal, the latter a leading scholar of Lahontan and French literature; Debbie Dodero of the Inter-library Loan staff, Montrose Public Library; David Kessler, Bancroft Library; René Chartrand, Muséoplume Inc., Gatineau, Quebec; Dale Henning, an archaeologist from West Des Moines, Iowa; Brother Patrick McSherry of the Capuchin Provincial Archives in Detroit; Dirk dePagter, dePagter Collection, Telluride, Colorado; and the late Robert S. Weddle of Bonham, Texas.

Jeremy Ward and other staff of the Canadian Canoe Museum in Peterborough, Ontario, shared information as did Patricia LaBounty of the Union Pacific Railroad Museum in Council Bluffs. Others who assisted were Gary Krapu and Dave Brandt of the Northern Prairie Wildlife Research Center of the USGS, William Iseminger of Cahokia Mounds State Historic Site in Illinois, and Stephen Veit of Grand Portage National Park. Professor of Anthropology, Ian Brown, at the University of Alabama graciously read and commented on portions of the manuscript. Professor José António Brandão of the Department of History, Western Michigan University and director of the Michilimackinac Papers Project, was of critical assistance in this project. He shared information, recommended important source materials, and encouraged and befriended me. I am deeply indebted to him.

Others who assisted me were historian Dennis Reinhartz, now of Santa Fe, who helped with cartographic history. Geologist, Jim Swinehart, formerly of the University of Nebraska, provided important information on the ephemeral lakes that are thought to have formed along the Platte River. These are relevant to the baron's poorly understood Lake of the Apaches shown on the map of 1699 attributed to him. Tom Tiesen, formerly of the National Park Service, Lincoln, Nebraska; E. Steve Cassells, Cheyenne Community College; and others, including my ever-patient wife, Nancy Ellen, have also been most helpful. Thanks also to John Wilson of Las Cruces, New Mexico for his ongoing encouragement and help in translating. As usual, my close friend and colleague, historian and editorial consultant Rick Hendricks, provided sage advice in preparing this volume.

Steven G. Baker
Montrose, Colorado
April 25, 2024

• List of Illustrations •

1

• LAHONTAN'S LONG RIVER PUZZLE •

by

STEVEN G. BAKER

This volume reappraises one of the most long-standing and puzzling mysteries of early inland North American historical discovery; namely the French Baron Lahontan's narrative of his Long River exploration of 1688–1689. His lengthy canoe trip, in an unsuccessful search for an inland passage to the Pacific Ocean, took him from "old" Michilimackinac near St. Ignace on Lake Huron in Canada all the way to the Platte River in Nebraska. He continued westward on the Platte far out onto the Great Plains almost to the Rocky Mountains. (Figure 1). No European is known to have visited that region before him. He said he claimed it for France and erected a monument along the river as testimony to that event.

The baron was a bright and ever inquisitive young French marine officer who could make major contributions to the history of colonial New France and the initial exploration of the central Plains while simultaneously making rash and very consequential mistakes. These youthful missteps helped lead historians to cast him as little more than an infidel and liar, especially with respect to his Long River narrative which he published in 1703. His personal errors have kept him, as it today appears he should have been, from being considered one of the more important participants in New France's early exploration of inland North America.

Not only did Lahontan come to challenge the authority of the French Crown, he was also audaciously outspoken against the then powerful Jesuits and is said to have slandered the character of those French women who became the colonial mothers of New France. To cap it all off, he blatantly lied about the location of the Long River; seemingly as a great deceptive feint to help protect his potential for further exploring it and finding an inland passage as he very clearly did propose. Other self-destructive matters finally led him to desert from his king's service and become an exile from the French realm. These, together with his feint, also resulted in having his Long River narrative deemed fictitious as a historical "fact" at the highest levels of Canadian and American scholarship where it has remained until this writing.

The Puzzling Long River Narrative

The mystery of Lahontan's Long River narrative arose from the difficulty critics, of whom many of the most important ones were products of the Victorian Era and quite ethnocentrically biased in their outlooks, encountered in trying to confirm whether he even made the trip as he claimed. Although much of the narrative appeared to be authentic, no one has ever before convincingly equated the Long River, as the baron mapped and wrote about its location (Figure 2), with any existing river. Through the years his critics have also found it difficult to believe that his descriptions of what seemed to be unrealistic and exotic Native Americans were accurate accounts of real people. These are the primary reasons why Lahontan's narrative has remained such an enigma. The nature and extent of these problems with his narrative are exemplified in the following quote from the noted historian, Bernard DeVoto (1897-1955). The words of this respected scholar are similar to those of most of Lahontan's numerous other critics over the years.

> The Baron provided geography with another kind. He was a first-rate soldier and a courageous explorer, a trustworthy historian, a shrewd and sharp critic, a penetrating and cynical intelligence but a literary man. With a single chapter he befogged a large area of geography for half a century. Poetry or a formula for bestsellers came upon him and he created a big lake of salt water in the interior West and discovered on its shores an Indian culture as ornate as the Byzantine [sic].
>
> Fact graciously fulfilled this fiction with the Great Salt Lake, but no [sic] Byzantines, more or less where he had said it was. It was otherwise with the Long River, which Lahontan caused to flow among impossible tribes [sic] across a landscape from the dark side of the moon. The Long River as art but it ministered to desire, for it might be the water route to the Pacific, which was even more urgently wanted in 1703 than before. [emphasis added] So it twisted across the maps and the printed page, sometimes paralleling the Missouri river, whose exploration is affected, sometimes creating from its own substance large province for the truth to get lost in.[1]

The baron wrote only an abbreviated narrative of his trip, although for his time it was still comparatively substantial. He did this immediately upon his return to Michilimackinac from the Long River in the spring of 1689. It is suspected that that document, or some version of it, was initially written so quickly to serve as the required debriefing for the intendant and governor of New France. Lahontan stated that he debriefed these men about his travels the first day after his arrival back in Montreal.[2]

Lahontan's narrative was eventually published, possibly in attenuated form, as Letter XVI in a much larger work in French. That publication detailed a host of the other travels, exploits, and observations he made about New France while there in military service to his mother country. He published this in 1703 in Holland as *Nouveaux Voyages de Mr. Le Baron de La Hontan, dans l'Amerique Septentrionale.*[3] He published an English version of his narrative that same year, again as part of his classic book *New Voyages to North America*.[4] To this day Lahontan's book, despite the unresolved puzzle of his Long River travels, is generally considered to be a rare and invaluable seventeenth-century resource for the history of colonial New France as well as for aspects of the French Canadian cultural and literary heritage.[5]

The Baron Lahontan, initially only a teenage cadet and then a junior officer in the French Ministry of Marine, was in New France in the 1680s assisting the colony in the Beaver Wars it was fighting against the English-backed Iroquois Confederacy. While posted at the original Michilimackinac on Lake Huron, the baron said that he left there in the fall of 1688 and led his small detachment of marines and a few Natives on an extended canoe expedition far up a substantial westerly tributary of the Mississippi River. He referred to that river, as it continued westward as the Platte of today, as the "Long River." In addition to seeking an inland passage across North America, he also held an ancillary goal of obtaining information on the Spaniards of New Mexico. That was because France was just then on the cusp of commencing hostilities with England, Spain, and their allies in the Nine Years War. This became known as King William's War in its North American theatre.[6] The immediacies of the Iroquois wars and protecting the fur trade were then the most pressing concerns for the colonials of New France.

It appears that Lahontan attempted, seemingly without official specific orders or sanction from the Crown, to find an inland passage by trying unsuccessfully to travel to the source of the Long River. Finding such a passage was considered by Louis XIV and his officials governing in New France to be one of the highest priorities for the small colony. The prevailing opinion among the explorers and leaders of the colony was that such a passage would most likely be found by following the great Long River toward its source, then only meaning the Missouri.[7] That opinion held all the way up through the travels of Lewis and Clark and their US sponsors at the dawn of the nineteenth century.

The baron's trip was, however, unsuccessful in that he neither reached the source of the Long River nor discovered an inland passage. By being the first Frenchman to travel very far up the lower Missouri and far out westward on the Platte, experience good relations with many Native peoples and safely return to the colony with all his men, certainly still made him a most intrepid and successful major explorer.

Because of its potential to enhance the colony's vitally important fur trade, the discovery of an inland passage that would ease travel into the Pacific and on to the fur markets of Asia was why such a passage was still ardently desired by the French Crown. To that end the king had long been offering a substantial reward to its discoverer. Had Lahontan found such an important passage, news of it would have quickly been forwarded to the king and been mentioned in the highest levels of official period correspondence relating to New France. Although he stated that he laid claim to new lands for France, other than his own narrative there are no known records substantiating his trip or the claim and monument he made for them.[8] Likewise, there are also no known records that support any refutation of his claimed journey or to the newly discovered lands he claimed.

As detailed in chapter 15, in his narrative the baron tried to hide the river's location through a great deception. Lahontan's Long or *"Morte"* (Dead) River as described in his narrative was certainly the Platte in combination with the lower Missouri to the south of it. The Platte's existence was then apparently unknown to the French. It is worth noting, however, that the Platte and lower Missouri have at times been seen as the primary river, with the upper Missouri beyond the Platte being considered only a tributary to it.[9] This is despite the fact that the Natives had canoed it for eons. No European is known or even suspected to have traveled the Missouri up to the Platte before the baron. It appears that when he learned that the Platte led westward (Figures 1, 12), likely when he first noted it as he reached it, he followed it. He also followed the Osage for a short distance from the Missouri in anticipation that it might lead him to an inland passage or to new Native people who might know about one or about the Spaniards of New Mexico.

Lahontan claimed his journey commenced in late September 1688. By his account, and this revised interpretation of portions of it, his journey took him southward from old Michilimackinac out onto Lake Michigan which was then known as Lake Illinois. He then traveled down to Green Bay (*Baye du Puants*) and on by way of the Fox and then the Wisconsin Rivers down to the Mississippi. (Figures 1, 4). From there he passed southward, and not northward, as he has very successfully misled virtually all his past-readers into believing, down the great river, then up the lower Missouri, and then far up its west to east flowing Platte tributary in present-day Nebraska.[10] He then traveled the Missouri back downriver to a portion of the Osage River before returning to the Mississippi and then briefly detouring on south to explore part of the Ohio River, then known as the Wabash. (Figure 1). He then turned back to the Mississippi and headed upriver. He returned to Michilimackinac in May 1689 by way of the Illinois River and Lake Michigan after an eight-month absence and there immediately wrote his Letter XVI.

The Beginnings of the Lahontan Puzzle

The persistent mystery in Lahontan's Long River narrative began to evolve because he intentionally obscured the identity of the Long River, namely that when he started it was actually the Missouri. The fact that there was no such river then or ever known to have been located where he mapped it (Figure 2) to the north of the Wisconsin River was the first thing the baron's critics noticed. Although this was apparently recognized by the late eighteenth century, the falsehood became more widely obvious by the nineteenth, and because of that few if any critics attempted further study of the narrative. The geography and ethnology of the Plains and the Platte were also only barely even becoming known until long after the baron wrote and published his narrative. From the outset the baron's deception led to him being broadly branded a liar. His narrative also significantly befogged the early cartography and historiography of North American discovery, particularly relative to French exploration and the central Great Plains.[11]

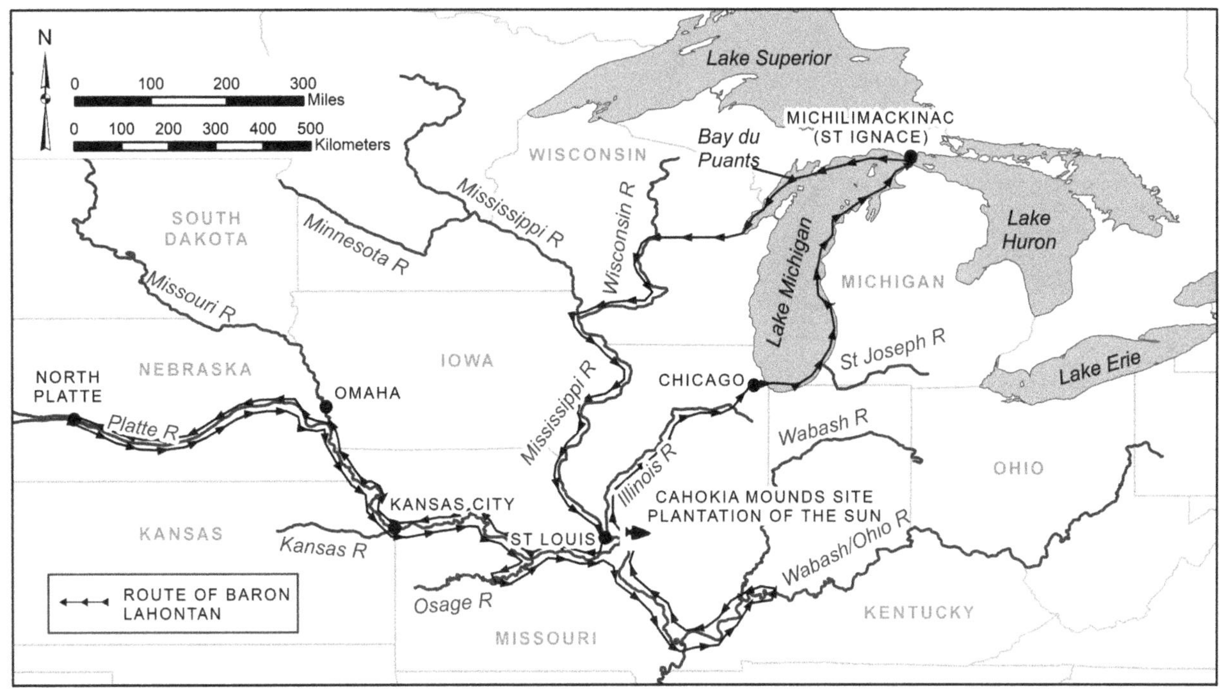

1. Map of Lahontan's 1688–1689 travel route from old Michilimackinac on Lake Huron to the Platte River in Nebraska and his return from there.

During the early portion of his tour of active duty (1683–1689) as a cadet and junior officer in New France, the baron was often out and about the Great Lakes. Much of his last year in that region encompassed his Long River expedition. Except for when he was on that trip, Lahontan stated that he had penned a series of letters to a regular, although never identified, correspondent in France.[12] He had begun this correspondence the moment he arrived at Quebec in 1683. The ever curious and observant young man's letters described all kinds of things he noted about the French colonists; their history, Canada's geography, and various topics of natural history including its Natives, as well as its politics, philosophy, economics, and many other aspects of the nascent colony. His book, largely consisting of these letters, was very popular in Europe well into the eighteenth century and was truly a bestseller.[13] Lahontan's Letter XVI contained his Long River narrative.[14]

2. A portion of Lahontan's 1703 General Map of New France... showing his misleading mapping of the Long River's location relative to that of the Wisconsin River ("Ouisconsine").

Demand became so strong for the baron's book that it was translated into multiple languages and by about 1900 had gone through a great many editions, as listed by both Victor Paltsits and A. H. Greenly, and has spawned innumerable additional writing since then.[15] Overall, the volume was initially considered authoritative, even though some French clergy, politicians, and later generations of French Canadians did not like the way the notably cynical baron sometimes portrayed their ancestors, particularly the Jesuit priests and the women of New France, as well as the conditions and the history of the early colony. The early eighteenth-century Jesuit historian, Charlevoix, although charged with assimilating all he could about the potential for finding an inland passage, gave Lahontan's account no credit.[16] The baron had been so outspoken in his book against the Jesuits that it is little wonder that Charlevoix did not credit him. Perhaps the Jesuits in snubbing the baron commenced the diminishment of his contributions. It is not obvious that his travels were even mentioned in the *Jesuit Records*.

Lahontan's Critics and Their Times

With the exception of the Long River narrative, Lahontan's book is generally considered to be quite reliable as to facts and events, many of which were his own eyewitness accounts.[17] Instead of being honored among other famous explorers for this major trip and his claimed discoveries, the baron has long been "branded as a liar and a cheat, as but a mere idle-brained Munchausen incapable of truth."[18] Today, due to his poor reputation, he has been largely forgotten by historians and critics who rarely even "mention him except to accuse him of lying and of ignorance."[19] This is most unfortunate because his narrative is, overall, truthful and describes things about the Natives which no one ever again witnessed and wrote about.

In addition to his very creative and remarkably successful deception about the river's location, the baron has been criticized about his descriptions and praise of Natives whom he claimed to have encountered along the Long River. Lahontan was an obvious and impetuous maverick in French society who appreciated Native society and nearly "went native." He could readily have spent his life among them and ultimately claimed to prefer living out in the wilds in their company than to be bound by the constraints of marriage and French society.[20]

The eminent American Victorian historian, Rueben Gold Thwaites, generally credited the baron with considerable veracity in all his other accounts but doubted the Long River narrative. Nevertheless, Thwaites also believed that the baron's thinking was far in advance of his age.[21] As it truly was! He was obviously highly intelligent, if not a true genius. French and German critics have usually focused on his writings, other than the Long River narrative, through literary analysis, philosophy, and the evolution of Enlightenment thought. Among all the other junior French Marine officers who fought for their country in the New World and elsewhere, Lahontan stands out for his literary contributions that mark him as an exceptionally bright officer, one of the few whose name is recalled and mentioned.

American historians, however, appear to have been most interested in the historiography of colonial New France and the Beaver Wars with the Iroquois people. They have never really been able to resolve the puzzle of the Long River and have largely dismissed it.[22] Anthropologists have also basically ignored that narrative. These issues tend to hang on the question of whether he even made the trip to the Long River, which some have doubted.[23] Assuming he made the trip, the major issue has been to determine what real river and Native peoples he was describing.

Unfortunately, many writers have judged his narrative as a work of literature rather than geography and anthropology learned in the applicable ethnology and archaeology of the Great Plains. These fields of study did not even begin to emerge until the nineteenth century. It was only about mid-century that the geography of the Platte River drainage and the central Plains were beginning to be explored. It was even later that the Indian Wars on the Plains were being concluded, and Native peoples were giving up ancient territories and being resettled on distant reservations.

Stephen Leacock, a highly regarded Canadian writer and Lahontan scholar, has been the most ardent of the baron's sparse defenders from the ranks of historians. Among those who have attempted to evaluate the baron's narrative, he appears to have been the wisest and most judicious. He wrote that:

> ...the book succeeded because it deserved to succeed, the product of a bright clear mind, written with absorbing interest, with that strange quality of being readable, so easy to the master's hand, so impossible for most.[24]

Regarding the criticism ultimately directed toward Lahontan, Leacock further stated:

> The truth lies in exactly the opposite direction. The great value of Lahontan's writing, or of ninety-nine-one-hundredths of it, lies in its exactness, in the picture which it produces of the actual facts, the actual conditions of the life, the wars, the dangers and the hardships of the colony of New France. Lahontan wrote with a lack of conscious effort, with no anxious striving for style or effect. So wrote Xenophon and Julius Caesar and John Bunyon, telling what they saw and knew, and unconcerned with the manner of their narration.[25]

There appears to be a bit of an academic schism between American and Canadian scholars regarding Lahontan. Canadians, particularly those of French descent, do not regard him with much respect in large part due to the problems in understanding the Long River narrative and his negative comments about early New France.[26] Because they wrote off his Long River narrative, they tend to focus on the philosophical and literary aspects of his writings and the French component of Canadian society.

Thwaites believed Lahontan's book had a double purpose, as both a satire upon European life and civilization and as a narration of the author's adventures in new and previously unknown realms.[27] At its heart the Long River narrative is essentially a descriptive ethnographic study most relative to the history of the US, which was a rare contribution for so early a date. It is similar to the later classic volume by Antoine Simon Le Page du Pratz, *History of Louisiana*, which still provides rare and vivid early ethnographic information on the Natchez people and other complex Mississippian Native societies of Louisiana prior to their major cultural changes wrought by their post-contact experiences.[28] His book details some of the kinds of observations which Lahontan also made about these Mississippian peoples, which were so heavily criticized.

Charlevoix, the Jesuit priest and historian, was among the first to criticize the baron's Long River narrative. He branded Lahontan's Long River trip spurious because of his incorrect mapping of the river, even though he had been charged with investigating the many rumors about the "existence and location of a western sea" between the New World and Asia. By the time he had concluded his investigations and traveled in the *pays d'en haut* in ca. 1721, Charlevoix was considered an authority on the subject.[29]

Thwaites discusses how other people, like Charlevoix, of the eighteenth century, who came to know the Mississippi and its tributaries soon after Lahontan published, began to recognize that there was no river like the one he described in the location he indicated in his mapping.[30] Such realizations did not, however, diminish the interest in the baron's book within the popular market for travelogues.

Nineteenth-century American historians began to note the baron's work as they started compiling histories of US and Canadian exploration.

American Victorian historians of New France, such as Francis Parkman in 1869 and Thwaites in 1905, as well as DeVoto in 1952, came to directly question Lahontan's work and inflicted extreme damage on the veracity of his Long River narrative.[31] The well-known notary, journalist, politician, and historian, Joseph Edmond Roy, a French Canadian and member of Canada's Royal Society, effectively destroyed the reputation of Lahontan and his Long River narrative among his countrymen. He did so by means of a very biased *coup de grâce* that was administered before The Royal Society's membership in 1894.[32]

These and other men were primary sources in the ruination of Lahontan's reputation and, particularly so, in regard to his Long River travels. None of the early critics, however, seem to have been students of the modern field of ethnography or even its place as part of the natural history of their times.[33] Despite their lack of these appropriate backgrounds for judging ethnographic studies, they have been keys among the many otherwise regarded scholars who have not reviewed the baron's Long River narrative kindly or even respectfully. Because of the power of authority inherent in their scholarly voices, and those of many others, even though they lacked anthropological knowledge, the Long River narrative has almost universally been regarded as only a fanciful tale.

Such negative voices from important scholars have unfortunately stood the test of time, persisting to this day and inspiring a veritable legion of additional and secondary condemnations by various writers from diverse disciplines. Despite it being a major early ethnographic study of America's Natives that has inappropriately been condemned, modern scholars have not yet realized that most of what his critics have said was wholly unfounded.[34] Lahontan's original doubters were unfortunately encouraged by the baron's well-crafted deception. Despite his many obvious contributions to history, he destroyed his own credibility and reputation.

To this day Lahontan's Long River narrative has never been recognized as a credible account written by a highly intelligent early Enlightenment thinker and student of natural history.[35] But in the light of today's anthropological thinking and knowledge of Great Plains archaeology and ethnography it appears to be an accurate first-hand account of some precontact Mississippian Native societies. According to the baron's observations, they were still at least partially functioning in traditional, although perhaps attenuated, form in the very earliest moments in the twilight of their precontact lives as they gained their first experience with Frenchmen or any other Europeans.

When seen from such a precise viewpoint, the narrative reads like an eyewitness account of a most ephemeral and very first instance of Native and European interaction and a critical source in that rare genre of North American and world literature.[36] The apparent authenticity of his detailed ethnographic and geographic observations forcefully argues that no Frenchman of his time could have invented them from whole cloth. They were obviously works produced by an educated person such as the baron, who was, like him, very familiar with Native Americans. Unlike most of his fellow Marine officers, Lahontan had spent much time among the Natives, lived among them, liked them, and viewed them comparatively from the perspective of a student of natural history. He knew them and observed them on the Plains far earlier than any of his critics even learned about them. He was thus far more of an authority on the American Natives than any of his critics have ever been.

Virtually all the earlier major and most influential criticisms of the baron's narrative, including those of Parkman, Thwaites, Roy, DeVoto and many others, were cast from a posture of superiority toward Natives as well as the baron himself.[37] They reveal the pedantic and racially biased overtones of the Victorian Era, which characterized so much of North American thought during those critics' lifetimes.[38] Their views from well over a century ago are now badly out of date given modern advancements in our understanding of the geography and historical ethnography of the Great Plains and the sophistication to which some Mississippian societies there had risen before their declines and/or destruction.

It is an old historical conundrum, largely formed within his critics' Victorian mindsets, that has today commonly been overlooked by scholars. No evidence has to date been noted that any unbiased scholars of Lahontan, other than possibly Stephen Leacock, have attempted to understand the baron's deception. No one has tried to comprehensively re-evaluate his narrative from a more modern perspective of natural history or anthropology and any appreciation for what were complex and highly developed Native societies. However, in his attempt to dissect the baron's Long River narrative, even Leacock failed to detect the baron's deceptive feint. Therefore, as a result, he, like others, attempted to evaluate it from the perspective that the baron traveled northward on the Mississippi River to Minnesota and then traveled up the river of that name. That doomed his effort from the start and required that he force his interpretations with insufficient evidence. He did, however, resolutely believe that the baron had made the Long River trip.[39]

Leacock believed the legend of Lahontan as a liar simply grew and solidified until it was uncritically accepted as a fact. In Leacock's opinion, if his Long River narrative could be proven to be true, which he believed it was, Lahontan's name should be honored along with other famous early French Canadian explorers for having canoed the farthest beyond the confines of any previous exploration in the old Canadian frontiers.[40] The baron was the first European to document, let alone travel and describe, the Platte River and its valley, which are major landmarks of the Great Plains and still one of the most important old travel corridors in the US and all of North America. The honor for discovering the Platte has long been granted to Etienne de Veniard, sieur de Bourgmont who saw the river in 1714 and gave it the Otoe name of "*Nebraskier*" or "flat water."[41] Bourgmont, however, did not travel up the Platte to any extent if at all.

Lahontan should be accorded that honor, and a new chapter should be added to the history of French exploration, the central Great Plains, and Nebraska and its seventeenth-century Native residents. In this regard Leacock, as far back as 1933, objectively stated that:

> It is time that some real historian should trace out the truth in regard to Lahontan. The writing of history today is full of "vindications," in which the legendary villains of history become the real fathers of the nation.[42]

This volume aspires to be such a long-overdue, and hopefully credible, revisionist, and vindicating account. It challenges the long-held and widespread notions that the baron was one of the greatest travel liars of all time and that the Native societies he encountered on the Long River could not have appeared and functioned as he described.[43] This challenge is rooted in a few, and only recently recognized, Spanish colonial documents which support the authenticity of some of the baron's most seriously questioned descriptions of unusual Native Americans and the geography of the Great Plains and other involved regions, including the Great Salt Lake area of Utah. These documentary sources derive from the early history of New Mexico and have only recently been published by this writer.[44]

The discovery of these Spanish documents led directly to the preparation of this study.[45] It was only due to serendipity that their importance was noted and how they demanded that someone revisit the baron's Long River narrative under the new light they provide. That conclusion was reached during the research for the recently published volume on the 1765 Spanish expeditions of Juan Rivera. Rivera was sent northward from New Mexico to find out about bearded Caucasian-looking men who were suspected of being Europeans. These Natives lived in the province of *"Teguayo,"* which appears to have been Lahontan's land of *"Mozeemlek"* or that of *"Tahuglauk"* from near the Great Salt Lake.[46] Lahontan had also encountered and described Caucasian-looking Natives with beards from there.

It was not much more than a decade ago that the importance of Spanish documents, as confirmation of some of the baron's supposedly most outlandish observations, such as regarded the bearded ones, were noted. Until the book about Juan Rivera's travels and his journals was published in 2015, not even any well-informed anthropologists and historians were truly believing in the existence of the so unusual-bearded men from Teguayo. These people, some of whom the baron met among the Plains Apaches on the Platte River, were real! These indigenous stone-age peoples were known to the French and other Europeans only as *"sauvages américains."*[47] Europeans believed these peoples to be racially inferior and incapable of elevating themselves to any appreciable level of civilization.

The baron's early scholarly critics were only familiar with post-contact Native societies that had been reduced over many generations to mere shadows of their former elaborate and sophisticated precontact forms. These Victorian writers held only disdainful and racially prejudiced views of these so badly reduced peoples.[48] They looked down on them and had no conception of the levels of sophistication their complex societies had once attained. It of course followed that they had no idea about what the baron observed or heard about regarding those societies while on the Long River. They were in no position to competently judge what he related in his narrative but judge they did.[49]

Some of the baron's worst critics believed he never left Michilimackinac and instead spent the time he purported to have been away on his trip waiting out the winter of 1688–1689 there while he conjured it up.[50] Almost all of his critics failed to see through his ruse and followed his misleading information regarding the direction of travel on his maps and their supporting narrative. These writers, if they believed he even made the trip, like Leacock, have postulated that Lahontan journeyed northward, as he very effectively led them to believe, up the Mississippi to the Minnesota River in present-day Minnesota and then lied about what he witnessed there.[51]

The baron's narrative thus became the great enigma it has remained because of all these several factors, including the ease and complacency with which his critics believed his ruse and never looked for alternate explanations for his mapping. They also jumped to conclusions, failing from the outset to accord him any credibility because of their total lack of familiarity with the central Great Plains and the Platte River and because they failed to apply analytical rigor in their analyses. The latter included neither closely reading his narrative (truly listening to what he said or believing any of it) nor recognizing the obvious pattern of the contradictions in it.

That pattern involved two major elements. When he was on the Long River his narrative closely conforms with what is known of the geography and Natives of the lower Missouri and Platte. Everything he stated relative to his river's location and any landmarks that might have helped his contemporaries identify it with the Missouri were, however, obscured. The Platte was of course not, or barely, known to exist before he published his book and would not be at all well known for another hundred years. Because of these factors, his critics could not detect and see through his deception. His critics were but men of their times, however, and cannot be faulted for their world views and lack of information about an unexplored continent and its peoples which fueled their disbelief.

Goals and Problem Orientations

The primary goal of this study is to fulfill the long-delayed need, as exemplified by Leacock's old call, for an intensive reexamination of Lahontan's Long River narrative and of the major criticisms that have been leveled against it.[52] This study is strictly limited in scope and explicitly treats only the Long River narrative since it is the only one of the baron's many personal narrations to be condemned as fraudulent. It considers none of his other written works and does not evaluate the narrative from a perspective of fiction focused on French literature and the Enlightenment as has commonly been done.[53] In this regard his other contributions are widely recognized as "invaluable to the history of New France" and considered "essential" to the "evolution of the travel literature genre, as well as the libertarian movement that swept over Europe during the Enlightenment of the eighteenth century."[54]

It is important to reemphasize that the baron's Long River narrative is only an abbreviated text that provides nothing more than extracts from a larger journal that Lahontan said he kept but which has not come to light.[55] By his admission it also covers only those standout events he believed were worthy of mention and thus omits much day-to-day detail. There is thus no complete account of his Long River travels.[56] Furthermore, this study is not a detailed or comprehensive ethnohistorical or archaeological study of the Native peoples he encountered. It only identifies and introduces them and provides their earliest known ethnographic profiles.

One of the major criticisms of the baron through time relates to his descriptions of the physical appearance and Mississippian culture/customs of America's Native societies he encountered.[57] According to one of his more modern critics, Percy G. Adams, "No one has ever been able to find this rivière Longe." It was much "too big, too long, and too straight to be the Minnesota, and its junction with the Mississippi was much too far north [(Figure 2)] (as he mapped it) for it to be the Missouri." [emphasis added] In fact, Lahontan claimed in Letter XVI to have explored part of the Missouri. "But stranger than the appearance and geographical position of his river were the curious tribes of Indians who lived near its banks-the Essanapes, the Gnacsitares, and the Mozeemleks."[58] Adams obviously did not even closely read the account because Lahontan never said the Mozeemleks lived near the Long River, only that they were from far to the west near the great lake of salt, just as they proved to have been.

Taken as a whole, the evidence lends considerable weight to a belief that Lahontan's narrative is authentic and contains a great deal of truth just as all his other accounts do. This book should readily demonstrate the consistency of the truth the baron maintained throughout his descriptive writings. It is indeed unfortunate that there are, other than for his book itself, no known contemporary French documents, such as his daily logs, to confirm or deny whether he made the trip.[59]

The problems that had to be dealt with in this study to begin to fairly judge the baron's narrative after more than three hundred years were multiple and complex. They involved translations, which were at times seriously imperfect, of multiple Native languages into the baron's French and then into English. The important points to be kept in mind relative to the narrative are the demonstrably true things that were mentioned by the baron as opposed to the clearly untrue/misunderstood ones. Even more important, there are those that were totally ignored but which should have been mentioned if he had not been trying to obscure the location of the Long River. On any subject it is also critical to determine whether the baron was reporting from his own direct observations or from information imparted to him by others, most notably Natives by means of at times extremely poor and multiple translations.

Although Lahontan never mentioned an inland passage, it must be remembered that he did note that he was seeking to explore all the way to the source of the Long River/Missouri.[60] It is precisely that river which was, during his time and even much later, widely believed to be the most likely way to such a passage. Further, the baron was preoccupied with his own sad financial plight and standing with the Crown and French society during most of his time in New France. Since the Crown was offering financial reward to whomever could find the passage it was then a great priority for the colony.[61] One thus must conclude that the possibility of reaping such a reward helped motivate the notably poor baron to desert his posting and launch such a major, expensive, and potentially dangerous expedition and rely largely on the king's resources in doing so. As the Fox chieftain told him, the baron obviously had some sort of discovery in mind by undertaking the trip, and the baron again mentioned his goal of making a discovery while on the Osage River near the end of his Long River travels.[62]

The levels of scorn heaped upon the baron for his observations along the Long River have seldom been piled upon any other early explorers who, exactly like him, have otherwise been regarded as quite credible witnesses to historical events. Even his most ardent critics have acknowledged this when they still described him as a liar, insubordinate, a braggart, spiteful, a coward, and a slanderer when it came to his Long River narrative.[63] This has been done by critics who knew far less than he about the things of which he wrote.

There are literally thousands of works in print or on the internet containing information or comments relating to the Baron Lahontan and/or his Long River. The number of these works testify to the lasting importance of his contribution. They do vary greatly in quality and span a variety of disciplines over a span of three hundred or more years. Given this amount of material, it has been necessary to herein cite only selected key works from various disciplines which lie at the root of so much writing and best exemplify what has been said about the baron's Long River. For present purposes the comprehensive study by historian Rueben Gold Thwaites remains the single most useful English language source for the baron and his Long River narrative.[64] Insightful biographies of Lahontan by David Hayne and Réal Ouellet are available on-line and provide additional references.[65] Readers who wish to follow the historiography of denunciations of Lahontan's Long River narrative will find the heart of it in his great deception discussed in chapter 15.

The terms "American Native" and "Native" rather than "Native American or" "American Indian," "savages," or "First Nations" are employed in referring to the indigenous peoples the baron encountered. In most cases the spellings for names of these peoples have been standardized in keeping with the usage of the *Handbook of North American Indians* published by the Smithsonian Institution.[66]

Major criticisms by Lahontan's detractors are the subject of some chapters herein. These chapters should be considered independent case studies. Some of these rely on some of the same information or evidence which is also germane to other topics similarly considered. There is, therefore, some repetition of information through this volume as it moves from one individualized subject to another. Due to the number and diversity of the topics involved and the long time since Lahontan wrote, there appeared to be no better way to structure this volume so as to avoid this repetition and still demonstrate the veracity of his narrative in as definitive a manner as possible. The mystery of the baron's Long River has, hopefully, finally, and definitively, been put to rest through thoughtful discussion and reliance on a host of readily verifiable reference source materials.

NOTES:

1. DeVoto, *Course of Empire*, 64.

2. Lahontan, *New Voyages*, 219-20.

3. Lahontan, *Nouveaux Voyages.*

4. Lahontan, *New Voyages,* 1703 English edition and 1905 and 1970 reprints. Victor Paltsits assembled a very comprehensive bibliography of the various editions and translations of Lahontan's book. Palsits, "Lahontan Bibliography." It is a very extensive listing included in the 1905 English reprint by Rueben G. Thwaites (reprinted 1970) that carries the bibliography up to about the time that Thwaites published his reprint of the original 1703 English translation of *New Voyages.* A. H. Greenly also published a comprehensive bibliography as "Lahontan: An Essay and Bibliography" in 1954. If one wishes to learn more about all the complex of translations and reprints of the baron's famous work one should first check these sources or that of Réal Ouellet, which is written in French. Ouellet, *Oeuvres Complétes;* e.g. Ouellet, "Baron of Lahontan."

5. Leacock, *Lahontan's Voyages*, vi; Ouellet, "Baron of Lahontan," 1.

6. King William's War was the North American theater of the Nine Years War (1688–1697), https://

en.wikipedia.org/wiki/Nine_Years%27_War. also known as the War of the Grand Alliance or the War of the League of Augsburg. Although the Spanish were part of the League pitted against France, in North America the contest was primarily between France and England. The war was the first of the French and Indian Wars fought before France finally ceded its mainland territories to the east of the Mississippi in North America to England in 1763. *Wikipedia*, "King Williams War."

7. Dablon, "Discovery of the Mississippi," (58), 108; Frontenac, "General Memorandum," (IX), 16-21; Marquette, *Father Marquette's Journal*, 13; *Voyages of Marquette;* Parkman. *La Salle and Discovery*, 762.

8. Lahontan, *New Voyages*, 197. Many have written about the Baron Lahontan and combed through the historical records of New France. Other than for his own book, no period documents are known to either support or deny his claim to having made the Long River trip or even discuss his other activities while on active duty with the French Ministry of Marine. Writing in the late eighteenth century, Peter Pond, who could have read the baron's book, did, however, refer to the fact that Lahontan had canoed to the Mississippi from lake Michigan but erred when he said he was the first to do so by way of the Fox River. Kent, *Rendezvoux*, (I), 504.

9. Norall, *Bourgmont*, 123.

10. Virtually all the writers who have attempted to study the baron's narrative have followed the feint or misinformation he built into it and have never questioned that he had not traveled north toward Minnesota as he wanted them to believe. The notion that he traveled south is considered in detail in Chapter 15 and in Lahontan, *New Voyages*, 177-80.

11. DeVoto, *Course of Empire*, 62; Karpinski, *An Historical Atlas*, 49; Reinhartz, *Herman Moll*, 28-30; Thwaites, "Introduction," xxxviii; Wheat, *Mapping the Transmississippi,* 61-62.

12. All that Lahontan said of his correspondent was that he was "a*n old Biggoted Relation of mine*." Lahontan, *New Voyages*, 10.

13. Lahontan, *New Voyages; Nouveaux Voyages.*

14. Lahontan, *New Voyages*, 176-215.

15. Palsits, "Lahontan Bibliography;" Greenly: "Lahontan, An Essay...."

16. Charlevoix, *History and General Description;* Hayne, "Charlevoix."

17. In his book, Percy G. Adams, *Travelers*, 55-63; as well as Thwaites, "Introduction;" and Leacock, *Lahontan's Voyages*, 339-44; and others, have well-summarized the nature and sources of the major criticisms of Lahontan's account of his travels on the Long River. According to Adams, an early traveler in New France, one Claude Le Beau, was the first to challenge the veracity of the baron's account. Adams does not provide a date or citation for this view and did not give much credit to that particular critic. He did, however, still follow the ever-popular trend and entirely discredited the veracity of the account. Adams ranks him as one of the greatest of the "travel liars" of all time and one of the most "notorious" of the eighteenth-century adventurers. Adams provides a good summary of the history and nature of the challenges to the baron's narrative even though he could not adequately address or resolve the major

issues with it. *See* Ouellet, "Baron of Lahontan, 4;" Ouellet, *Oeuvres,* 43-82; Lahontan's narrative of his "Dialogue with Adario" has, however, been the subject of much discussion and speculation relative to its place in French literature, Lahontan, *New Voyages*, vol. 2:512-17.

18. Leacock, *Lahontan's Voyages*, v.

19. Ouellet, "Baron of Lahontan," 5.

20. Thwaites, "Introduction," xxviii, xxx, xliv.

21. Thwaites, xlvii.

22. Ouellet, "Baron of Lahontan."

23. Brandao, "Introduction;" Hayne, "Lom D'Arce;" Thwaites, "Introduction, xl-xlii; Adams, *Travelers,* 55-60.

24. Leacock, *Lahontan's Voyages*, 340.

25. Leacock, vi.

26. Lahontan, *New Voyages*, 36.

27. Thwaites, "Introduction," xxxvi.

28. du Pratz, *History of Louisana*.

29. Hayne, "Charleviox;" Charlevoix, *History;* Thwaites, "Introduction," xxxix.

30. Thwaites.

31. Parkman, *La Salle and the Discovery*, 1051; Thwaites, "Introduction," xxxvii-xliii.

32. Roy, *Le Baron*, 109-165.

33. Hébert, "Roy;" Parkman, *La Salle and Discovery*, (I):1051; Thwaites, *New Discoveries*, xviii; Roy.

34. Oulette, "Baron of Lahontan," 6.

35. Thwaites, "Introduction," xlvii.

36. Barlowe, "Barlowe's Narrative of the First Voyage;" Connolly and Anderson, *First Contact*.

37. Parkman, *La Salle and the Discovery;* Thwaites, *New Voyages;* Roy, *Le Baron de Lahontan*.

38. Howe, "Victorian Culture," 24.

39. Leacock, *Lahontan's Voyages*. 340-44.

40. Leacock, *Lahontan's Voyages*, vi, "Lahontan in Minnesota."

41. Norall, *Bourgmont;* Wikipedia, "Platte River."

42. Leacock, *Lahontan's Voyages*, vi.

43. Adams, *Travelers.*

44. Baker, et al., *Juan River's Colorado;* Rivera, "Diario del reconocimiento."

45. Bolton, *Pageant in the Wilderness;* Chávez and Warner, *Domínguez and Escalante.*

46. Baker et al., *Juan Rivera's Colorado*, 13-34.

47. Berkhofer, "White Conceptions," 53. Dickason, "Myth of the Savage;" Gagon, "Introduction," 74; Sayre, *Les Sauvages Américains,* xvii; Senior, "Translator's," 262n11.

48. Howe, "Victorian Culture;" Parkman, *California and Oregon Trail.*

49. Sayre, *Les Sauvages Américains.*

50. Adams, *Travelers*, 54-62; Brandão, "Introduction;" Thwaites, "Introduction," xxxix-xlii.

51. Adams, *Travelers*; Leacock, *Lahontan's Voyage,* "Lahontan In Minnesota;" Ouellet, "Baron of Lahontan;" Thwaites, *New Voyages.*

52. Leacock, *Lahontan's Voyages*; "Lahontan in Minnesota."

53. Ouellet, "Baron of Lahontan," *Oeuvres Complétes;* Sayre, *Les Sauvages Américains.*

54. Ouellet, "*Baron of Lahontan," 1.*

55. Lahontan, "Concerning the Relationship...," 215, 224.

56. Lahontan, *New Voyages*, 209.

57. Adams, *Travelers;* Sayre, *Les Sauvages Américains.*

58. Adams, *Travelers*, 57.

59. Norall, *Bourgmont;* Wikipedia, "Platte River."

60. Lahontan, *New Voyages*, 176.

61. Heidenreich, *Early French Exploration*, 126; Colbert to Talon (9), 89.

62. Lahontan, *New Voyages*, 176, 202.

63. Ouellet, "Baron of Lahontan."

64. Thwaites, *New Voyages.*

65. Hayne, "Lom D' Arce;" Ouellet, "Baron of Lahontan;" *Oeuvres Complétes.*

66. Sturtevant, *Handbook.*

2

• NEW FRANCE AND THE LURE OF THE WESTERN SEA •

by

STEVEN G. BAKER

The fur trade and New France's closely related search for an inland water passage to the Pacific Ocean (Western Sea), as well as intelligence gathering on the Spanish at the start of the Nine Years War, were the primary historical contexts within which Lahontan undertook his Long River expedition. Even the ongoing hostilities with the Iroquois, which sapped so much of the colony's energy, also centered around the fur trade. The baron's expedition was one of the early efforts in what became a long, drawn-out search for an inland passage. Although they had profound impact on the history of North American discovery, those searches have in large measure been forgotten. Lahontan's Long River story, however, can neither be told nor understood without summarizing the history of the searches for that passage, the existence of which the English, French, Spanish, Americans, and others ardently believed.

Francis Parkman discussed how the French explorer, René-Robert Cavelier Sieur de La Salle (1643–1687), developed his passion for finding an inland passage. He noted that after coming to New France in 1666, with his new home surrounded by nothing but the deep forests of Canada, La Salle questioned what might lie further to the west. Like Champlain and other Frenchmen had done in the earliest days of New France, "he dreamed of a passage to the Western Sea, and a new road for commerce to the riches of China and Japan."[1] According to Parkman, this dream set a firm resolve in La Salle for exploration that he thought might lead him to discover such a passage. Champlain had early on sought the support of the Crown for such an endeavor and believed it could be easily achieved by way of the St. Lawrence River. He further believed that if one could be found, New France could greatly increase its revenues far beyond those derived from the fur trade alone by placing customs duties on other goods passing through an inland passage.[2]

In the 1670s the Crown became increasingly interested in westward exploration and locating what would ultimately prove to be only a mythical passage. In June 1672 the king's minister, Jean-Baptiste Colbert, sent a letter to the colonial government in Quebec emphasizing how important discovery of such a passage would be for France and its little Canadian colony. The king considered this so important that he promised to handsomely reward its discoverer.[3] By Lahontan's time the desirability of locating an inland passage had become established within the French government, as well as among the populace and government of New France, particularly those involved in the fur trade. Once he arrived there in 1683, the young and ultimately financially strapped Lahontan would have quickly understood this desire and the promised reward. By the middle of the eighteenth century this had led many French expeditions from New France to seek such a passage.[4]

The Western Sea

Following establishment of their first settlements in North America, finding a way to the Pacific as an expedient route to Asia remained a major interest of France, England, and Spain.[5] For New France it was believed that Asia would provide profitable markets for the bounty of furs coming out of Canada's expansive wilds. If a direct route to the Pacific could be discovered and furs shipped out more easily, France's foothold in North America would be strengthened. Along with the desire for territorial expansion, new sources of furs, and the Jesuits' passion for saving souls, this economic interest became the driving force behind inland exploration from New France in the seventeenth century.[6]

In New France's early years knowledge of the geography of the distant interior to the west and south of the Great Lakes, despite still being vague and often unreliable, was being consolidated in the collective knowledge of the colony and encouraged further explorations into that tierra incognita.[7] Although the existence of the Pacific and its many adjoining seas was to some extent known, it was then referred to as the "Western,""Southern,""Vermillion," or "China" sea. No matter what name was used, if it could be reached directly by water, ships could sail onward in many directions to many countries by any number of sea routes.

Seldom is an incipient body of collective knowledge about unexplored distant places, like the North American interior of the seventeenth century, written down. Much of the information passed by word of mouth and involved significant issues in translating a variety of Native languages into French. America's Natives possessed a deep collective memory passed down through ancient oral traditions.[8] They traveled widely or heard stories about distant lands from other Natives, such as traders or enslaved people who might come among them from afar. Lahontan encountered captive Natives from the vicinity of the Great Salt Lake, hundreds of miles from where he met them on the Platte River in Nebraska, and whence they tried to describe their distant homeland to him.[9]

Some Natives had surprisingly good grasps of the major features of the landscape of the New World and could provide basic information, including the general directions of travel, relative approximations of distance measured, and basic descriptions of what was there or on the way. To a Frenchman who knew absolutely nothing about the hinterlands of the New World, this information might appear "vague and unreliable;" contain both "reasonable and fantastic ideas," and involve both "practical and impracticable plans of action."[10]

Natives had known and traveled the Mississippi and its Missouri River tributary long before they became known to the French. The first known European to visit the Mississippi and document its presence was the Spanish explorer, Hernando de Soto, who, traveling westerly from Florida, was slipped into eternal rest in its waters in 1542.[11] In the end, however, his discovery of the "father of waters" had little impact on future French exploration.

The first Frenchman known to have learned that the rumored Mississippi was a reality appears to have been Jean Nicollet sometime in the period 1635–1638. He was sent as an ambassador of peace to the Winnebagoes then living at the head of Green Bay (*Baye des Puants* or Bay of the Stinks) on the southwest side of Lake Michigan. These people were at war with the Hurons, important allies of the French until the Iroquois along with European-introduced disease decimated them.[12] Lahontan traveled beyond the Winnebagoes, ascended the Fox River, and then took the portage to the Wisconsin. (Figure 4). He followed it down to a point very near the Mississippi. This was the traditional route which the Baron Lahontan also later traveled. Nicollet initially believed the great river was part of the Western Sea because his guide is said to have called it the "great water."[13]

Following Nicollet a few other men were said to have reached the Mississippi or its branches, including a Colonel Wood of Virginia in ca. 1654 and a Captain Bolton in 1670. According to Parkman the evidence for these explorations was not sufficient to sustain these claims.[14] In 1658 two French traders reached Lake Superior where they wintered and then returned to the colony with tales of the Sioux and the great western river in their homeland in present-day Minnesota. With the onset of the colony's wars with the Iroquois ca. 1640, however, French exploration westward beyond Lake Superior was largely curtailed. The French king, Louis XIV, who began his long reign in 1643, and many of his functionaries were not in its early years disposed to favor expansion of the fur trade or exploration and settlement far from the heart of the colony along the Saint Lawrence.

Thus, while the French were becoming aware of the great river's existence, by mid-century they are not known to have visited it and still had little information about it. The Jesuit, René Ménard, tried to establish a mission on the south shore of Lake Superior but perished there. He was succeeded by Father Claude-Jean Allouez who explored parts of the lake and heard more about the river from the Sioux who knew it by the name of "*Messipi*."[15]

By about the middle of the seventeenth century, there was more and more exploration around the Great Lakes. Better knowledge of the Lake Superior region and areas to the west was rapidly accumulating. This was largely through the efforts of the Jesuit missionaries on the colony's far western margin, as well as the illicit traders (Coureurs de Bois) who were ranging farther and farther into more remote regions in seeking furs. In 1659 Charles Lallemant prepared the Jesuits' annual report and spoke of information that was coming in from the west of Lake Superior.[16] In addition to the notion that North America was bounded by a sea to the west (Pacific), that report introduced the notion of the desirability of finding "a passage into this great sea" into the records of the colony.[17]

Another early French visitor to the Mississippi River area was Father Louis Hennepin, a comrade of La Salle, between 1679 and 1680. He only traveled northward up the great river from its confluence with the Illinois, which is just north of the Missouri's, perhaps as far as Minnesota, although details of his discoveries are not certain. He was captured and held by the Sioux and ultimately rescued by Daniel Greysolon, Sieur Dulhut (a.k.a. "Duluth"), a famous Coureur de Bois, in 1680 and returned to the colony. He then quickly headed back to France. There he wrote a popular travel book about his exploits, but it is typically regarded as fanciful.[18] He is generally even more poorly regarded than Lahontan, but he explored parts of the upper Mississippi that Lahontan never came close to seeing.

In about 1680 Dulhut was among the Sioux in present-day Minnesota trading and attempting to rescue Father Hennepin. He learned of a great body of salty water that was unfit to drink. Presuming that his Sioux informants were speaking of the Western Sea, he dispatched three Frenchmen and some Sioux to try to find it. They reported that it was only a great lake, some twenty days' travel by foot, to the westward. Rather than the Pacific, it seems they had discovered the Great Salt Lake, which was a major feature of the landscape and likely gave rise to the early cartographic indications of an inland sea in that region. This appears to be the first documented mention of the Great Salt Lake.[19] Other bits and pieces of information about a large river and the Western Sea began to drift steadily to French ears. Their thoughts, including those of the Jesuits, thus began to focus more on the "Messipi" as a possible route to the Pacific.

Between 1678 and 1681 and later, Dulhut likely added to his store of lore about the Western Sea from information he obtained from the Sioux and other Natives and Coureur de Bois. He would obviously have been as well informed as any Frenchman about where the inland passage might be found. He later became Lahontan's comrade when they were traveling together and garrisoning Fort St. Joseph and when they were about Michilimackinac.[20] He would certainly have conversed with the baron and helped him become one of the better-informed men in New France about what might lie out in the far west and southwest of the Great Lakes.

The French were intrigued and wished to learn where this river Messipi flowed and if it might lead them to the Western Sea.[21] The desire to answer these questions grew and ultimately spawned a new period of discovery from New France. It seems that there was never doubt among the French that an inland passage existed and that they had to and could find it. This belief led to exploration of the Mississippi and to the discovery of the even longer Missouri. Ultimately, within a few decades, it led to Lahontan's explorations on the Missouri and westward up the Platte River.

By 1672 the Crown was becoming more and more concerned with the need to expand New France's economy. The fur trade was the one way this could most expediently be accomplished. The crown's thoughts on growth of the colony and settlement of the interior of New France were shifting and had begun to make western exploration and finding an inland passage a higher priority. Louis de Buade, Count of Palluau and Frontenac (1622–1698) (Figure 3), commonly simply referred to as only "Frontenac," was appointed governor of New France for two terms (1672 to 1682 and 1689 to1698). He was not yet there in June 1672 when Minister Colbert wrote to the intendent of the colony, Talon, on behalf of the king. Colbert, stated that:

> The King ... ordered me to communicate his intentions to you ... next to the increase of the Colony of Canada, there is nothing more important for that country and his Majesty's service than the discovery of the passage to the South Sea, his Majesty wishes you to offer a large reward to those who shall make that discovery.[22]

Frontenac had a huge impact on the course of French exploration and the search for the passage to the Western Sea.[23] He became personally involved in the fur trade through business partnerships including with Dulhut and Durantaye, commander of the Coureur de Bois at Michilimackinac.[24] Most all of these men and others ultimately became close to the baron. They formed a business cartel to control much of the fur trade in the west. Some, such as the Tontys were cousins of Daniel Greysolon Dulhut as well as Claude Greysolon del La Tourette; all appear to have been part of the La Salle/Frontenac cartel.[25] This group along with Frontenac and his policies, and Dulhut's information, likely encouraged the baron's Long River adventure. Ultimately, there may well have been some strong association among Lahontan, Dulhut, and Frontenac relative to the western lands and the fur trade.[26]

Frontenac was a force in the court of Louis XIV and had strong views on how important exploration and occupancy of interior lands, as well as advancement of the fur trade, was to the long-range success of New France, both for the crown and individual entrepreneurs, including himself. These views at times pitted him against those of his king whose policies at that time did not favor western exploration and expansion of the colony. Perhaps Frontenac had a heavy hand in getting these policies changed in such a dramatic way that the Crown would turn one-hundred eighty degrees and begin to encourage westerly exploration intended to find the passage.[27] By 1751, twenty-six of fifty-three known exploratory expeditions that set out from New France had endeavored to locate an inland water route to the Pacific.[28]

3. Ca. 1895 conjectural drawing by James L. Wiseman of Governor Frontenac (1622-1698) at center left with French marines at one of the fortifications of New France, courtesy of Bibliothèque et Archives Nationales du Québec / 52327/1958459, Canadian public domain.

The king's instructions were passed on to Frontenac when he arrived at Quebec in 1672, and he rapidly began to liberally carry them out. In search of profits for himself, his associates, and the colony, the governor began to actively encourage searches for the passage and more sources of furs. Much to the chagrin of the Montreal fur merchants, as part of the cartel he personally became deeply involved in the trade. He also encouraged settlement of more remote areas distant from Montreal and Quebec. These actions and other transgressions led to his recall to France in 1682.[29]

Historian W. J. Eccles, one of Frontenac's biographers, credited him with many faults and mistakes made under his watch as governor. Regarding his business intrigues in the fur trade, he stated: "There can be no doubt that Frontenac took every advantage of his position to profit from the fur trade but unfortunately there is no evidence to indicate the amount of his profits."[30] Eccles went on to state:

> the most serious consequence of Frontenac's activities in the fur trade was the division of the colony into two hostile factions, the Frontenac-La Salle group [cartel] and the Montreal traders... at a time when external threats to the colony, from the English in the north and the Iroquois in the south, made unity most essential.[31]

While Frontenac was building up his role in the fur trade, the subject of an inland passage for many years remained important in the colony with its small population of only about 11,000 French people.[32] The first target of exploration beyond Lake Superior under Frontenac's administration was the Mississippi, and among his first major steps was authorizing Marquette, Jolliet, and La Salle to investigate it. Although the French were certainly aware that there was a big river west of the Great Lakes, the first certain documentation of the Mississippi's existence and course was not accomplished until Marquette and Jolliet had canoed down it in 1673 under a plan Frontenac devised, ordered, and supervised directly.[33] With the Crown's standing orders, he was the force behind the scenes and responsible for the early explorations of the great river.

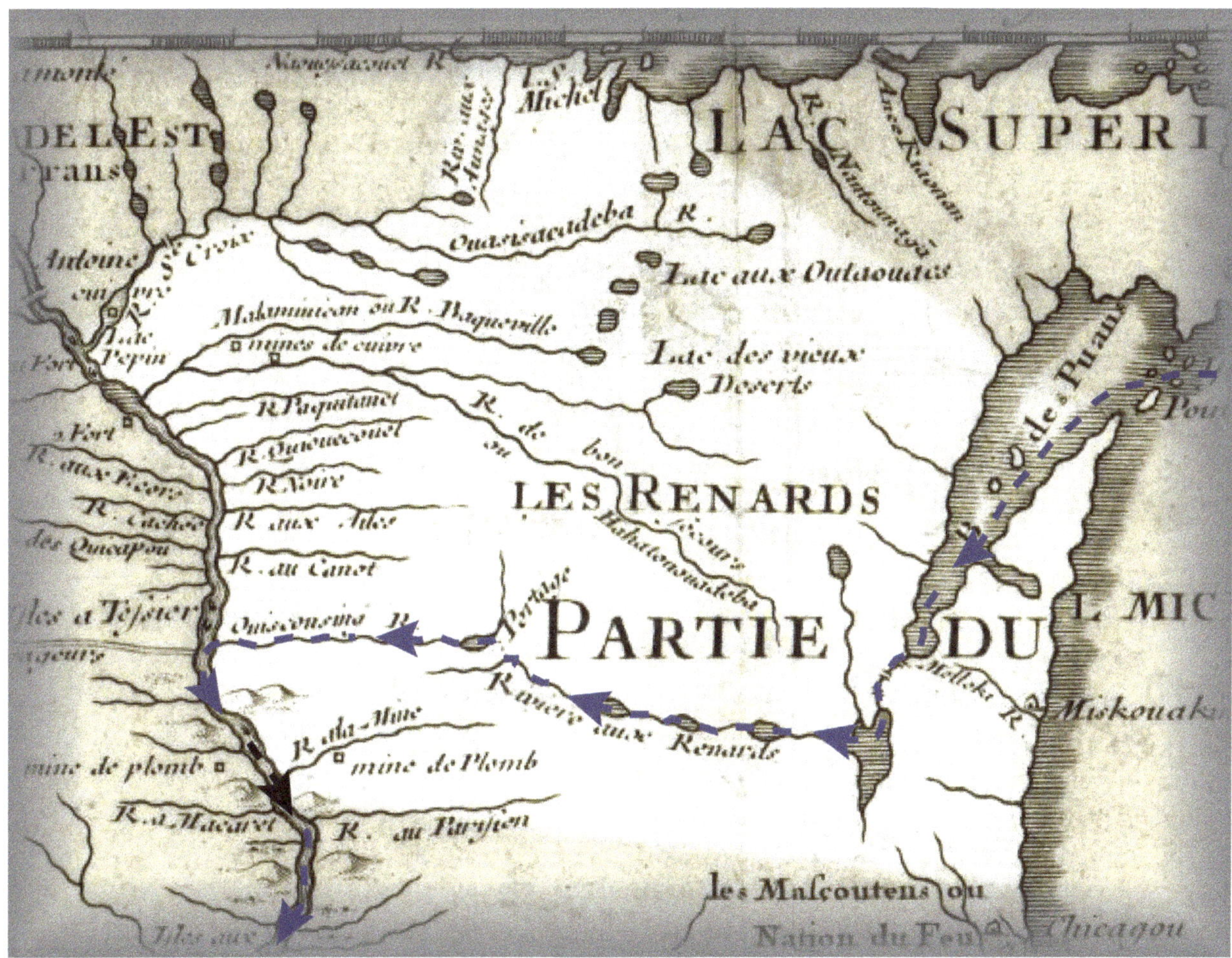

4. Map of Lahontan's travels from Green Bay on the west shore of Lake Illinois (Michigan) to the Mississippi River in 1688. Map detail adapted from 1755 Parte occidentale de la noubelle France ou du Canada, courtesy of US Library of Congress, US public domain.

Marquette and Jolliet followed the same path from Green Bay on Lake Illinois (Michigan) to the Wisconsin River and down it to the Mississippi that Nicollet had utilized, and Lahontan later described as the route he traveled. (Figure 4) They of course did not travel to its mouth on the Gulf of Mexico. When he reached it, Marquette initially and very joyously believed the Mississippi might well lead to the Western Sea, but he and Jolliet became the first to question that notion as they traveled downriver and that hope quickly crumbled away entirely.[34] Although they had solved one mystery, they brought on yet another when they discovered the Missouri at its confluence with the Mississippi near present-day St. Louis, Missouri. (Figures 1, 5) With this discovery they spawned another idea about an inland passage that held sway for over one hundred more years and helped lead Lewis and Clark on their journey to the source of the Missouri and on to the Pacific. Natives who had known of it for eons described the Missouri's great length, size, and ferocity to Marquette and Jolliet.

The map in Figure 5 is commonly attributed to Father Marquette, but was seemingly prepared by Melchisedech Thévenot following the Father's original one, with the then still unnamed Missouri River on which the Missouri Indians lived indicated near the map center at about 37 degrees north. This version of the so-called "Marquette Map," was apparently not widely published until 1852 when historian John Shea did so. Although the attribution and history of this map is a bit confusing, it is generally believed to be a relatively accurate version of the map first published by Thévenot, seemingly in Paris. While greatly simplified, it also well conforms to the very detailed and slightly earlier colored version directly attributed to Marquette in the National Archives of France and to the even earlier and more primitive one that was published in the *Jesuit Relations.*[35]

Although they did not ascend the Missouri, which they called the *"Pekitanouï,"* Natives informed the explorers about it. Father Marquette's description of the mouth of the river during its annual rise is consistent with its nature.[36] What Marquette and Jolliet learned and wrote about appears to have been the first information the French obtained about the Missouri and other western tributaries of the Mississippi.

When he realized that the Mississippi could not lead to the Western Sea, Father Marquette began to believe that the Pekitanouï might do so. He had noted its great size and that it was an even mighter stream than the Mississippi. He wished to explore the Pekitanouï in the hope that it might lead him to an inland passage.[37] Given the size of the Pekitanouï in comparison to the Mississippi, Marquette and Jolliet would have recognized that the Mississippi was only a tributary of the main stream, and thus held promise of leading far into the interior.

In introducing Marquette's journal of his voyage down the Mississippi in 1673, Father Claude Dablon, who edited it, stated:

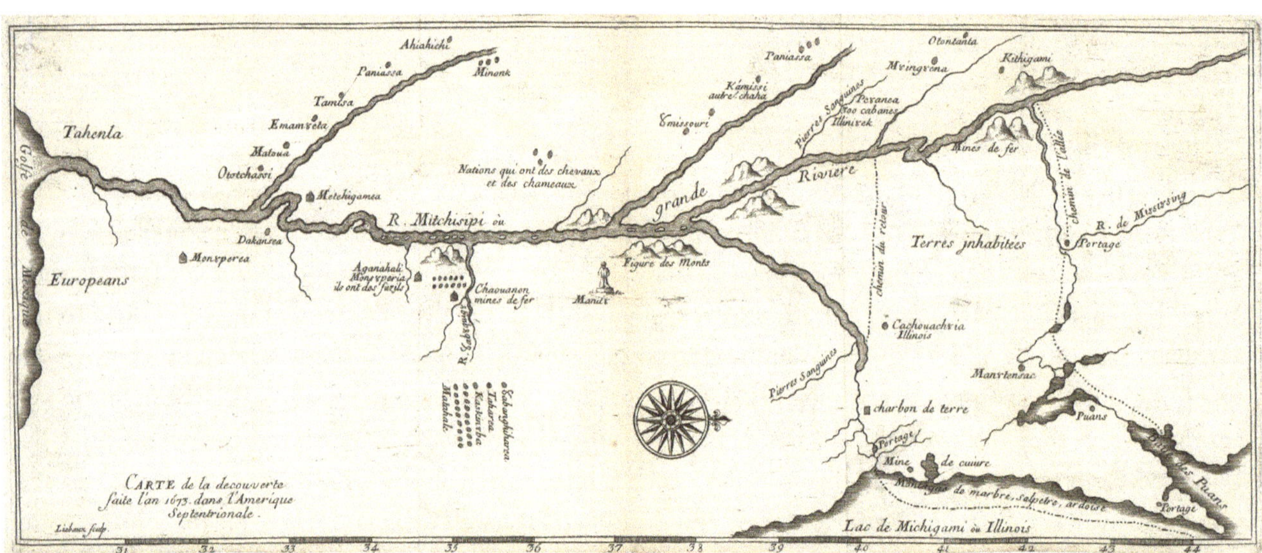

5. Ca. 1673 Marquette Map of the Mississippi River. Map from Thévenot, Recueil de Voyages ca. 1691, US public domain.

> In The year 1673, Monsieur the Count De Frontenac, Our Governor, and Monsieur Talon, then Our Intendant, Recognizing the Importance of this discovery, - either that they might seek a passage from here to the sea of China, by the river that discharges into the Vermillion, or California Sea; or because they desired to verify what has for some time been said concerning the two Kingdoms of Theguaio [*"Teguayo"*] And Quiuira [*"Quivera"*], which Border on Canada, and in which numerous gold mines are reported to exist.[38]

Marquette never returned to the colony; he died among the Illinois people in 1675 but not before forwarding his journal to Father Dablon in Montreal. It reposed there in the Jesuit archives for many years before being published in *The Jesuit Relations*....[39] Jolliet returned to Montreal but in a canoe mishap in the Lachine Rapids he lost all his papers and maps he had made while on the expedition. Dablon interviewed him, and the intendant and Frontenac may have done so as well. Late in 1674 the governor wrote to Minister Colbert in his memorandum "On the State of the Colony."

> Sieur Joliet whom Monsieur Talon advised me, upon my return from France, to dispatch for the discovery of the South Sea, has returned three months ago, and discovered some very fine Countries, and a navigation so easy through the beautiful rivers he has found...He has been within ten days' journey of the Gulf of Mexico, and believes that water communications could be found leading to the Vermilion' and California seas, via the river that flows from the West [obviously the Missouri] into the Grand River [the Mississippi] that he discovered, which runs from North to South, and is as large as the Saint Lawrence opposite Quebec.[40]

Dablon also spoke about the trip of Marquette and Jolliet when he prepared his own brief on it for the *Jesuit Relations* in 1674.[41] This was primarily based on his interviews with Joillet. Although he made clear the disappointment that came from not yet having Marquette's journal and the loss of Jolliet's field records, he spoke about some of the positive things that the expedition had demonstrated in its exploration of the Mississippi. Foremost among them was that it had opened up a whole new Native population for missionization and conversion by the Jesuits. It also indicated that the river terminated at the Gulf of Mexico and was not a route to the Vermillion Sea. He further pointed out how disappointing it was that the expedition did not find an inland passage.[42]

When finally returned to Montreal, Marquette's journal confirmed Jolliet's opinion that the large tributary river, the Pekitanouï, would most likely be the way by which any inland passage could be found. Jolliet pointed out that he hoped he would be able to explore it.[43] That opinion about the newly discovered river reinforced a strong belief among both Jesuits and colonial authorities that it might be the way to a passage. Upon hearing of the discovery of Marquette and Jolliet, Dablon became convinced that it was the route to follow in searching for one.[44]

The next formal information on the Mississippi drainage is believed to have come through La Salle who traveled down the Illinois River to the Mississippi, perphaps for a second time, in 1682. La Salle, a Quebec trader, knew Frontenac as well as Jolliet and Marquette and was versed in their travels. For some years after their 1673 expedition, which did not take them all the way down to the great river's mouth, he is said to have contemplated completing it by traveling all the way to the Gulf of Mexico. It seems unclear whether La Salle reached the Mississippi on his first trip, but he would at least have gained further information about it and conveyed it to Quebec where it would have been folded into the accumulating collective lore of the great river.[45]

In 1681 La Salle had led an expedition down the Mississippi all the way to its mouth in the Gulf of Mexico in his own quest to find a passage. His large company consisted of some 31 Natives and 23 Frenchmen, including several priests. He also passed and only barely commented on the confluence of the river with the Missouri. In April 1682 he claimed Louisiana, then in Spanish territory, and the Mississippi and its drainage for France before returning to Canada.[46]

Historians have presented some rivalry in the claims between La Salle's first expedition and that of Marquette and Jolliet as to which of them should be credited with the discovery of the Mississippi. La Salle claimed to have visited the river before Marquette and Jolliet. This question has apparently never been resolved, although the two seem to have been commonly credited with the clearest evidence for first discovery.[47] They do, however, appear to have been the first Frenchmen to have seen the Missouri River.

In 1683 the lure of the Mississippi led Father Zenobius Membré to follow La Salle's route down the Illinois River. Six leagues below its confluence with the Mississippi, which he referred to as the "Colbert," Membré found the mouth of the Missouri, which he referred to as the "Osage." He noted that the river was at least as large as the Mississippi and carried water that was hardly drinkable. Local Natives informed him that the river was fed by many tributaries which rose in far distant mountains, and was populated by a number of different Native nations with many villages. It was said to pass through prairies with abundant bison and beaver; and poured so much mud into the Mississippi that, despite the addition of clearer water from other rivers, it was never again clear all the way to the Gulf of Mexico.[48] Because of Frontenac's encouragement, in addition to Marquette and Jolliet, Membré; Henri Tonty, and La Salle also observed the mouth of the Missouri before Lahontan.

By the late fall 1683 when Lahontan was just arriving in Quebec, La Salle was back there also. He was about to sail for France to seek the Crown's permission and sponsorship for establishing a colony at the mouth of the Mississippi in part to thwart Spanish interests in the region. Unfortunately, there was not time for Lahontan to meet La Salle before he sailed for France the day following the baron's arrival. Had he done so the baron might have learned something more about the Missouri from him even if he had not traveled it.[49]

La Salle achieved what he sought from the Crown and sailed for the Gulf of Mexico in 1684, but he ultimately came to ruin and lost his life.[50] It took years for the survivors of La Salle's last expedition to straggle back north to Michilimackinac in the spring of 1688 where the Baron Lahontan received them.[51] Lahontan had traveled to Fort Saint Joseph with Tonty, La Salle's trusted lieutenant, in the fall of 1687 and could have learned much about the Mississippi and Missouri from him, as well as from Dulhut.

By the time of the baron's trip in 1688 La Salle, Membré, and others, including Marquette and Jolliet, had already learned that the Mississippi was not a route to the Pacific.[52] By then the French had only documented with some certainty the location, including latitude, of the confluence of the Missouri/Pekittanouï and the Mississippi.[53] Until Lahontan's 1688 travels there was little or no additional documentation of the Mississippi or the Missouri Rivers

The Pekittanouï was for a time known as the "Long River" apparently because of the way the Natives had described it. One can be certain, however, that Frenchmen, or their Native trading partners, were trading well into the Illinois River drainage and toward the Mississippi by that time. The extent to which they might have penetrated down the Mississippi and up the lower Long River/Missouri is not known, although it does not appear to have been very far up the latter, if at all, according to Lahontan's narrative and that of Bourgmont.[54]

The Frenchman, Le Page du Pratz, lived in Louisiana for sixteen years including eight among the Natchez people and wrote the important early eighteenth-century volume, *The History of Louisiana.*[55] In speaking of the years he lived there (1718–1734) he noted that that there were then many Native peoples with a variety of inconsistent names living along the Missouri River as it by then had finally become known. He further noted that the river was little visited during those years and even by the early eighteenth century the French had only penetrated upstream from the Mississippi for about 300 leagues (900 miles). This was apparently more than the distance to the Platte, which he did not mention. Until now the discovery of the Platte—as opposed to merely knowledge of its existence—has been accorded to the Seir de Bourgmont in 1714, although he did not travel up it.[56] Le Page du Pratz noted that the largest river then known to join with the Missouri was the "*Canzas*" ("Kansas" now often referred to as just the "Kaw") in the territory of the Canzas people.[57] This was in eastern Kansas, with the confluence near present-day Kansas City, far downstream below the Platte.

The fact that Le Page du Pratz spoke of the Kansas River and made no mention of the Platte, which is even larger, suggests that the latter was still essentially unknown. It also indicates that French exploration and trade to and beyond the Platte was not well established if at all by the early 1700s. It may be that the potentially hostile and numerous Natives of the Upper Missouri may not have been quite as welcoming as those the baron encountered on the Platte. It is to be noted that the Fox leader cautioned the baron not to go too far up the Long River because of the potential for hostilities from these people. The defensive preparations Lahontan ultimately recommended in his plan for traveling beyond the Platte to the source of the Missouri/Long River included heavy portable leather barriers for protection against arrows. In reviewing his proposal, this point appears to have been a salient concern for him and likely later potential travelers who might venture up the Missouri.[58]

Frontenac was reappointed governor of New France in 1689. In October he was enthusiastically received by some upon his arrival back in the colony. New France was then still deeply troubled by the ongoing wars with the Iroquois as well as by threats from the English. The fur trade had largely been curtailed by the Iroquois hostilities as well as by stringent new regulations that had been imposed on it by Denonville, Frontenac's predecessor. This led Frontenac to aggressively take the fight to the Iroquois and commenced some years of further conflict.

Vast amounts of valuable furs had been stranded at remote trading posts by what amounted to an Iroquois blockade of the river transportation routes. Frontenac finally broke this blockade, and the furs were canoed down to Montreal. The populace then saw him as "their father and deliverer." The governor also improved the local militia and so successfully prosecuted warfare against the Iroquois and their British allies that they finally sought peace, thus ending their threats to the colony.[59]

Among North American rivers, the Missouri is the longest and most deserving of being named the "long" one. It had obviously become known to Lahontan by that name prior to his trip as he referred to it that way on October 13 before he even reached the Mississippi.[60] By that time Natives had already described it to Jolliet and Marquette in 1673 and Membré in 1682, in terms of its great length.[61]

Lahontan and Period Knowledge of the Missouri River

When Lahontan departed from Michilimackinac for the Long River in September 1688, the Missouri/Long River was known to exist, its latitude at its mouth had seeminglybeen recorded, and it was widely considered to be the most likely route to an inland passage.[62] Lahontan probably even had Melchisedech Thévenot's book, *Recueil de Voyages de Mr. Thevenot,* with its copy of the map supposedly based on Marquette's and Joliett's travels down the Mississippi.. (Figure 5). This map showed the confluence of the Mississippi and the Missouri.[63] The baron could have had access to this after he arrived in Quebec, and due to his strong interest in Canada, perhaps even before he left France.[64]

Interest in finding an inland passage to Asia was common knowledge. The rapids on the Saint Lawrence River just above Montreal were first named the *"Sault St. Louis"* by Champlain in about 1611 in memory of one of his men who had been lost there. They were apparently renamed *"Lachine"* during La Salle's time by his detractors who derided his travel up them in his quest for the passage to the Western Sea and China. The word "Lachine" means "China" and helps to illustrate just how pervasive the idea of a possible inland passage to Asia was within New France.[65]

The baron could hardly have overlooked such important speculation. After making his trip in pursuit of the headwaters of the Long River, he remarked to his regular correspondent in France that he would never have made the trip "if I had not been fully instructed in everything that related to it and conveyed by a good guard."[66] This collective knowledge gathered from the wide variety of sources gave him a solid idea of where he wanted or needed to go, how to get there, and at least some idea of the major considerations he should have been aware of in trying to do so.

More immediate and specific knowledge was conveyed to the baron after he started his trip. This included the danger the Sioux poised and especially the point that he could travel in safety from hostile savages at least as far south on the Mississippi as the "Plantation of the Sun." This was certainly a reference to the site of the former prehistoric Mississippian city of Cahokia near Saint Louis near where the Missouri joins the Mississippi. In the baron's day the Natives' collective memory would certainly have retained knowledge of this most major ancient cultural landmark. In earlier times Cahokia had been the home of a paramount "great Sun" leader. It was also the largest prehistoric settlement in North America north of Mexico and would have been easily known far and wide due to its many huge mounds and cultural importance. Cahokia would have been as as far south as the baron was intending to go because it was where he would have to turn into the Long River. He was also warned of the potential danger posed by the large populations of Natives living on the upper Long River.[67]

Immediately prior to his travels toward the Long River, the baron stated that he was planning to travel through "the southern countries I have so often heard of (emphasis added)" and to explore all the way up to the source of the Long River.[68] These statements are critical in interpreting the baron's narrative and were overlooked by his many critics.

It seems obvious that Lahontan was especially interested in exploring to the far distant headwaters of the Long River because he was looking for something important there. As the Fox chief stated to him, the baron "had some discovery in my view" rather than trading, which he could easily have done without attempting such a long and dangerous journey.[69] He certainly did not have to go that far to find good fur trading opportunities or to substantially advance knowledge of the area to the west and or south of the Great Lakes. There was something beyond simple curiosity about the New World that was driving him to target the source of the Long River. The answer is simple enough given the context of the time. Because of the baron's poor finances and his family's loss of standing with the Crown, the rewards that might flow to him would have been a powerful incentive to seek an inland passage to the Pacific.

Notes:

1. Parkman, *La Salle and Discovery*, 731-32; Eccles, "La Mer de l'Ouest."

2. Eccles, "La Mer de l'Ouest," 1.

3. Heidenreich, "Early French Exploration," 126; Colbert to Talon, "His Majesties Intentions," (9), 89.

4. Brandão, "Introduction," xxiv; Chappell, *History of the Missouri River*, xxiii-xxiv, 2-4; Eccles, "La Mer de l'Ouest," 4-6; Heidenreich, "Early French Exploration," 126; Mapp, *Elusive West*, 101; Parkman, *La Salle and Discovery*, 735-45; Wood, *Prologue*, 10.

5. Eccles, "French Exploration," 144-520; *La Mer de l'Ouest;* Burpee, *Search For,* xiii -xix; Crouse, *In Quest of the Western Ocean;* Flint and Flint, *Coronado Expedition;* Heidenreich, "Early French Exploration," 66; Mapp, *Elusive West*, 4.

6. Crouse. *In Quest of*, 310 -348; Heidenreich, "Early French Exploration," 66-69, 147.

7. Kingston, *"Western Sea,"* 133-34; Crouse, *In Quest of*, 232-88.

8. Lovis and Donahue, "Space, Information, and Knowledge."

9. Lahontan, *New Voyages*, 193-95.

10. Kingston, "Western Sea,"133-34.

11. Hudson, *Knights of Spain*, 349-52; Parkman, *LaSalle and Discovery*, 725.

12. Crouse, *In Quest of*, 253; Parkman.

13. Parkman.

14. Parkman, 726.

15. Parkman, 726.

16. Kupfer and Buisseret, "Seventeenth-Century Jesuit Explorers."

17. Kingston, "Western Sea," 137.

18. Hennepin, *A New Discovery*.

19. Kingston, "Western Sea," 134; Parkman, *La Salle and Discovery*, 905-9; Zoltvany, "Greysolon Dulhut." Historians generally credit the discovery of the Great Salt Lake to mountain man, Jim Bridger, in 1820. Among these, Hubert H. Bancroft adamantly denied the credibility of Lahontan's account of the lake. Bancroft, *History of Utah*, 18-20. Utah historian, David Miller, also credits the discovery of the lake to Bridger and does not even mention the baron. Miller, "Fur Trade," 64-65; Also see Baker et al., *Juan Rivera's Colorado*, 33n22,

20. Lahontan, *New Voyages*, 73, 139, 140, 216; Thwaites, "Introduction," xviii.

21. Parkman, *La Salle and Discovery*, 736.

22. Heidenreich, "Early French Exploration," 126; Colbert to Talon, "His Majesty's Intentions...," (9), 89.

23. Eccles, *Frontenac;* Parkman, *La Salle and Discovery*,760-800.

24. Eccles, *Frontenac*, 78-87, 98, 160, 183-84, 280-82, 289-90; Fortier, "Juchereau;" Lahontan, *New Voyages*, 164; Parkman, *Count Frontenac*, 54-56, 111, 144; Oslier, "Tonty;"Thwaites, "Introduction," xviii; Weilbrenner, "Morel de la Durantaye;" Zoltvany, "Greysolon Dulhut;"

25. Osler, "Tonty, Henri."

26. Zoltany, "Greysolon Dulhut."

27. Eccles, *Frontenac;*" Heidenreich, "Early French Exploration," 130-133. Parkman, *La Salle and Discovery*, 760.

28. Brandão, "Introduction," xxiv.

29. Eccles, *Frontenac*, 130-133; Heidenreich, "Early French Exploration," 130-33; Parkman, *La Salle and Discovery*, 760; Zoltany, "Greysolon Dulhut."

30. Eccles, *Frontenac*, 98.

31. Eccles, 98.

32. Canada, *Statistics Canada*, "Early French settlements (1605 to 1691)."

33. Marquette, *Father Marquette's Journal*, 13, *Voyages of Marquette;* Marquette and Dablon, "Of the First Voyage," 139-41; Parkman. *La Salle and Discovery*, 762.

34. Crouse, *In Quest of the Western Ocean*, 277; Marquette, *Father Marquette's Journal*, 15; Marquette and Dablon, "Of the First Voyage," 139-41.

35. Jolliet, Louis, Associated Name, and Jacques Marquette. *Map of the New Discovery Made by the Jesuit Fathers in and Continued by Father Jacques Marquette, from the Same Group, Accompanied by a Few Frenchmen in the Year 1673, Named "Manitounie".* [Place of Publication Not Identified: Publisher Not Identified, 1673] Map. https://www.loc.gov/item/2021668635/. US Library of Congress, control number 2021668635.

36. Chappell, *History of the Missouri River*, 2-6; Marquette, *Father Marquette's Journal*, 13; Parkman, *La Salle and Discovery*, 768-69.

37. Marquette, 13. Crouse, *In Quest of the Western Ocean*, 276-79.

38. Dablon, "Relation de la descouverte," (CXXXI), 108.

39. Marquette and Dablon, "Of the First Voyage."

40. Frontenac to Colbert, "General Memorandum," (ix), 16-121.

41. Dablon, "Discovery of the Mississippi," 108.

42. Dablon, 108.

43. Marquette and Dablon, "Of the First Voyage," 139-41.

44. Marquette and Dablon, 141-43; http://moses.creighton.edu/kripke/jesuitrelelations/_59html-edn34.

45. Chappell, *History of the Missouri River*, 5-6; Heidenreich, *Early French Exploration*, 130-33; Parkman, *La Salle and Discovery*, 760-91.

46. Chappell, *History of the Missouri River*, 1-9; Marquette, *Father Marquette's Journal;* Parkman, 921-29.

47. Parkman,742-43, 831-41.

48. Chappell, *History of the Missouri River*, 6; Parkman, 920-21.

49. Lahontan, *New Discoveries*, 32; Thwaites, "Introduction," xii; Weddle, *The French Thorn*.

50. Parkman, *La Salle and Discovery*, 713-1054; Weddle. *Wreck*; Also see *French Thorn*.

51. Lahontan, *New Voyages*, 144-45; Parkman, 954-1035.

52. Marquette, *Father Marquette's Journal;* Parkman, 766-69, 886, 921-27.

53. Marquette, "Map of the New Discovery;" Thévenot, *Recueil de Voyages.*

54. Norall, *Bourgemont*, 25-27.

55. du Pratz, *History of Louisana*.

56. Norall, *Bourgemont*, 25-27.

57. du Pratz, *History of Louisiana*, 59.

58. Lahontan, *New Voyages*, 176, 209-15.

59. Eccles, "Brisay De Denonville."

60. Lahontan, *New Voyages*, 174-76.

61. Chappell, *History of the Missouri River*, 1-6; Marquette, *Father Marquette's Journal*, 15; Parkman, *La Salle and Discovery*, 768.

62. Kingston, *Western Sea*, 134-35; Marquette, *Father Marquette's Journal;* Marquette and Dablon, "Of the First Voyage," 139-41.

63. Thévenot, *Recueil de Voyages.*

64. Thwaites, "Introduction," xi.

65. Lahontan, *New Voyages*, 67n.

66. Lahontan, 301.

67. Lahontan, 175-77.

68. Lahontan, 164-65, 176.

69. Lahontan 176.

3

• THE BARON LAHONTAN: A YOUNG MARINE IN NEW FRANCE •

by

STEVEN G. BAKER

On Tuesday, November 8,1683 the weather was cold and blustery as a French troop ship finally anchored at the port of Quebec on the Saint Lawrence River in New France. The *Tempest*, transporting three companies of French marines (Figure 6) consisting of about two-hundred fifty to three hundred men, had sailed from La Rochelle in southwestern France on August 29. The Crown sent these soldiers to bolster its colony's ability to fend off the Iroquois Confederacy, which was then seriously threatening it during what came to be known as the long and ongoing French and Iroquois or Beaver Wars.[1]

Episodic fighting occurred on-and-off through the seventeenth century between the colony with its Native allies, including Algonquian speakers, and the Iroquois in large part over control of the all-important fur trade along the Saint Lawrence River and adjacent regions about the Great Lakes. Since that trade was then New France's central economic driver, defeating the competing Iroquois with their close British alliance was thus a major strategic consideration for the French. These conflicts are commonly seen as among the most violent and bloodiest of the Indian Wars fought in North America.[2]

LAHONTAN'S PRE-LONG RIVER TRIP BIOGRAPHY

The marine contingent that anchored at Quebec included a tall, thin, and pale seventeen-year-old of noble birth named Louis-Armand de Lahontan d'Arce. (June 9, 1666 –ca. April 21, 1716). The young marine was then still only a cadet but also bore the inherited French title of le Baron de Lahontan et Heslèche (a.k.a. *"d'Esleich"*). He was the eldest son of Isaac de Lom d'Arce and his second wife, Françoise Le Fascheux de Couttes. In formal terms this young man has emerged to history as the "Lom d'Arce de Lahontan" but is more commonly known as the "Baron Lahontan" or just "Lahontan." Foregoing formalities, he often just simply signed his name "Darce."[3]

6. A French Marine officer as served in Canada in the late 17th century, courtesy Parks Canada, via René Chartrand (retired), Canadian Public Domain.

The baron was born at the Barony of Lahontan in the domain of Esleix in the French department of Basses-Pyrénees.[4] Lahontan's father had been a noted French engineer who was awarded those lands by the Crown in recognition of his efforts to make the waterway known as the *Gave de Pau* navigable. Unfortunately, his father died a deeply indebted old man when the baron was only about eight years old.[5] His creditors would in time become major nemeses for Lahontan.

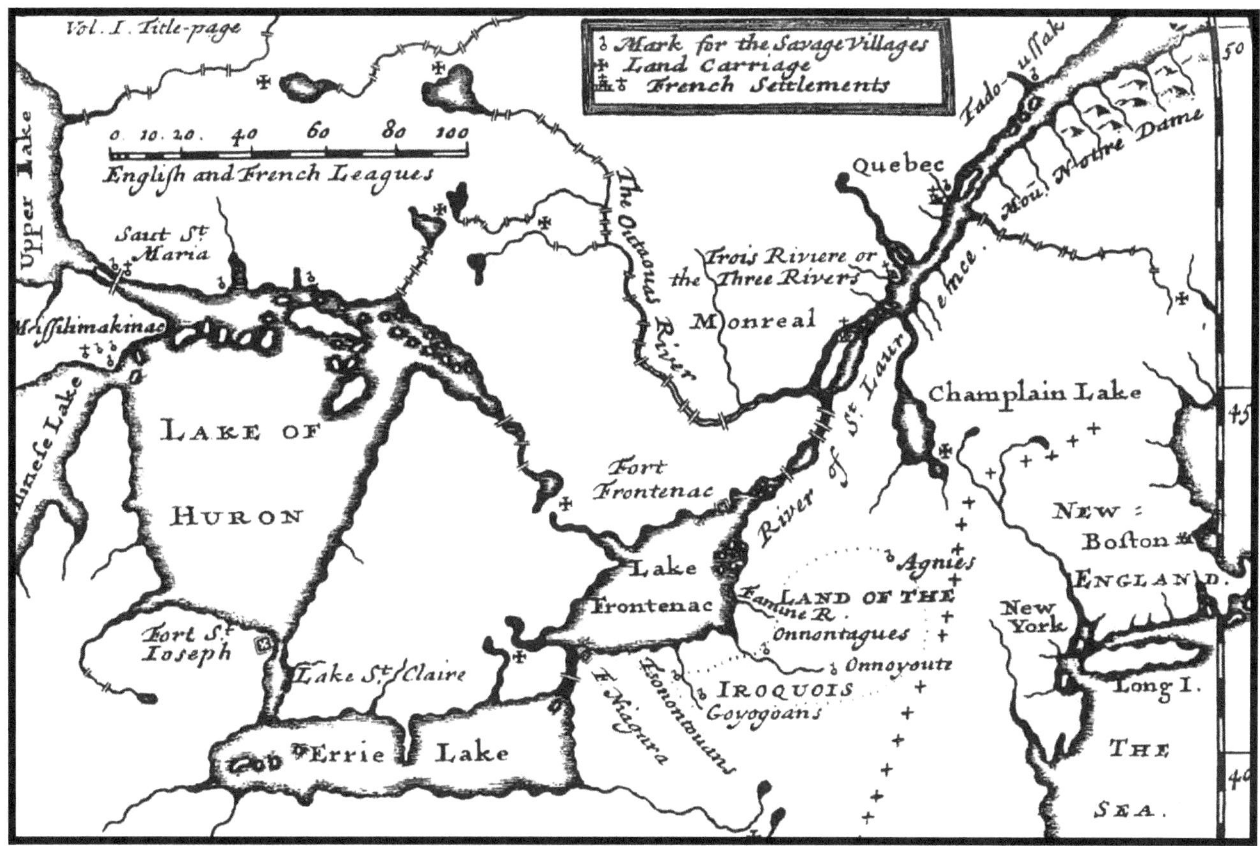

7. A portion of Lahontan's 1703 General Map of New France showing locations that are important in his biography of the time he spent there.

When the baron arrived in port at Quebec (Figure 7), he was already relatively well-educated for his years and had been destined for a military career from birth. To prepare him for such a future, the young nobleman was enrolled as a cadet in the prestigious Bourbon regiment. He was eventually appointed to the *compagnie de Saint-Circq* in the Ministry of the Marine, which was responsible for the care and defense of France's colonies. He was apparently part of that company when he arrived in New France and may have sought the posting to see and learn about Canada, which he obviously remained keen to do prior to and throughout his service there.[6]

Just as the baron was arriving in Quebec, the great French explorer of the Mississippi River, La Salle, was there also and preparing to sail for France the next day. La Salle had only recently returned to the colony from his initial exploration down that great river. To thwart Spanish interests there he was sailing back to France to try to muster the Crown's approval and sponsorship for establishing a colony near the river's mouth on the Gulf of Mexico. Although he would certainly have been aware of La Salle's early exploits, upon his arrival in Quebec, Lahontan would have had no inkling that his interests and paths of the next few years would become associated, at least in a tangential way, with his. That was through men they both knew, such as La Salle's compatriots who survived his 1687 ill-fated attempt at colonization.[7]

8. A ca. 1673 image of an Ottawa warrior as accompanied Lahontan and his marines on the Long River travels. From Louis Nicolas, Codex canadensis, ca. 1700, courtesy Wikipedia Commons, https://commons.wikimedia.org/wiki/Main_Page.

Lahontan had long been keen to learn all he could about the things he was hearing in France about the Canadian colony. He ultimately crossed paths with other famous French explorers of the period including Tonty, Henri Joutel, Anastase Douay, John Cavalier, Durantaye, and Dulhut (Duluth), all of whom were La Salle's cohorts. Among many, including Natives of all kinds and the Coureurs de Bois, these men became a major source of information about distant lands for the young baron.

Lahontan had an abiding interest in natural history and became well known as an early naturalist from the observations he made on the Natives, flora, fauna and a host of other topics that caught his attention in Canada. All his writings indicate that Lahontan was not just a brilliant, educated, and precocious young fellow. He was also naturally curious, morally guided, high-minded, humane, and refined in his thinking. He had certainly studied the classics and had at least a passing familiarity with Latin. He was also a gifted, somewhat compulsive, writer. He was truly an early child of the Enlightenment noted for his attempts at rational thought and questioning of authority, particularly that of the Church and Crown.

As one noted early historian pointed out, in his thinking he was a "generation in advance of his age." [8] He readily gained wilderness survival, fighting, linguistic, and travel skills from the Natives he encountered and actually traveled and lived among. These skills enabled him to stand out among the other officers of the French marines sent to New France and made him an especially important asset to the Crown in battling the Iroquois. These special skill sets also well served him and his men on his travels to the Long River.

By the time he reached Quebec, winter was rapidly setting in and the primary fighting season with the Iroquois was over. Lahontan could only look forward to being stuck in winter quarters with his marine comrades in the outlying settlements around the city. Even after his long voyage from France and the discomfort of a the fast-approaching frigid Canadian winter, he was not at all disheartened when he arrived at Quebec except that he felt it was "mortally cold" there. His interests in exploring his new environs remained strong and led him on several expeditions including the one that would take him to the Long River and the very heart of the central Great Plains. Almost as soon as he arrived, he wrote: "Tis true, the Passage [from France] is in some measure long [70 days]; but then the hopes of viewing an unknown Country, atones for the tediousness of the Voyage."[9]

Although he eventually became preoccupied with his family's increasingly endangered financial affairs in France, this was not yet an obvious major concern for him when he arrived in Canada. Seemingly unfettered by such matters, the young baron was eager to learn all he could about the colony and commenced writing about the history, geography, and living conditions there as soon as he had landed at Quebec.[10]

Along with a multitude of other things he observed, he described the Saint Lawrence River and visited and described the friendly Ottawa Natives (Figure 8) living in the vicinity of the city of Quebec. He described the city, its population and fortifications. He wrote about the nature of the Iroquois and the history of their ongoing wars with the colony. He described travel in the Canadian wilderness and how snowshoes and canoes made it possible. He wrote of Montreal and its role in the fur trade. Little of significance about the colony escaped either his gaze or his pen in both his writings and drawings. Even a casual reading of his book reveals the extent of his profuse knowledge, enlightened nature of his writing and seemingly a skillful artistic ability. He claimed to have penned at least 25 letters to a never-identified correspondent in France from the time of his arrival in Canada in 1683 and to have kept copies of all of them as well as the travel journals from which he extracted them.[11]

Following his arrival in Canada, the baron spent most of his time for the next few years in routine garrison duty within the settled parts of New France, namely about Quebec and Montreal. He spent much of his time hunting and fishing with local Ottawa Natives. He roamed the woods with them for long periods. even in the depths of winter. He became a pioneer ethnographer of some merit and was particularly interested in the Natives' cultures. He immersed himself in their ways, soaking up all that he could learn from and about them. He became a skilled woodsman and learned to live and travel as they did. He also learned to speak dialects of Algonquian, the language of so many of the colony's Native allies, including the Ottawas with whom he spent so much time. When combined with his military skills, these additional abilities greatly enhanced his usefulness in defending the colony against the Iroquois.

Because of his skills and unique knowledge, he became so important to the defense of the colony that on multiple occasions he found himself barred from returning to France to manage his family's financial affairs. Against his wishes and, in spite of permission from the Crown to return home, he was kept in active service in Canada until his family's affairs had deteriorated to a point that he was left in near penury. This situation also left him with enduring mistrust and hostility to the Crown, lawyers, bankers, and the kind of politicians who had ignored his family's past services to France and, to his thinking, usurped its wealth, including what he hoped to inherit.

Throughout his service in Canada, and even after he left there, the baron longed for an opportunity to have his wealth and social status in France restored. Following his Long River expedition, the desire to restore his wealth and reputation seem to have provided the strong motivation for the further exploration he hoped to make of the Missouri/Long River as a potential route to an inland passage and the Western Sea.

With few official duties to occupy him, he was content to spend much of his early time in New France out in the wilderness with his local Native friends. In the spring of 1684 he was finally ordered to join an expedition being sent against the Iroquois from Fort Frontenac on Lake Ontario. (Figure 7). Lahontan describes this failed expedition in Letter VII.[12]

In September 1685 Lahontan was sent to quarters in Boucherville on the south shore of the Saint Lawrence River opposite Montreal. He was quartered there for the next year and a half, apparently with few official military duties to perform. He seems to have enjoyed ample free time to explore by canoe and to hunt, particularly for moose.

The baron's routine returned to more formal military duties in the spring of 1687 while he was posted at Saint Helens near Montreal. (Figure 7). At about this time he received a letter from his correspondent in France, which informed him of the extreme plight of his family fortunes and recommended that he return home as soon as possible if he wished to salvage anything from them. At this point, the baron's demeaner seemed to change. Although he remained keen to learn all he could about Canada, he appears to have begun to worry, and his writing devoted more thought to his plight and to finding a way to get back to France.

To help facilitate his return, the baron's relatives went to great lengths in petitioning the minister of the Marine, Jean-Baptiste Colbert, marquis de Seignelay, to grant him the necessary permission. Letters bearing word of their success in obtaining permission and orders to newly appointed governor Denonville on the matter reached the baron from Seignelay' s office on or about June 8,1687, while the young officer was still at Saint Helens.

Denonville had turned his attention to finally defeating the Iroquois and planned to field an expedition that would be the largest ever sent against these irrepressible hostiles. Eight hundred regular soldiers newly arrived from France doubled the number in the colony. This army was assembled on the island of Saint Helen in the Saint Lawrence River opposite Montreal. (Figure 7). The governor, however, refused to allow Lahontan to leave Canada because his special skills were needed in the pending campaign. Instead, he promised the baron that he would be free to sail for home as soon as the summer campaign was over. That expedition of 1687 invaded Iroquois territory and burned Seneca villages and crops. Although Denonville's army was large it accomplished little.

When the governor's campaign ended the baron again anticipated that he would be allowed to finally return to France as promised. Despite the Crown's orders to allow him to return, Denonville, once again refused him permission to do so because his "knowledge of native languages and his skill in forest diplomacy" were then still sorely needed.[13] Lahontan was understandably exasperated by the governor, but he could not disobey him.

Denonville's expeditionary force also built a new fort at Niagara in hopes of thwarting future Iroquois attacks. Fort Niagara was located near the south shore on the Niagara River near its confluence with Lake Ontario (a.k.a. Lake Frontenac). (Figure 7) This is near present-day Youngstown, New York, across the lake opposite Toronto. This period and its campaign are discussed in Lahontan's Letters XII -XIV.

The baron was next sent to Fort Niagara and apparently helped in its further construction. There he witnessed the extreme torture and enslavement of Native prisoners, one of whom was his friend. He was sympathetic to their plights, writing about them in his Letter XIII.[14] In one case he believed the torture was completely inhumane and unjustified. He subsequently punished some of the torturers and by doing so aroused considerable Native anger toward himself. This intervention also nearly got him killed by the Natives for interfering with their customary brutal treatment of prisoners. For this, higher ranking authorities punished him with confinement[15]

Instead of sailing for France as he was anxiously anticipating, the baron found himself in command of a detachment of marines, about thirty or perhaps as many as sixty strong.[16] He had by then received a promotion from cadet to lieutenant. As before, he could not disobey the governor and therefore began preparing for a substantial campaign far from Montreal and Quebec.

He and his men were dispatched to go assist the colony's Huron and Ottawa allies in the vicinity of Lake Huron, then a vast and little-known region of what was then the "Northwest" portion of New France. La Durantaye had claimed this region for France in June 1687 when he erected the arms of France at the head of the strait between Lake Huron and Lake St. Clair.[17] Lahontan left Niagara on

August 3 and eventually found himself garrisoning the small fort of Saint Joseph on the south shore of Lake Huron during the winter of 1687–1688. (Figure 7)

For his trip into the distant northwest, Lahontan was provided with good healthy soldiers, large new canoes, and as guides two Frenchmen who emerged as very important people in the history of New France. These were Dulhut (Duluth) and M. de Tonty, the close associate of La Salle. Both were experienced woodsmen from whom the baron certainly learned a great deal. As was typical, he also had some Native allies with him.

Dulhut had built the small defensive post, Fort St. Joseph, the previous year (1686) on the governor's order. It was a simple bastioned log blockhouse on the strait between Lakes Huron and Erie. (Figure 7) It was part of chain of posts the French established to block Iroquois and English incursions into the fur country and to control the ever-wandering Coureurs de Bois, the illicit/unlicensed French fur traders. The baron left Fort Niagara on August 3 with his men and headed to St. Joseph as ordered. Lahontan considered his mission dangerous and was fearful of being attacked and perhaps captured and tortured by the Iroquois who were so expert at using fire to that purpose and even eating their victims' flesh while they still lived. As he stated: "To die is nothing but to live in the midst of Fire is too much."[18]

The baron's company arrived at St. Joseph on September 14 with fall fast closing in. Lahontan relieved the Coureurs de Bois that Dulhut had left to garrison the post. These men quickly disappeared into the woods to commence trading for furs. Dulhut and Tonty stayed with the baron at the fort for a few days, which provided ample opportunity for him to get to know these men and learn more from them about distant lands. The baron and his detachment then spent the fall hunting and socializing with friendly Native parties that passed through the post. Winter then set in, and it was so cold and snowy that it kept the men indoors, preventing them from venturing outside even to hunt.

This experience appears to have soured the baron on being shut in by snowy winters on the frontier of New France. Within a year it helped motivate him to abandon the north woods during the winter and head out to explore warmer, more southerly regions and his Long River. His experience at Fort St. Joseph is discussed in his Letters XIII and XIV.[19]

By April 1688 Lahontan was so weary of being snow bound at Fort Saint Joseph that he found an excuse to depart the remote post as early as the ice-out was underway. In an attempt to procure corn for his detachment from friendly Hurons and Ottawas, he set out for Michilimackinac by canoe. That outpost was then a small yet important trading station on the north shore of the Strait of Mackinac over two-hundred miles to the northwest. (Figure 7) Lahontan and his detachment arrived at Michilimackinac on April 18.

Denonville had already twice denied the baron an opportunity to return to France. Lahontan, back at Michilimackinac, wrote directly to Colbert and implored him to assist him further. In this letter, which he apparently sent by way of his regular, unnamed correspondent, he recited the services his father had rendered to the Crown. These included the deepening of some rivers. He also summarized the injustices that had been done to his rights of inheritance since his father's death and his absence from France. He attributed these injustices to the fact that he was not present but was in the "sag end of the

World" far from where he could defend his rights against what he believed were corrupt creditors and individuals in the parliament.

Lahontan implored Colbert to again grant him permission to return to France the next year. The baron appears to have been optimistic that, due to his good reputation and conduct in service in New France, the request would finally be honored. He discussed the circumstances and reprinted his letter in his Letter XIV.[20] By the time his 1688 field duties were fulfilled, and the baron was free to head back down to Montreal and Quebec, the fall season was already so far advanced that it was no longer possible to attempt that long, dangerous canoe journey before the next year. There was just no way that he could get there and catch a ship home before summer 1689. After previously being snowbound at Fort Saint Joseph, he faced the prospect of being locked in at Michilimackinac through yet another seemingly eternal winter in the long cold nights of the Canadian wilderness.

While he was at Michilimackinac the survivors of La Salle's failed colonization attempt finally straggled into the post on May 6,1688, after traveling for many months and over 800 leagues (roughly 2400 miles) to get back to the colony. These men included Jean Cavelier, the brother of La Salle; Anastase Douay, a priest as well as La Salle's nephew; and Henri Joutel, one of La Salle's pilots. The baron hosted them for about two weeks while they recuperated and then headed them downriver toward Quebec escorted by ten men from his detachment in canoes he provided.[21]

Prior to their departure, the baron appears to have spent considerable time with these individuals, presumably listening to their tales about the distant lands they had seen and heard of as well as the events in their travels. They were likely one of Lahontan's primary sources of information about the "Southern Countries" he would endeavor to explore when he finally embarked on his trip down the Mississippi.

Lahontan was already acquainted with Tonty who had been one of La Salle's close partners in his fur cartel and with whom he had explored remote territories. The baron had previously spent considerable time with both him and Dulhut during expeditions against the Iroquois and at Fort Saint Joseph. Charles de Juchereau de Saint Denys was temporarily in command at Michilimackinac in 1688 while Durantaye, the regular commander, was absent. Thus, when the baron was preparing for his expedition and then left, he clearly did so under the watch of St. Denys, a leading figure in the fur trade and another close associate of La Salle in his trading ventures in the Illinois country.[22] Lahontan wrote about these experiences in his Letters XII and XIII.[23] These men had also seen other southern areas and likely told Lahontan what they had personally observed as well as learned about them from Natives.[24]

Once he had procured some sixty sacks of corn at Michilimackinac, Lahontan was ordered to take his detachment to Saint Mary's Fort (Figure 7) to raise allies from among the Chippewas living in proximity to that post. He was instructed to persuade them to join his forces and proceed into Iroquois country around Fort Saint Joseph, which he was ordered to once again garrison.

The baron and his detachment departed for Fort Saint Mary's on June 2, 1688, and after coasting eastward from island to island and then crossing to the south shore of Lake Huron, arrived back at Saint Joseph on July 1. Lahontan then quickly led his forces into Lake Erie and the Iroquois country by canoe.

They immediately built a temporary defensive redoubt on the River Conde in what is now believed to be New York and went to look for the enemy. After encountering what his men believed to be a large Iroquois force, they fled in a rout back to their redoubt. Fearing he was greatly outnumbered, the baron and his forces retreated and canoed back toward Saint Joseph. Despite some encounters and scares on the way, they reached the post safely on August 29, 1688.

While at Saint Joseph, the baron learned that Governor Denonville was planning to make peace with the Iroquois and had already abandoned Fort Niagara. With this information he concluded that the fort was no longer of any strategic value. He also had only enough rations and ammunition there to last his men for two months and would ultimately have to abandon the post and retreat to Michilimackinac. Since he had no fresh orders from the governor, he felt it within his duty to make his own decisions. His men were also fearful they might have to spend another long, cold, and snowy winter there without sufficient resources. They were, accordingly, pleased to hear that they were going to abandon the post. At the end of August Lahontan burned St. Joseph and set his canoes northwesterly back toward the Straits of Michilimackinac. He arrived there on September 10. The Baron discussed these activities in his Letter XV. [25]

When he arrived at Michilimackinac he found new orders from Denonville stating that he was to return to the colony if it was not too late in the season to make that long and dangerous canoe trip. If he could not make it back to Montreal, he was to remain until spring and then return. Along with these orders the governor sent, perhaps as part of a normal supply shipment for the post, pay and provisions for his detachment so that it could overwinter there if necessary.

The baron and his French and Native associates all agreed that it was already too late to commence the trip. He further noted that his marine detachment, while able to satisfactorily work the canoes on calm waters, was not as adept at running fast, difficult rivers as such a trip required. His inability to return to the colony in 1688 ensured that the baron could not possibly get back to France to deal with family affairs until the summer or fall of the following year at the earliest. Even that would depend on any new orders he might receive from the governor. Lahontan would certainly have been crestfallen when he realized this, but it could not be helped. He discussed these events in his Letter XV. [26]

Before closing his letter, the baron informed his correspondent of his plans to explore the "countries" south of Michilimackinac and Lake Illinois (Michigan). Carrying out this vaguely stated plan would lead him to the Long River. [27] Since he wrote his Letter XV in September 1688, after it was too late for a canoe trip back down to Montreal, let alone Quebec, that communication could not have even reached his correspondent until well into 1689.

Notes:

1. Unless otherwise noted, the information for this chapter was drawn from the Baron Lahontan's book, *New Voyages to North America* and Rueben Gold Thwaites's "Introduction" to the 1905 reprint of the

baron's original 1703 English version of it augmented by the on-line biographies prepared by Hayne, "Lom D'Arce De Lahontan;" and Ouellet, "Baron of Lahontan." Crompton, *Glimpses of Early*, xii-xiii; Kent, *Rendezvous*, 70; Lahontan, 25-28.

2. Brandão, *Your Fyre Shall Burn; Brandão and Starna, Treaty of 1701;* Eccles, *Fur Trade*, 324-34; Moore, *Colonization and Conflict*,138- 46; Neave, "Lahontan and the Long River," 124-47; Parkman, *France and England*, 541-620; Phillips, *Fur Trade*, (I), 220-45.

3. Fournier, *Les Officiers*,425; Hayne, "Lom D'Arce;" Crompton, *Glimpses of Early*, xi.

4. Lahontan, *New Voyages*, 6.

5. Allan, "Baron Lahontan," 1.

6. Allan, 1. Fournier, *Les Officiers;* Lahontan, *New Voyages*, 25.

7. Weddle, *The French Thorn.*

8. Thwaites, "Introduction," xlvii.

9. Lahontan, *New Voyages*, 25.

10. Lahontan, 25.

11. Lahontan, 300.

12. Lahontan, 66-87.

13. Thwaites, xvii.

14. Lahontan, *New Voyages*,121-34.

15. Hayne, "Lom D'Arce."

16. Various personal e-mail and telephone communications between René Chartrand, a French-Canadian military historian from Muséoplume, Gatineau, Quebec, with Steven G. Baker, Centuries Research, Inc., Montrose, Colorado, 2008. Neave, "Lahontan and the Long River,"137. Kent notes that the first contingent of marines in 1683, which would have apparently included Lahontan, contained only 156 men in three companies with only 120 being fit for service and with much unserviceable equipment. This suggests that each company may have had roughly 40 men in it. Kent, *Rendezvous*, 70.

17. Lahontan in a similar manner to that of La Durantaye laid claim for France to distant lands on the Great Plains by erecting a monument along the Platte River in Nebraska. Lahontan, *New Voyages*, 197.

18. Thwaites, "Introduction," xix.

19. Lahontan, *New Voyages*,121-34.

20. Lahontan, 135-51.

21. Lahontan, 144-45; Cavelier, *Journal*, 129; Thwaites, "Introduction," xxi.

22. Fortier, "Juchereau."

23. Lahontan, *New Voyages*, 124, 133,139, 144, 145.

24. Eccles, *Frontenac*, 78-87, 98, 160, 183-84, 280-82, 289-90; Fortier, "Juchereau." Parkman, *Count Frontenac*, 54-56, 111, 144; Oslier, "Tonty." Thwaites, "Introduction," xviii; Weilbrenner, "Morel de la Durantaye;" Zoltvany, "Greysolon Dulhut."

25. Lahontan, *New Voyages*, 152-66.

26. Lahontan, 152-66.

27. Lahontan, 164.

4

• LAUNCHING THE LONG RIVER EXPEDITION: LAHONTAN AT MICHILIMACKINAC, 1688 •

by

STEVEN G. BAKER

In 1688, Michilimackinac, New France's critically important fur trade center, was located at present-day St. Ignace, Michigan, on the north side of the narrow Straits of Mackinac, which connect Lake Michigan—then known as Illinois Lake—and Lake Huron. Today the Straits separate lower and upper Michigan. (Figures 7, 9) Because of this strategic location on the Straits relative to canoe travel, Michilimackinac played a central role in the fur trade and the baron's Long River trip. It was the seat of the trade in the early years of New France and the starting point for nearly all exploration into the "*pays d'en haut*." In the seventeenth century the French term "pays d'en haut" simply meant the "upper country" west of Montreal. This region included the western Great Lakes (Huron, Michigan/Illinois, and Superior) as well as surrounding wilderness areas to the west, south, and north of them, including the Mississippi drainage area.[1]

MICHILIMACKINAC: A PORTRAIT

Michilimackinac was usually reached from Montreal by canoeing up the Ottawa River from the Saint Lawrence River to Georgian Bay on Lake Huron and then on westward by way of Lake Huron to the Straits of Mackinac. (Figure 9) This trip was roughly 500 miles long; Quebec was another 150 miles downriver below Montreal. As the portal from the lower Great Lakes to the western territories of the pays d'en haut, the Straits were a prime gathering point for Native and French traders. The pays d'en haut was thus a critical region for the fur trade. It had plentiful fur-bearing animals, such as the highly desired beaver, and a large Native population to trap and hunt for furs and hides. It also had an extensive system of lakes and rivers that served as the canoe routes, which were vital in transporting furs and trade goods. Almost everyone headed to or from Lake Illinois or into the pays d'en haut or beyond passed through Michilimackinac. The French came to use the term Michilimackinac to refer to the region about the Straits as well as the Straits and the post itself.

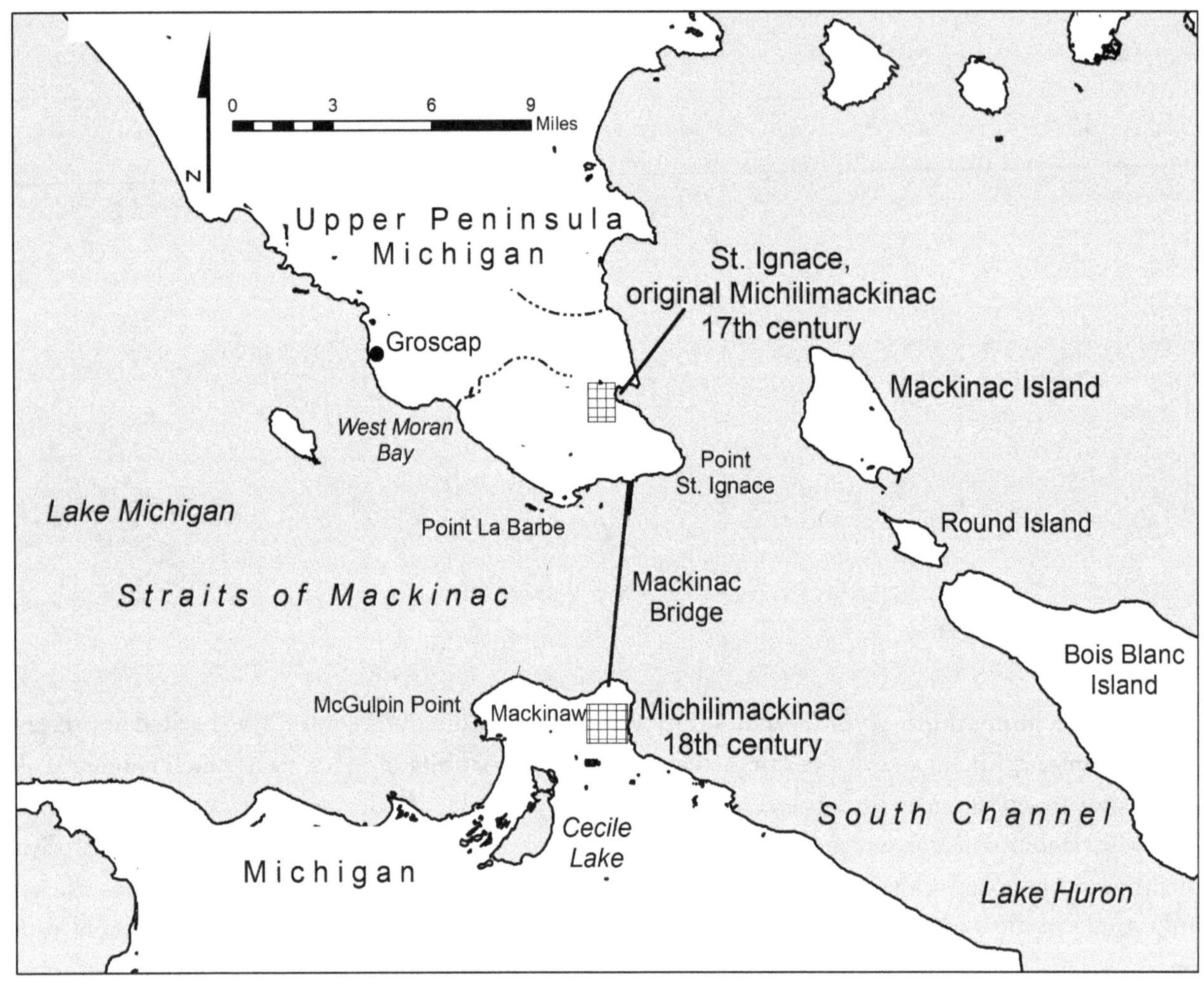

9a. Map of the Straits of Mackinac and locations of Michilimackinac.

Michilimackinac was also presumed to be on the way to any possible inland passage and the Western Sea.[2] It was thus the scene of important diplomatic and economic events in the colony's early history. It was not only an active trading post but also the supply hub for all those involved in more remote western fur trading. It was also the transportation center for much of the all-important fur and other peltries shipped from Canada by way of Montreal. Lahontan emphasized that the post was not only essentially the capital of the Northwest but also the "staple of all the goods" traded to the Natives to the south and southwest of Lake Illinois.[3]

Other than what Lahontan provided, there is little information available about the original seventeenth-century post. No remains of it have to date been found archaeologically in the vicinity of St. Ignace. (Figures 9a, 9b,10) Michilimackinac was also the residential base of some Coureurs de Bois and housed a Jesuit mission as well as a village of Ottawas, a major ally of the French, and one of the Hurons and other friendly Natives. The Natives and the French lived in close proximity there. Later, it may also have been the site of a Crown fortification known as Fort de Baude. The main settlement is believed to have been moved to the south shore of Lake Michigan in the early eighteenth century as shown in Figure

9b. This newer site has been archaeologically investigated, reconstructed, and interpreted as a major public heritage resource park by the Mackinac State Historic Parks Department.[4]

Prologue to Lahontan's Long River Expedition

In planning his trip Lahontan was certainly reflecting on his miserable experience in overwintering at Fort Saint Joseph.[5] Ever true to his adventurous spirit, and with no way to reach Montreal or Quebec, he had a lot of time to kill ahead of him. These circumstances led the young baron to state:

> In the meantime, I am upon the point of undertaking another Voyage, for I cannot mew my self up here all this Winter. I design to make the best use of my time, and to travel through the Southern Countries that I have so often heard of, having engag'd four or five good Huntsmen of the Outaouais [Ottawas] to go along with me." [emphasis added][6]

Except for his narrative of his Long River travels, there is no information about the baron for the period September 24, 1688, to May 22, 1689, when he said he arrived back at Michilimackinac. Except for when he had hunted moose with Ottawas out of Boucherviller for much of the winter in1686–1687, there is no other similarly extended period during his years in New France when he did not write to his correspondent in France.[7]

True to his well-demonstrated habits as a rather compulsive writer, it is highly unlikely that if Lahontan had remained "mewed up" by the coming winter, as he had been afraid might happen, and some critics have accused him of doing, at Michilimackinac, that he could have stilled his pen for so long. He would have found something to relate to his correspondent. His abruptness in breaking his well-established writing habit lends credence to the idea that he was not at Michilimackinac during the winter of 1688–1689. Some have suggested that he may have been away from the post on a prolonged moose hunt with the Natives during this time. This runs counter to the idea Lahontan implied that he was determined to avoid the cold and snow such as he and his men had painfully experienced at Fort Saint Joseph the previous winter.

Such an assertion by his critics also unjustifiably questions the truthfulness of his statement that he was going to travel to the "southern countries" and seek the source of the Long River. There are no indications in the known records of the colony suggesting that he was present at Michilimackinac or that region during this period instead of being on the Long River.[8]

Prior to his departure for the Long River, fortune had certainly smiled even more brightly on the baron by way of his unforseeable posting to Michilimackinac for an entire winter. He could not have planned the trip in advance because he could not have known where or when he might be posted. He could not have anticipated a time when he would have had no official duties or have at his disposal the resources for making a long trip of exploration.

Michilimackinac's location presented Lahontan with fortuitous opportunities to spend time with many of the men who traveled into the interior and the Mississippi drainage.[9] Michilimackinac was not only a place where Lahontan could gather the freshest intelligence about distant lands, it was also the best departure point for expeditions headed into them. By being posted there the baron was given a marvelous and very rare opportunity that would never come to him again. He could not have mounted such an expedition toward the Long River from either Montreal or Quebec as easily because they were so far away. There was one other consideration. In North America, King William's War, part of the Nine Years War or War of the Grand Alliance (1688–1697), was then brewing. Because France was going to war against Spain, Michilimackinac was the best place from which to launch an expedition to gather intelligence on Spanish activities to the south of the Great Lakes and the regions north of Mexico.

At the right place and time and with the availability of his detachment and its supplies, Lahontan made the most of it and went forward. Locating an inland passage and gathering intelligence on the Spanish certainly raised the importance of the baron's mission to a high level on behalf of the Crown's interests. If all these elements had not come together for him in the fall of 1688, there probably would not have been a Long River expedition. It was an unexpected set of circumstances. Lahontan was not slow to realize this and sieze full advantage of the situation. When he departed from Michilimackinac, Lahontan probably had the most up-to-date information available to the French on the course and drainage of the Mississippi and the southern countries he hoped to explore, including the Long River. He may well have been the best, or one of the best, informed Frenchman in New France on these matters.

The Long River as the way to an inland passage was certainly Lahontan's primary target.[10] He had his marine company and reliable Native guides to accompany, protect, and translate for him. His company began the expedition with new canoes "loaded with Provisions and Ammunition, and such commodities as are proper for the savages."[11] Although he never said how he obtained these things, particularly the items for gifting and trading, which were critical elements in any explorations in New France at that time, he should have had little problem obtaining what he needed at Michilimackinac.[12]

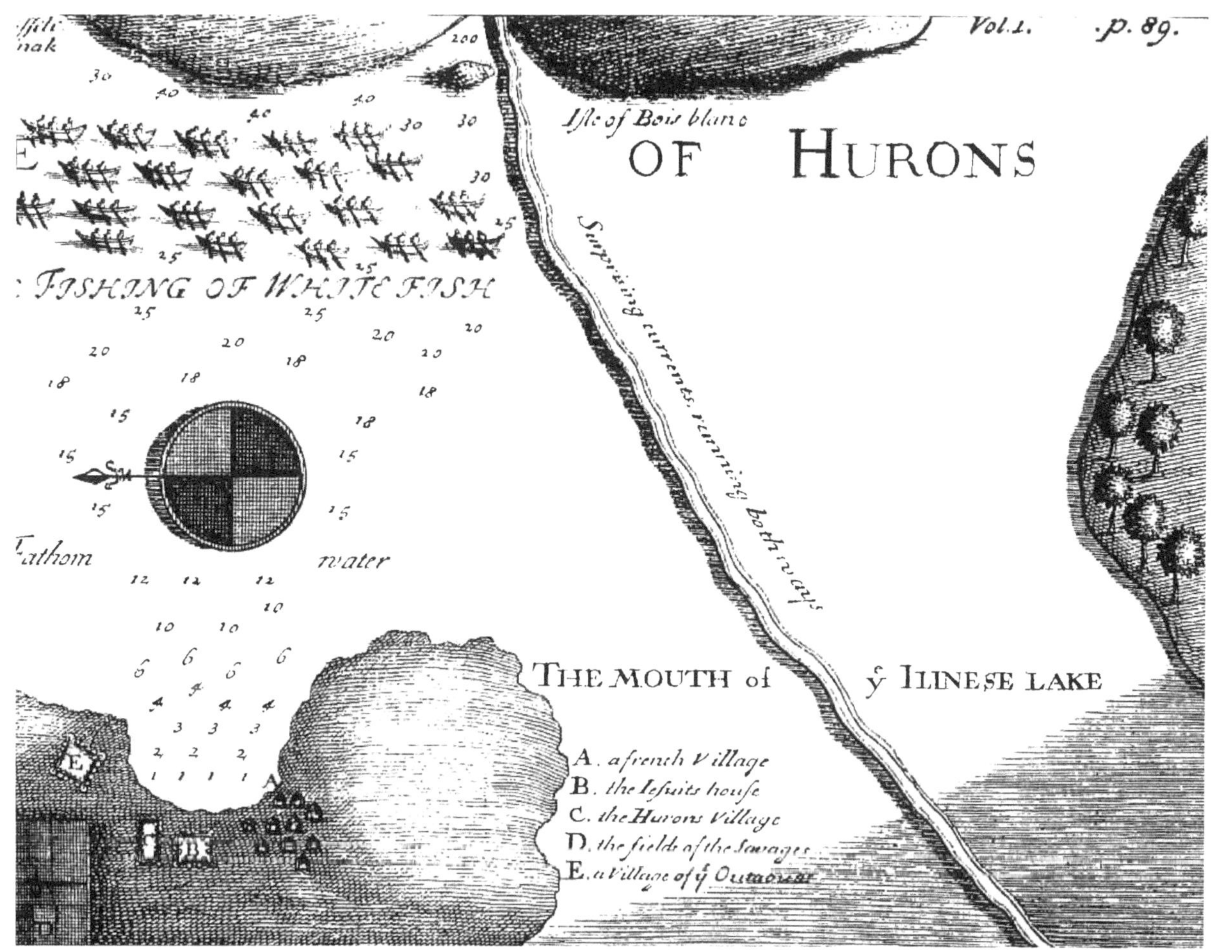

10. Lahontan's 1703 Map of the Straits of Mackinac showing the French and Native settlements there in 1688.

As noted on the map of the Long River in his narrative (Figure 18), Lahontan could determine his approximate latitude from the stars and knew how to use and owned an astrolabe.[13] Even the Thevenot version of Marquette's map of 1681 (Figure 5) recorded the latitude, which Marquette or Jolliet—who apparently had an astrolabe with them—first recorded.[14] The baron knew about where he needed to go!

When the baron departed for the Long River, he knew the Mississippi was not a route to the Pacific. Although he needed to travel down it some distance, he would not have been planning to explore it all the way to its mouth; by that time a pointless exercise. As he explicitly stated, he was targeting something else in its drainage between the Wisconsin River and the lower Mississippi—the Missouri/Long River.[15] He was looking to go west! After traveling up the Missouri, the Platte would have emerged as an obvious choice for him once he became aware of it and its valley as a likely great natural route toward the Western Sea.

In the end, the Platte proved a disappointment; it neither led the baron to the source of the Long River nor to any inland passage. The unexplored Missouri northward beyond the Platte, however, beckoned him onward after his first failed effort. It still held the potential to lead him to what he was seeking, just as Marquette and Jolliet, Frontenac, and others long believed it would. It also motivated Bourgmont's and Lewis and Clark's expeditions upon its waters. It was an attractive target over the many years. His narrative indicates that he was the first Frenchman to explore the Missouri River to any extent. He probably came to temporarily understand its lower portion below the Platte better than anyone other than Natives.

Because of the number of men thought to have been in his company, perhaps at least thirty or more marines and several Natives, Lahontan is believed to have used the large canoes that came to be known as "*batards*." As Lahontan described them, these craft measured about twenty-eight feet in length and up to four and a half wide, could carry a ton of freight, and hold up to fourteen people. These canoes were the best suited for martial expeditions and long voyages. They were, however, smaller than the quite large and well-known *"Montreal"* variety or "*canot du maître"* canoes (Figure 11) that came to be used on large rivers and lakes, including the Great Lakes, beginning around 1729 or earlier.

Lahontan indicates that he had multiple canoes. It has, however, been inaccurately reported that his company utilized six new ones.[16] Because of their large cargo capacity, larger ones were used rather than the smaller, classic "North Canoes" or "*canot du nord"* used by the voyageurs for traveling on small lakes and rivers into the Canadian wilderness from the primary transportation route of the Great Lakes.[17] Although Lahontan regularly speaks of "rowing" his canoes with the use of "oars," the appropriate terms would have been "paddling" his canoes with "paddles." Canoes of the time were not rowed.

After he started up the Platte, the baron changed to Native "*pirogues"* (a.k.a. known to the French in Louisiana as *"pettaugres*)," dugouts made from hollowed-out logs.[18] He borrowed these from Pawnees, presumably because his fragile birchbark canoes could not be operated in the icy and shallow water conditions typical of the Platte in winter. They were too easily damaged.[19] Dablon described the pirogues Marquette and Jolliet saw among the Natives on the Mississippi. He noted that they were made from cottonwood trunks of extraordinary girth and height. These graceful one-piece canoes were up to fifty feet long and three wide and could carry thirty men with all their baggage. Pirogues, likely of various sizes, were so plentiful among the Natives that a single village was said to perhaps have as many as 280 of them.[20]

11. A replica of a large Montreal-style canoe under sail on Lake Superior during a 2016 reenactment by the US Grand Portage National Monument. This is just the way which Lahontan often traveled. This canoe is ca. 28 ft. long and likely similar to those used by Lahontan, courtesy of US Grand Portage National Monument, Minnesota, US public domain.

On September 24,1688, the baron and his company departed Michilimackinac, almost certainly with the full awareness of its temporary commander, St. Denys. They first sailed their big birchbark canoes (Figure 11) southwesterly across Lake Michigan toward the Mississippi River and the river route to the "southern countries." On October 13, after passing south through Green Bay, Lahontan' company reached the village of the leader of the friendly Algonquian-speaking Outagami or Fox people. There he clearly divulged his specific plan to travel to the Long River, which he intended "to trace up to its source."[21]

Notes:

1. Brandão, "Introduction," *Mémoires*, xxiii-lxv.

2. Brandão, "Introduction," xxiii-lxv, lxix; Thwaites, *George Rogers Clark*, 203-05.

3. Brandão, *Mémoires*, xxiii-lxv; Kent, *Rendezvous*, (1), 26-116; Lahontan, *New Voyages*, 146.

4. Brandão, "Introduction," *Mémoires*. José António Brandão, a professor of history at Western Michigan University and director of the Michilimackinac Papers Project, coedited *Edge of Empire: Documents of*

Michilimackinac, 1671–1716 by Peyser and Brandão. He wrote the most useful "Introduction" to that volume and authored *Mémoires of Michilimackinac,* which, along with Timothy Kent's, and Lahontan's *New Voyages*, are the main sources of much of the early history of Michilimackinac reiterated here. Brandão's end notes contain a listing of key source materials relative to Michilimackinac. Thwaites has also discussed the physical evolution of Michilimackinac as its location shifted over time. Thwaites, *George Rogers Clark*, 204-05. The role of Michilimackinac within what has sometimes been called the "Middle Ground" is discussed by Richard White in *Middle Ground*. e.g. Skinner, *Upper Country*, 48-49. 2008.

5. Relative to his planning for his Long River trip, in Letter XV the baron commented that he was planning to travel to the southern colonies "for I cannot mew myself up here all this winter." Lahontan, 164.

6. Lahontan, 164-65.

7. Lahontan, 106.

8. Adams, *Travelers*, 63; Brandão, "Introduction," *Mémoires*, xxix-xxx; Lahontan, *New Voyages,* 143. Thwaites, "Introduction,"xxxix-xlii. White, *Middle Ground,* 47-49.

9. Brandão, "Introduction," *Mémoires*; Cavelier, *Relation of M. Cavelier*. Lahontan, *New Voyages*,144. Parkman, *La Salle and Discovery*, 977-1015, 1032.

10. Lahontan, 176.

11. Lahontan, 167; Heidenreich, "Early French Exploration," 65-66.

12. Lahontan, *New Voyages*, 146, 164-67, 207. The expedition obviously lived largely off the land and the largess of the Natives it encountered who provided it with lots of wild meat, corn and other plant foods.

13. Lahontan, *New Voyages*, 285.

14. Thevenot, *Recueil de Voyages;* Dablon, "Discovery of the Mississippi," 58, 108; Marquette, "Map of the New Discovery;"Thévenot, *Recueil de Voyages;* Father Dablon mentions that Marquette and Joliet had descended the Mississippi to about 38 degrees of latitude when they encountered the Missouri. Both Marquette's original and the Thévenot copy of the map in Figure 5 give relatively precise latitude for this confluence.

15. Lahontan, *New Voyages*, 176.

16. Lahontan, 62, 167, 183; Kent, *Birchbark*, (I), 97. On several occasions the baron indicated that he had multiple canoes and noted that he needed four pirogues to replace his canoes and haul his company when he left the Essanapes and headed up the Platte toward the Gnacsitares. The Canadian Virtual Museum of History, "Louis Armand de," states that he had six canoes but provides no reference for the statement. In July 2021 Jean-François Lozier, curator of French North America at the Canadian Museum of History, concurred with Steven Baker by e-mail that there is no known documentation for the notion that the baron had six canoes and the VieruL museum will be correcting that information.

17. In 1684 and early in his Canadian career, before he had much canoeing experience, the baron described the canoes he was then familiar with and pointed out that only the larger freighting canoes then in use were suitable for long voyages while the smaller North canoes were not. Kent, *Birchbark*, (I), 97; Lahontan, *New Voyages*, 62-65, 64n1; Nute, *Voyageur*, 24; Poling, *Canoe*, 58-63. The great Montreal canoes, workhorses of the developed fur trade in the eighteenth century, were, however, up to 36 to 40 or more feet long, weighed perhaps 600 pounds when empty, could carry 6,000 pounds of freight and 2,000 pounds of crew and supplies. Such a boat would typically have a crew of about 15 voyageurs. Nute, *Voyageur*, 24; Poling, *Canoe*, 58-63. The baron, however, appears to have used some large canoes of at least the "*batard*" or Montreal size on his Long River trip as he speaks at various times of them carrying substantial numbers of Frenchmen and Indians.

18. du Pratz, *History*. 221.

19. Lahontan, *New Voyages*, 187-88.

20. Dablon, *Relation de la descouverte*, (CXXXI), 97.

21. Lahontan, *New Voyages*, 176.

5

• THE PLATTE RIVER AND ITS VALLEY: THE MAJOR GREAT PLAINS TRAVEL CORRIDOR •

by

Steven G. Baker

Descriptions of the Platte River and its valley clearly demonstrate that Lahontan was on the Platte amid the Sandhills of western Nebraska when he turned back toward Michilimackinac. (Figures 1, 12, 16) His narrative further indicates that there, in January 1689, he met and accurately described the unusual bearded Native men from the distant lands of Mozeemlek and Tahuglauk. Descriptions of these lands located near the Great Salt Lake, far and directly west from Lahontan's location on the Platte, and their bearded men were the keys which helped unlock the mystery of Lahontan's Long River narrative.

Anyone familiar with the Platte, as are two coauthors of this book (Baker and Wood), should readily conclude that Lahontan was on the Platte. The accuracy of his descriptions also demonstrates that his detractors were not at all acquainted with the river since it was not well documented until the early to middle nineteenth century.[1] They further demonstrate that his Long River descriptions were entirely in keeping with the great fidelity the baron maintained in all of his reported observations and information reported to him by Natives.

The Platte River Valley-The Major Great Plains Travel Corridor

The focus of Lahontan's Long River narrative is the central Great Plains. (Figure 12) Spaniards had briefly explored them as far as Quivera and Etzanoa in south central Kansas in the sixteenth and seventeenth centuries.[2] Lahontan's Platte River travels were, however, the first known French incursions into the larger region of the central Plains west of the Mississippi. His descriptions of the geography and ethnography of the central Plains are among the earliest accounts and the first known for the valley of the Platte.

The Great Plains form an immense geomorphic province which divides the area of the US to the west of the Missouri River between it and the Rocky Mountains.[3] The Missouri and Platte Rivers are major hallmarks of the region. These extensive grassy prairielands stretch northward from Texas across the central US all the way into Canada. (Figure 12) They encompass Texas, Oklahoma, Kansas, Nebraska, South Dakota, North Dakota, and portions of Colorado, New Mexico, Montana, and Wyoming, as well as the Canadian provinces of Alberta, Manitoba, and Saskatchewan. The central portion of the Great Plains enfolds portions of Texas and Nebraska as well as all of Kansas and Oklahoma. Overall, the Plains are generally known as a broad plain largely covered in prairies, steppes, and grasslands. This vast region is roughly five hundred miles wide east to west and two thousand miles long north to south. Until the early twentieth century it was commonly known as the High Plains which contrast with the lower Prairie Plains of the Midwestern states further to the east.[4]

Numerous rivers drain the runoff of the Plains and the north-south trending Rocky Mountains that border them on the west. These rivers generally run eastward from the mountains toward the Missouri, the Mississippi, or the Gulf Coast. The lower Missouri, or those primary rivers that drain into it, are the only rivers of interest here since the baron was clearly not following out the Mississippi below the Missouri as a potential westerly water route to the Pacific Ocean. Those major rivers above the confluence of the Mississippi and Missouri include the Kansas, Platte, and the Yellowstone, as shown in Figure 12.

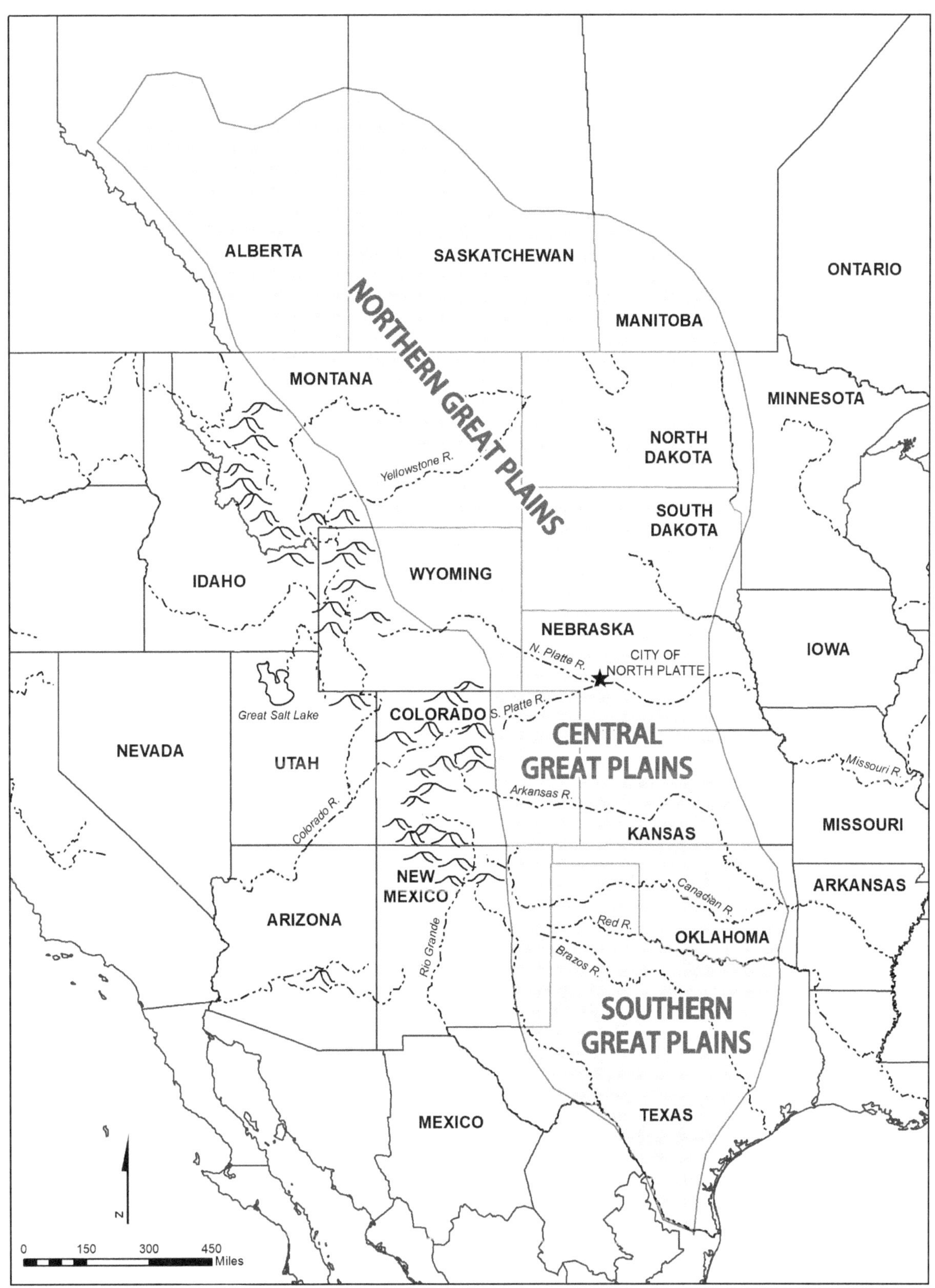

12. Map of North America's Great Plains with the Platte River in Nebraska as visited by Lahontan. North Platte about where Lahontan turned homeward is shown by the star.

The Platte was given its name by other early French explorers who followed Lahontan.[5] It has been said that "*Platte*" was their translation into French from the Otoe or Omaha name for the river, which was "*Nebraska*" as supposedly descriptive of its exceptionally flat, broad, shallow and braided nature.[6] This great American west-to-east-flowing river dominates Nebraska geography, which it essentially bisects. (Figures 12-16)[7]

Merrill Mattes described the Platte River and its valley in his classic study of the Great Platte River Road.[8] This was part of the route that many emigrants traveled in the nineteenth century during the period of US westward expansion. Mattes' book includes eye-witness accounts and personal impressions of early travelers which are in many cases similar to those characteristics mentioned by the baron and which well match those of the Platte. These descriptions in no way describe any other rivers Lahontan might have explored, and particularly not the Minnesota River.

The Platte Valley was an almost perfect natural travel corridor leading deep into the western frontier. Because of its long flat nature, the valley of the Platte was destined to become the route of the Union Pacific portion of the first transcontinental railroad.[9] Grenville Dodge, a primary force behind the construction of the Union Pacific, stressed that the Platte Valley was as fine a natural highway to the mountains and Pacific Ocean as existed.[10] Lahontan for a time must also have realized the potential of the Platte Valley as a possible route to the Pacific.

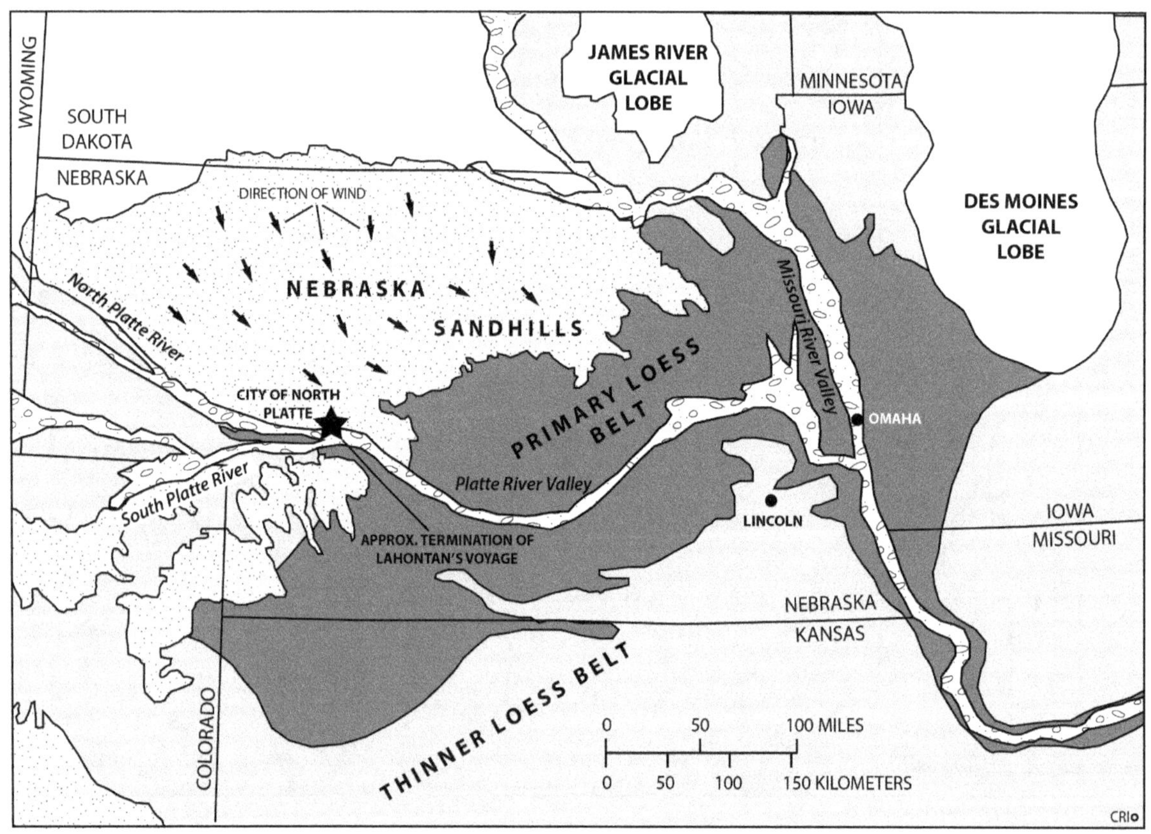

13. Map of the surficial geology of Nebraska and the valley of the Platte River.

14. Northward looking photo of the Platte River taken near Cozad Nebraska (near North Platte) in October of 1866 during an excursion by Union veterans of the Civil War on the then still uncompleted Union Pacific portion of the transcontinental railroad, courtesy of US Geological Survey, Denver, US public domain.

Because he had traveled through the area, it is surprising that historian Francis Parkman failed to realize that the baron was describing the Platte River and its valley in his subsequent condemnation of the baron's narrative. Parkman recorded his first impression of the valley of the Platte when he traveled the Oregon Trail in 1846. As his party prepared to drop into the valley from the south he stated:

> ...the long-expected valley of the Platte lay before us.... For league after league, a plain as level as a frozen lake, was outspread beneath us; here and there the Platte, divided into a dozen thread-like sluices, was traversing it, and an occasional clump of wood, rising in the midst like a shadowy island, relieved the monotony of the waste...we were passing up the center of a long narrow sandy plain, reaching like an outstretched belt, nearly to the Rocky Mountains. Two lines of sand-hills, broken often into the wildest and most fantastic forms, flanked the valley at the distance of a mile or two on the right and left; while beyond them lay a barren, trackless waste.[11]

Mattes quoted another early traveler who believed Nebraska and its Platte would only prove useful as a route to the Pacific Ocean.[12] This is a telling statement and likely a major reason the baron ended up on the Platte. Here was the most likely place to look for such a passage to the Pacific.[13] Even if it was not initially part of the Long/Missouri River he had originally been intending to explore, (which is still an open question) it is little wonder that Lahontan would have followed the Platte once he encountered it since it may have appeared to be the main stream of the Missouri River.

From its confluence with the Missouri to its sources in the mountains of Wyoming, the Platte and its North Platte tributary are over 1,000 miles long. From its mouth to the confluence of its North and South Platte major tributaries in western Nebraska where Lahontan turned homeward it is roughly 300 or more miles. Its length from Omaha near its mouth to the Wyoming state line is roughly 500 miles. The South Platte is nearly 450 miles long and rises in South Park high in the mountains to the southwest of Denver, Colorado.

The Platte could abruptly change its character. From slowly running shallow waters with many sandbars (Figure 15), it could quickly flood to become a huge, wide and rapidly flowing stream of varying depths up to fifteen feet. (Figure 14) It could range from such dangerous depths to notable shallows with braided channels that could easily be waded.[14] The slow-moving Platte seems to have been what led Lahontan to also refer to it as the "*Morte*" or Dead River.[15] The notoriously shallow, although wide and island and sandbar-ridden, Platte was never well suited to navigation. The baron's account of his upriver travels on the Platte supports this view and indicates that it took him some fifteen days to travel from the Pawnee villages upriver to Gnacsitare territory, no more than about 150 miles.[16] He made only about ten miles a day at most while pushing (stemming) against the river's flow and likely fighting his way through sandbars. The river was and still is suitable only for pirogues, canoes and shallow draft boats as Lahontan noted while he was among the Essanapes on December 3.[17]

15. 2010 winter overview of the Platte River with its braided channels, sandhill crane flocks, and its valley looking west from near the west end of Mormon Island near Grand Island, Nebraska, courtesy of Jeff Drahota, US Fish and Wildlife Service, Nebraska, US public domain.

In western Nebraska beyond Kearney, the famed Sandhills (Figure 13), a major, large and distinctive landform that in the region exists only in Nebraska, rise above the valley on the north, and somewhat on the south, and follow it westward all the way to the Wyoming border.[18] They form a giant dune field presently stabilized by prairie vegetation.[19] This unique landform, along with small natural lakes or ponds, helped characterize the region before the advent of agricultural tilling of the valley floor. These small, naturally formed marshes or wetlands drew Lahontan's attention in his journal entries of December 4, 8-9, 1688. There he appropriately referred to them as "fens."[20] The hills rise in elevation west of Kearney and reach their maximum elevation on the south side of the river just below the confluence of the North and South Platte Rivers.[21] The Sandhills are notable in the way that they depart from the more typical "plain-like" nature of the high Plains. The Sandhills cover roughly 24,000 square miles in northwestern Nebraska with dunes dominating the topography in a maze of mounds and ridges.[22] After Lahontan entered the Sandhills region he noted that the prairie-like countryside of the valley floor contained nothing much more than marshes covered with reeds, clay, and bare fields.[23]

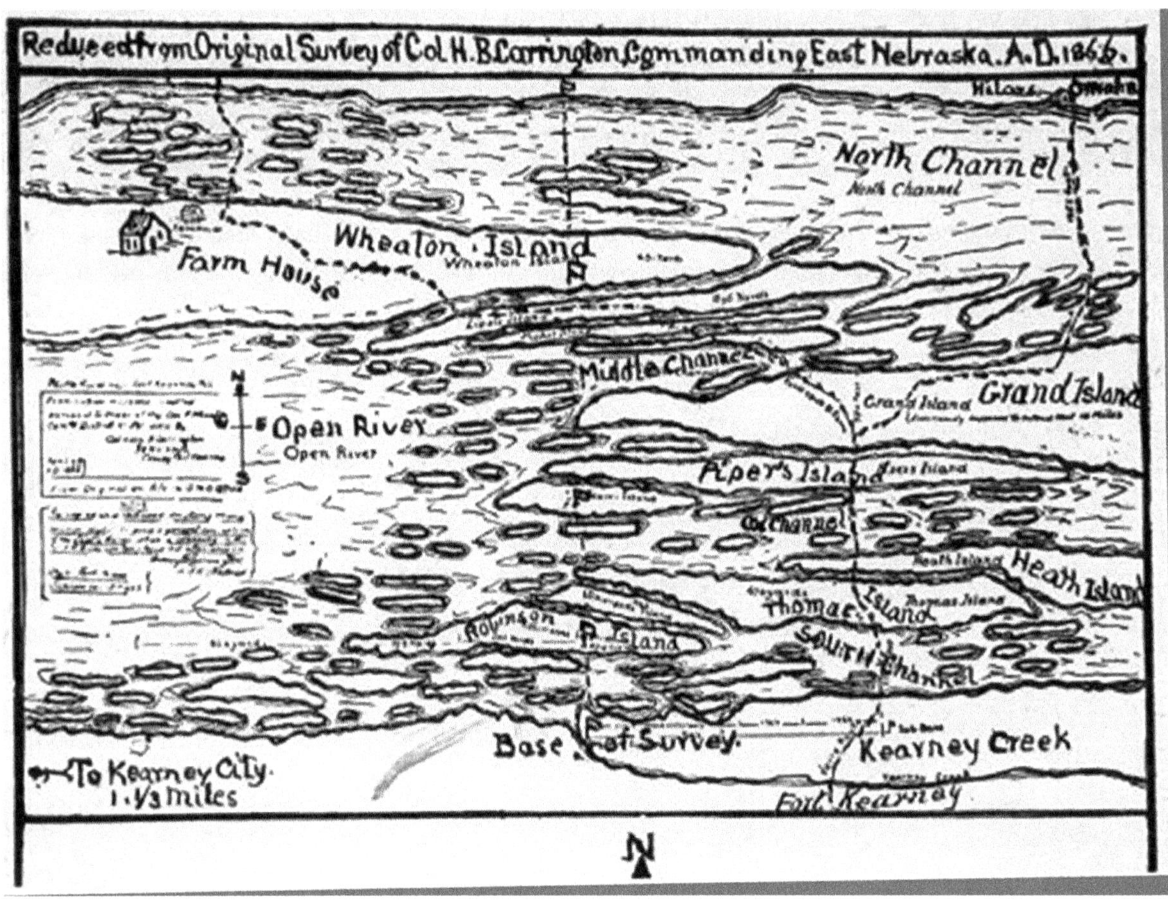

16. 1866 map of the islands and channels of the Platte River near Kearney, Nebraska, courtesy of Nebraska State Historical Society, Lincoln.

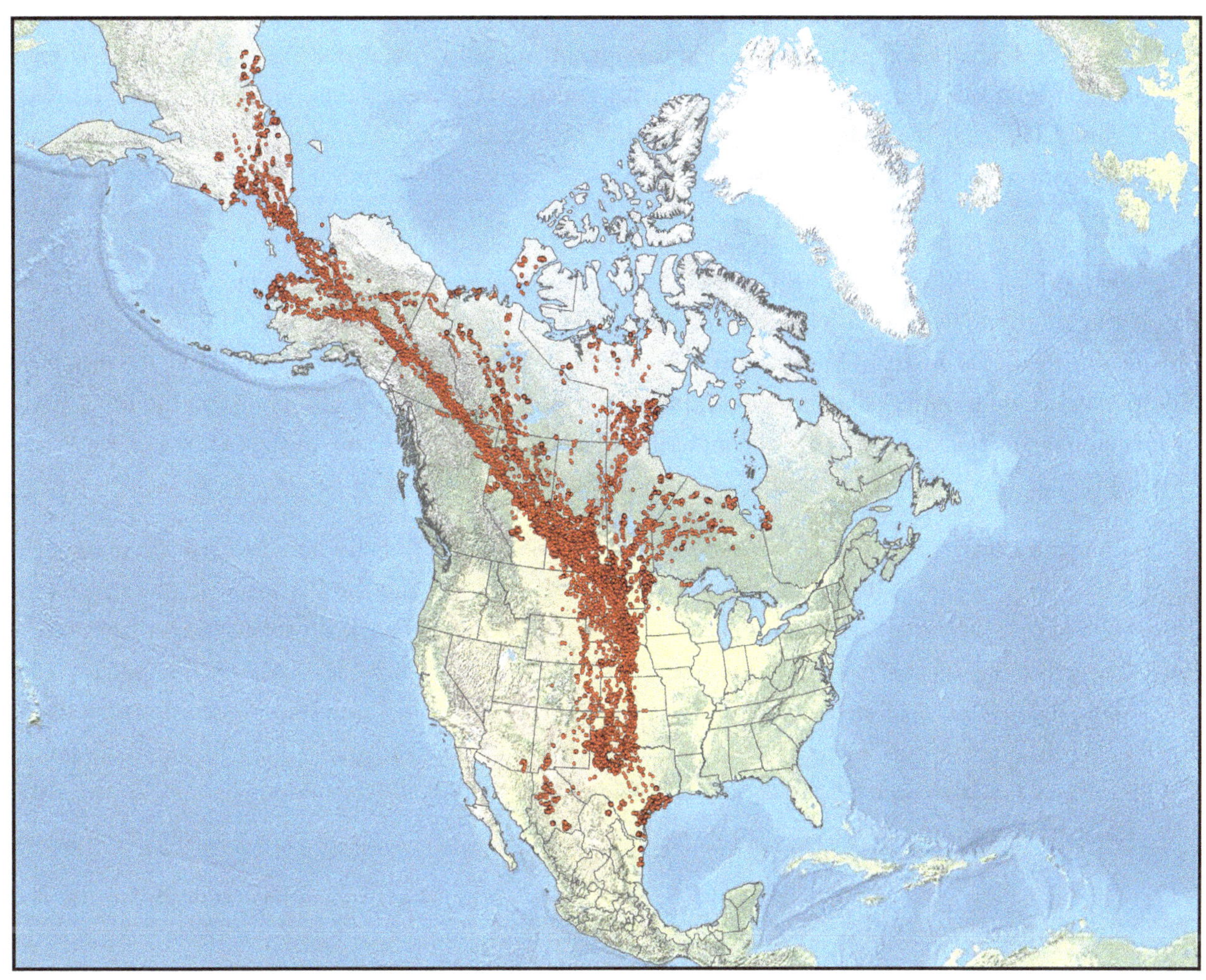

17. Map of the Great North American Central (waterfowl) Flyway, courtesy of David Brandt, Northern Prairie Wildlife Research Center, US Geological Survey, North Dakota, US public domain.

The scarcity of timber in the Sandhills, about which the baron spoke on December 4, was later attributed to frequent prairie fires started by Natives, lightning, and careless travelers along the Platte River route. Historical sources tell us that even the Pawnees living along the Platte were forced to rely on the burning of dried buffalo dung (chips) because of the scarcity of wood in the region.

The Platte Valley offered a rich and diverse biomass of wildlife. This was dominated by the American bison or "buffalo." Larger mammals such as bears, wolves, elk, deer, and pronghorn antelope, would also have been present along with a host of smaller species. Prairie dogs were abundant and characteristic residents of the valley. The Platte's valley was sometimes so full of bison that it was, as far "as the eye could reach," said to have been "black with herds" of them.[24] Exceptionally large numbers of bison congregated about the confluence of the North and South Platte Rivers in extreme western Nebraska and eastern Colorado. Lahontan did not say much about seeing bison other than noting their presence and that they were hunted.

The valley of the Platte teemed with migrating waterfowl during the baron's winter trip, as it still does to this day. This is particularly so in the spring and fall when it becomes a major stop-over in the annual migrations of massive numbers of many species. This area of the Platte in central Nebraska near Grand Island is in the heart of the great Central Flyway, one of the most impressive and important natural corridors in North America for migrating geese, ducks, and cranes. (Figure 17)[25]

Both now and historically, many species of waterfowl either overwinter or take prolonged rests there in the Platte Valley well into the winter. On November 26, 1688, and February 5, 1689, the baron alluded to the flyway. His Native escorts hunted waterfowl intensively as they followed him along on the shores of the Platte. On or about January 26 he noted the plentiful waterfowl the Essanape chieftain provided to him.[26] The immense number of waterfowl Lahontan alluded to on the Long River in December and January is entirely consistent with placing him within the great North American Central (Platte River) Flyway in central Nebraska. (Figure 17)[27]

Long after his voyage but before he published his book, in 1699 Lahontan developed a map of the Long River (Figure 24), as it was composed of the lower Missouri and the Platte, which he named the "*Masotanta River*."[28] This map and the one he published in 1703 (Figure 19) illustrates the villages of the Gnacsitares as being located on what he understood to be a lake he named the Lake of the Apaches *(Lago de los Apache)*. It is unclear if he actually saw this lake or was only told about it as it seemingly lay to the west some distance beyond "Lahontan's Limit" as he denoted it in his map of 1703. If he actually saw it, the baron may not have seen a real lake but just one of the many shallow braided channels of the river, which may have appeared to him to be a lake.

The lake shown on that map has long been a major conundrum which has confounded the few scholars who have even seen it since it is not well known. The only lake known in that location is the present-day Lake McConaughy, nine miles north of Ogallala, Nebraska, and just west of North Platte. This is a man-made lake created by the Kingsley Dam between 1936 and 1941. Therefore, the lake Lahontan placed on his 1699 map and the one derived from the map the Gnacsitare's prepared for him on a deerskin (Figures 18, 19) could not be Lake McConaughy, although it is in about the correct location relative to the mountains and rest of the river.

Geologists studying Nebraska's Sandhills and Platte River have noted that a series of ancient ephemeral lakes formed along the channels of the Platte and its tributaries in the region.[29] These lakes are believed to have formed repeatedly through time during dryer periods when portions of the Sandhills sluffed off and collapsed into the channel, forming impermanent lakes that came and went with local climatic changes. Geologists believe one such massive dam blocked the Platte near Lake McConaughy for perhaps 1,000 years some 12,000 to 14,000 years ago as determined by the chemistry of the local dune sand.[30] This is a potential explanation for the presence of the lake or otherwise island-strewn "lake-like" appearing body of water on the upper Platte region mapped by the baron and the Natives once on or near the location of Lake McConaughy. Geologist Jim Swinehart tends to favor a theory that what might have appeared to Lahontan and later travelers as lakes were most likely nothing more than large, flooded, old-damned up braid channels instead of true dune dams. (Figure 15)[31]

Good chronologies and locations where the dune damming may have taken place are not yet available, but there is apparently geological evidence that such events were taking place in the Sandhills region of the Platte drainage through time. There are, therefore, seemingly rational explanations for the Lake of the Apaches, as illustrated by both the baron and the Gnacsitares/Plains Apaches but which has by now disappeared.

NOTES:

1. Benson, *From Pittsburg;* Mattes, *Great Platte.*

2. Bolton, *Coronado*; Flint and Flint, *Coronado Expedition*; Malakoff, "Searching for Etzanoa."

3. Dort and Jones, *Pleistocene and Recent*; Kay, "Great Plains Setting;"Thornbury, *Regional Geomorphology.*

4. Thornbury, 287; Wikipedia, "Great Plains."

5. Johnsgard, *Platte*, 25; Staley and Wayne, "Epeirogenic and Climatic;" Stansbury, *Exploration of the Valley*, 29.

6. Long, *Account*, 173; Mattes, *Great Platte*, 161.

7. Johnsgard, *Platte,* xiv.

8. Mattes, *Great Platte.*

9. Ambrose, *Nothing Like It*, 3, 36, 37, 140-43; Fremont, "A Report on Exploration;" Perkins, *Trails, Rails and War;* Preuss, *Topographic Map.*

10. Ambrose, *Nothing Like It*, 36.

11. Parkman, *California and Oregon Trail*, 105-6.

12. Mattes, *Great Platte*, 238.

13. Mattes, 239.

14. Eschner et al., "Hydrologic and Morphologic," A15.

15. Lahontan, *New Voyages*, 285.

16. Lahontan, 189-90.

17. Lahontan, 187-88. The baron recorded the month as November in error. Allin, "A Mile Wide;" Boss, "Keelboat, Pirogue;" Mattes, *Great Platte*, 247; *See also* Frémont, *A Report on an Exploration,* June 28, 1843.

18. Bleed and Flowerday, "Atlas of the Sandhills;" Stansbury, *Exploration of the Valley*, 33 Thornbury,

Regional Geomorphology, 306.

19. Loope and Swinhart, "Thinking Like a Dune Field."

20. Lahontan, *New Voyages*, 189-90.

21. Lahontan, 189-90; Mattes, *Great Platte*, 242-47.

22. Thornbury, *Regional Geomorphology*, 306

23. Lahontan, 190.

24. Stansbury, 29.

25. Johnsgard, *Platte,* 41-4; Eschner et al. "Hydrologic and Morphologic," A1; Shoumatoff, "Flight Club."

26. Lahontan, *New Voyages*, 183, 187, 197.

27. Johnsgard, *Platte*.

28. Lahontan, 1699, *Mappa del Missisip*.

29. Loope, et al., "Dune-dammed Paleovalleys;" Loop and Swinehart, "Thinking Like a Dune.

30. Loope, et al.; Loop and Swinehart.

31. Personal e-mail communication from geologist Jim Swinehart, formerly of the University of Nebraska, May 18, 2021. *See also* Loop, et al. and Loop and Swinehart.

6

• LAHONTAN'S LONG RIVER NARRATIVE •

by

Claude J. Fouillade and Steven G. Baker

Introducing Lahontan's Narrative

When preparation of this study commenced it was understood that Lahontan's first English version of his *New Discoveries*...with its Long River narrative had apparently never again been translated into English from his original French version. Thwaites did not appear to pass judgment on the quality of that original translation. Old translations are, however, known to vary greatly in quality and their faithfulness to the writer's original words and intentions. Although the baron stated that someone else had done the translation it was, therefore, not known how closely it hewed to the original French.[1] The two new translations by Fouillade and Wilson, however, demonstrated that the original translation had been done quite well and spoke best to the language of Lahontan's time.[2] The authors thus worked from Thwaites's 1905 reprinting of the original 1703 English version in preparing this work.[3]

The information conveyed in the following designated "reference sections" of the baron's Letter XVI help prove that he was on the Platte River. Other chapters support the comparative discussion of his observations and those of the Franciscans Domínguez and Vélez de Escalante on the people of Teguayo, Mozeemlek, and Tahuglauk as well as other topics.[4] The referenced quotations were designated at appropriate points so that the reader would not have to page through the entire English translation to find the sources for the observations. These most pertinent reference sections are designated "**RS 1, 2, 3**," etc.

Table 1:

Native American Peoples and Their Languages Involved in Lahontan's Long River Trip

LOCATION	NATIVE AMERICAN NATIONS SPEAKING	LANGUAGE GROUP
Lake Michigan West Shore and South toward Wisconsin R. and Mississippi	Algonquian	Ottawa, Pottawatomie, Sauk, Menoni-mee, Kickapoos, Outagami (Fox)
In Minnesota west of Mississippi	Siouan	Nadouessis (Sioux)
Lower Missouri River first people encountered there (these people pose special problems)	Siouan	Eokoros (Missouris and/or Otoes)
Platte River and/or area of its confluence with Missouri River	Caddoan	Essanapes (Pawnee)
Platte River below forks of North and South Platte	Athabascan	Gnacsitanes (Plains Apache/Kiowa?)
Encountered on Platte but from area about Great Salt Lake in present Utah	Numic-Ute?	Mozeemleks (Bearded Utes)
On Mississippi below Missouri	Siouan ?	Otentas (pose special problems)
On return to lower Missouri	Siouan	Missouris
On return to lower Missouri region	Siouan	Osage
On return to lower Missouri region	Iroquoian	Iroquois
On return to lower Missouri/ Osage region mentions Panima-ha, Panessa, and Panetonka, are unknown and special problems exist with these.	(Skiri Pawnee?)	
On the Missouri or Osage River	Algonquian	Arkansas/Quapaw
Upper Missouri and Plains	Siouan	Panimoba (Omaha)?
Kansa/Kaw River tributary of Missouri	Siouan	Kansas/Canza
The Illinois River	Algonquian	Illinois
Miami River near Chicago	Algonquian	Oumami (Miami)

The Baron Lahontan's Long River Narrative

What follows is a direct transcription of the baron's original 1703 English narrative. Readers will note that significant words or phrases are at points inserted in **bold** within the baron's text in bold brackets (such as a **[word or phrase]).** Such insertions indicate how the word or phrase used in the new translations from the French differed from the baron's original English one. Although the original French as translated into English has been relied upon, the updated word or phrase has been offered for clarification, and not always as a strict direct substitution. This was done in deference to those readers' who may not be acquainted with what certain words meant in the baron's context and time. Additional explanatory information, such as the modern name of a river, the identities of Native peoples (Table 1), animals, historical comments, or distances and such, are inserted in brackets without bold print within passages quoted from Lahontan (such as [25 miles for leagues traveled or other explications]). Simple underling in a quote indicates that emphasis was added. Scrupulous efforts were made to avoid changing any of Lahontan's original English text as transcribed here directly from Thwaites 1905 reprint which was itself an exact transcription of the original.[5] All page numbers reference the baron's English volume as reprinted by Thwaites in 1905 and not to the pagination in the original 1703 volume. The baron italicized some words in his narrative and that pattern has been preserved. Lahontan had no maps to guide him beyond the Mississippi, and his navigational toolbox was limited to a compass and probably a watch, but seemingly did not include the astrolabe which he said he owned. His compass likely had its principal points boxed or named in a clockwise order.[6]

Because Lahontan seemingly did not have his astrolabe on the Long River, he had no way to accurately measure latitude. He measured his travel distances in terms of leagues. Although variable, typically, a land league of the period was calculated as the distance one traveled in one hour by horseback over level terrain at a walking speed equaling roughly 2.63 miles today. Although he did not discuss how he determined his travel distance on water, to effectively calculate leagues by this method when canoeing, one must have a suitable means of measuring time so he must have had a watch. Lahontan, however, equated his leagues traveled to three English miles. That is the equation used in this analysis.

Lahontan's Letter XVI. His Entire Journal of his Departure and Return from the Long River

PRELUDE: A PORTION OF LAHONTAN'S *LETTER XV* INTRODUCING HIS PLANS FOR TRAVELINGTOTHE "SOUTHERN COUNTRIES". (September 18, 1688 at Michilimackinac on Lake Huron)

Toward the end of this letter, Lahontan discusses his plans for returning to Montreal the next year since it is by then too late for him to make the long dangerous trip across Lake Huron and down the Ottawa and Saint Lawrence to the colony. He had spent all the past winter (1687–1688) snowbound at Fort St. Joseph and stated:

/Page 164/

Upon my Arrival in this Place, I found here Mr. de la Durantay, whom Mr. Denonville [then governor of New France] has invested with the Commission of Commander of the Coureurs de Bois that trade upon the Lakes, and in the Southern Countries of Canada. The Governour has sent me Orders to return to the Colony if the Season and other Circumstances permit; or to tarry here till the Spring if I foresee unsurmountable Difficulties in the Passage. In the mean time he has sent me Effects to answer the Pay of my Detachment, and to subsist 'em in the Winter. These Orders would be extream acceptable to me, if I could but contrive how to return to the Colony; but that seems to be absolutely impossible, and both the French and the Savages agree that it is so. There are in that Passage so many Water-falls, Cataracts, and Places where there's a necessity of tedious Land-carriages, that I dare not run such Hazards with my Soldiers, who cannot work the Boats but upon stagnating Water. Upon that consideration I have thought it more proper to halt here till the next Year; at which time I design to take the Advantage of the Company of some Frenchmen and Savages, that promise to take into each of their Canows one of my Men. In the meantime, I am upon the point of undertaking another Voyage, for I cannot mew my self up here all this Winter. I design to make the best use of my time, and to travel through the Southern Countries [emphasis added] that I have so...

/Page 165/

...often heard of, having engag'd four or five good Huntsmen of the Ontaouas [Ottawas] to go along with me.

LAHONTAN'S LETTER XVI CONTAINING HIS ENTIRE "JOURNAL OF A REMARKABLE VOYAGE UPON THE LONG RIVER"

/Page 167/

LETTER XVI. *Dated at Missilimakinac, May 28, 1689. Containing an Account of the Author's Departure from, and Return to,* Missilimakinac. *A Description of the Bay of* Puants, *and its Villages. An ample Description of the* Beavers; *follow'd by the Journal of a remarkable Voyage upon the Long River, and a Map of the adjacent Country.*

(May 28, 1689 at Michilimackinac)

SIR, THANK God, I am now return'd from my Voyage upon the *Long River,* which falls into the River of *Missisipi.* I would willingly have trac'd it up to its Source, if several Obstacles had not stood in my way. I set out from hence the 24th of *Sept.* accompany'd with my own Detachment [seemingly of 30 to 60 marines at maximum], and the five [Ottawa] Huntsmen I mention'd in my last; who indeed did me a great deal of Service. All the Soldiers were provided with new Canows loaded with Provisions and Ammunition, and such Commodities as are proper for the Savages. The Wind, which stood then in the North, wafted me in three days [at roughly 40 miles per day] to the Bay of *Pouteouatamis* [Pottawatomie Bay/Green Bay on Lake Michigan] (**Bay of Puants/Stinks)**, that lay forty Leagues [120 miles] off. The mouth of that Bay is in a manner choak'd with Isles, and the Bay it self is ten Leagues broad [30 miles], and twenty five Leagues [75 miles] long.

(September 29, 1688 on the Fox River near South End of Green Bay)

/Page 168/

The 29th we came to a little deep sort of a River, which disembogues at a place where the Water of the Lake swells three foot high in twelve hours, and decreases as much in the same compass of time. Our tarrying there three or four days gave me an opportunity of making this Remark. The Villages of the *Sakis* [Sauk or Sac], the *Pouteouatamis* [Pottawatomies], and some *Malominis* [Menonimees], are seated on the fide of that River, and the Jesuits have a House or College built upon it. This is a place of great Trade for Skins and *Indian* Corn, which these Savages sell to the *Coureurs de Bois*, as they come and go, it being the nearest and most convenient Passage to the River of *Missisipi*. The Soil of this Country is so fertile, that it produces (in a manner without Agriculture) our *European* Corn, Pease, Beans, and several other Fruits that are not known in *France*. As soon as I landed, the Warriours of these three Nations came by turns to my Apartment, to regale with the *Calumet-Dance,* and with the *Captains-Dance*; the former being a signification of Pease and Friendship, and the latter of Respect…

/Page 169/

…and Esteem. I return'd the Compliment with a Present of some Rolls of *Brasil* Tobacco, which they value mightily, and some strings of *Venice* Beads, with which they embroider their Coats. Next Morning I was invited to a Feast with one of the three Nations; and after having sent to 'em some Dishes and Plates [of food], pursuant to the Custom of the Country, I went accordingly about Noon. They began with congratulating my Arrival, and after I had return'd them thanks, fell a singing and dancing one after another, in a particular manner, of which you may expect a circumstantial account when I have more leisure. The Singing and Dancing lasted for two hours, being season'd with Acclamations of Joy and Jests, which make up part of their ridiculous Musick. After that the Slaves came to serve, and all the Company sat down after the *Eastern* fashion [meaning cross-legged on the floor?], every one being provided with his Mess, just as our Monks are in the Monastery-Halls.

First of all four Platters were set down before me, in the first of which there were two white Fish only boil'd in Water; in the secund the Tongue and Breast of a Roe-buck [small male deer as opposed to the larger elk or stag-like animal?] boil'd; in the third two Woodhens **[Hazel Hens]** [partridges?], the hind Feet or Trotters of a Bear, and the Tail of a Beaver, all roasted; and the fourth contain'd a large quantity of Broth made of several forts of...

/Page 170/

...Meat. For Drink they gave me a very pleasant Liquor, which was nothing but a Syrrup of Maple beat up with Water; but of this more elsewhere. The Feast lasted two Hours; after which I intreated one of the Grandees to sing for me; for in all the Ceremonies made use of among the Savages, 'tis customary to imploy another to act for 'em. I made this Grandee a Present of some pieces of Tobacco, in order to oblige him to act my part [*stay]* till Night. Next day, and the day after, I was oblig'd to go to the Feasts of the other two Nations, who observ'd the same Formalities. The most curious thing I saw in the Villages, was ten or twelve tame Beavers, that went and came like Dogs from the Rivers to the Cottages, without stragling out of the Road. I ask'd the Savages if these Animals could live out of the Water; and receiv'd this answer, that they could live ashoar as well as Dogs, and that they had kept some of 'em above a year, without suffering them to go near the Rivers: From whence I conclude that the *Casuists* are out in not ranging Ducks, Geese, and Teals, in the number of Amphibious Animals, as the Naturalists are wont to do....

(Pages 170-173)

...contain an interesting but lengthy discussion of beavers intercalated within but irrelevant to the baron's Long River travel narrative. That discussion is not included here.)

(Approximately October 3rd or 4th with Potawatomies on the Fox River)

/Page 173/

To return to my Voyage. After our arrival in the Bay of *Pouteouatamis,* we bid adieu to the Navigation upon the Lakes of *Canada;* and setting out *September* 30, arriv'd *October* 2, at

the foot of the fall of *Kakalin* (on Fox River), after stemming some little Cur-...

/Page 174/

...rents in the River of *Puants* [*River of Stinks*]. The next day we acconmplish'd the small Land-carriage, and on the 5th arriv'd before the Village of *Kikapous* [Kickapoos], in the Neighbourhood of which I incamp'd the next day, in order to receive Intelligence. That Village stands upon the brink of a little

Lake, in which the Savages fish great quantities of Pikes and Gudgeons [pickerel ?]. I found only thirty or forty Men fit for War in the place, for the rest were gone a Beayer-hunting some days before. The 7th I reimbarq'd, and rowing hard made in the Evening the little Lake of *Malominis* (Menonimee Lake), where we kill'd Bucks and Bustards [crane or rail-like birds of the family Gruiformes-likely meaning cranes] enough for Supper. We went ashoar that Night, and built Hutts for our selves upon a point of Land that shoots out; by break of day I went in a Canow to the Village, and after an hours Conference with some of the Savages, presented 'em with two Rolls of Tobacco, and they by way of Acknowledgement, made me a present of two or three Sacks of Oatmeal [wild rice]: For the sides of...

(October 9th to ca. 19th with Outagamis (Fox) on Wolf or Fox (?) River)

/Page 175/

...the Lake are cover'd with a fort of Oats [wild rice], which grows in tufts with a tall Stalk, and of which the Savages reap plentiful Crops. The 9th I arriv'd at the foot of *Outagamis* (Foxes) Fort where I found but few People; however, they gave me a very kind Reception, for after dancing the *Calumet* before the Door of my Hutt, they made a Present of Venison and Fish. Next day they convey'd me up the River, to the place where their folks were hunting the Beavers. The 11th we imbarq'd, and landed the 13th upon the shoar of a little Lake, where the Head of the [Fox] Nation resided. After we had rear'd up our Hutts, the General gave me a Visit, and inquir'd which way I intended to move. I made answer, that I was so far from designing to march toward the *Nadouessious* [Sioux] his Enemies, that I should not come near 'em by 100 Leagues [300 miles]; and to con-...

/Page 176/

...firm the innocence of my Intentions, I pray'd him to send six [of his Fox] Warriours <u>to accompany me to the long River</u> [a really important phrase with emphasize added], <u>which I design'd to trace up to its Source</u>. [This is a critically important comment by the baron as it is the first mention of the Long River in his narrative and the first indication that it was the preselected target in his explorations of the "southern countries." He was obviously well informed about it and was intending to head to the Long River from the outset even before leaving Michilimackinac. No one among his many critics appears to have ever noted, let alone mentioned this.] He reply'd that he was extream glad to find that I carry'd neither Arms nor Cloaths to the *Nadouessious* [Sioux]; that he saw I had not the equipage of a *Coureur de Bois*, but that on the contrary, I had some discovery in my view. At the same time he caution'd me not to venture too far up that Noble River, by reason of the multitudes of People that I would find there, though they have no stomach for War: He mean'd, that some numerous Party [*large band*] might surprise me in the Night-time. In the mean time, instead of the six Warriours that I desir'd, he gave me ten, who understood the Lingua, and knew the Country of the *Eokoros* [Otoes and/or Missouris regarding which there are special problems of identity], with whom his Nation had maintain'd a Peace of twenty years standing. I stay'd two days with this General, during which time he regal'd me nobly, and walk'd about with me to give me the Satisfaction of observing the disposure of the Cottages of the Beaver hunters; a description of which, you may expect in another place; I presented him with a Fusee [flintlock muzzle-loading shoulder fired long gun], twelve Flint-stones [gun flints], two pound of Powder, four pound of Ball, and a little Axe, and I gave each of his two Sons a great Coat, and a Roll of *Brasil* Tobacco. Two of the ten Warriours that he gave me, could speak the Language of the *Outaouas* [Ottawas], which I was well pleas'd with; not that I was a stranger to their own Language, for between that and the *Algonkin* there is no great difference,...

/Page 177/

...but in regard that there were several words that puzzled me. My four *Outaouas* were transported with this little Reinforcement, and were then so incouraged, that they told me above four times, that we might venture safely so far as the Plantation [House] of the Sun [Apparently the massive Missippian culture "Cahokia" mounds site near Saint Louis, Missouri very near where the Missouri/Long River joins with the Mississipp][emphasize added]. I embarqed with this small Guard the 16th about Noon, and arriv'd that Night at the Land-carriage [portage] of *Ouisconsinc* [Wisconsin River], which we finish'd in two days, that is, we left the River of *Puants* **[Stinks]**, and transported our Canows and Baggage to the River *Ouisconsinc*, which is not above three quarters of a League [just over 2 miles] distant, or thereabouts. I shall say nothing of the River we left, but that 'twas Muddy, full of Shelves, and inclosed with a steep Coast, Marshes, and frightful Rocks.

(October 19th to October 22nd on Wisconsin River to Mississippi)

The 19th we embarqu'd upon the River *Ouisconsinc,* and being favour'd by a slack Current, arriv'd in four days at the place, where it empties it self into the River *Missisipi*, which is about half a League broad in that part. The force of the Current, and the breadth of that River, is much the same as that of the *Loire* [a major river in France]. It lies North-East, and South-West; and its sides are adorn'd with Meadows, lofty Trees and Firs. I observ'd but two Islands upon it, though there may be more,...

/Page 178/

...which the darkness of the Night hid from us as we came down. The 23*d* we landed upon an Island in the River *Missisipi*, over against the River I spoke of but now [Wisconsin], and were in hopes to find some wild Goats [it is unclear to what animal he is here referring to] there, but had the ill fortune to find none. The day after we crost to t'other side of the River, sounding it every where, as we had done the day before, and found nine foot water in the shallowest place. The 2*d* of *November* we made the Mouth of the *Long River*, having first stem'd several rapid Currents of that River [this is where Lahontan first begins laying down his "great deception" discussed in chapter 15 regarding his direction of travel (emphasis added)], though 'twas then at lowest Ebb. In this little passage we kill'd several wild Beeves (American bison/buffalo) which we broil'd, and catch'd several large Dabs [*catfish*]. On...

(November 3rdThrough November 21st Among the Eokoros (Missouris [and/or Otoes?]) **on the Lower Missouri Portion of the Long River)**

/Page 179/

...the 3*d* we enter'd the Mouth of the *Long River* (Missouri), which looks like a Lake full of Bull-rushes; we found in the middle of it a narrow Channel, upon which we steer'd till Night, and then lay by to sleep in our Canows [this description does not well fit that of the mouth of the Missouri and it appears that this may have been another step in furthering his "great deception"]. In the Morning I enquir'd of my ten *Outagamis* [Foxes], if we had far to sail before we were clear of the Rushes, and receiv'd this answer, that they had never been in the Mouth of that River before, though at the same time they assur'd me, that about twenty Leagues (60 miles) higher, the Banks of it were clad with Woods and Meadows. But after all we did not sail so far, for about ten a Clock next Morning the River came pretty narrow, and the Shoar was cover'd with lofty Trees; and after continuing our course the rest of that day, we had a prospect of Meadows now and then. That same Night we landed at a point of Land, with a design to dress [prepare or warm?] our broil'd Meat, for at that time we had none fresh. The next day we stop'd at the first Island we saw, in which we found neither Man nor Beast; and the Evening drawing near, I was unwilling to venture far into it, so we e'en contented our selves with the catching of some sorry Fish. The 6th a gentle Gale sprung up, which wafted us to another Island about 12 Leagues [36 miles] higher, where we landed. Our passage to this place was very quick, nothwithstanding the great calm that always prevails upon this River, which I take to be the least rapid River in the World. But the quickness of the passage was not the only surprisal, for I was amaz'd that I saw no Harts [elk or stags?], nor Bucks [roebucks, male deer?], nor Turkeys, having met with 'em all along in the other parts of my Discovery.[7] The 7th the same Wind drove us to a third Island, that lay ten or twelve Leagues [30 to 36 miles] off the former,...

/Page 180/

...which we quitted in the Morning. In this third Island our Savages kill'd thirty or forty Pheasants, which I was not ill pleas'd with.

The 8th the Wind proving unservicable to us, by reason that 'twas intercepted by Hills cover'd with Firs, we ply'd our Oars [*paddles*]; and about two in the Afternoon, descry'd on the left Hand large Meadows, and some Hutts at the distance of a quarter of a League from the River. Upon this Discovery, our Savages and ten of the Soldiers jump'd upon the shoar, and directed their course to the Houses, where they found fifty or sixty Huntsmen prepar'd to receive 'em, with their Bows and Arrows. As soon as the Huntsmen heard the voice of the *Outagamis* [Foxes], they threw down their Arms, and presented the Company with some Deer that they had just kill'd, which they likewise help'd to carry to my Canows. The Benefactors were some of the *Eokoros* [Otoes and/or Missouris], who had left their Villages, and come thither to hunt. I presented 'em, more out of Policy, than Acknowledgment, with Tobacco, Knives and Needles, which they could not but admire. Upon this, they repair'd with expedition to their Villages, and gave their Associates to understand, what a good sort of People they had met with; which had so much influence, that the next day towards the Evening, there appear'd upon the River side above two thousand Savages, who fell a dancing as soon as they descry'd us. There-upon, our *Outagamis* went ashoar, and after a short Conference, some of the principal Savages imbarq'd on board of our Canows, and so we all steer'd to the chief Village, which we did not reach till Midnight. I order'd our Hutts to be made...

/Page 181/

...up on a point of Land near a little River, at the distance of a quarter of a League from the Village. Though the Savages press'd me extremely to lodge in one of their Villages, yet none went with 'em but the *Outagamis*, and the four *Outaouas,* who at the same time caution'd the Savages not to approach to our Camp in the Night-time. Next day I allow'd my Soldiers to refresh and rest themselves; and went my self to visit the Grandees of this Nation to whom I gave Presents of Knives, Cissars, Needles, and Tobacco. They gave me to understand, that they were infinitely well pleas'd with our arrival in their Country, for that they had heard the Savages of other Nations speak very honorably of the *French.* I took leave of 'em on the 12th, and set out with a Convoy of five of six hundred Savages, who march'd upon the shoar, keeping pace with our Canows. We pass'd by another Village that lay to the right Hand, and stop'd at a third Village that was five Leagues [15 miles] distant from the first, but did not disimbarque: For all that I design'd, was to make a Present to the leading Men of the Village, from whom I receiv'd more *Indian* Corn, and broil'd or dry'd Meat, than I had occasion for. In fine, I pass'd from Village to Village without stopping, unless it were to incamp all Night, or to present the Savages with some Trinkets; and so steer'd on to the last Village, with a design to get some Intelligence. As soon as we arriv'd at the end of this Village, the Great Governour, who indeed was a venerable old Gentleman, sent out Hunters to bring us good Cheer. He inform'd me, that sixty Leagues higher [180 miles] I should meet with the Nation of the *Essanapes* (Pawnee), who wag'd War with him; that if...

/Page 182/

...it had not been for their being at War, he would have given me a Convoy to their Country; that, however he mean'd to give up to me six Slaves of that Country, which I might carry home, and make use of as I saw occasion; and that in sailing up the River, I had nothing to fear, but the being surpriz'd in the Night-time. In fine, after he had instructed me in several useful Circumstances, I immediately made every thing ready for my Departure.

The Commanders of this People acquainted me, that they had twelve Villages peopled by 20000 Warriours; that their number was much greater before the War, which they wag'd at one time with the *Nadonessis* [Sioux], the *Panimoba* [Omaha?], and the *Essanapes* [Pawnee]. The People are very civil, and so far from a wild Savage temper, that they have an Air of Humanity and Sweetness. Their Hutts are long, and round at the top, not unlike Those of our Savages [typical house type for people of that region including those known as associated with the "Oneota" archaeological culture]; but they are made of Reeds and Bulrushes, interlac'd and cemented with a sort of fat Earth **[clay]**. Both the Men and the Women go naked all over, excepting their Privities. The Woman are not so handsom, as those who live upon the Lakes of *Canada*. There seems to be something of Government and Subordination among this People; and they have their Houses fortified with the branches of Trees (palisades made with upright branches placed into a trench), and Fascines [tree limbs and bundled branches] strengthen'd with fat Earth [*clay*].

The 21st we imbarqu'd at the break of day, and landed that Night in an Island covere'd with Stones and Gravel, having pass'd by another at which I would not put in, because I would not slight the opportunity of the Wind, which then stood very fair. Next day the Wind standing equally fair, we set out...

/Page 183/

...and continued our course all that Day, and the following Night; for the six *Essanapes* inform'd us, that the River was clean, and free from Rocks and Beds of Sand. The 23 we landed early in the Morning on the right side of the River, in order to careen one of our Boats that sprung a Leak. While that was a doing, we drest [*prepared/cooked*] some Venison that had been presented me by the Commander of the last Village of the *Eokoros*; and the adjacent Country being replenish'd with Woods, the Savages of our Company went a shooting in the Forests; but they saw nothing but small Fowls, that they did not think fit to shoot at. As soon as we reimbarqu'd, the Wind fell all of a sudden, and so we were forc'd to ply the Oars; but most of the Crew having slept but little the Night before, they row'd but very faintly, which oblig'd me to put in at a great Island two Leagues higher; the six *Essanapes* Slaves having inform'd me, that this Island afford great plenty of Hares, which I found to be true. These Animals had a lucky Instinct in taking shelter in this Island, for there the Woods are so thick, that we were forc'd to set fire to several places, before we could dialodge 'em.

Having made an end of our Game, my Soldiers fed heartily, and thereupon fell so sound asleep, that I could scarce get 'em wak'd upon a false Alarm, occasion'd by a Herd **[pack]** of Wolves that made a noise among the Thickets upon the Continent. We reimbarqued next day at ten a Clock in the Morning, and did not run above twelve Leagues [36 miles] in two days, by reason that the Savages of our Company would needs walk along the River side with their Guns, to shoot Geese and Ducks; in...

/Page 184/

...which they had very good Success. After that we incampt just by the Mouth of a little River on the right Hand, and the *Essanapes* [Pawnee]Slaves gave me notice, that the first of their Villages was not above sixteen or eighteen Leagues [48 to 54 miles] off. Upon this Information, I sent, by the advice of the Savages of our Company, two of the Slaves to give notice of our arrival. The 26th we row'd briskly, in hopes to reach the first Village that day; but being retarded by the huge quantities of floating Wood, that we met in several places, we were forc'd to continue all Night in our Canows. The 27th about ten or eleven a Clock we approach'd to the Village, and after putting up the great *Calumet* of Peace **[large Pipe of Peace]**[8] upon the Prow of our Canows, lay upon our Oars. Upon our first appearance, three or four hundred *Essanapes* [Pawnees] came running to the shoar, and, after dancing just over against us, invited us ashoar. As soon as we came near the shoar, they began to jump into our Canows; but I gave 'em to know by the four *Essanapes* Slaves, that I desir'd they should retire, which they did immediately. Then I landed, being accompany'd with the Savages of our Company, namely, the *Outagamis* [Foxes], and the *Outaouas* [Ottawas], and with twenty Soldiers.[9] At the same time I gave orders to my Sergeants, to land and post Centries. As we stood upon the shoar, all the *Essanapes* prostrated themselves three or four times before us, with their Hands upon their Foreheads; after which we were convoy'd to the Village with such Acclamations of Joy, as perfectly stun'd us. Upon our arrival at the Gate, our Conductors stop'd us, till the Governour ([of the Essanapes]), a Man of fifty years of Age,...

/Page 185/

...march'd out with five or six hundred Men arm'd with Bows and Arrows. The *Outagamis* [Foxes] of my Company perceiving this, charg'd 'em with Insolence in receiving Strangers with their Arms about 'em, and call'd out in the *Eokoros* [Missouri and/or Otoe] Language, that they ought to lay down their Arms. But the *Essanapes* [Pawnee] Slaves that I had sent in the day before, came up to me and gave me to understand, that 'twas their custom to stand to their Arms on such occasions, and that there was no danger in the case. However, the obstinate *Outagamis* [Foxes] oblig'd us to retire immediately to our Canows: Upon which the Leading Officer, and the whole Battalion [that of the Essanapes], flung their Bows and Arrows aside all on a sudden. Then I return'd and our whole Company enter'd the Village with their Fusees in their Hands, which the [Essanape] Savages admir'd mightily. The Leader of the Savages conducted us to a great Hutt, which look'd as if no body had liv'd in it before. When I and my twenty Soldiers [10] had enter'd the place, they stop'd the *Outagamis* [Foxes], affirming, that they did not deserve the priviledge of entering within the Cottage of Peace, since they had endeavour'd to create a difference, and occasion a War between us and the *Essanapes*. In the mean time I order'd my Men to open the Door, and to call out to the *Outagamis*, that they should offer no manner of Injury **[insult]**: But the *Outagamis* in stead of coming in, press'd me to return with all expedition to the Canows, which accordingly I did, without loss of time, and carry'd with me the four *Essanapes* Slaves, in order to leave 'em at the first Village we came to. We had no sooner imbarqued, then the two other Slaves **[who were in a pirogue** [dugout canoe made from a tree trunk]**]** to acquaint me that the Governor would stop me in his River; **[with fifty men came to tell me that the Chief was blocking his River]**, to which the...

/Page 186/

...*Outagamis* made answer, that he could not do that, without throwing a Mountain into it. In fine, we did not stand to dispute the matter; and tho' 'twas then late, we rowe'd straight to the next Village, which lay about three Leagues [9 miles] off. During the time of this passage, I us'd the precaution of taking from my six Slaves an exact information of the Constitution of their Country, and particularly of the principal Village. They having asur'd me, that the Capital Canton [main village or capital] was seated upon a fort of a Lake [this was likely an abandoned braided channel of the Platt River], I took up a Resolution of not stopping at the other Villages, where I should only lose time, and lavish my Tobacco, and steering directly to the *Metropolitan* [main village] in order to complain to their Generalissimo [main or head chief].

We arriv'd at the Capital Canton on the 3rd of *November* [correct date was December 3], and there met with a very honourable Reception. The *Outagamis* [Foxes] of our Company complain'd of the affront they had receiv'd; but the Head General [head chief] being already inform'd of the matter, made answer, that they ought to have carry'd off the Governour or Leading Officer [who had so offended them], and brought him along with them. In passing from the first Village to this we run fifty Leagues [150 miles], and were follow'd by a Procession of People, that were much more sociable than the Governour that offer'd us that Affront. After our Men had fitted up our Hutts at the distance of a Cannon shot from the Village; we went in a joynt body with the *Outagamis* and the *Outaouas,* to the *Cacick* [chief] of that Nation; and in the mean time the *Essanapes* Slaves were brought before him by ten of my Soldiers.

/Page 187/

[RS1] I was actually in the presence of this petty King, when these Slaves spent half an hour in prostrating themselves several times before him. I made him a Present of Tobacco, Knives, Needles, Cissars, two Firelocks [guns]with Flints, some Hooks, and a very pretty Cutlas. He was better satisfied with these trifling things, which he had never seen before, than I could have been with a plentiful Fortune. He testified his Acknowledgment of the Gift, by a Counter-present that was more solid, though not much more valuable, as consisting of Pease, Beans, Harts [male, buck, or stag deer but probably referring to Elk], Roe-bucks [male small deer?], Geese and Ducks, of which he sent great plenty to our Camp: And indeed, we were extreamly well satisfied with such a seasonable Present. He gave me to know, That, since I design'd to visit the *Gnacsitares* [Plains Apaches/Kiowa Apaches], he would give me a Convoy of two or three hundred Men: That the Gnacsitares were a very honest sort of People; and that both they and his People were link'd by a common interest in guarding off the *Mozeemlek* [seemingly Numic-speaking Bearded Utes], which were a turbulent and warlike Nation. He added, that the Nation last mention'd were very numerous; that they never took the Field without twenty thousand Men at least: That to repres the Incursions and Insults of that dangerous Enemy, the *Gnacsitares* and his Nation [Essanape/Pawnee] had maintain'd a Confederacy for six and twenty years; and that his Allies [The Gnacsitares] were forc'd to take up their Habitation in Islands, where the Enemy cannot reach 'em. I was glad to accept of his Convoy, and return'd him many thanks. I ask'd four Pirogues [canoes made out of hollowed out tree trunks which can be quite large] of him, which he granted very frankly, allowing me to pick and choose that number out of fifty. Having thus concerted my Measures, I was resolv'd...

/Page 188/

...to lose no time; and with that view order'd my Carpenters to plane the Pirogues; by which they were thinner and lighter by one half.[11] The poor innocent People of this Country [that of the Essanape/Pawnee], could not conceive how we work'd with an Axe; every stroke we gave they cry'd out, as if they had seen some new Prodigy; nay, the firing of Pistols could not divert 'em from that Amazement, though they were equally strangers both to the Pistol and the Axe. As soon as my Pirogues were got ready, I left my Canows with the Governour or Prince, and beg'd of him that they might remain untouch'd by any body; in which point he was very faithful to me.

I cannot but acquaint you in this place, that the higher I went up the River, I met with more discretion from the Savages. But in the mean time I must not take leave of the last Village, without giving some account of it. 'Tis bigger than all the rest, and is the Residence of the Great Commander or Generalissimo [Head or highest ranking chief], whose Apartment is built by it self towards the side of the Lake [an abandoned braided river channel?], and surrounded with fifty other Apartments, in which all his Relations are lodg'd. When he walks, his way is strow'd with the leaves of Trees: But *commonly he is carry'd by six Slaves* [emphasis added because his critics have seized on this as a lie though Mississippian cultures routinely did this for their royalty as will be discussed]. His Royal Robes are of the same Magnificence with those of the Commander of the *Okoros* [Otoes and/or Missouris]: For he is naked all over, excepting his lower parts, which are cover'd with a large Scarf made of the barks of Trees. The large extent of this Village might justly intitle it to the name of a City. The Houses are built almost like Ovens [referring to classic Pawnee and other Plains peoples' earth lodges] but they are large and High; and most of 'em are of Reeds cemented with fat Earth [*clay*]. The day before I left this place, as I was walking about, I saw...

/Page 189/

...thirty or forty Women running at full speed; and being surpris'd with the spectacle, spoke to the *Outagamis* to order my four Slaves [the Essanapes/Pawnees] to see what the matter was; for these Slaves were my only Interpreters in this unknown Country. Accordingly they brought me word, that 'twas some new married Women, who were running to receive the Soul of an old Fellow that lay a dying. From thence I concluded, that the People were *Pythagoreans*; [believers in the philosophies of the 6th Century Creek philosopher, Pythagoras, who believed in the transmigration of the soul and in numbers as the ultimate elements of the universe] and upon that Apprehension, ask'd'em how they came to eat Animals, into which their Souls might be transfus'd: But they made answer, that the Transmigration of Souls is always confin'd to the respective Species, so that the Soul of a Man cannot enter into a Fowl, as that of a Fowl cannot be lodg'd in a quadruped, and so on. The *Okoros* [Otoes and/or Missouris], of both Sexes, are as handsom and as clever, as this People.

December the 4th, I took leave of this Village, having ten Soldiers on board of my Pirogue, besides the ten *Oumamis* [misprint and should read Outagamis as no Miamis were with him], The four *Outaouas* [Ottawas], and the four *Essanapes* [Pawnee] Slaves, that I have mention'd so often [a total of 29 men so it was quite a large pirogue]. Here ended the Credit and Authority of the *Calumet* of Peace, for the *Gnacsitares* are not acquainted with that Symbol of Concord. The first day we had enough to do to run fix or seven Leagues [18 to 21 miles], by reason of the Bulrushes with which the Lake is incumber'd. The two following days we sail'd twenty Leagues [60 miles]. The 4th day a West-North-West wind surpris'd us with such a boisterous violence, that we were forc'd to put ashoar, and lay two days upon a sandy Ground,...

/Page 190/

...(Though a bit uncertain this was likely in the vicinity of Grand Island, Nebraska?) where we were in danger of starving for Hunger and Cold; for the Country was so barren, that we could not find a chip of Wood wherewith to warm our selves, or to dress out **[cook]** Victuals; and as far as our Eye could reach, there was nothing to be seen but Fens cover'd with Reeds and Clay, and naked Fields. Having indur'd this Hardship we set out again, and row'd to the little Island, upon which we incamp'd, but found nothing there but green Fields; however, to make some amends we fish'd up great numbers of little Trouts, upon which we fed very heartily. At last, after sailing six days more, we arriv'd at the Point or Lands-end of that Island which you see mark'd in my Map with a Flower-de-luce [Maps 12, 13]; It took him 15 days to work his way up river and reach the first Gnacsitare villages from the principal village of the Essanapes but, unfortunately we do not know where that point was.]. 'Twas then the 19th day of *December*, and we had not yet felt all the rigorous Hardships of the Cold. As soon as I had landed and fitted up my Tents or Hutts, I detach'd my *Essanapes* Slaves to the first of the three Villages that lay before us; for I had avoided stopping at some Villages in an Island upon which we coasted in the Night-time. The Slaves return'd in a great Alarm, occasion'd by the unfavourable Answer they receiv'd from the *Gnacsitares* [Plains or Kiowa Apache], who took us for *Spaniards*, and were angry with them for conducting us to their Country. I shall not be minute in every Particular that happen'd, for fear of tyring your Patience. 'Tis sufficient to acquaint you, that upon the Report of my Slaves I immediately embark'd, and posted my self in another Island that lay in the middle between the great Island [it seems doubtful that this could be a reference to the "Grand Island" of the Platte which is only about 50 miles from the core of the Pawnee villages near Columbus, Nebraska.] and the Continent; but I did not suffer the *Essanapes* to be in my Camp. In the mean time the *Gnacsitares* sent expeditious Couriers to the People that live eighty...

/Page 191/

...Leagues [240 miles] to the Southward of them [probably, to El Cuartelejo in extreme west-central Kansas] to desire they would send some of their number to examine us: for that People were suppos'd to be well acquainted with the *Spaniards* of *New Mexico*. The length of the Journey did not discourage 'em, for they came as cheerfully as if it had been upon a National Concern: and after taking a view of our Cloaths, our Swords, our Fusees, our Air, Complexion, and manner of Speech, were forc'd to own that we were not true *Spaniards?* These Considerations, join'd to the Account I gave 'em of the Reasons upon which I undertook the Voyage [namely to find the source of the Long River and inland passage and gain information on the Spaniards of New Mexico], of the War we were ingag'd in against *Spain*, and of the Country to the Eastward that we possess'd; these, I say, had so much influence, as to undeceive 'em. Then they invited me to encamp in their Island, and brought me a fort of Grain not unlike our Lentils [probably goosefoot/*Chenopodium berlandieri* or *quinoa*, a routine wild Native American food grain], that grows plentifully in that Country. I thank'd 'em for their Invitation, and told 'em that I would not be oblig'd to distrust them, nor give them any occasion to distrust me. However, I cross's with my Savages and ten Soldiers well arm'd; and after breaking the Ice in certain places (for it had freez'd hard for ten or twelve days) I landed within two Leagues of one of their Villages, to which I walk'd up by Land. 'Tis needless to mention the Particulars of the Ceremony with which I was receiv'd, it being the fame with what I describ'd upon other occasions; I shall only take occasion to acquaint you, that my Presents made a wonderful Impression upon the Minds of these people, whom I shall call a rascally Rabble, tho' at the same time they are the politest Nation I have yet seen in this Country. Their Governour bears the...

/Page 192/

...Figure of a King more than any of the other Commanders of the Savages. He has an absolute Dominion over all the Villages which are describ'd in my Map. In this and the other Islands I saw large Parks, or Inclosures **[***meadows***]**, stock'd [*containing*] with wild Beeves [bison] for the use of the People. I had an Interview for two hours together with the Governour, or the *Cacick*; and almost our whole Conference related to the *Spaniards* of *New Mexico*, who, as he assured me, were not distant from his Country above twenty *Tazous,* each of which is three Leagues [thus about 180 miles]. I must own indeed, I was as curious upon this Head as he was; and I wanted an Account of the *Spaniards* from him, as much as he did from me: In fine, we reciprocally inform'd one another of a great many Particulars relating to that Head. He requested me to accept of a great House that was prepar'd for me; and his first piece of Civility consisted in calling in a great many Girls, and pressing me and my Retinue to serve our selves. Had this Temptation been thrown in our way at a more seasonable time, it had prov'd irresistible; but 'twas not an agreeable Mess for Passengers that were infeebled by Labour and Want. *Sine Cere & Baccbo friget Venus* **["Without Ceres and Bacchus, Venus Withers"]**. After he made us such a civil Proffer, the Savages, upon my instance, represented to him, that my Detachment expected me at a certain hour, and that if I stay'd longer, they would be in pain for me. This Adventure happen'd on the 7th of *January* [1689].

[RS2] Two days after, the *Cacick* came to see me, and brought with him four hundred of his own Subjects, and four *Mozeemlek* Savages, whom I took for *Spaniards.* My Mistake was...

/Page 193/

...occasion'd by the great difference between these two *American* Nations; for, the *Mozeemlek* **[RS3]** Savages were cloath'd, they had a thick bushy Beard, and their Hair hung down under their Ears; their Complexion was swarthy, their Address was civil and submissive, their Meen grave, and their Carriage engaging. Upon these Considerations I could not imagine that they were Savages, tho' after all I found my self mistaken. **[RS4]** These four Slaves gave me a Description of their Country, which the *Gnacsitares* represented by way of a Map upon a Deer's Skin; as you see it drawn in this Map [Maps 12, 13]. Their Villages stand upon a River that springs out of a ridge of Mountains (Wasatch Range at the western edge of the Rocky Mountains), from which the Long River likewise derives its Source, there being a great many Brooks there which by a joint Confluence form the River. When the *Gnacsitares* have a mind to hunt wild Beeves [bison], they set out in Pirogues, which they make use of till they come to the Cross mark'd thus (†) in the Map, at the Confluence of two little Rivers. The Hunting of the wild Bulls [American bison], with which all the Valleys are cover'd in Summer, is sometimes the occasion of a cruel War: For the other Cross (†) which you fee in the Map is one of the Boundaries or Limits of *Mozeemlek*; and if either of these two Nations advances but a little beyond their Limits, it gives Rise to a bloody Engagement. The Mountains I spoke of but now, are six Leagues broad [this is obviously not a correct distance at all in referencing the width of the Rocky Mountains to the west of the Platte as they include the Wasatch], and so high that one must cast an infinity of Windings and Turnings **[many large detours]** before he can cross 'em. Bears and wild Beasts are their only Inhabitants.

[RS5] The *Mozeemleck* Nation is numerous and pussant. The four Slaves of that Country [Mozeemlek] inform'd me, that at the distance…

/Page 194/

…of 150 Leagues [450 miles but an obviously incorrect distance] from the Place where I then was [near North Platte, Nebraska?], their principal River empties it self into a Salt Lake of three hundred Leagues [900 miles] in Circumference, the mouth of which is about two Leagues [6 miles] broad: That the lower part of that River is adorn'd with six noble Cities, surrounded with Stone cemented with fat Earth [*clay*]: That the Houses of these Cities have no Roofs, but are open above like a Platform, as you see 'em drawn in the Map [language problems appear to be involved in this strange description]: That besides the abovemention'd Cities, there were above an hundred Towns, great and small, round that sort of Sea, upon which they navigate with such Boats as you see drawn in the Map: That the People of that Country made Stuffs, Copper Axes, and several other Manufactures, which the *Outagamis* [Foxes] and my other Interpreters could not give me to understand, as being altogether unacquainted with such things: That their Government was Despotick, and lodg'd in the hands of one great Head, to whom the rest paid a trembling Submission: That the People upon that Lake call themselves *Tahuglauk,* and are as numerous as the Leaves of Trees, (such is the Expression that the Savages use for an Hyperbole:) That the *Mozeemlek* People supply the Cities or Towns of the *Tahuglauk* with great numbers of little Calves, which they take upon the abovemention'd Mountains: and, That the *Tahuglauk* make use of these Calves for several ends; for, they not only eat their Flesh, but bring 'em up to Labour [*they train them for farming*] [a questionable misunderstanding by Lahontan of what he was hearing in the Numic language]**,** and make Cloaths, Boots, &c. of their Skins. They added, That 'twas their Misfortune to be took Prisoners by the *Gnacsitares* in the War which had lasted for eighteen Years; but, that they hoped a Peace would be speedily concluded,…

/Page 195/

...upon which the Prisoners would be exchang'd, pursuant to the usual Custom. **[RS6]** They glory'd in the possession of a greater measure of Reason than the *Gnacsitares* could pretend to, to whom they allow no more than the Figure of a Man; for they look upon 'em as Beasts otherwise. To my mind, their Notion upon this Head is not so very extravagant; for I observ'd so much Honor and Politness in the Conversation of these four Slaves, that I thought I had to do with *Europeans*: But, after all, I must confess, that the *Gnacsitares* are the most tractable Nation I met with among all the Savages. One of the four *Mozeemlek* Slaves had a reddish sort of a Copper Medal hanging upon his Neck, the Figure of which is represented in the Map. I had it melted by Mr. *de Tonti's* Gun-smith, who understood something of Mettals; but it became thereupon heavier, and deeper colour'd, and withal somewhat tractable. I desir'd the Slaves to give me a circumstantial Account of these Medals; and accordingly they gave me to understand, that they are made by the *Tahuglauk*, who are excellent Artizans, and put a great value upon such Medals. I could pump nothing farther out of 'em, with relation to the Country, Commerce and Customs of that remote Nation. **[RS7]** All they could say was, that the great River of that Nation runs all along Westward, and that the salt Lake into which it falls is three hundred Leagues in Circumference, and thirty in breadth, its Mouth stretching a great way to the Southward. I would fain have satisfied my Curiosity in being an eye-witness of the Manners and Customs of the *Tahuglauk*; but that being impracticable, I was forc'd to be instructed at...

/Page 196/

...second hand by these *Mezeemlek* Slaves; who assur'd me, upon the Faith of a Savage, that the *Tahuglauk* wear their Beards two Fingers breadth long; that their Garments reach down to their Knees; that they cover their Heads with a sharp-pointed Cap; that they always wear a long Stick or Cane in their hands, which is tipp'd, not unlike what we use in *Europe*; that they wear a sort of Boots upon their Legs which reach up to the Knee; that their Women never shew themselves, which perhaps proceeds from the same Principle that prevails in *Italy* and *Spain*; and, in fine, that this People are always at War with the puissant Nations that are seated in the Neighbourhood of the Lake; but withal, that they never disquiet the strowling Nations that fall in their way, by reason of their Weakness: An admirable Lesson for some princes in the World who are so much intent upon the making use of the strongest hand.

[RS8] This was all I could gather upon that Subject. My Curiosity prompted me to desire a more particular Account; <u>but unluckily I wanted a good Interpreter: and having to do with several Persons that did not well understand themselves, I could make nothing of their incoherent Fustian</u> [emphasis added to this important information]. I presented the poor miserable Slaves with something in proportion to the Custom of that Country, and endeavour'd to perswade 'em to go with me to *Canada*, by making such Offers as in their esteem would appear like Mountains of Gold: but the love they had for their Country stifled all Perswasion; so true it is, that Nature reduc'd to its just Limits care but little for Riches.

[January 26th to March 2nd, 1689 Homeward Down the Platte to the Essanape and on Down the Lower Missouri to the Mississippi]

/Page 197/

[RS9] In the mean time it began to thaw, and the Wind chop'd about to the South-west; upon which I gave notice to the great *Cacique* of the *Gnacsitares*, that I had a mind to return to *Canada*. Upon that occasion I repeated by Presents; in compensation of which, my Pirogues were stow'd with Beef as full as they could hold. This done, I embark'd, and cross'd over from the little Island to the Continent, where I fix'd a great long Pole, with the Arms of *France* done upon a Plate of Lead. I set out the 26th of *January* and arriv'd safe on the 5th of *February* in the Country of the *Essanapes*. We had much more pleasure in sailing down the River, than we had in going up; for we had the agreeable diversion of seeing several Huntsmen shooting the Water-Fowl, that are plentiful upon that River. You must know, that the Stream of the Long River is all along very slack and easie, abating for about three Leagues between the fourteenth and fifteenth Village; for there indeed its Current may be call'd rapid. The Channel is so straight, that it scarce winds at all from the Head to the Lake. 'Tis true 'tis not very pleasant; for most of its Banks have a dismal Prospect, and Water it self has an Ugly Taste: but then its Usefulness attones for such Inconveniences; for, 'tis navigable with the greatest ease, and will bear Barques of fifty Tun [here he has to be referring to the Missouri portion of the Long River and not the Platte unless he is attempting to mislead as part of his feint and proposal to further explore to the source of the Missouri], till you come to that place which is mark'd with a Flower-de-luce in the Map [see Maps 12, 13], and where I put up the Post that my Soldiers christen'd *la Hontau's Limit. March* 2. I arriv'd in the *Missisipi*, which was then much deeper and more rapid than before, by reason of the Rains and Land-floods. To save the Labour of Rowing, we then…

(March 2nd, 1689 Sojourn Down the Mississippi to the Osage/Otentas)

/Page 198/

…left our Boats to the Current, and arriv'd on the 10th in the Island of *Rencontres*, which took its Name from the Defeat of 400 *Iroquese*, accomplish'd there by 300 *Nadouessis.* The Story of the Encounter is briefly this: A Party of 400 *Iroquese* having a mind to surprise a certain People in the Neighbourhood of the *Otentas* (of whom more anon) march'd to the Country of the *Illinese,* where they built Canows, and were furnish'd with provisions. After that they embark'd upon the River *Missisipi*, and were discover'd by another little Fleet that was sailing down the other side of the same River. The *Iroquese* cross'd over immediately to that Island, which is since call'd *Aux Rencontres.* The *Nadouessis, i.e.* the other little Fleet, being suspicious of some ill Design, without knowing what People they were (for they had no knowledge of the *Iroquese* but by Hear-say); upon this suspicion, I say, they tugg'd hard to come up with 'em. The two Armies posted themselves upon the point of the Island, where the two Crosses are put down in the Map [Maps 12, 13]; and as soon as the *Nadouessis* came in fight, the *Iroquese* cry'd out in the *Illinese* Language, *Who are ye?* To which the *Nadouessis* answer'd, *Some body*; and putting the like Question to the *Iroquese,* receiv'd the same Answer. Then the *Iroquese* put this Question to 'em, *Where are you a going?* To hunt Beeves, reply'd the *Nadouessis. But pray,* says the *Nadouessis, what's your business? To hunt Men,* reply'd the *Iroquese. 'Tis well*, says the *Nadouessis, we are men and so you need go no further*. Upon this challenge the two Parties disembark'd, and the Leader of the *Nadouessis* cut his Canows...

/Page 199/

...to pieces; and after representing to his Warriours that they behov'd either to Conquer or Die, march'd up to the *Iroquese*; who receiv'd 'em at first Onset with a Cloud of Arrows: But the *Nadouessis* having stood their first Discharge, which kil'd 'em eighty Men, fell in upon 'em with their Clubs in their hands, before the others could charge again; and so routed 'em entirely. This Engagement lasted for two hours, and was so hot, that two hundred and sixty *Iroquese* fell upon the spot, and the rest were all taken Prisoners. Some of the *Iroquese* indeed attempted to make their Escape after the Action was over; but the victorious General sent ten or twelve of his Men to pursue 'em in one of the Canows that he had taken: and accordingly they were all overtaken and drown'd. The *Nadouessis* having obtain'd this Victory, cut off the Noses and Ears of two of the cliverest prisoners; and supplying 'em with Fusees, Powder, and Ball, gave 'em the liberty of returning to their own Country, in order to give their Country-men to understand, that they ought not to employ Women to hunt after Men any longer.

The 12th we arriv'd at the Village of the *Otentas,* where we took in a plentiful Provision of *Turkey* Corn, of which these People have great store. They inform'd us, that their River was pretty rapid, and took its Rise from the neighbouring Mountains; and that the upper part of it was adorn'd with several Villages inhabited by the People call'd *Panimaba,...*

/Page 200/

...*Paneassa*, and *Panetonka* [no name equivalents are known for these peoples]. But considering that I was straitned for time, and that I saw no probability of learning what I wanted to know with reference to the *Spaniards*, I took leave of 'em the next day, which was the 13th, and in four days time, by the help of the Current and our Oars, made the River of the *Missouris.* This done, we run up against the Stream of that River, which was at least as rapid as the *Missisipi* was at that time; and arriv'd on the 18th at the first Village of the *Missouris*, where I only stop'd to make the People some Presents that procur'd me a hundred Turkeys, with which that People are wonderfully well stock'd. After that, we row'd hard against the Stream, and landed next night near the secund Village. As soon as I arriv'd, I detach'd a Sergeant with ten Soldiers to convoy the *Outagamis* to the Village, while the rest of my Crew were busied in fitting up our...

/Page 201/

...Hutts and unloading our Canows. It happen'd unluckily that neither the Soldiers nor the *Outagamis* could make the Savages understand 'em; and the latter were just ready to fall upon 'em, when an old Fellow cry'd out, that the Strangers were not without more company, for that he had discover'd our Huts and Canows. Upon this, the Soldiers and the *Outagamis* retir'd in a great Consternation, and advis'd me to keep a strong Guard all night. About two a clock in the Morning two Men approach'd to our little Camp, and call'd in *Illinese,* that they wanted an Interview; upon which the *Outagamis,* being extremely well satisfied that there was some body among 'em who could understand what they said, reply'd in *Illinese,* that they should be very welcome as soon as the Sun appear'd in the horizon. Nevertheless, the *Outagamis* resented the former Affront so much, that they importun'd me all night long to set fire to the Village and put all the scoundrel Inhabitants to the Sword. I made answer to 'em, that' twas our business to be wiser than they, and to bend our Thoughts, not upon a fruitless Revenge, <u>but upon the Discovery that we were then in quest of</u> [namely a inland passage and information on the Spaniards, emphasis added]. At the break of Day the two Adventurers of the Night came up to us, and after putting Interrogatories to us for the space of two hours, invited us to come up to their Village. The *Outagamis* reply'd, that the Head or Governour of their Nation ought to have saluted us sooner: and this oblig'd 'em to go back to give him notice. After that we saw no body for three hours: but at last, when our Impatience was just beginning to boil, we perceiv'd the Governour, who accosted us in a trembling Posture. He was...

/Page 202/

...accompany'd with some of his own Men, who were loaded with boil'd or dry'd Meat, Sacks of *Turkey* or *Indian* Corn, dry'd Raisins, and some speckled or particolour'd Buck-skins. In consideration of this Present, I made 'em another of less consequence. Then I brought on a Conference between the *Outagamis* of my Company and the two Night Messengers, in order to make some discovery of the Nature of the Country; but they still stop'd our Mouths with this Answer, that they knew nothing of the Matter, but that the other Nations that liv'd higher up were able to inform us. Had I been of the same mind with the *Outagamis*, we had done noble Exploits in this Place: but I consider'd that 'twas my business to purchase the Knowledge of several things, which I could not obtain by burning the Village. To be short, we re-embark'd that same day, about two a clock in the Afternoon, and row'd about four Leagues up the River, where we made the River of the *Osages*, and encamp'd by its Mouth. That Night we had several false Alarms from the wild Beeves [American bison], upon which we made sufficient Reprisals afterwards; for the next day we kill'd many of 'em notwithstanding that it rain'd so heavily that we could scarce stir out of our Hutts. Towards the Evening, when the Rain was over, and while we were transporting two or three of these Beeves to our little Camp, we spy'd an Army of the Savages upon a full March towards us.

/Page 203/

Upon that, my Men began to entrench themselves, and to unload their Pieces with Worms [gun worms or screw devices for removing undischarged balls from muzzle loading muskets], in order to charge ‘em afresh; but one of the Pieces happening to go off, the whole Body of the Enemy disappear’d, some straggling one way, and some another: for these people were upon the same foot with the Nations that lived upon the Long River, forasmuch as neither of them had ever seen or handled Fire-Arms. However, this Adventure mov’d the *Outagamis* so much, that to satisfie them, I was oblig’d to re-embark that very night, and return the same way that I came. Towards Midnight we came before a Village, and kept a profound Silence till Day-break, at which time we row’d up to their Fort; and upon our entering there, and discharging our Pieces in the Air, the Women, Children, and superannuated Men, were put into such a Consternation, that they run from place to place calling out for Mercy. You must know, all their Warriours were abroad, and ‘twas a Body of them that offer’d to attack us the day before. The *Outagamis* perceiving the Consternation of the Women and Children, call’d out, that they behov’d to depart the Village, and that the Women should have time to take up their Children. Upon that the whole Crew turn’d out, and we set fire to the Village on all sides. This done, we pursu’d our Course down that rapid River, and enter’d the River *Missisipi* on the 25th, early in the Morning: the 26th, about three a clock in the Afternoon, we descry’d three of four hundred Savages employ’d in the Hunting of Beeves, which swarmed in all the Meads to the Westward. As soon as the Hunters spy’d us, they made a sign that we should make…

/Page 204/

…towards ‘em. Being ignorant who, or how numerous they were, we made a halt at first; but at last we put in about a Musket-shot above ‘em, calling out to ‘em that they should not approach to us in a Body. Upon that, four of their number came up to us with a smiling Countenance, and gave us to know, in the *Ilinese* Language, that they were *Arkansas* [Quapaws]. We could not but credit their Report, for they had Knives and Scissars hanging upon their Necks, and little Axes about’em, which the *Ilinese* present ‘em with when they meet. Infine, being assur’d that they were of that Nation, which Mr. *de la Salle* and several other *French-men* were intimately acquainted with, we landed at the same place; and they entertain’d us first with Dancing and Singing, and then with all sorts of Meat. The next day they shew’d us a Crocodile that they had knock’d in the head two days before, by a Stratagem that you’ll find describ’d in another place: After that they gave us the diversion of a Hunting Match; for ‘tis customary with them, when they mean to divert themselves, to catch the Beeves [bison] by the different Methods laid down in this Cut. I put some Questions to ‘em relating to the *Spaniards*, but they could not resolve ‘em. All that I learn’d from ‘em was, that the *Missouris* and the *Osages* are numerous and mischievous…

/Page 205/

…Nations, equally void both of Courage and Honesty; that their Countries were water’d with very great Rivers; and in a word, were too good for them.

After we had spent two days with them, we pursued our Voyage to the River *Ouabach* [Wabash as the Ohio was originally known], taking care to watch the Crocodiles very narrowly, of which they had told us incredible Stories. The next day we enter'd the Mouth of that River, and sounded it, to try the truth of what the Savages reported of its depth. In effect, we found there three Fathom and a half Water; but the Savages of our Company alledg'd that 'twas more swell'd that usually. They all agreed, that 'twas Navigable an hundred Leagues up, and I wish'd heartily, that my time had allow'd me to run up to its Source; but that being unseasonable, I sail'd up against the Stream [of the Mississippi], till we came to the River of the *Illinese*, which we made on the 9th of *April* with some difficulty, for the Wind was against us the first two days, and the Currents was very rapid.

(April 9th to May 22nd, 1689 Up the Illinois River and Back to Michilimackinac)

All I can say of the River *Missisipi*, now that I am to take leave of it, is, that its narrowest part is half a League over, and the shallowest is a Fathom and a half deep; and that...

/Page 206/

...according to the information of the Savages, its stream is pretty gentle for seven or eight Months of the year. As for Shelves or Banks of Sand, I met with none in it. 'Tis full of Isles which look like Groves, by reason of the great plenty of Trees, and in the verdant season of the year afford a very agreeable prospect. Its Banks are Woods, Meadows and Hills. I cannot be positive, whether it winds much in other places; but as far as I could see, its course is very different from that of our Rivers in *France*; for I must tell you by the way, that all the Rivers of *America* run pretty straight.

The River of the *Illinese* is intitled to Riches, by virtue of the benign Climate, and of the great quantities of Deer, Roe-Bucks, and Turkeys that feed upon its brinks: Not to mention several other Beasts and Fowls, a description of which would require an intire Volume. If you saw but my Journal, you would be sick of the tedious particulars of our daily Adventures both in Hunting and Fishing divers species of Animals, and in Rencounters with the Savages. In short, the last thing I shall mention of this River, is, that the Banks are replenish'd with an infinity of Fruit-Trees, which we saw in a dismal condition, as being strip'd of their verdure; and that among these Fruit-Trees, there are many Vines, which bear most beautiful Clusters of very large Grapes. I ate some of these Grapes dry'd in the Sun [raisins], which had a most delicious Taste. The Beavers are unfrequent in this, as in the long River, where I saw nothing but Otters, of which the People make Furs for the Winter.

I set out from the *Illinese* River on the 10th of *April*, and...

/Page 207/

...by the help of a West-South-West Wind, arriv'd in six days at the Fort of *Crevecoeur* [this had to have been the new post that replaced *Crevecoeur* which had seemingly been destroyed by then], where I met with Mr. *de Tonti*, who receiv'd me with all imaginable Civility, and is justly respected and honour'd by the *Iroquese* [did he not mean to say the Illinois since Tonti would not have been honored by the Iroquois?].[12] I stay'd three days in this Fort [could he have been doing some trading also?], where there were thirty *Coureurs de Bois* that traded with the *Illinese*. The 20th I arriv'd at the Village of the *Illinese*; and to lessen the drudgery of a great Land-carriage of twelve great Leagues [36 miles], ingag'd four hundred Men to transport our Baggage [seems like a lot of baggage and suggests that Lahontan may have been trading for furs along the way but did not wish to mention it], which they did in the space of four days, being incourag'd by a Bribe of a great Roll of *Brasil* Tobacco, an hundred pound weight of Powder, two hundred weight of Ball, and some Arms, which I gave to the most considerable Men of their number. The 24th I arriv'd at *Chekakou* [Chicago on Lake Michigan], where my *Outagamis* took leave of me in order to return to their own Country, being very well satisfied with a Present I made 'em of some Fusees, and some Pistols. The 25th I reimbarqued, and by rowing hard in a Calm, made the River of the *Oumamis* [Miamis located on the east shore of Lake Michigan] on the 28th [Map 1]. There I met four hundred Warriours, upon the...

/Page 208/

...very same place where Mr. *de la Salle* had formerly built a Fort. These Warriours were then imploy'd in burning three *Iroquese*, who, as they said, deserv'd the Punishment; and invited us to share in the pleasure of the Show; for the Savages take it very ill if one refuses the diversion of such real Tragedies. The Tragical spectacle made me shrink, for the poor wretches were put to inconceivable Torture; and upon that I resolv'd to reimbarque with all expedition; alledging for an Apology, that my Men had great store of Brandy with 'em, and would certainly make themselves drunk, in solemnifing their Victory, upon which they would be apt to commit disorders, that I could not possibly prevent. Accordingly I went immediately on board, and after coasting along the Lake [east shore of Lake Michigan], cross'd the Bay *de l'Ours* **[Bay of Sleeping Bears]** [Grand Traverse Bay, Michigan], and landed at *Missilimakinac* the 22*d*.

(Lahontan's Epilogue to Letter XVI and Recommendations for Further Exploring the Long River)

I am inform'd by the Sieur *de S. Pierre de Repantigni* [Jean-Paul Le Gardeur, sieur de Repentigny was an explorer and lieutenant for New France who served with Dulhut], who travel'd from *Quebec* hither upon the Ice, that Mr. *de Denonville* has took up a resolution of making a Peace with the *Iroquese,* in...

/Page 209/

…which he means to comprehend the other Nations that are his Allies; and with that view had given notice to his Allies, that they should not infest the *Iroquese*. He acquaints me further, that Mr. *de denonville* has sent orders to the Governour of this place, to perswade the *Rat*, (one of the Commanders of the *Hurons*) to go down to the Colony, with a design, to have him hang'd; and that the Savage General being aware of the design, has made a publick Declaration, that he will go thither on purpose to defie him. Accordingly he designs to set out to Morrow with a great body of Outaouas, and some *Coureurs de Bois*, under the command of Mr. *Dulhut*. As for the Soldiers of my Detachment, I have dispers'd 'em in several Canows among the Savages, and the *Coureurs de Bois*; but having some business to adjust in this place, I am oblig'd to tarry my self seven or eight days longer. [What business could he have had for so long remaining at Michilimackinac and could it have involved trading or settling up with any who may have assisted him in launching his expedition or to prepare his trip report for the governor?]

This, Sir, is the true account of my little Voyage. I have related nothing but the Essential Circumstances; choosing to overlook the rest, which are so trifling, as to be unworthy of your Curiosity. As for the *Illinese* Lake [Lake Michigan], 'tis three hundred Leagues [900 miles] in Circumference, as you may see by the Scale of Leagues upon the Map. 'Tis seated in an admirable Cli-…

/Page 210/

…mate; its Banks are cloath'd with fine and tall Trees, and have but few Meads. The River of the *Oumamis* [Miamis] is not worth your regard. The Bay *de l'Ours qui dort,* is of an indifferent large extent, and receives the River upon which the *Outaouas* are wont to hunt Beavers every third year. In short, it has neither Shelves, Rocks, nor Banks of Sand. The Land which bounds it on the South side, is replenish'd with Roe-bucks, Deer, and Turkeys. Farewel, Good Sir: And assure your self, that 'twill always be a sensible pleasure to me, to amuse you with an account of the greatest Curiosities I meet with. But now, Sir, I hope you will not take it ill, that the Relation I here give you, is only an Abridgment of my Voyage: For, in earnest, to be minute upon every particular Curiosity, would require more time and leisure than I can spare. I have here sent you a view of the substantial part; and shall after wards hope for an opportunity of recounting to you by word of Mouth, an infinity of Adventures, Rencounters, and Observations, which may call up the reflecting faculty of thinking Men. My own Thought is too Superficial to philosophise upon the Origin, the Belief, the Manners and Customs of so many Savages; or to make any advances with reference to the extent of this Continent to the Westward. I have contented my self with offering some thoughts upon the causes of the bad success of the Discoveries [here alluding to the search for an inland passage?], that several experience'd Men have attempted in *America*, both by Sea and Land: And I flatter my self, that my thoughts upon that head are just. The fresh Instances of Mr. *de la Salle*, and several other unlucky Discoverers, may afford a sufficient and seasonable caution to…

...those, who for the future shall undertake to discover all the unknown Countries of this New World. 'Tis not every one that's qualify'd for such an Enterprise, *non licet omnibus adire Corinthum* **[Not everyone is allowed to go to Corinth]**. 'Twere an easie matter to trace the utmost limits of the Country that lies to the West of *Canada*, provided it be gone about in a proper Method. In the first place, instead of Canows, I would have such Adventurers to make use of certain Sloops of a peculiar Structure, which might draw but little Water, and be portable, as being made of light Wood; and withal carry thirteen Men, with 35 or 40 hundred weight of Stowage, and be able to bear the shock of the Waves in the great Lakes. Courage, Health, and Vigilance, are not sufficient of themselves to qualifie a Man for such Adventures; he ought to be possess'd of other Talents, which are rarely met with in one and the same Person. The Conduct of the three hundred Men that accompany'd me upon this Discovery, gave me a great deal of trouble **[Leading three hundred men with whom one could undertake these discoveries seem arduous enough]** [the baron did not lead 300 men on the Long River]. It requires a large stock of Industry and Patience, to keep such a Company up to their Duty. Sedition, Mutinies, Quarrels, and an infinity of disorders frequently take place among those, who being in remote and solitary Places, think they have a right of using force against their Superiours. One must dissemble, and shut his Eyes upon occasion, least the growing Evil should be inflam'd: The gentlest Methods are the surest, for him that commands in Chief; and if any Mutiny or Seditious Plot is in view, 'tis the business of the inferior Officers to stifle it, by perswading the Mutineers, that the discovery of such things to the Commanding Officer, would create a great deal of uneasiness. So the chief Officer must still make as if he were ignorant of what passes, unless it be, that the flame breaks out in his Presence; then indeed he lies under an indispensible Obligation, of inflicting speedy and private punishment, without his prudence directs him to put off the Execution, upon an apprehension of some pernicious consequences that may insue thereupon. In such Voyages he must overlook a thousand things, which upon other occasions he has all reason to punish. He must counterfeit a downright ignorance of their Intrigues **[liaisons]** with the She-Savages, of their Quarrels among themselves, of their negligence in not mounting the Guard, and not observing the other points of Duty; in a word, he must pretend to know nothing of an Infinity of such Disorders, as have no direct tendency to a Revolt. He ought to use the precaution of singling out a Spy in his little Army, and reward him handsomly for a dexterous Intelligence as to all that happens; to the end that he may remedy the growing disorders either directly or indirectly. This Spie may be good management, and due secrecy find out the Ringleader of a Club or Cabal; and when the Commanding Officer has receiv'd such satisfaction upon the matter, that there's no room left to doubt of the Criminal's Demerit; 'twill then be very convenient to make away with him, and that with such management, that no body should know what became of him.

Farther: He ought to give 'em Tobacco and Brandy now and then, to ask their advice upon some occasions, to fatigue 'em as little as possible, to call'em up to dance and make merry, and at the same time to exhort'em to live in a good understanding with one another. The best Topick he can make use of for inforcing their Duty, is Religion, and the Honour of their Country, and this he ought to descant upon himself: For though I have a great deal of Faith in the power of the Clergy; yet I know that sort of Men do's more harm than good, in Voyages of this nature; and for that reason I'd choose to be without their Company. The Person who undertakes to go upon a Discovery, ought to be very nice and cautious in the choice of his Men: for every one is not fit for his business. His Men ought to be between 30 and 40 years of Age; of a dry Constitution **[temperate with alcohol]**, of a peacable Temper, of an active and bold Spirit, and inur'd to the fatigues of Voyages. This whole Retinue must consist of three hundred Men; and of that number there must be some Ship-Carpenters, Gun-smiths, and Sawyers with all their Tools; besides Huntsmen, and Fishermen with their Tackling. You must likewise have Surgeons among 'em, but their Chest ought to contain nothing but Razours, Lancets, External Medicines for Wounds, Orvietan and Senna. All the Men of the Detachment, ought to be provided with Buff-Coats and Boots [heavy leather garments?] to turn the Arrows; for, as I intimated above, the Savages of the unknown Countries are strangers to Fire-Arms. They must be arm'd with a double barrel'd Gun, a double barrel'd Pistol, and a good long Sword. The Commanding Officer must take care to provide a sufficient quantity of the Skins of Deer, Elks, and Beeves, in order to be sew'd together, and hung round his Camps...

/Page 214/

...upon certain Stakes fix'd at convenient distances from one another. I had **[should have had?]** as many as would go round a square of thirty Foot every way; for each Skin being five Foot deep, and almost four Foot broad, I made **[would have made?]** two pieces of eight Skins a piece, which were **[would be]** rais'd and extended in a Minute [these were merely his recommendations not something he had with him on the Long River]. Besides these, he ought to carry with him some Pot-Guns [large shot guns] of eight Foot in length, and six [sic] in breadth; with two Hand-Mills for grinding the *Indian* Corn, Nails of all sizes, Pickaxes, Spades, Hatchets, Hooks, Soap, and Cotton to make Candles of. Above all, he must not forget to take in good store of Powder, Brandy, *Brasil* Tobacco, and such things as he must present to the Savages whose Country he discovers. Add to this Cargo, an Astrolabe, a Semicircle, several Sea-Compasses, some Simple, and some of Variation, a Load-stone [magnet], two large Watches of three Inches Diameter; Pencils, Colours, and Paper, for making Journals and Maps, for the designing of Land-Creatures, Fowl, Fish, Trees, Plants, Grain, and in a word, whatever seems worthy of his Curiosity. I would like-wise advise him to carry with him some Trumpeters and Fiddlers, both for animating his Retinue, and raising the admiration of the Savages. With this Equipage, Sir, a Man of Sense, Conduct, and Action, I mean, a Man that's Vigilant, Prudent Cautious, and above all, Patient and Moderate, and qualify'd for contriving Expedients upon all occasions; a Man, I say, thus qualify'd, and thus fitted out, may boldly go to all the Countries that lye to the West of *Canada*, without any apprehension of danger. As for my own part, I seriously declare,...

/Page 215/

...that if I were possess'd of all these qualities, I should esteem it my happiness to be imploy'd upon such an Enterprise, both for the Glory of his Majesty, and my own Satisfaction; For the continu'd diversity of Objects, did so charm me in my Voyages, that I had scarce time to reflect upon the fatigue and trouble that I underwent. I am,

SIR, Yours, &C.

(End of Lahontan's Long River Narrative)

A Retrospective on the Long River Narrative

Lahontan's recommendations for the necessary supplies and equipment needed for his proposed further exploration up the Missouri to its source demonstrate just how thoughtfully and knowingly they had been prepared. In the nineteenth century The Royal Geographical Society of Great Britain prepared a series of guidelines for explorers.[13] These contained lists of the kinds of things and participants that should be carried on expeditions into unknown lands, particularly where there might be hostile indigenous peoples. The similarities between what the baron recommended and what the Society recommended some two hundred years later are surprising in their equivalency.[14] In addition to his proposal for a continuation of his search for an inland passage via the Long River, the baron is known to have prepared a number of other substantive plans for France as well as Spain and England.[15]

The baron had returned to Michilimackinac on May 22, 1689, but he did not finish or at least date Letter XVI with its Long River narrative for his correspondent until the 28th. It is not known whether he immediately sent it with the next canoe brigade headed down the lakes toward Montreal and Quebec or carried it with him when he departed for Montreal on June 8. On that trip he was with twelve Ottawas in two canoes loaded with those Natives' own furs. He discussed that journey in Letter XVII.[16] He finally arrived back in Montreal on July 9 after a month of hard paddling and running a lot of fast "fearful cataracts" or rapids, making numerous portages, and nearly being drowned in the dangerous *Lachine* (China Town) rapids just above Montreal where so many canoeing parties came to ruin. Jolliet lost all his papers there in a similar canoe mishap following his explorations on the Mississippi with Marquette. When Lahontan's canoe upset one of the baron's Native companions drowned and all the furs lost. The baron was saved only by the quick intervention of the Chevalier de Vaudreuil whose brigade of canoes was by chance close by.

The day following his arrival in Montreal on July 10, Lahontan met with governor Denonville and the crown's intendant, Mr. de Champigni. True to the requirements made of all explorers in New France, he "gave an account of my voyages."[17] The only voyages he had made which these superiors would not have been aware of were those involving the Long River expedition. They were certainly aware of the travels they had ordered for him in early 1688 and his return to Michilmackinac since they sent him a dispatch there along with the supplies for the winter. It seems inconceivable that given his official position the baron would not have reported his exploits on the Long River to the Crown's highest representatives in New France. This would particularly have been the case for a junior military officer posted to an important facility, particularly if he was hoping for sponsorship of further exploration, as he clearly was. The baron had sent members of his detachment downriver ahead of his own return to Montreal. Thus, men who had been with him on the Long River were back in the colony ahead of him. It would seem to be very unlikely that they would have kept mum about their recent adventures.

The trip to the Long River was a substantial and costly expedition. Too many people would have had to have known about it for it to have been kept a secret, including all his marines and the other French personnel at Michilimackinac; his Native companions; and the post commanders, first St. Denys and then Durantaye, the trader with whom Lahontan was well acquainted.[18] Lahontan made no mention of the outcome of his reporting. This is despite the fact that the recalled governor, Denonville, and his immediate successor, Frontenac, who arrived only a month after the baron arrived back in Quebec (October 1689), had to have eventually learned about the Long River trip.

If Lahontan had indeed submitted a written report to the governor, it may not have been mentioned in official documents, such as the governor's or intendant's reports to the Crown, because the expedition was not at all successful in meeting its goals of locating the source of the Long River or an inland passage or learning much about the Spaniards. It was essentially a failed expedition as well as one that the Crown had not officially sanctioned. In this regard it bears similarities to the unsuccessful explorations of Juan Rivera out of New Mexico in 1765. Because of their importance to the interests of the Spanish Crown, the governor of New Mexico quietly sanctioned Rivera's activities in the absence of formal approval from his superiors.[19] As with the baron's travels, there were no contemporary records other than Rivera's journals to demonstrate that he made the trips. One must speculate that the baron may not have had the Crowns' authorization for his trip but only the tacit approval of the local colonial authorities (governor and intendant). If he did not have such local approval, it would appear that he could have been charged with desertion from his posting and even the unauthorized use of the Crown's resources such as canoes, men, and supplies. Since he made his report and was not so charged, his superiors must not have been too aggrieved about his Long River expedition.

A significant unanswered question is whether fur trading played any part in Lahontan's travels to the Long River? He described how Dulhut had started out for the colony before him, seemingly from Michilimackinac, with a brigade of voyageurs that was obviously carrying furs down to Montreal.[20] This brigade may have been nothing more than the routine annual transport of the previous year's accumulation of furs, but Lahontan may have obtained at least some of them on his return. On that trip Lahontan explained that he had to hire the four hundred Illinois people to transport the expedition's baggage and canoes over one great thirty-six-mile portage he had to make before finally reaching Lake Michigan.[21] That portage took the company four days and strongly suggests that he had a large cargo that could hardly have been made up of anything other than furs.

Lahontan's back load was much, much larger than he had started out with as evidenced when he spoke of his short portage to the Wisconsin River from the Fox villages.[22] He accomplished that in only two days but with far fewer men than he needed to make that last long carry back to Lake Michigan. Since furs were so valuable and, given the common fur trade intrigues of the time in New France, it would appear likely that there was some surreptitious fur trading going on, even though Denonville was attempting to strictly regulate it. He was the "King's man" and normally tried to carry out his orders to the letter.[23]

Nevertheless, at times Denonville was known to have allowed soldiers on the frontier to trade for furs.[24] As discussed in chapter 2 he could hardly have been unaware that the king had instructed colonial authorities to encourage the discovery of an inland passage and offered to substantially reward whomever could find it.[25] Since it was still the king's wish that explorations be made to locate the desired passage, it would not appear to have been inappropriate for Denonville to quietly look favorably on the baron's Long River expedition. Whether Denonville would have been personally involved in the fur trade is an open question since he worked to curb the abuses then prevalent in that commerce, which made him quite unpopular within the colony.[26]

By contrast, when Frontenac replaced Denonville as governor in the fall of 1689 he would certainly have been interested in continuing his involvement in the trade. If Lahontan failed to tell Denonville about his Long River trip, he quite likely did tell Frontenac. Frontenac could hardly have been kept ignorant of the baron's travels in search of an inland passage since they ultimately became such close comrades and he was involved with the baron in getting at least some of his book published.[27] In addition to befriending and financially supporting Lahontan, he was also keenly interested in westward exploration and the fur trade with which he had been so deeply involved from his early days in Canada.

Historian W. J. Eccles wrote about Frontenac and his involvement in the fur trade. His words apply to far more people in power in New France than just Frontenac: "There can be no doubt that Frontenac took every advantage of his position to profit from the fur trade."[28]

Notes:

1. Thwaites, "Introduction," xxiv.

2. Fouillade, "Translation; Wilson, "Translation."

3. Lahontan, *Nouveaux Voyages de;* Thwaites, *New Voyages*.

4. Chávez and Warner, *Domínguez-Escalante Journal*.

5. Thwaites, *"Introduction,"* xlviii.

6. The named points on a boxed compass are formed by the initials of the cardinal directions and their intermediate ordinal directions. This system, called a "wind rose" or more commonly a "compass rose," is of ancient Mediterranean origin. The boxed points are useful in referring to compass headings in a colloquial fashion without resorting to computing or recalling angles. Although there are up to 128 named points on a compass, the baron never directly mentioned his direction of travel. Although he noted that he was traveling to the "southern" colonies he never mentioned that he was ever traveling north or south. Likewise, he never mentioned if he ever was traveling east or west. On one occasion he noted that the wind was blowing from "West-North-West" or 292.60 degrees and another time by "West-South-West" or 247.50 degrees.

7. One issue that consistently cropped up in Lahontan's narrative was with the mix of terms he used for large animals that were used for food such as "harts," "roe-bucks," "bucks," etc. It appears that Lahontan's translator, who seems to have been a European unfamiliar with the North American fauna, was at times at a loss to know just what animals the baron was referring to and he had obviously never encountered them and could only name them by the European terms that best described them. This led to some confusion in attempts to equate the names for such given by the baron with modern animals with which readers should be familiar. In such cases the most likely common name has been given in brackets. Toward the end of *Letter XVI* Lahontan lists two large mammals, that appear to encompass all those he hunted or referenced from the "Southern Countries" during his Long River travels and whose hides might be capable of turning the arrows of the Indians. These were "Deer" and "Beeves." He also

mentions "elks" but he did not report seeing these on that trip. Rather, he does report on hunting them in Canada, and he is quite obviously describing "moose" as "Elk" or "Originals" as he called them and not the "wapiti" or "elk" as they are now known, although they are commonly considered as but another form of the cloven-hoofed deer. Among other names of big game from the south he referred to were "harts" which dictionaries refer to as "mature male deer" with substantial antlers, otherwise known as a "stag." By this term it appears that he is speaking of the large true so-Lordly elk or wapiti which can look like a stag with their huge sets of multiple-tined antlers. The best term available to him would have been the large "harts" or "stags" of Europe. This becomes more evident in his use of the term "roe-bucks" which refers to the small "roe deer" of Europe. The baron's attention to differentiating between these various animals is believed to be testimony to his consistency, as a dedicated student of natural history, in adhering to the most honest descriptive detail he could muster in his various narratives. A "Roe-buck" would, therefore, be a small male deer, seemingly a white tail deer, with antlers that were obviously smaller than those of a "hart" or similarly antlered Elk/wapiti. That would well describe the white tail deer as it has long been known from the Eastern woodlands and Great Plains. Lahontan's reference to "Beeves" or "wild bulls" of the Plains is obviously his attempt to describe the well-known "American bison" or "buffalo." He also referred to just "bucks" and one can only presume that he was referencing male deer.

8. Marquette and Dablon, "Of the First Voyages," "Voyages of Marquette," "Description of the Calumet." "There remains no more, except to speak of the Calumet. There is nothing more mysterious or more respected among them. Less honor is paid to the Crowns and scepters of Kings than the Savages bestow upon this. It seems to be the God of peace and of war, the Arbiter of life and of death. It has but to be carried upon one's person, and displayed, to enable one to walk safely through the midst of Enemies -who, in the hottest of the Fight, lay down Their arms when it is shown. For That reason, the Ilinois gave me one, to serve as a safeguard among all the Nations through whom I had to pass during my voyage. (Figure. 24) There is a Calumet for peace, and one for war, which are distinguished solely by the Color of the feathers with which they are adorned; Red is a sign of war. They also use it to put an end to Their disputes, to strengthen Their alliances, and to speak to Strangers. It is fashioned from a red stone, polished like marble, and bored in such a manner that one end serves as a receptacle for the tobacco, while the other fits into the stem; this is a stick two feet long, as thick as an ordinary cane, and bored through the middle. It is ornamented with the heads and necks of various birds, whose plumage is very beautiful. To these they also add large feathers,-red, green, and other colors, -wherewith the whole is adorned. They have a great regard for it, because they look upon it as the calumet of the Sun; and, in fact, they offer it to the latter to smoke when they wish to obtain a calm, or rain, or fine weather. They scruple to bathe themselves at the beginning of Summer, or to eat fresh fruit, until after they have performed the dance, which they do as follows: The Calumet dance, which is very famous among these peoples, is performed solely for important reasons; sometimes to strengthen peace, or to unite themselves for some great war; at other times, for public rejoicing. Sometimes they thus do honor to a Nation who are invited to be present; sometimes it is danced at the reception of some important personage," http://moses.creighton.edu/kripke/jesuitrelations/relations_59.html - _edn27.

9. This is the maximum number of soldiers that the baron ever directly enumerates as being in his detachment with him on the Long River. Thus, we know that he had at least twenty and probably more

with him, likely forty to sixty. There were at least two sergeants, and he surely was indicating that he left them and some of his men on shore to guard his canoes while he took 20 others with him to meet the Essanape leaders of the village. Lahontan, *New Voyages*, 184.

10. Once again Lahontan mentions that he had twenty men of his detachment with him as only a part of this shore party. Lahontan, 185.

11. The Natives made their dugouts or pirogues from cottonwood trunks of extraordinary girth and height. These were commonly made by burning and then chipping out the charred interiors of the logs. These graceful, one-piece canoes were up to 50 feet in length and three in width and some could carry thirty men with all their baggage. They were very plentiful among the Indians living along the rivers. Dablon, *Relation de la descouverte (Relation de la descouverte), (*CXXXI) 97.

12. The original Fort Crevecoeur had been built by La Salle on the Illinois River in 1680 but was destroyed by his mutinous men the same year. A new trading facility, Fort S. Louis, was built upriver from the original one in 1682 and that is where the baron would have been visiting when he encountered his old comrade Tonty. It is certainly possible that the newer post could at times have been inadvertently referred to as "Crevecoeur" also. There are some contradictions apparent in the accounts of these posts but the baron reported that he met Tonty there on his way back to Michilimackinac. Lahontan, *New Voyages*, 207n1, n2.

13. Freshfield and Wharton, *Hints to Travellers;* Grann, *Lost City*, 69-71.

14. Lahontan, *New Voyages*, 209-15.

15. Lahontan, "Brief Discours qui," "Concerning the Regulation of the Limits…," 215, 224, Haney, "Lom D'Arce de;" Towle and Rawlyk, "A new Baron De Lahontan Memoir…"

16. Lahontan, *New Voyages*, 216-29.

17. Lahontan, 219-20; Talon to the King, "Extracts of a Memorial," (9) 64.

18. Lahontan, 125, 144, 164; Thwaites, "Introduction," xviii; Weilbrenner, "Morel de la Durantaye."

19. Baker, et al., *Juan Rivera's Colorado*, vii, 74-75, 44, 150-51.

20. Lahontan, *New Voyages*, 216.

21. Lahontan, 207.

22. Lahontan, 177.

23. Eccles, "Brisay de Denonville."

24. Kent, *Rendezvous at the Straits*, (I), 1, 99, 103.

25. Heidenreich, *Early French Exploration*, 126; Colbert to Talon, "His Majesties Intentions."

26. Eccles, “Brisay de Denonville.”

27. Eccles, “Comte de Frontenac;” Lahontan, *New Voyages,* 9.

28. Eccles, *Frontenac*, 98.

7

• PLACING LAHONTAN ON THE PLATTE RIVER •

by

STEVEN G. BAKER AND W. RAYMOND WOOD

This chapter concerns Lahontan's description of the land of the Gnacsitares (Table 1 in chapter 6) along the Platte River, and the lands of the Mozeemlek and Tahuglauk near the Great Salt Lake in Utah. Lahontan gathered this information while he was on the Platte among the Gnacsitares and their bearded Mozeemlek captives.[1] This is the most critical part of the baron's Long River narrative since it goes far beyond just helping to confirm the—elusive identity of his Long River. When compared to the Spanish descriptions of *"Teguayo"* from the documents of Fathers Domínguez and Vélez de Escalante, it also proves that his ethnographic descriptions of the unusual people of Mozeemlek and Tahuglauk were highly credible. [2] Lahontan's information conveyed within the designated reference sections in Letter XVI herein show why it is known that he was speaking of the Platte.

JANUARY 1689 WITH THE GNACSITARES

Lahontan wrote that in January of 1689 he was among the Gnacsitare people. He was then in the vicinity of today's North Platte in the Sandhills region of western Nebraska. He was close to and just below the confluence of the North and South Platte Rivers, his "two little rivers" (**RS 4)**, as indicated in his maps. (Figures 13, 18, 19)[3] These Gnacsitares were occupying an area now known to have then been the territory of the Plains Apache people. They were responsible for the culture archaeologists refer to as the Dismal River aspect. As currently understood, this was located about the valley of the Platte River in western Nebraska from ca. 1400 to 1700 CE.[4]

All evidence indicates that the baron became an honored guest of these people in their villages, some of which were situated on islands in the river or the ephemeral lake or "lake-like" bodies of water once present there.[5] Their island villages helped protect them from the incursions of the war-like Mozeemlek people from near the Great Salt Lake (entry of December 3, 1688, not November **RS 1**). This is where he met the four heavily bearded European-looking captives from the far distant land of Mozeemlek. (**RS 2, 4, 5**)

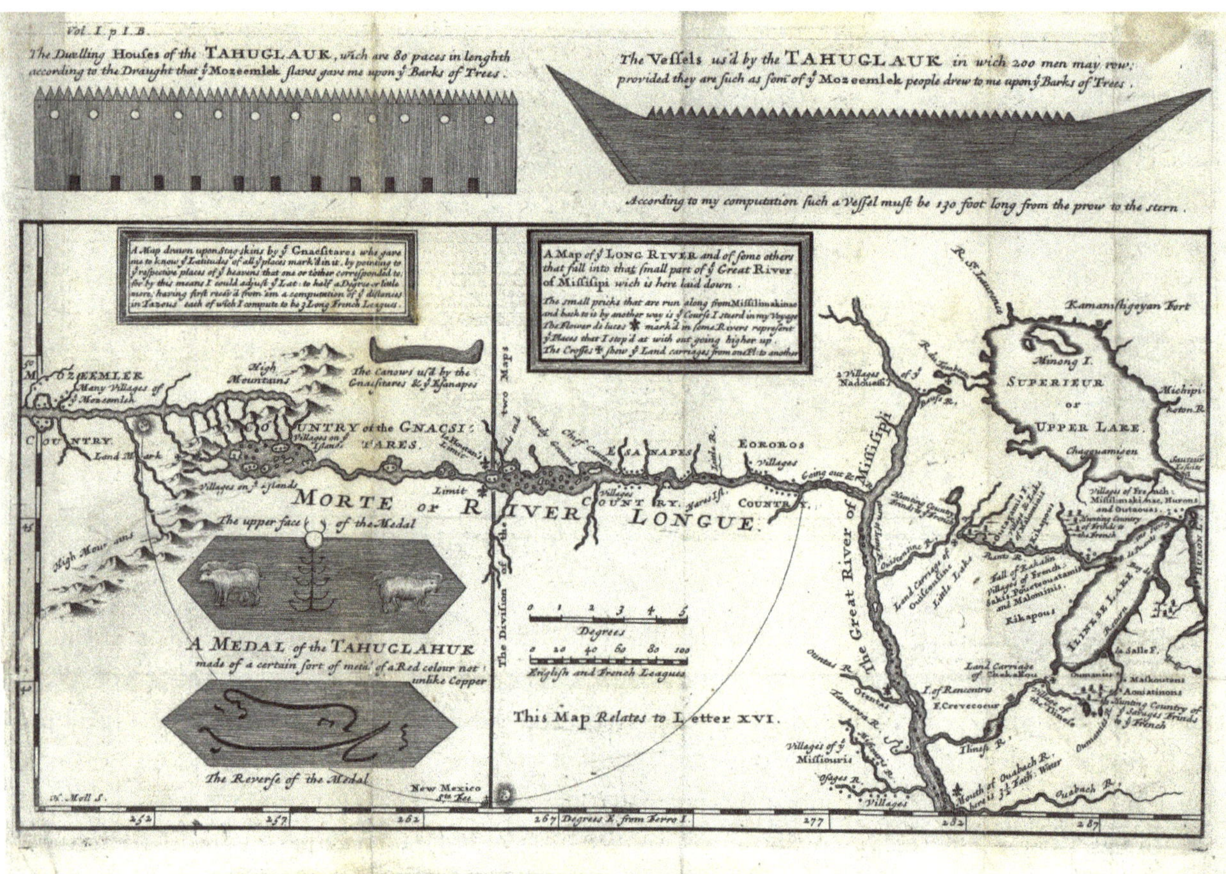

18. Lahontan's 1703 composite English Map of the Long River showing both his own map of where he visited (to right of the dividing line) and the map he based on one drawn by the Natives with charcoal on a deer skin (to the left of the dividing line). Also see Figure 19.

Placing Lahontan on the Platte is in large measure possible because of common denominators present in both his narrative and that of Vélez de Escalante discussed in chapter 10 in relation to the province of Teguayo.[6] The first of these, as noted by the baron, was that bearded men he knew as "Mozeemlek" and "Tahuglauk" lived beyond a range of mountains near a large salt lake far and directly west of his location on the Platte. (**RS 4, 5, 7**) Father Vélez de Escalante observed that the similarly bearded men of Teguayo also lived near this large salt lake on the west side of the Rocky Mountains.

Here are supporting references not only to the very unusual-bearded men the baron emphasized, but also to the Great Salt Lake, near where they lived. (Figures 18 -20) The salt lake serves as a very credible and highly specific reference point in the accounts of both Lahontan and Fathers Domínguez and Vélez de Escalante.

Vélez de Escalante also reported that there was a special region in the distant interior far to the north beyond the New Mexico colony. This was to the north of the Colorado River and west of the mountains and was known as "Teguayo". (Figure 27) As Lahontan reported, in the vicinity was the large salt lake near which there were strange, heavily bearded men who looked more like Europeans than the Natives with whom the two Franciscans were familiar. Lahontan's and Vélez de Escalante's accounts described these men in nearly identical terms. This corroborating information from two accounts widely separated in time allows for specific placement of the bearded men near the Great Salt Lake. The caption Lahontan placed on the portion of Figure 19 which the Natives initially prepared read as follows:

> A Map drawn upon stag-skins by ye Gnacsitares who gave me to know ye Latitudes of all ye places mark'd in it, by pointing to ye respective places of ye heavens that one or t'other correspondsed to; for by this means I could adjest ye Lat; to half a Degree or little more; [sic] having first recev'd from 'em a computation of ye distances in Tazous each of which I compute to be 3 Long French Leagues.[7]

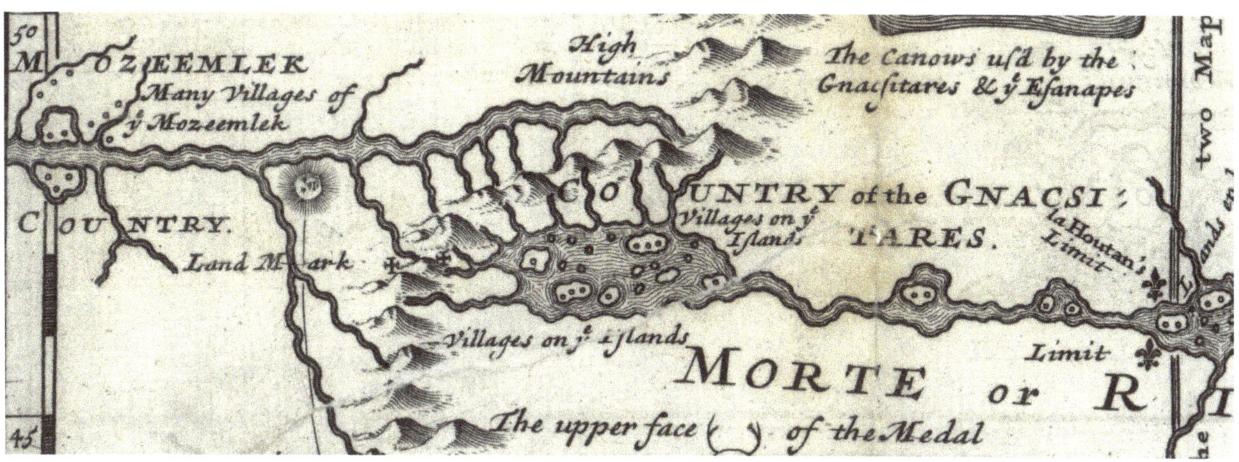

19. Derivative detail from the 1703 English Map of the Long River Lahontan derived from one drawn by Natives which became a portion of his composite map of the area to the west where he did not travel as shown in Figure 18.

There is additional information in the narrative that proves that Lahontan was describing the Platte. As also shown in Figures 18 and 19, he clearly indicated that his Long River was generally flowing west to east from the Rocky Mountains, which were also the source area of the river of the Mozeemlek which flowed to the west. Natives provided him with the rough map drawn with charcoal on a deer hide, (**RS 4**) which he and his engravers obviously redrew, embellished, and then placed alongside and as a continuation of his own map reproduced in his narrative.

Figures 18-20 show the land of the Mozeemlek to the west and directly across the Rocky Mountains opposite the Long River, exactly where the Great Salt Lake is located. Although the maps show the Mozeemlek territory, the baron obviously misunderstood or misstated the distances he reported between his location and the lake. (**RS 5 and 7**) The maps are still quite accurate in the relative placement of the key features. They are also relatively accurate in the latitudes shown for the Long/Platte River as well as the Great Salt Lake at roughly 48 degrees north.

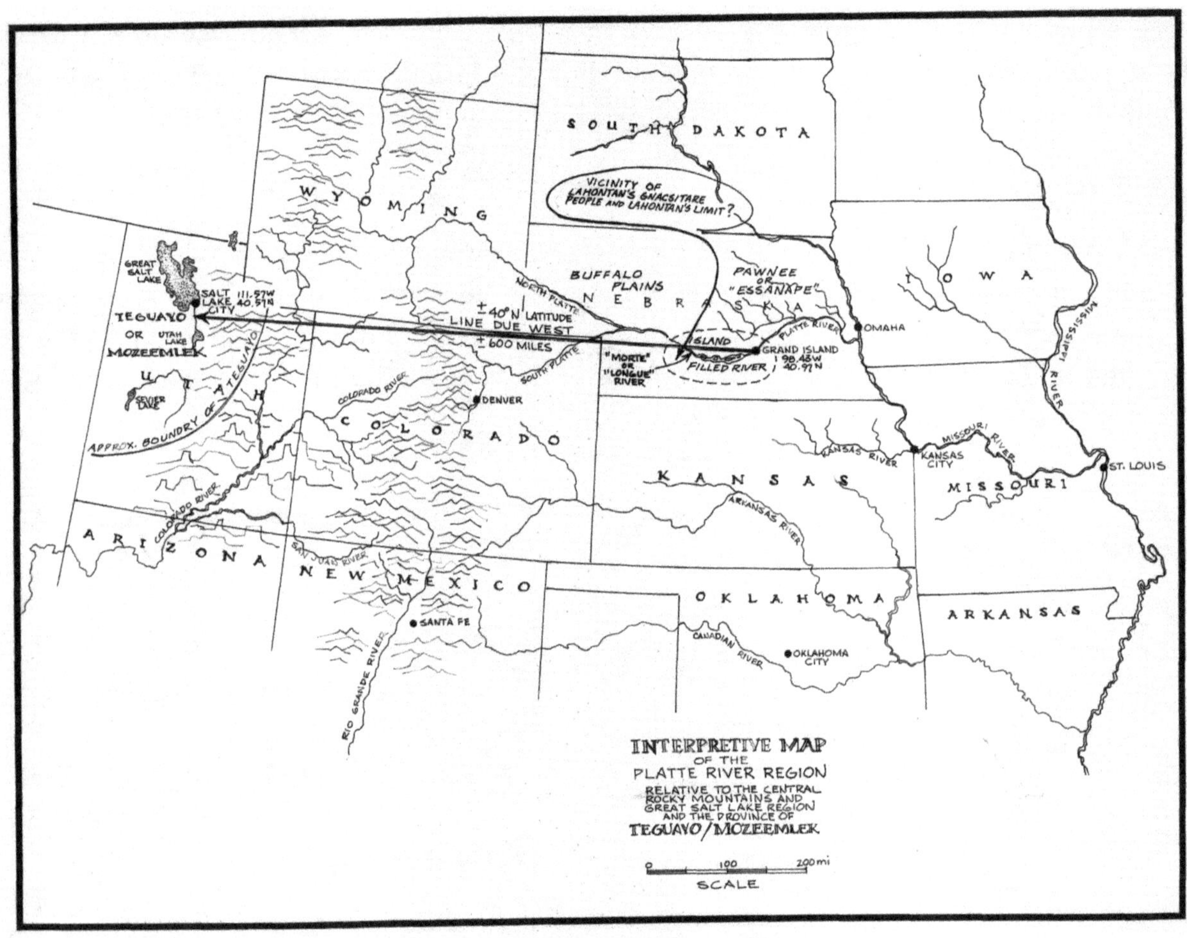

20. Interpretive map of the Baron Lahontan's travels on the Platte River during his Long River expedition of 1688–189. Based on all referenced French, Indian, American, and Spanish information herein.

The caption Lahontan placed on the portion of the map (Figure 18) that originated with him and based on his own direct observations read as follows:

A Map of y[e] LONG RIVER and some others that fall into that small part of ye Great River of Mississippi wich is here laid down. The small pricks that run along from Missislimakinac and back to it by another way is y[e] Course I steerd in my Voyage. The Flower de luces marked in some Rivers represent ye Places that I stop'd at with out going higher up. The Crosses Show ye Land Carriages from one Pt; to another.[8]

Although he carried an astrolabe during his campaign against the Iroquois in 1687, there is no evidence that he had one on the Long River. It is obvious, however, that he knew how to use one and even how without one to approximately calculate latitude from the position of the stars.[9] This is clear from the annotation on the Gnacsitares' map of the Long River originally drawn by Natives on the deerskin as shown in the left portion of Figure 18.

Unfortunately, in his general location maps (Figures 2, 18) for the Long River the baron may have accidentally miscalculated its latitude, as well as those of other places, as approximately 46 degrees north. He also may have been attempting to further obfuscate and hide the true position of his Long River by indicating it was well north of his true location on the Platte. Although his map does not give very precise latitude for the Platte, its west to east course is shown basically straight on a line corresponding to roughly ca. 46-47 degrees north. The correct latitude of the Platte River at North Platte, Nebraska, is only 41 degrees and four minutes north. Salt Lake City, Utah, and the Great Salt Lake are found very close to this at about 40 degrees and 36 minutes north.

These latter determinations are so close that the relative north-to-south relationship of the Long River and the land of the Mozeemlek, namely nearly equal, on the Natives' map are surprisingly accurate and true to the actual geography. Lahontan's calculations for the latitude of the Long River's location are, however, significantly in error by about five or six degrees.

Despite this question about latitude, the map whose origins were attributed to the Natives' deerskin map (Figures 18, 19) were obviously redrawn by Lahontan and likely enhanced, then professionally engraved at an unknown level of fidelity. Most were certainly elaborately altered to some extent. Despite these multiple steps in its production, it is surprisingly accurate in its representation of the relative north-to-south position of the Land of Mozeemlek and the Long River, which simple geography demonstrates is obvious and could only have been the Platte.

There are no other possible candidate rivers between Kansas and South Dakota that remotely fit the geography, the baron's descriptions, and basically flow eastward on a generally straight line toward the lower Missouri which Lahontan had to have navigated. (Figures 1, 12) To the south it could not have been the Kansas or smaller rivers such as the Republican or the Solomon. To the north is could not be the Niobrara, the White, or the Cheyenne, let alone the Minnesota. None fit his descriptions as the Platte does so well.

The baron's descriptions of the Sandhills and the lack of firewood also help to confirm the Platte location. The famous builder of the Union Pacific Railroad, General Grenville M. Dodge, once spoke about the natural east to west travel corridor provided by the valley of the Platte as followed by Lahontan. It is little wonder that he would have followed it as a likely way to an inland passage. Dodge stated that:

> There was never any very great question, from an engineering point of view, where the line, crossing Iowa and going west from the Missouri river, should be placed. The Lord had so constructed the country that any engineer who failed to take advantage of the great open road out the Platte valley, and then on to Salt Lake, would not have been fit to belong to the profession. [emphasis added][10]

The baron had left the main village of the Essanapes/Pawnees in the eastern portion of the Platte, which he described as being on "some sort of Lake." Soon after working through that reed-filled lake, likely a shallow braided cut-off channel of the Platte, the baron entered an area he described as a "sandy Ground." It was so barren that the company could scarce "find a chip of wood wherewith to warm our selves, or to dress our Victuals." He described the countryside all around as far as one could see as nothing but "naked fields **[prairies]**" and "Fens **[marshes]** covered with Reeds and Clay **[filled with sludge and reeds]**." This is a classic and very accurate description of the grassy prairie and the Loess Belt of Nebraska through which the Platte flows as illustrated in Figure 13.[11] Further, the baron described the extensive waterfowl that were present along the river in the depths of winter. This appears to be indicative of the waters of the Central Flyway which remain open on the Platte in winter while those further north, such as the Minnesota, freeze solid. (Figure 17)

Just as explained to the baron, the map prepared by the Natives (Figures 18, 19) shows the "Mozeemlek Country" and "many Villages of Mozeemlek" as being located directly west of and across "High Mountains" from the "Country of the Gnacsitares."[12] It also shows the lake or lake-like braided waters and islands below the confluence of the North and South Platte where the Gnacksitares had taken refuge to protect themselves from the distant Mozeemleks with whom they had been at war for so many years. (**RS 1, 4, 5**) This is the region where early travelers said they could not readily identify the Platte's main channel. Although the Gnacsitares prepared the portion of Figure 19 that Lahontan attributes to them in its caption, they had nothing to do with writing that caption. The baron certainly added that information from the Natives' descriptions he was trying so hard to understand.[13]

It is important to stress Lahontan's acknowledgements of the language difficulties he experienced with the Gnacsitares and the Mozeemleks and how his comprehension of what he was being told and recorded was at times compromised. It is also important always to differentiate between what the baron was directly observing with his own eyes and what he was being told about by the people he struggled to understand (**RS 7, 8**). There are, therefore, some things that make little or no sense in terms of what ethnologists and archaeologists know, or think they know, about some subjects, such as the use of young bison in agriculture and roofless houses (**RS 5**). This type of misinformation is not unusual in accounts like this where there were serious translation issues involved. The need for accurate interpreters was crucial on voyages of discovery among the Natives.[14]

None of Lahontan's long list of critics is known to have ever alluded to the different ways that he received his information and the language challenges he encountered on his Long River trip. This is despite his forthright acknowledgement of them, and the fact that they most certainly account for some of the more unlikely things he described. Such admissions should contribute to the exoneration of any explorer who faced the complications the baron did. As extracted from the earlier long quote, the baron stated: "I would fain have satisfied my curiosity in being an eye-witness of the Manners and Customs of the Tahuglauk; but that being impracticable, I was forced to be instructed at second hand by these Mozeemlek Slaves."[15] He then added:

> This was all I could gather on the Subject. My Curiosity prompted me to desire a more particular Account; but unluckily I wanted a good interpreter: and having to do with several Persons that did not well understand themselves, I could make nothing of their incoherent Fustian."[16] [**RS 6, 8**]

Relative to the location of the captives' homeland in Mozeemlek, Lahontan stated:

> These four Slaves gave me a Description of Their Country…Their Villages stand upon a River that springs out of a ridge of Mountains, from [generalized statement of the combined Rocky Mountains and Wasatch Range in Utah] which the Long River likewise derives its Source. [**RS 5**]

He then added that:

> The Mozeemlek Nation is numerous and pussiant [**powerful**]. The four Slaves…inform'd me, that at the distance of 150 leagues [sic 450 miles as the baron determined by his measurement of leagues] from the Place where I then was [the Platte] their principal River, [seemingly the Jordon River connecting Utah Lake with the Great Salt Lake or possibly even the upper Colorado] empties itself into a Salt Lake of three hundred Leagues [900 miles] in Circumference, the mouth of which is about Two Leagues broad…"[17] (**RS 5**)

These quotes indicate that the Mozeemlek lived near the Great Salt Lake since it is the only such major lake in the interior west and was in the vicinity of where the Spanish Franciscans later found the bearded men living. Their journal provides primary historical documentation for this critical element in Lahontan's narrative and was the key to unlocking its mysteries.[18] It is obvious that the baron had not crossed the Rocky Mountains and that Mozeemlek was on the west side of the mountains far opposite of his position, even though the distance the baron provided between them were obviously too little. The river in Mozeemlek near the Great Salt Lake originated from several small streams incorrectly shown to be in the same general range as the source of the baron's Long River, which was made by the joining of two small rivers. The latter are quite easily identified as the North and South Platte Rivers, which join in western Nebraska directly east from the Great Salt Lake. (Figures 18-20)

Lahontan's description of the way in which the boundaries of the Mozeemlek and Gnacsitare hunting grounds adjoined one another west of the forks of the Platte indicates how vast an area was involved. This seeming contiguity suggests that they bordered one another. The baron's map (Figure 18) shows the boundary between the Mozeemlek and Gnacsitare core territories. In keeping with the baron's description, this region in southeastern Wyoming, western Nebraska, and northeastern Colorado was a major bison hunting range in both prehistoric and historic times just as he described.[19]

Lahontan recorded the distance between his location and the place to the west where the main river of the Mozeemlek flowed into the Great Salt Lake as being only 150 leagues or about 450 miles. It is actually about 600 miles. He also incorrectly recorded that the mountain range separating the sources of the rivers of the Mozeemleks (Jordon River in Utah) and the Long River of the Gnacsitares (Platte in Nebraska) was only six leagues or about eighteen miles wide. This is certainly an indication that he was misunderstanding his Native informants and of course he did not travel into the mountains.

This mistake is clear from the narrative, which states that the mountains were so high "that one must follow large detours to cross them" and that: "They are only inhabited by bears and wild animals." This is certainly a highly generalized reference to the Rocky Mountains rather than a small range only a few leagues across.[20] After synthesizing all the baron's information discussed here, including the final published version of the Natives' deerskin map with Lahontan's annotations, it was possible to prepare the interpretive map shown in Figure 20. It demonstrates how Lahontan was clearly on or referring to the Platte River at the apogee of his trip.

Notes:

1. Butler, "Some Thoughts"; Gunnerson, *An Introduction to Plains*, "Plains Apache Archaeology," "Plains Village Tradition;" Hill and Trabert, "Reconsidering the Dismal River;" Levy, "Kiowa."

2. Chávez and Warner, *Domínguez-Escalante Journal*.

3. Lahontan, *New Voyages*, 192-97.

4. Butler, "Some Thoughts;" Gunnerson, *An Introduction to Plains;* "Plains Apache Archaeology," "Plains Village Tradition;" Hill and Trabert, "Reconsidering the Dismal River;" Levy, "Kiowa."

5. Lahontan, *New Voyages*, 187.

6. Chávez and Warner, *Domínguez-Escalante Journal;* Baker et al. *Juan Rivera's Colorado;* Bolton, *Pageant in the Wilderness.*

7. Lahontan, *New Voyages*, 285, *A Mapp of the Long River.*

8. Lahontan.

9. Lahontan,133, 401.

10. Grenville Dodge as quoted in Perkins, *Trails, Rails and War,* 199.

11. Lahontan, *New Voyages*, 189-90.

12. Lahontan, 193.

13. Lahontan, 195-96.

14. Heidenreich, "Early French Exploration," 65-66.

15. Lahontan, *New Voyages*,196.

16. Lahontan.

17. Lahontan, 193.

18. Bolton, *Pageant in the Wilderness;* Chávez and Warner, *Domínguez -Escalante.*

19. Newton, "Using Euro-American Hunting," "Native Place, Environment."

20. Lahontan, *New Voyages*, 192-93.

8

• AMONG THE LONG RIVER NATIONS AND HOMEWARD •

by

Steven G. Baker

In the second volume of his book Lahontan compared the Algonquian-speaking Natives of Canada that he knew so well with those newly discovered ones from the area to the west of the Mississippi; pointing out how they contrasted in major ways.[1] His critics did not quibble about his descriptions of the former but were near universally dismissive of his narrative of the Natives he discovered on the actual Long River portion of his journey. These dismissals were not only due to the confusion his deception caused relative to the river's identity and location.[2] It also derived from his descriptions of the seemingly exotic peoples he encountered on his Long River as it included both the lower Missouri and Platte. These peoples included the bearded Mozeemleks from the distant region of the salt lake as well as the Eokoros, Essanapes and Gnactsitares along the Platte who were never again referred to by these names.[3]

It is now obvious that even though Lahontan intentionally obscured the location of the Long River, he credibly reported his observations of real Native peoples living along its lower Missouri and Platte Rivers segments, as well as those in the vicinity of Lake Illinois/Michigan. Further, it is only here that it is possible to equate these peoples with now well-known nations from the areas where the baron traveled. To best grasp details and nuances in Lahontan's narrative of the entire expedition, in this chapter it is critical to discuss the ethnicities and locations of the societies that he passed through on his trip.

Unlike many other exploratory expeditions in North America, Lahontan's Long River trip was almost entirely by canoe on major waterways. (Figure 1) He only briefly traveled overland when he had to portage his canoes and cargo or walk to Native villages near rivers.[4] His trip was accomplished in only about eight months and was about 2,500 miles long, including the mileage involved in his return trip and his side trip south to the Wabash. Just to reach the Platte near present-day North Platte, Nebraska, the baron's company had to canoe far from Michilimackinac by riding the currents, sailing, and paddling for extended periods. There were many long canoe voyages throughout the course of Canadian discovery, but Lahontan's ranks among the greatest of the early river voyages into what became the US. His travels took him through the territories of Native peoples (Table 1) who spoke a variety of languages drawn from at least four language families, many of which were mutually unintelligible. He directly encountered languages from the Algonquian, Siouan, Caddoan, and Athabascan families (Figure 26) as well as the Numic one.

Some of the peoples Lahontan mentioned, such as some of the Illinois, had already been in contact with the French for some time.[5] This was particularly true for the Algonquian speakers from the vicinity of Lake Michigan southward toward the Wisconsin River. As he pushed southward down the Mississippi, the baron passed through the territory of the Siouan-speaking Iowas until he was close to the mouth of the Missouri near present-day St. Louis.[6] Some Iowas had already had contact with the French, but the baron does not appear to have met any of these people. Some peoples the baron met were geographically remote; others, such as many Algonquian speakers living closer to French settlements, were well accustomed to the presence of Europeans. This difference is readily apparent in the baron's narrative of the very remote peoples of the Platte, most notably the Pawnee/Essanape and the Plains Apache/Gnacsitare.

Lahontan understood and described Native societies quite well from the perspective of natural history just as he did the flora and fauna.[7] He wrote about both those of New France, such as the Ottawas, and the seemingly more complex ones he encountered on his Long River from a well-informed and intellectually organized perspective. His descriptions of the various nations are quite sound since they were written by a man who had seen things that changed early and rapidly, which few other Europeans ever witnessed, understood, or let alone even wrote about. This chapter does not consider the Canadian Natives since they were not located anywhere near the Long River.

Lahontan's Native Nations Beyond the Mississippi

European explorers, including the baron, commonly referred to Native societies as different "nations."[8] This naming practice is out of favor with many ethnologists today. This chapter discusses the various nations Lahontan recognized as he sequentially canoed the waters which flowed through their territories to the west of the Mississippi. Now that it is known where he ended up, it is possible to demonstrate with fair precision where some of the nations were situated when he encountered them.[9]

There is no single set of standardized, accurate, and widely recognized synonymies of names for all Native American nations.[10] This is particularly so for the earliest eras of exploration and discovery when the plentiful numbers of nations were being greatly reduced in size, and many died away completely or were absorbed into other ones. Nations were typically named according to the way in which their members identified themselves, as other Native nations identified them, and often according to the language they spoke. Their names were also at times drawn from geographical landmarks or by distinctive attributes of a nation's culture. Hearers of Native languages with no or little knowledge of the language often recorded names erroneously. This is evident in the Long River narrative.

Through time Native American peoples have also commonly come to be thought of as "tribes." Some ethnologists are as uncomfortable with this term as they are with "nations."[11] The concept of tribes and the names early explorers assigned to them have sometimes survived to the present day and are still used to identify and differentiate them. Some names have not survived, and there is no way that some peoples mentioned in early documents can confidently be related either to a surviving Native people/tribe/nation or to a people mentioned in early documents that may have become extinct. Gordon Sayre notes in his study, *Les Sauvages Américains*:

> Because aboriginal North America was home to so many small, autonomous societies, identifying and separating (which amounts to the same thing as naming) each one or groups thereof is extremely difficult. "At least sixty-eight mutually unintelligible tongues" were spoken among the eastern North American woodlands tribes..., and these groups constantly moved, assimilated, and split apart from one another, even before European contact. Any name such as Algonquian or Miami does not have a fixed referent but appeals to geography, linguistics, or history to constitute a group of a size located somewhere between the universality of "human" and the specificity of each dialect's version of that word.[12]

Despite these challenges, ethnologists and linguists have sorted out many of the individual peoples and assigned them to various linguistic categories, thus forming relatively accurate templates within which speakers of different languages can be identified and associated with certain geographical territories over time. Relative to Lahontan's narrative it has proven possible to determine the identity of his Eokoros, Essanapes, Gnacsitares, and Mozeemleks which have long been considered figments of his imagination. They have been so overlooked through the years that they were not even mentioned among the "Enigmatic Groups" of the Plains in the authoritative *Handbook of North American Indians*.[13] Sayre advocated using the old names when writing about early Natives. Although at times a difficult task, that is the approach taken here with the Long River narrative.[14]

The Baron's Progress Down to the Long River

Upon leaving Michilimackinac the baron's company had a favorable wind and quickly sailed its big laden canoes down and across Lake Illinois/Michigan to Green Bay. This was Lahontan's "Bay of Pouteouatamis" along the lake's west shore. In the early part of the expedition before reaching the Mississippi River, the company spent time with Pouteouatamis/Pottawatomies, Sakis/Sauks, Outagamis/Foxes, Kikapous/Kickapoos, and Malominis/Menominees (Table 1) who were all post-contact Algonquian speakers and already known to the French. After visiting with Pottawatomies on Green Bay, the company ascended the Fox River and entered a Kikapous village on the shores of a small lake. From there it traveled on to another small lake to a Menonimee village.[15]

On October 9 the baron reached the fort of the Outagamis/Foxes (Figure 4), apparently on the Wolf River of Wisconsin.[16] Among these friendly people the baron obtained ten additional Native men to bolster the strength of his party. It is important to note that the Fox chieftain was at least somewhat familiar with the Long River.[17]

The Algonquian-speaking Fox men were particularly helpful because they not only knew about the Long River in the land of the Siouan-speaking Eokoros/Otoes. A few could also speak their language. Some of these men later demonstrated some direct knowledge of the river. The Fox had maintained a peaceful relationship with the Eokoros for twenty years. Along with the baron, they also spoke an Algonquian language at least similar to that of his four original Ottawa companions. As the company proceeded up the Lower Missouri, these ten men proved to be invaluable to Lahontan as he began treating with Eokoros and other distant peoples who spoke different languages that he did not know.[18]

When he was leaving the Fox/Outagami people, his ten new recruits and his own four Ottawas traveled together in one canoe large enough to hold all fourteen and their cargo. Despite the Fox headman's warning about not traveling too far up the Long River, these Algonquian speakers were not fearful and seemed to have been encouraged by the prospects of the trip. In their exuberance they stressed to the baron on more than four occasions that "we might venture safely so far as the Plantation of the Sun [emphasis added]."[19] Fouillade translated the baron's French as saying the company could travel to the "house of the sun without having to fear anything." The Natives' information was specifically directed and not just offered as an aside.

From an ethnological perspective this is an extremely telling comment since it was a repeated "call out" to a specific site as an obvious cultural landmark that stood out in the Fox speakers' minds and one that the baron could or should have been able to rely on as a reference point.[20]

There were once many Mississippian mound sites along the course of the Mississippi and its tributaries all the way down to the Gulf of Mexico. There is, however, only one very prominent mound site to the south that is on the baron's route to the Missouri and worthy of being designated the residence of a "Sun." That could only have been the great temple mound city of Cahokia and its environs, once the largest Native city in North America north of Mexico (Figures 1, 21), and the place where the company would have to turn west onto the Missouri.

Among anthropologists the term "Sun" has a very special meaning in relation to the great-chiefdom-level Mississippian mound building societies, as best known from the Southeastern region of the US and the Mississippi drainage.[21] The leaders of these commonly large and highly sophisticated ranked societies, and the focal personage(s) in the entire Mississippian Ceremonial Complex, were known as "Suns."[22] This complex involved religious mechanisms that were the pillars supporting local chieftains. These high-ranking individuals were all-powerful and believed by their people to have descended from the "Sun family," probably from a special "Sun lineage."[23]

21. Archaeological artist's conceptual painting of how the great Mississippian Native city of Cahokia with its many great mounds (seemingly Lahontan's "Plantation of the Sun") might have looked during the height of its power and extensive regional influence, courtesy of Bill Isminger, Cahoka Mounds Historic Site, Collinsville, Illinois.

Although past its prime and thought to have been largely depopulated by 1688, Cahokia would certainly have not been lost in the collective memory of Native Americans throughout an extremely wide area.[24] This massive site complex is focused on the Illinois side of the river near St. Louis and the confluence of the Missouri and Mississippi. Lahontan's Algonquian companions were almost certainly telling him he could travel safely to the mouth of the Missouri River.

After leaving the Fox village on the Fox River on October 16, the baron's company proceeded upriver to the important portage over to the Ouisconsinc/Wisconsin River. (Figure 4) He noted that this land-carriage of just over two miles was a "long" one. It took the company two days to complete, presumably because of the weight of the canoes, trade goods, and other supplies. Once on the Wisconsin, the company started down it on the 19th and reached the Mississippi in four days. The baron did not mention meeting any Natives during his time on the Wisconsin or the Mississippi before entering the mouth of the Missouri on November 3. He also never again mentioned the plantation or home of the Sun and since he did not describe it, he apparently did not visit it. The baron's trips from Michilimackinac to the Mississippi followed a well-traveled canoe route (Figure 4), and today a well-understood one, used since the early days of New France.

It was the way people went from Lake Illinois to the Mississippi to go northward to the territory of the Nadouessis or Sioux of Minnesota or southward toward the Gulf of Mexico. Although he quibbled over some of the distances and time frames noted by the baron, Thwaites did not challenge the baron's narrative of this portion of his travels. He believed the baron fabricated his Long River narrative but also appears to have believed that Lahontan had traveled the Wisconsin down to the Mississippi and suitably described that portion of his travels.[25] Thwaites is the authority on this portion of Lahontan's narrative to the Mississippi but no further.

Down the Wisconsin to the Mississippi

After reaching the Mississippi by way of the Wisconsin on October 23, the baron's company briefly tarried there to hunt before departing toward the Long River on the 24th.

As Lahontan pushed southward downriver, he passed along the eastern edge of the Iowas' territory until he was near the mouth of the Missouri at present-day St. Louis. He was probably at least sometimes ashore at night while in the territory of the Iowas, but he did not mention them. The Iowas are believed to have been occupying much of present-day Iowa and southern Minnesota during the baron's time.[26] Their neighbors to the east across the Mississippi were the Illinois. The baron also did not mention encountering any of them on his way downriver.

Lahontan stated that the company reached the mouth of the Long River on November 2, which indicates that it took some eight days to travel approximately 450 miles. In the entry for November 3 the baron described the mouth of the Missouri, or a portion of it, where he entered it as being like a lake full of "Bull-rushes" with a narrow channel that he followed upriver all day before the company slept the night in the canoes.[27] It is difficult to understand this description, since the mouth of the Missouri is huge and not choked with vegetation unless the baron was along its periphery at extremely low water when channels may have been changing. It may have been no more than some lapsed memory, confusing notes, or have been an intentional additional comment to help bolster his great deception. Once on the Missouri he was heading toward the territory of what most anthropologists believe were the Siouan-speaking Missouri people then of the lower Missouri River.[28] He did not, however, report meeting any of these people until he was well into his return trip. This may have again been an attempt to lead others away from the Missouri as part of his deception.

From the broad mouth of the Missouri, the company quickly moved some distance upriver by taking advantage of favorable winds and sailing the canoes. (Figure 1) The winds slacked on November 8 and forced the company to begin paddling. After traveling hard upriver for six days, the company had covered a considerable—yet unknown—distance. It finally encountered some Eokoros in a village in a meadow on the west bank of the Missouri about a quarter of a league from the river. They were the first Natives he mentioned on the Missouri. The baron sent a party of Natives and soldiers into the village where they were met by surprised men who were prepared to receive them with bows and arrows readied. Fortunately, no hostilities erupted once the Eokoros heard the baron's Fox companions who spoke their language. This caused the men to drop their arms and through the giving of gifts; including tobacco, knives, and needles, the company made friends with them.[29]

The best information indicates that Lahontan's Eokoros were Otoes. (Table 1) These people were the ones with whom the baron's Fox companions were familiar and friendly. But the Missouris and not the closely related Otoes are the only people thought by historians and anthropologists to have been living along the lower Missouri near its mouth in the baron's time. In support of this point, Michael Dickey cited a letter written by Father Gabriel Marest to Louisiana's governor, Pierre Lemoyne d'Iberville, in June 1700.[30] The Jesuit noted that the Missouri River, formerly known as the Pekitanouï (and to Lahontan as the Long River), was given its name because the Missouris were the first Natives one met after leaving the Mississippi. In the latter part of the seventeenth century the Otoes are generally believed to have been living around the mouth of the Platte and from there a bit lower down along the Missouri but still north of the Missouris.[31]

It is quite probable that the baron bypassed a major Missouri village before meeting the Eokoros as he proceeded up the Missouri. This would have been the important Utz archaeological site on the west bank of the Missouri River near its confluence with the Chariton River in Saline County of north-central Missouri. This is some two hundred or more miles from the river's mouth. In the view of most archaeologists, including co-author Wood who well knows the site, Utz has been definitively identified with an occupation by Missouri people in the late seventeenth century, although dating is not precise enough to prove it was occupied in the year 1688.[32] It is certainly possible that the baron missed it because it might have been only a seasonally used site and not occupied when he passed through the area. It also seems plausible that it could have been occupied by Otoes who were culturally and linguistically very closely related to the Missouris. Both Missouris and Otoes are represented in the Oneota archaeological tradition.

The Oneota tradition is well-known from the lower Missouri River in the region Missouri people occupied as well as the Otoe did further upstream. Utz was abandoned by about 1700CE. French trade began in this area soon after the baron's visit.[33] Dickey suggests that although the Missouris once occupied the area near the river's mouth, they may have moved further upriver to escape internecine warfare or for some other reason (s), such as avoiding newly introduced disease. In keeping with this long-held interpretation, the Missouris should have been the first Native Americans the baron encountered as he traveled upriver. Lahontan clearly distinguished between the Missouris and the Eokoros/Otoes (Table 1), however, thus indicating that although closely related they were different peoples living in separate locations in 1688. He did not report encountering any Missouris by that name until he had gone back down the Long River near the end of his trip. Perhaps he just slipped past the Missouris without noticing them or being noticed by them. The first people he reported meeting on it were clearly Eokoros.[34]

The company's introduction to the Eokoros was so successful that word of the visitors was sent out to their villages. By the next evening, November 9, as many as two thousand had gathered to meet the company. A few continued up the river in the company's canoes to direct it to their chief village. The company reached the village at midnight, and the baron set up camp on a point of land about a half-mile away. Although the Eokoros pressed the baron to lodge with them, only his Foxes and Ottawas chose to do so after warning their hosts not to go near the French camp at night. The following day Lahontan allowed his men to rest and gave gifts of knives, scissors, needles, and tobacco to his hosts who expressed their pleasure at meeting the Frenchmen. Up to that time these Eokoros appear to have only heard about the French from other Natives. They reported that these indirect sources had spoken "very honorably" of them. [35]

The company left this main village on November 12 escorted by five or six hundred Eokoros who marched along the river shore and kept up with the canoes. He passed another Eokoro village and then stopped at yet another just long enough to give presents to its leading men. They reciprocated by providing the company with more Indian corn and cooked and/or dried meat than it needed. The company then passed on from one Eokoro village to another as they canoed upriver without stopping, except at night, or just long enough to give out gifts.

It is not possible to calculate how far upriver he was before the baron encountered the first Eokoro/Otoe village since he was sailing and therefore moving fast. Perhaps with hard effort he could have traveled 50 miles per day? He was, however, obviously at least some 200 or 300 miles upriver from the mouth of the Missouri before he encountered his first village of Eokoros. Their last village was well beyond the first, which he encountered after several days of canoe travel. This implies that he was far up the Missouri by the time he left the last village. There, he spoke with its "Great Governor" who informed him that the territory of the Essanapes/Pawnees commenced 50 more leagues (150 miles) upriver from his village. [36]

The Eokoro leader, whom Lahontan described as "a venerable old Gentleman," explained that he was then at war with the Essanape nation. Otherwise, he would have given the company an escort to their country. Instead, he provided six Essanape slaves, presumably war captives, to accompany the company upriver to their home country. This Eokoro explained that his people had 20,000 warriors available throughout its twelve villages. He added that the nation's strength in warriors had been greatly reduced by the hostilities with not only the Essanapes but also with the Panimoba/Omaha and Nadonessis/Sioux. Lahontan noted that the Eokoros were "far from wild" and had an air of politeness. He also commented that there appeared to be some form of social and political ranking or subordination among the people that was typical of ranked societies such as the Mississippian chiefdoms. [37]

Lahontan made an important observation on the architecture of the Eokoro houses in that village. He noted that their villages were fortified with palisades, vertical log walls set into the ground, and their huts were long and round on top, like some of the long houses of Canadian Natives. (Figure 22) The huts were made of reeds and bulrushes interlaced and cemented over with a "sort of fat earth" or clay. This is a nearly classic description of a long house of the once very widespread Oneota archaeological tradition within which both the Otoes' and Missouris' cultures were reflected. [38] It is noteworthy that their villages were also fortified. [39]

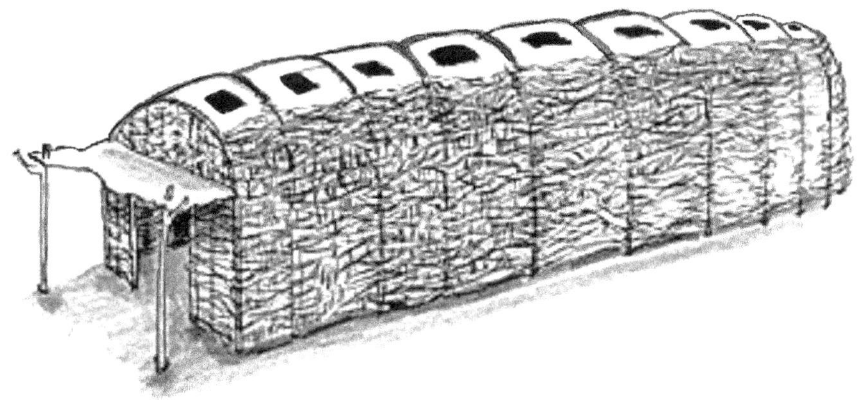

22. Conceptual sketch of a Oneota style long house as described among the Otoe Indians by Lahontan along the lower Missouri River, courtesy of Centuries Research, Inc.

The baron departed from this Eokoro village at dawn on November 21 and once again relied upon the wind to sail his canoes until night. Taking advantage of another fair wind, the company sailed all the next day and on through that night since the "river was clean, and free from rocks and beds of sand." On the 23rd the company was forced to stop and repair a leaking canoe. When they were back on the water the wind suddenly slackened, and the company was forced to again take up its paddles. The men were, however, tired from lack of rest and did not paddle with any vigor. This forced the company to go ashore on a large island where it hunted and ate rabbits until the men fell into a sleep so sound that they could not be roused, even with a false alarm. Finally, at ten o'clock the next morning the company put its canoes back onto the river but was unable to move upriver more than 12 leagues (about 36 miles) that day and the next. It made so little distance because the company's Native escorts were slowly walking the shores shooting geese and ducks, which were still plentiful there in the great North American Central flyway. (Figure 17)[40]

On November 24 or 25, the company set up its tent camp on the righthand bank of the Missouri. There, the newly acquired Essanape/Pawnee companions informed the baron that the first of their villages was not more than about 16 or 18 leagues (about 38 to 54 miles) ahead. Two of the Essanape slaves were sent ahead to alert their people that the French were coming. On the 26th the company paddled steadily and fast in hopes of reaching the first Essanape village that day, but they were unable to do so and could not go ashore because of large quantities of logs floating in the river. The men had to spend the night in their canoes. On the morning of the 27th the company finally neared the first village. The baron was cautious and placed "the great calumet of peace" on the bow of his canoe and had his men paddle hard toward the village on the shore.[41] (Figure 23)

The calumet was the venerable Native American "peace pipe" so often referenced in their history and which was commonly made of red catlinite stone. Lahontan described this great symbol quite well and in the way ethnologists generally still do.[42]

The *Calumet of Peace* is made of certain Stones, or of Marble, whether red, black or white. The Pipe or Stalk is four or five foot long; the body of the *Calumet* is eight Inches long; and the Mouth or Head in which the Tobacco is lodg'd is three Inches in length; its figure approaches to that of a Hammer. The red *Calumets* are most esteem'd.

The Savages make use of 'em for Negotiations and State Affairs, and especially in Voyages; for when they have a *Calumet* in their hand, they go where they will in safety. The *Calumet* is trimmed with yellow, white, and green Feathers and has the same effect among Savages, that the Flag of friendship has amongst us; for to violate the Rights of this venerable Pipe, is among them a flaming Crime, that will draw down much mischief upon their Nations.[43]

Among the Long River Nations and Homeward

23. Artist's old conjectural view of how Father Marquette likely displayed the calumet pipe of peace when greeting new Indian peoples, just as Lahontan said he did, courtesy of Centuries Research, Inc.

At about this point in his travels, the baron's company entered the Platte River from the lower Missouri. Unfortunately, he never mentioned the confluence of these great waters. The most likely explanation for this is that, like Bourgmont later noted, Lahontan found that the mouth of the Platte was obviously larger than that of the Missouri there and followed the larger one thinking it was the continuation of the Missouri rather than just a tributary.[44] His Native companions would probably have informed him that the river turned westward, which was the direction in which an inland passage to the Western Sea was then widely believed to be located. The baron could have easily misunderstood the situation and believed he was following the Missouri in the direction of the sea.

Lahontan was on the Platte and in the territories of the Essanapes/Pawnees/Pani and the Gnactaries/Plains Apache as indicated by the relative ordering of the peoples in his narrative and the placements of the "Lago de los Apache" in his 1699 map. (Figure 24)[45] Although he did not visit them, Marquette also had recorded the presence of the Pani in about this position on the Platte in his map of 1673. (Figure 5)[46]

Although French traders were probably penetrating all the way to the Platte by the early 1700s, there is no record of any other such visits other than Lahontan's until Le Seuer Bourgmont's in 1714.[47] By 1701 the Platte had apparently not yet been so named, but it was known to Le Seuer, who learned of its existence as the "River of the Panis" but did not visit it.[48] On his 1714 ascent of the Missouri, Bourgmont noted in his log that the Pani were residing in ten villages about 30 leagues (90 miles) up the Platte from its mouth.[49] This places them in the area around the confluence of the Loup and the Platte Rivers, which is almost universally attributed to them by anthropologists and historians and seemingly where Lewis and Clark were told they were living during their journey at the opening of the nineteenth century.[50]

At the first Essanape village the baron came close to experiencing serious Native hostilities. As soon as the villagers noted the company's presence, three or four hundred rushed to the shore and danced in excitement and then tried to jump into the canoes. The Essanape slaves were able to convince these people not to board them. They backed off and invited the company to come ashore. After posting sentries to guard his canoes, the baron, escorted by his fourteen Native companions and twenty marines, went ashore to meet the local Essanape leader. As they landed all the village people repeatedly prostrated themselves before the baron's entourage with their hands against their foreheads as a seeming ritualized greeting sign of friendship and respect. Exuberant in their delight at receiving their visitors, these people then happily "convoyed" them into their village. It was then that armed conflict was only very narrowly avoided.[51]

The village was palisaded and gated. Once through the gate the company was held back by his hosts until the village leader, whom Lahontan called the "governour," "marched out" to confront the company with five or six hundred men armed with bows and arrows. Lahontan's Native men "charg'd 'em with insolence" for the appearance of this armed troop which seriously concerned the baron's Fox companions. They could only speak to the Essanapes in the language of the Eokoros, since they could not speak the Essanapes' Caddoan tongue. They insisted that the Essanapes lay down their arms.[52]

24. Lahontan's 1699 Mappa del Rio Missisipi which he prepared for the Spanish Duke of Jovenza, courtesy Archives of Centuries Research, Inc. and Robert S. Weddle Collection.

The Essanape slaves explained that it was their people's custom to carry their weapons when meeting strangers, and the baron should not be afraid. The Fox were not convinced that there was no danger and urged Lahontan to immediately take his escort back to the canoes. When the Essanape leader realized the baron was leaving, he and his men suddenly dropped all their weapons, likely because they did not want to miss out on gifts from the French. The Essanape slaves would have observed the French giving gifts in the downriver Eokoro village where they were being held when the baron visited there, and presumably they would have so informed this Essanape village.[53]

When the villagers dropped their weapons, the baron and his escort returned and reentered with their guns, which the Natives "admir'd mightily," at the ready. The baron and his twenty-soldier escort were then led into a "great hutt," which Lahontan thought was not a residence since it did not appear to have been lived in. This suggests it was some form of council house or other ceremonial structure. The Essanapes identified it as the "Cottage of Peace," and they would not allow the Fox escorts inside. The hosts considered them unworthy since they thought they had tried to instigate a fight between them and the company. The baron then ordered his Fox companions to stand back and not slight or insult their hosts.[54]

The Fox men remained concerned and continued to pressure the baron to take his escort and hurry back to the canoes. He finally acquiesced and headed the shore party and the four Essanape slaves back to the river. He was planning to take the slaves upriver and release them at the next village. Although his visit to the first village had nearly ended in hostilities that might well have resulted in the company's demise, it was able to get back onto the river safely. As soon as they departed, the two additional Essanape slaves from the village caught up with them. They carried a message to the effect that the leader of the village would try to stop the company in the river, apparently perturbed that Lahontan had left so suddenly and would not be giving gifts to him and his people. The baron's Fox companions answered that there was no way he could stop them in a river as big as the one they were on without throwing "a Mountain into it."[55]

Now there were six Essanape slaves traveling with the company, all of whom had been obtained from the Eokoros. The company paddled straight toward the next village, which was not too far upriver, hoping to reach it yet that day. On this part of his trip, the baron quizzed the slaves about their nation. He particularly wanted to learn all he could about their principal village. They explained that it was located on a "sort of lake." The baron decided not to stop at any more villages and determined to head straight for the principal one. He felt if he stopped at all the other villages on the way he would squander his supplies of tobacco and other gift items. He wished to conserve these until he met the highest-ranking leader of the Essanapes and could give them to him when he complained about his bad treatment by the headman at the first village.[56]

The company set up camp near the principal village, and Lahontan went to see the Essanape headman with an escort that included his Ottawas and Foxes. The baron referred to this headman as a "petty king." It is not clear if this was the same leader that the Foxes initially complained to, but it is clear that the petty king was the leader of the Essanape nation. His subjects who had been slaves demonstrated their subordination and veneration of this individual (a Sun?) when they met him by spending half an hour prostrating themselves many times. This behavior is not at all out of place in ranked Mississippian societies and what Lahontan had witnessed when he visited the first Essanape village.[58]

25. A typical Pawnee earth lodge winter village from the nineteenth century similar to the ones observed earlier by the Baron Lahontan. courtesy of archives of Centuries Research, Inc.

The baron gave extensive gifts to this high-ranking leader, including rolls of tobacco, knives, needles, scissors, two firelocks with flints, some fishhooks, and "a pretty cutlass."The baron felt that the man was very pleased with these "trifling" gifts and added that he had never before seen such things. This is significant because it indicates that the baron was likely the first European to enter Pawnee territory. This does not mean that they had not heard of the French or felt negative pressures from the protohistoric contact experience through other Natives and such things as increased internecine warfare, forced physical dislocation, or exotic diseases caught from them.[59]

Following typical Mississippian chiefly greeting ceremonials, this leader reciprocated and gave the company prodigious gifts of peas, beans, harts, roebucks, geese, and ducks, which the baron considered quite valuable and for which he was very grateful.[60] But Lahontan wished to move on upriver and visit the Gnacsitares whom the Pawnee leader described as honest people.[61] Again, following chiefly protocols for greeting strangers, this headman offered Lahontan an escort of two or three hundred warriors to accompany him to the Gnacsitares.

The Essanape headman explained that his people and the Gnacsitares had been allied for 26 years for protection from raids from the hostile and numerous Mozeemleks from the salt lake area. According to the baron's understanding of what he heard the headman say, the Mozeemleks never took the field with less than twenty thousand men. Perhaps the baron did not capture the headman's meaning correctly because this would have been a very large force. Lahontan was further told that the pressure from the Mozeemleks was so great on the Gnacsitares that they had placed some of their villages on islands "where the enemy cannot reach 'em" as he illustrated on his map of the Long River. (Figures 18, 19, 24) The baron seems to have gladly accepted the offer of the large Essanape escort and prepared to depart upriver, probably with most of his escort following by land.

The Essanape headman loaned Lahontan four pirogues as temporary replacements for his fragile birchbark canoes. This would have been necessary due to the shallow nature of the Platte with its many sandbars and the fact that it was late in the season and the river was or soon would be icing up. Lahontan was allowed to choose the dugouts he wanted from over fifty made available to him. The headman promised to guard Lahontan's canoes until the company returned to his village; and which he did.[62]

Before departing for Gnacsitare country, the baron set his men to work with iron axes to plane down and lighten up the pirogues. They accomplished this so well that they made the crafts thinner and only half as heavy as they were initially. The baron made a point about how surprised the Essanapes were while they watched the men work on the dugouts with their axes and fire their pistols. With every stroke of the axes, the Natives would cry out "as if they had seen some new Prodigy." This is one of the baron's more telling observations as it indicates that the Pawnees were not yet acquainted with the most basic items of their protohistoric era, namely metal tools and firearms. This tends to support the view that by late 1688 no European had traveled and/or traded into the Pawnee territory along the Platte River.

Lahontan described the village of the Pawnee head chief ("Great Commander or Generalissimo)," and more of the Mississippian-like ceremonial behaviors of the people. Of particular importance he described how six slaves carried this paramount leader on a litter. This is a specific point that was heartily scoffed at by at least one of Lahontan's great critics, even though it was common behavior among the ranked Mississippian societies.[63] The baron described the Essanape village, its large, classic, earth lodge homes (Figure 25) and how they were laid out in relation to the kinship of the paramount chief, just as one would expect in such a ranked society. Overall, he provided the first ethnographic observations on this Mississippian-like nation.[64]

The next Native territory along the Platte west of the Essanapes was that of the Gnacsitares. In the lightened pirogues Lahontan led his company forward toward them on December 4th. His craft was large enough to hold him, ten soldiers, and ten Foxes. In the narrative the baron mistakenly stated that there were also Oumanis (Miamis). He, however, had none of these people with him. That vessel also held his four Ottawas and four remaining Essanape slaves the Otoes had given him, making a total of 28 men and their gear in one very large pirogue.[65] In leaving the Essanape country Lahontan stated that the calumet would no longer serve to protect him upriver, and he said nothing about displaying it like he did when he approached the Pawnee villages.[66]

It was obviously slow going for the company as it made its way in the heavy pirogues up the shallow sandbar-ridden Platte. By the fourth night they entered the distinctive Loess Belt (Figure 13) along the Platte and were shore bound for two days on "sandy ground," which begins to characterize the river valley floor in the vicinity of Grand Island and Kearny, Nebraska.[67] Here, Lahontan and virtually all later travelers found firewood so scarce that they could hardly cook their meals and had to resort to using buffalo chips for fires. This region was where he emphasized that the landscape was so barren that all one could see were naked fields with fens or small ponds covered in reeds and clay.[68]

The company finally entered Gnacsitares territory on December 19 after what must have been a grueling fifteen-day trip upriver from the Essanape's main village. They had obviously not been making good time working their way up the notably difficult Platte. On his way back downriver in late January, Lahontan commented on how much more enjoyable it was to travel downstream with the slack current than it had been in working upstream against it.[69]

In1805 Lewis and Clark were told the Kiowa-speaking Apaches (Gnacsitares) lived on the Platte. By the middle of the nineteenth century, and perhaps much earlier, Cheyennes and Sioux had driven them south of the Platte country.[70] While still there they would have been the people responsible for what archaeologists refer to as the Dismal River Phase or "aspect" of the Plains Village Tradition along its western periphery.[71]

Although there has been some debate on the matter, the general archaeological consensus is that the Dismal River Phase was focused on the valley of the Platte River in western Nebraska in the late seventeenth century and extended for some distance north and south of the river.[72] Lahontan thus witnessed the Dismal River Phase near the end of its duration in the region. The Dismal River people are not well documented historically from their time on the Platte. The baron appears to have been the first and perhaps the only European to have visited among their villages and written of them before they were driven from the region.

At least some of the Gnacsitares were then living on islands in the Platte for protection from hostile incursions by the Mozeemleks.[73] The baron's mapping (Figure 18, 19, 24) illustrates how these villages were situated. Having their villages on islands would have hampered archaeological studies over the years. Islands in the Platte come and go, as did the ephemeral lakes such as the "Lake of the Apaches" seemingly illustrated by the baron in 1699. (Figure 24)[74] Much of the Gnacsitares' occupational record may thus well have disappeared with the islands that once sheltered it. The baron did not describe their villages or houses and spoke little about their culture, since he was quite obviously most intrigued by their heavily bearded Mozeemlek captives. He did, however, note how despotic and authoritarian their leaders were.[75]

From an archaeological standpoint the Dismal River culture as it relates to the Gnacsitares is somewhat known from excavated sites. They reveal that the Dismal River people lived in fixed villages, made distinctive types of pottery, practiced some horticulture, and hunted, especially bison. Houses were clustered and of a unique style for the Plains, unlike the large Pawnee earth lodges. They were semi-subterranean with a pole and earthen roof supported by five main posts.[76]

After bypassing a few Gnacsitare villages along the river, Lahontan sent his Essanape slaves forward to make initial contact with these unknown people. The Gnacsitares they first encountered were fearful that the newcomers were Spaniards and were angry with the Essanapes for bringing them into their country. The baron therefore went on alert fearing that hostilities might erupt. The Gnacsitares sent messengers to some of their friends some two hundred miles or so to the southwest, likely among the

Apaches living in the area known as *Cuartelejo* (the barracks or quarters) in the vicinity of present-day Scott City in extreme west-central Kansas.

This Native territory with its small pueblo was on the outer limits of the sphere of Spanish influence at that time. It was located just about two hundred miles due south of North Platte, Nebraska just as the baron seems to have understood.[77] The people of Cuartelejo had experience with Spaniards and were asked to come and examine the baron's company to determine if that is who they were. These people quite willingly hastened to the Gnacsitares, probably by running, to examine the strangers.

Once these people determined that the strangers were not Spaniards, Lahontan was welcomed. He explained to his hosts about his mission, his country of New France, and its then pending war with Spain. Now relaxed and at ease with their unexpected guests, the Gnacsitares entertained them with dancing and other typical ceremonies of welcome, including providing plentiful food and offering the companionship of young women. The baron described the Gnacsitares and explained that their leader, or "governor" as he called him, appeared as a king more than any other of the leaders he had observed among the Natives and held "absolute dominion" over all their villages.[78]

Lahontan and the Gnacsitare leader discussed the Spaniards, apparently in regard to their activities out of New Mexico and perhaps about the mouth of the Mississippi. Neither one was able to provide very much information, and they may have not been aware that the Pueblo Revolt of 1680 had forced the Spaniards to abandon New Mexico. For all practical purposes, the New Mexico colony no longer existed as the Spanish residents had fled far to the south to El Paso del Norte or on southward beyond it.[79] Because of this there could not have been much information about New Mexico or even what was happening about the Gulf of Mexico.

The Gnacsitares hosted the company through January 9 when, in the vicinity of North Platte and today's Lake McConaughy near the confluence of the North and South Platte Rivers, the headman visited Lahontan in his camp. He was accompanied by four hundred of his people and the four Mozeemleks, whom the baron "took for Spaniards."[80]

Lahontan said he set up a pole with a lead plate on the bank of the Platte, in the vicinity of North Platte, whereby he claimed the region for France and which his men christened "Lahontan's Limit." (Figures 18, 19) He and his men set out back down the Platte towards the Essanape territory on January 26, 1689, arriving there on February 5. From the apogee of its travels, it took the company about ten days to return to Essanape territory, only some 150 miles back to the east in the vicinity of Columbus, Nebraska.[81] The baron spoke about the large number of waterfowl the Natives hunted along the river in the great central North American Flyway. (Figure 17) This information helps confirm that he was on the Platte and not a more northerly and by then frozen river like the Minnesota would have been.

The baron does not say how long or whether he may have tarried among the Essanapes. He obviously reclaimed his canoes and proceeded on down the Platte and back onto the lower Missouri. Here, his narrative becomes confusing, presumably because he was still working to shore up his deception and trying to lead his readers to believe that the Long River was not the Missouri. The narrative notes that he had arrived back on the Mississippi on March 2. That entry is immediately followed by an extraneous, intercalated description of an undated great battle, which he obviously did not witness and could only have heard of secondhand. This was between some Sioux and Iroquois at the Island of Recountres on the Mississippi where he said he arrived on March 10. This would have been some 31 days after he had arrived back in the Essanape territory. From that island he said he drifted southward downriver with the current and arrived at a village of the Otentas on March 12. If true, rather than just part of his elaborate deception, this placed Lahontan ten-days travel and quite far down the Mississippi. This would have been well south of the confluence of the Missouri and Mississippi and the documented territories of the Missouri and Osage on the lower Missouri and Osage Rivers, respectively.[82] If not a part of his great deception, it is at this point in the narrative that the baron's travel progression seems to have gotten out of order due to confusion in his notes or perhaps mingled with an indistinct memory of things which had taken place years before.

Once back on the Mississippi or near its confluence with the Missouri, the baron had obviously left the Long River behind him and his narrative provides little information on the peoples he dealt with from there on. This included the Missouris, Osages, and Otentas which are not discussed in detail here.

The Otentas provided the company with a good supply of turkey corn and explained that the river on which they lived originated in neighboring mountains. They said the upper part of their river was the home of peoples known as Panimah, Paneassa and Panetonka. Marquette's map (Figure 5) shows the Paniassa on the Missouri along with the Missouri people, but it does not show the Otentas. People denoted as "Otontanka" appear on that map on a river far north of the Missouri, and they may have been Otentas. The Otentas are among those Native peoples who are not at all well understood by ethnologists, likely because they were reduced early on in the post-contact years. They were a Siouan-speaking people probably closely related to or part of the Osages, some of whom lived at various places in and around the lower Missouri since they were first recorded. They may also have been associated with the Siouan-speaking Otoes/Eokoros whom Lahontan had met just before encountering the Essanapes.[83]

In keeping with the baron's confusing travel chronology at this point, he would have to have met the Otentas, Missouris, and Osage to the south of the confluence of the Missouri and Mississippi. This interpretation is, however, at odds with his next move where he states that he traveled further down the Mississippi by paddling with the current until he reached the Missouri River and there met Missouris and then Osages. According to this chronology, he appears to have been further attempting to demonstrate that the Long River, the Island of Recountres, and the Otentas were far north of the mouth of the Missouri and that he had to travel south of them to reach the Missouri people on the lower Missouri River. Nevertheless, he would have clearly found the Missouris and Osages on or around the lower Missouri and Osage Rivers of today.

The baron had hoped to learn what the Otentas knew of the Spaniards but concluded that he could get no information from them. He stated that he left the Otentas on March 13 and with the "help of the Current and our Oars" arrived at the Missouri River on about the 17th. He furthered his deception by stating that he then turned his canoes up the Missouri and arrived at the first Missouri village the next day and acquired some turkeys from them. Yet, he would have had to have reached this point on his return down the Missouri after leaving the Essanapes. He stated that the company continued to paddle upstream against the current until it arrived near the second Missouri village the next evening. No matter how he reached the Missouris, his actions among them appear reasonable and credible.

The baron sent out a small party to meet them, but no member of the company spoke the Missouris' language, which almost provoked them to attack. This was averted when the Missouris realized that the small greeting party was backed up by a larger force. Some of the Missouris could speak the Algonquin language of the Illinois, which some Natives in the company could also speak. Some additional negative diplomatic issues developed, and the baron's Natives wished to attack the Missouris. Eventually one of the leaders appeared and some gifts were exchanged.[84]

Using the Illinois language, Lahontan's Algonqian companions conversed with the Missouris and attempted to learn all they could about their country. The Missouris surprised the baron by professing a lack of knowledge about the subject and likely had no information about the Spaniards. His Algonquians were unhappy and wanted to burn the village, but Lahontan would not allow it. He felt it might spoil his chances to gain the intelligence he was seeking. At this point the company was not all that far up the Missouri and still below its confluence with the Osage, about 100 miles in from the Mississippi. In less than a day of travel, which covered about four leagues (12 miles) further up the Missouri, the company reached the mouth of the Osage and camped there. The next day the company killed some bison.[85]

While still camped near the mouth of the Osage, "an Army" of Missouris marched toward the baron's camp. Lahontan noted that these Missouris, like other Natives he had encountered on the Long River, were wholly unfamiliar with firearms. The baron's Fox companions were so concerned about a possible fight that they implored Lahontan to abandon his camp. Accordingly, the canoes were turned back down the Missouri where they silently came upon another Missouri village in the dark of night where the company quietly waited until morning.[86]

At daybreak the company entered the village and discharged its guns. This so alarmed the Natives that they ran about crying for mercy. The village warriors were absent and had been among those who had previously gathered to attack the company. The Fox took pity on the women and children and allowed them to leave before the company burned the village. Lahontan next turned his canoes back down the Missouri and entered the Mississippi early in the morning of March 26. Once back on the Father of Waters the canoes were turned downriver toward the Wabash as the Ohio River was then known.[87] From this point onward the baron's travels are again easily followed, perhaps because he felt he had satisfactorily disquised the fact that he had traveled so extensively on the Missouri.

After turning back onto the Mississippi, the company met a large group of Siouan-speaking Arkansas/Quapaw, which was hunting buffalo on the west bank of the river. Speaking in the Illinois language, the two parties became friendly, with the Natives dancing and singing for their guests while providing them with all kinds of meat. The Arkansas had iron axes and other trade items since they were already known to the French via La Salle and other traders. The baron questioned them about the Spaniards, but like the others they were unable able to answer his inquiries. The company was far enough down the Mississippi that it was in warmer country where crocodiles could be found. The Natives explained how they were hunted and pointed out that the Missouris and Osages were devoid of courage and honesty.[88]

Homeward Bound via the Illinois River

The company spent two days, until about March 28, with these Arkansas before proceeding downriver to the Wabash (Figure 1), which they traveled upriver for what seemed to be only a short distance before turning back down to the Mississippi. Lahontan wanted to follow the Wabash to its source, but he was becoming concerned about the time needed to get back to Michilimackinac. After returning to the Mississippi he headed back up it toward the Illinois River, just above St. Louis, Missouri, by which he was intending to return to Lake Michigan. By that time the weather should have begun improving enough that ice in the more northerly rivers would no longer pose any problem. He arrrived at the mouth of the Illinois on April 9 after fighting headwinds and a swift current for about a week.[89]

The baron started his company up the Illinois on April 10 and stopped for a few days at Tonty's fort and referred to it as "Fort Crêvecoeur," which La Salle had built in 1680, even though it was most likely Fort St. Louis where he met Tonty. The original Crêvecoeur is traditionally believed to have been destroyed the same year it had been built and seemingly replaced by Fort St. Louis in 1682. The baron stayed at that post as Tonty's guest. There were then thirty Coureurs de Bois who traded with the Illinois residing there. Lahontan appears to have used his time there to trade for furs because he took on a heavy cargo. From there he traveled upriver and entered and followed the tributary Des Plaines River toward the Chicago Portage that one had to make to reach the Chicago River and by means of it reach Lake Illinois. (Figure 1) Lahontan referred to this portage, the longest he made on his trip, as a "great Land-carraige."[90]

This portage took the baron to the Chicago (*Chekakou*) River, which emptied into Lake Illinois by which he could travel back to Michilimackinac. He reached a substantial village of the Algonquian-speaking Illinois people on April 20. At this village near the portage, he obtained four hundred Illinois to carry his canoes and cargo over its substantial length of 12 leagues (36 miles). He paid them with tobacco, gunpowder, ball, and some firearms. It appears that the company was still carrying a lot of cargo as well as their large canoes if it took this many people to carry it all. This strongly suggests that the baron must have obtained a quantity of furs during his travels, most likely at Tonty's post.[91] It would have been easy for him to have done so, and since he desperately needed money, this would have been a tempting opportunity. The four hundred Illinois were likely provided to him by their chieftain as was common Mississippian custom.[92] If, as suspected, he had obtained trade goods for his trip from people at Michilimackinac (members of the cabal?) he likely owed someone and one great way to pay debts was with furs.

Lahontan's company had made its long portage and reached Chekakou by April 24. There, his Fox men chose to return to their people, leaving the baron with only his marine contingent and his four original Ottawa companions with heavily loaded canoes. On the 25th the company then turned its canoes down the Chicago River toward Lake Michigan and crossed to its extreme southeastern shore where it reached the Oumamis (Miamis, now St. Joseph) River in Michigan. (Figures 1, 26) Lahontan met four hundred Miamis at the site where La Salle had once had a post. Warriors there were actively torturing Iroquois men. As it had previously done during his military activites in New France, this "inconceivable" deathly torture was hard for the baron to witness and it made him "shrink" and determine to leave the village just as soon as possible.[93]

Tracking back to Lake Michigan, the company followed its eastern shore as far as the *"Bay de l'Ours qui Dort"*(Bay of Sleeping Bears, today's Grand Traverse Bay, Michigan). Crossing the bay it then moved northward to the Straits of Mackinac and on to the north shore in the vicinity of today's St. Ignace where the original Michilimackinac was then located (Figure 9), Lahontan and his company arrived safely back at their post on May 22, 1689, after canoeing nearly the total 300 mile length of Lake Illinois/Michigan with their heavy loads. The baron then immediately began preparing his narrative as his Letter XVI.[94]

Notes:

1. Lahontan, *New Voyages,* 2:411-517

2. Although the baron's narrative of his Long River journey was apparently composed as extracts from his full trip journal in May 1689, it was not available to the public until he published it in 1703. Before that time the only people who might have read it were his correspondent in France, close friends of the baron, and perhaps government officials; assuming it was initially intended to serve as the official required report to the colonial authorities. This might have included Frontenac since he helped the baron prepare his book. Therefore, it appears that there could have been no written critiques or public knowledge of it until well after 1703. Further, the geography of the central Plains and the Platte and Missouri river tributaries of the Mississippi were not explored and understood until well into the eighteenth century or later. No one could have been certain that his Long River was misplaced, and that no river existed in the location he indicated until the geography was better understood. Even the Platte had not supposedly been revisited by the French after Lahontan until Bourgmont did so in the early 1700s and was thereafter credited for its discovery. The discovery of an inland passage continued as a popular hope among the colonists of New France for many years after the publication of Lahontan's book.

3. Thwaites, "Introduction," xlii.

4. These portages included one short one at rapids on the River of *Puants (*Stinks) at the head of Green Bay on the way to the Wisconsin River. He again had to portage from the Fox River to the Wisconsin, a distance of only three-quarters of a league (2.25 miles). Lahontan, *New Voyages,*174, 177, 207.

5. Marquette, *Father Marquette's Journal*.

6. Wedel, "Iowa," 432-33.

7. Lahontan, *New Voyages,* 2:411-512.

8. Sayre, *Les Sauvages,* xi-xvi; See also Dickason, *Myth of the Savage*.

9. Some anthropologists believe that "nation" implies too high a level of early historical sociopolitical development for North American Native polities. The subject is fraught with semantic difficulty in the modern era as it is deeply involved in treaties, land claims, and the legal issues between government and American Native tribes as they are known today as sovereign entities.

10. Parks, "Enigmatic Groups;" Sayre, *Les Sauvages,* xiii.

11. Helm, *Essays*.

12. Sayre, *Les Sauvages,* xi.

13. Parks, "Enigmatic Groups," 965-73.

14. Sayre, xvii, 41, 90-93; Adams, *Travelers;* Sayre, writing from the perspective of a literary critic rather than an ethnologist, erroneously believed that the names the baron gave to some Native peoples Lahontan encountered were products of his imagination with no basis in fact and that his account was nothing more than a travel hoax.

15. Lahontan, 167-70, 174-77.

16. Thwaites, *New Voyages*, 175n2.

17. Lahontan, 176.

18. Lahontan.

19. Lahontan, 177, ca. Oct. 19,1689.

20. Green and Rodell, "Mississippian Presence..."

21. Fogelson, *Southeast*.

22. Hudson, *Southeastern Indians*, 202-11, *Knights of Spain;* Rollingson, "Prehistory of the Central," 542-43; Wring Holder, *Southern Cult*.

23. Hudson, *Southeastern Indians*, 202-11; Hudson, *Knights of Spain*.

24. Pauketat, *Ancient Cahokia.*

25. Thwaites, *New Voyages*, 173-80, 178n1.

26. Wedel, "Iowa," 432-33.

27. Lahontan, *New Voyages*, 179.

28. O'Brien and Wood, *Prehistory of Missouri,* 345-57; Dickey, *People of the River's,* 33; Schweitzer, "Otoe and Missouria," 448.

29. Lahontan, *New Voyages*, 180.

30. Dickey, *People of the River's,* 33.

31. DeMallie, *Plains*, ix; Norall, *Bourgmont*, 94-98, 108-09; Schweitzer, "Otoe and Missourie," 447-48.

32. Dickey, *People of the River's,* 14-16; Henning, "Plains Village," 230-32; O'Brien and Wood, *Prehistory,*

346, 52; Ritterbusch, "Late Prehistoric Oneota;" Schweitzer, "Otoe and Missourie," 447.

33. Dickey, *People of the River's*, 16.

34. Lahontan, *New Voyages*, 180, 200.

35. Lahontan, 180-81.

36. Lahontan, 181-83.

37. Lahontan; Hudson, *Southeastern Indians*, 202-11.

38. Henning, "Plains Village Tradition."

39. Lahontan, *New Voyages*, 182.

40. Lahontan, 182-83.

41. Lahontan, 184-85.

42. Blakslee, "Origin and Spread;" Brown, "Calumet Ceremony."

43. Lahontan, *New Voyages,* 75-76.

44. Norall, *Bourgmont*, 123.

45. Lahontan, "Mappa del Rio."

46. Marquette's 1673 Map of the Mississippi from the *Jesuit Relations*, (LIX),108 is reprinted in Wedel, *Introduction to Pawnee Archeology*, Map 3. Also see page 11.

47. Norall, *Bourgmont*, 123.

48. Wedel reprinted Le Seuer's Map of 1701. Wedel, *Introduction to Pawnee Archeology*, Map 4. A very informative selection of rare maps of the Platte are reproduced by Wedel.

49. Norall, *Bourgmont*, 123.

50. Holder, *Hoe and the Horse*, 33, 35; Ludwickson, "Historic Indian Tribes," 136-40; Steinacher and Carlson, "Central Plains," 235-68; Wedel, *Introduction to Pawnee Archeology*, 3-7, 12; Parks, "Pawnee," 515; Roper, "Pawnee in Kansas," 233-35; Strong, *An Introduction to Nebraska;* Moulton, *Journals,* 399-400.

51. Lahontan, *New Voyages*, 185-87.

52. Lahontan.

53. Lahontan.

54. Lahontan.

55. Lahontan.

56. Lahontan, 186-87.

57. Lahontan.

58. Smith and Hally, "Chiefly Behavior;" Brown, "Calumet Ceremony."

59. Lahontan, *New Voyages*, 187.

60. Smith and Hally, "Chiefly Behavior;" Brown, "Calumet Ceremony."

61. Lahontan, *New Voyages*, 187.

62. Lahontan, 187-88.

63. Adams, *Travelers*, 57-8. Hudson, *Southeastern Indians*, 204-11.

64. Lahontan, *New Voyages*, 188.

65. "Pirogue" does not refer to any specific kind of boat; rather it is a generic old French term for native boats in regions once colonized by France and Spain, and particularly "dugouts" made from a single log. They were commonly made and used by various Native peoples throughout North America and ranged greatly in size with some being quite large, sometimes 50 or more feet in length. Neely, *Prehistoric Canoe*. There are many entries on the internet for them, including: https:lakeroland.org/wp-content/uploads/2018/09/dugout-canoe-2.pdf, accessed 1/3/21. https://www.cherokeeheritage.org/attractions/dugout-canoe/. Accessed 1/3/21. Florida Museum of Natural History, Dugout Canoes, https://.chickasaw.tw/videos/florida-museum-of-natural-history-dugout-canoes. Accessed 2/ 3/ 21.

66. Comment by Donald Blakslee from the audience at the 2006 Plains Anthropological Conference Annual Meeting in Topeka in response to Baker's presentation, "Spanish Documentary Confirmation." Blakslee of Wichita State University, a Plains archaeologist who had studied the history of the calumet, refuted the assertion that the calumet was not used among the Pawnees. But it cannot be established that his objection was correct, only that Lahontan made the comment.

67. Thornbury, *Regional Geomorphology*, 306.

68. Lahontan, *New Voyages*, 189-90.

69. Lahontan, 197.

70. Levy, "Kiowa," 907. It is to be noted that there are some contradictions evident in the writings about the little-known early history of the Plains or Kiowa Apache. Just how long they lived along the Platte is not solidly documented and not enough archaeology has yet been done on their sites to have a refined chronology for them. It is, however, obvious that they were there in the seventeenth century when Lahontan traveled far out onto the Platte and into the territory attributed to the Dismal River Tradition. Archaeology of the Pawnee has been far more intensively studied than that of the Plains Apache, in part

probably due to the more substantial nature of their associated archaeological sites.

71. Gunnerson, "Plains Village Tradition," 234.

72. Baker et al., *Protohistoric and Historic*, 88-91; Butler, "Some Thoughts." Gunnerson, *An Introduction to Plains*, "Plains Apache Archaeology," "Plains Village Tradition," 234, 239-42; Hill and Trabert, "Reconsidering the Dismal River," 198-222; Levy, "Kiowa," 907; Scheiber, "Late Prehistoric," 144-45.

73. Lahontan, *New Voyages*, 187.

74. Lahontan, "Mappa del Missisip."

75. Lahontan, *New Voyages*, 192.

76. Gunnerson, "Plains Village Tradition," 234, 239-42.

77. Butler, "Some Thoughts;" Gunnerson, "Plains Village Tradition," 239-40, 244; Hill and Trabert, "Reconsidering the Dismal;" Opler, "Apachean Culture," 389.

78. Lahontan, *New Voyages*, 191-92.

79. Hackett, *Revolt of the Pueblo;* Sando, "Pueblo Revolt;" Webber, *The French Thorn*.

80. Lahontan, *New Voyages*, 192.

81. Lahontan, 189-90.

82. Lahontan, 197-99.

83. The presumed Siouan-speaking Otentas seem to have died out early as a viable polity and to have likely been absorbed into the Missouri and/or Otoe. Although there are a few isolated mentions of them early on from the vicinity of the lower Missouri River, it is not possible to say much about them. Thwaites attempted to discuss them, but his discussion does not inspire much confidence in its credibility. Due to a lack of documentation the present authors have little to say about these early people other than that they did exist, apparently under that name, and in the vicinity of the lower Missouri River. Lahontan, *New Voyages*, 200 n2; e. g. Schweitzer, "Otoe and Missouria," 46; Swanton, *Indian Tribes*. Swanton's monumental listing of Indian Tribes does not mention them.

84. Lahontan, *New Voyages,* 200-02.

85. Lahontan, 200-03.

86. Lahontan, 203.

87. Lahontan, 203-05.

88. Lahontan, 204-05.

89. Lahontan, 205.

90. Lahontan, 206-07.

91. Lahontan, 207.

92. Smith and Hally, "Chiefly Behavior;" Lahontan, *New Voyages,* 207. Four hundred men seems a large number, but the original text has the number written out, which suggests that the figure is correct and not a misprint for "40."

93. Lahontan, 208.

94. Lahontan.

9

• THE LANGUAGES OF LAHONTAN'S NATIVES •

By

Steven G. Baker

Even though doing so should have enabled them to better understand his narrative; Lahontan's critics have rather cavalierly failed to address the ways in which he obtained his information about the Long River and its peoples. His best and most trustworthy descriptions were about things which he had personally observed. The least trustworthy often developed when he attempted to understand and discuss things that he was only told about by the Natives speaking various languages. However, in his attempts to accurately narrate his Long River journey, the baron still did a masterful job of chronicling the degree to which members of his company were able to communicate with these Native speakers. These aspects of his narrative are enhanced by the map of the Long River and its peoples he included in it (Figure 18) as well as the 1699 map he provided to the Spanish Crown. (Figure 24) Table 1 and Figure 26 list the languages and the identifiable individual peoples the baron encountered from the time he left Michilimackinac to the time that he departed homeward from the Mississippi by way of the Illinois River.

Since no one in Lahontan's company spoke or understood all the languages through which he received information, it is thus critical to note that most information communicated to him involved only translations. It is hard to believe that the baron's critics could not understand this point and take it into consideration in making their judgments! Often this involved a chain whereby multiple languages were involved, and information was lost or corrupted as it passed from one speaker to another whose native language was different. As the baron emphasized, the narrative of his time among the Gnacsitares and their likely Numic/Ute-speaking Mozeemlek captives was especially fraught with such language difficulties.[1] At no point in the narrative is there any indication of the use of a lingua franca or universally comprehensible language.

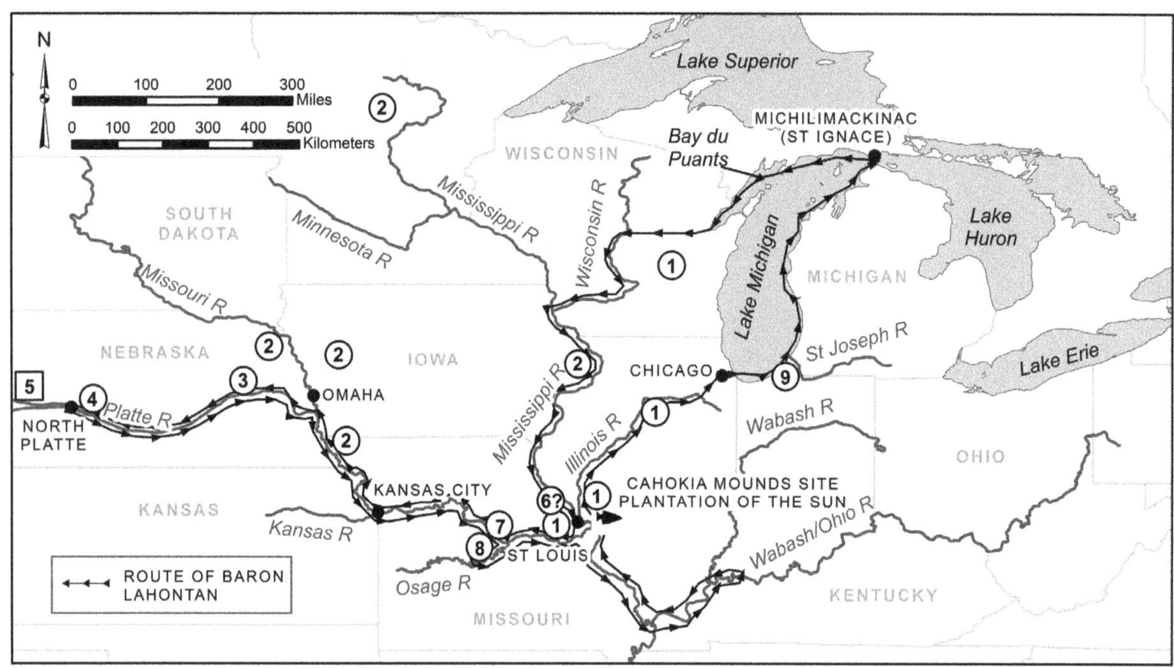

26. Map of Lahontan's Long River trip routing relative to the territories of the various Native language groups through which he passed, and which caused him so many translation problems as he candidly discussed. Key: 1) Algonquin/Ottawa, Pottawatomie, Sauk, Illinois, Menonimee, Kickapoos, Fox-Outagami; 2) Siouan/ Nadouessis-Sioux, Iowas, Eokoros/Otoes, Omahas; 3) Caddoan/ Essanapes-Pawnee; 4) Athabascan / Gnacsitares Plains Apache; 5) Numic/Ute far to west near Great Salt Lake not shown; 6) Siouan/Otentas?; 7) Siouan/Missouris; 8) Siouan/Osage; 9) Algonquian/Illinois, Miami.

The baron knew the basic Algonquian language as it would have been spoken by his Ottawa friends with whom he spent so much time. He also understood at least much of some variants of it as spoken by other peoples.[2] These included Kickapoos, Menonimees, Outagamis/Fox, Pottawatomies, and Sauk whom he dealt with on his outward trip. The territories of these people, other than the Ottawas, were around the south end of Lake Illinois and on toward the Mississippi. (Figure 26) Lahontan appears to have had little trouble in communicating with all these people. On his homeward trip up the Illinois River, he was back among the Algonquian-speaking Illinois and Miami with whom he should also have had little difficulty communicating.

The first inkling of potential communication difficulties in the baron's intended travels appears in the narrative of his stay among the Fox people at the south end of Lake Michigan near the headwaters of the Wisconsin River. The Fox leader explained that his own Algonquian-speaking people had been at peace with the Siouan-speaking Eokoros/Otoes or else the closely related Missouris, which archaeologists believe the baron would have encountered as he traveled up the Missouri.[3]

The Fox leader loaned the baron ten warriors to accompany him. He noted that some of these men not only knew something of the country of the Eokoros but also spoke their Siouan language, thus indicating that it was not understood by all his people. By adding these Natives to his company, Lahontan was assuring that he had, in keeping with conventional practices of French explorers, appropriate diplomats, protectors and translators who could assist him in traveling some considerable distance up the Long River.[4] The only times the Siouan-speaking Nadouessis/Sioux of Minnesota were mentioned in his narrative was when the baron was with the Fox leader and in the intercalated account of their battle with the Iroquois on an island in the Mississippi.[5] Lahontan had to assure the Fox leader that he would neither be traveling to the north nor trading with the Sioux since they were then at war with his people. Since the Sioux never appear in the narrative again, it seems certain that he did not venture northward on the Mississippi into Minnesota where they were located.

The Siouan-speaking Missouris and Otoes have been closely linked historically, ethnically, and linguistically. Some interpretations of their early history and territorial dispositions, however, appear to be contradictory unless they made very dramatic shifts in their occupational ranges, which was quite possible. According to the progression of his narrative, the baron's travels would have first taken him up the lower Missouri from its confluence with the Mississippi. This has long been considered to have been the territory of the Missouris in this time frame, although, as previously discussed, he only speaks of being among the Eokoros during this leg of his travels from November 2 to ca. 21, 1688.[6] He did mention the Missouris in the vicinity of the lower Missouri on his way home, implying he was making a distinction between them and the Eokoros. Such a notion, however, depends on whether Lahontan could actually tell the difference between the Eokoros and Missouris since they were so alike.

At least some members of the baron's Algonquian-speaking Fox contingent could speak directly with the Siouan-speaking Eokoros/Otoes. Since the baron did not apparently speak any Siouan, the Fox men would have been relaying information from them back to him and his Algonquian Ottawa contingent in Algonquian. It is possible that some of his Ottawas may well have also spoken some French and that may have factored into the dialogue as well. At least the baron was not evidencing any significant problems in communicating with the Eokoros through his Fox companions. His Ottawas apparently could not, however, speak Eokoro.

It is not apparent and doubtful that any of the baron's Algonquian-speaking Native companions could speak the Caddoan language of the Essanapes/Pawnees that were encountered after traveling farther up the Platte from the Eokoros. The Eokoros had reported that they had been at war with the Pawnee for some time and were holding some of their captured warriors as slaves. Some of these were freed in the care of the baron, and they would certainly have learned at least some of the Eokoro language during their captivity. Thus, even if none of the baron's original companions could speak the Pawnees' language, his company included a few men who would have spoken their own Caddoan language fluently. They could also have likely spoken at least a bit of the Eokoro that was also spoken by some of his Algonquian company. It is not known if the Pawnees as a group could speak Eokoro. Given this mix, it is important to try to tease out the basics of the complicated communication linkages that the baron would have had to have been relying on. Such an exercise, while not perfect, helps to exemplify the veracity of the baron's explicit comments about the language difficulties he encountered and thus how they handicapped his narrative and led many people to doubt its truthfulness.

In communicating with the Essanapes the baron's narrative implies that a three-way communication chain involved interpretating through an Algonquian Fox to and from Eokoro; the Siouan Pawnee to and from Eokoro; and then Eokoro to Algonquian and on to Lahontan through the Algonquian. Even though a complex and imperfect system, it would have been just workable and was likely augmented by signing. In this way the baron could communicate at a very basic level over the entire length of his travels until they took him beyond the limits of the Pawnee and on out to the Athabascan-speaking Gnacsitares in western Nebraska. At that point the baron began to experience some serious communication problems, which he clearly emphasized.[7]

The Gnacsitares and Mozeemleks that the baron met out on the Platte would, over the period of the latter's captivity among the former, most certainly have learned to understand each other at least somewhat. There was, however, probably no one in the French company including his Caddoan-speaking Essanape/Pawnee escorts if even still present, who could understand the language of either the Gnacsitares or the Mozeemleks. As the baron stated at the end of his stay with the Gnacsitares, he did not have a competent interpreter, and having to deal with several men that did not agree with each other, all the discussion resulted in a jumble of information, "incoherent Fustian" as he phrased it, "that forced me to stick with what I had heard."[8] This certainly lends credence to the notion that one must weigh Lahontan's descriptions by how they were obtained; either by his own observations or via imperfect translations.

The baron reiterated his misfortune of not having good interpreters when he described the Natives of Canada in his second volume in relation to others of North America and stated that:

> ...upon this Head I only speak of the Savages of Canada, excluding those that live beyond the River of Mississipi, of whose Manners and Customs I could not acquire a perfect Scheme, by reason that I was unacquainted with their <u>Languages</u>, not to menntion that I had not time to make any long stay in their Country. [emphasis added][9]

Lahontan could not have described the language situation more clearly or honestly than he did. His critics have never credited him for doing so! He not only acknowledged it but noted that because of these difficulties he had no choice but to accept and report what he was hearing out on the Platte, or at least thought he was hearing, since it appears that he must have been questioning some of its validity himself. His admission of this major difficulty is further testimony to the degree to which he attempted to maintain fidelity to the truth in his Long River narrative, just as he did in so many of his other letters.

Notes:

1. Lahontan, *New Voyages*, 190-97.

2. Lahontan, 176-77.

3. Lahontan, 176.

4. Heidenreich, "Early French Exploration," 65-66.

5. Lahontan 198-99.

6. Bray, "Utz Site;" Dickey, *People*, 1-8; Houck, *A History of*, 149-237; Nasatir, *Before Lewis and Clark*, 1-7; O'Brien and Wood, *Prehistory*, 347-50; Schweitzer, "Otoe and Missouri," 447-49.

7. Lahontan, *New Voyages*, 196, 414.

8. Lahontan, 196.

9. Lahontan, *New Voyages*, (2), 414.

10

• TEGUAYO AND MOZEEMLEK: THEIR LANDS AND BEARDED PEOPLE •

by

Steven G. Baker

In addition to the foregoing detail regarding the Platte River and its valley, other major evidence demonstrates that Lahontan was on the Platte when he ended his outward trip in January 1689. This can be done because of eighteenth-century and earlier Spanish documentation originating in New Mexico regarding the legendary land of Teguayo. This, which like Lahontan's lands of Mozeemlek and Tahuglauk, was near Utah's Great Salt Lake directly and far west of the Platte.[1]

Within the context of the legend of Teguayo it is possible to demonstrate the equivalency of its strange heavily bearded male Native populace with the similar one from the region of the Mozeemlek first described by Lahontan. His descriptions of them are some of the most interesting portions of his narrative and seem to have been among the origins of some of the key criticisms of it. These appear to have included those that assisted in comparing them to the *"Lilliputians"* and *"Brobdingnagians"* from Swift's 1726 novel about the travels of Mr. Gulliver.[2] Information in the Spanish documents is entirely consistent with that provided earlier by the baron. It proves that these so physically atypical Native people once existed in the same region and that any criticism by the baron's detractors regarding them was wholly unfounded.[3]

The Legend of Teguayo

The baron's description of the land of Mozeemlek, as it appears to have been known to the Spaniards a,s or related to, "*El Gran Teguayo*" (The Great Teguayo and *"TewaYo"*), has only quite recently proven to have been no myth and a critical element in understanding his Long River narrative. Since it was located in Spanish territory, Teguayo was already known to the Spanish earlier than it was to the even more distant French of Canada when Lahontan first described it from reports made to him by some of its native inhabitants. These reports were provided by the heavily bearded Mozeemlek war captives held by the Gnacsitares when the baron was their guest out on the Platte.

In the baron's eyes these unusual individuals looked more like Europeans than all the many other Native peoples he was used to. They were being held on the Platte quite far from their homeland near Utah's Great Salt Lake.[4] In the eighteenth century, similar, though at times vague and muddled rumors of such notably unusual, bearded Natives out in the distant hinterlands were still filtering all the way back to Montreal. "These tales were of a people in the far west who were supposedly white like Europeans, bearded, and lived in French-style houses." At least one French priest who heard the tales speculated that these bearded men must have been Tatars who had fled from the Japanese.[5]

By the middle of the eighteenth-century Spanish officials in New Mexico were becoming increasingly alarmed by the persistence of such rumors. They had long been circulating within that colony about a strange population of people living in the tierra incognita beyond the by then still wholly unexplored Colorado River, then known as the *Río Tizón,* far to the northwest of Santa Fe. The bearded men from there, like the baron's captive informants described, were in the tales being brought back to New Mexico. It was said that their heavy beards made them look more like Europeans than any other Natives with whom the Spaniards or regional Natives were familiar. Information on these unusual people had come to the attention of Spanish officials long before through Native accounts of the "great Teguayo." These people were sometimes referred to by both Spaniards, Natives, and later by some Frenchmen, as the "Spaniards of the Río Tizón."[6]

Spanish authorities were concerned that these supposedly European-looking men might be Frenchmen or Russians interloping in the dominions of their sovereign, Carlos III. These rumors had persisted for more than a century and had come to be the "Legend of Teguayo." No expeditions had, however, been sent northward to investigate their veracity until 1765 when Juan Antonio María de Rivera was explicitly charged to do so by New Mexico's governor, Vélez Cachupín. Although Rivera attempted to reach the Colorado River and Teguayo in that year, he did not succeed in his mission and only got as far as the Gunnison River in west central Colorado.[7]

It was not until 1776 that Fathers Francisco Atanasio Domínguez and Silvestre Vélez de Escalante completed Rivera's mission, at least as held in the mind of the latter man, and reached Teguayo. They confirmed the portion of the legend that indicated that the rumored strange- bearded men who, although still "savages," looked like Europeans and did live there near a great lake of salt. The fathers' impeccable documentation of these strange men, in association with the near vicinity of the Great Salt Lake, has become a central element in proving the veracity of Lahontan's narrative.

Native accounts of the province of Teguayo had first been heard by priests and conquistadors in earlier days of New Spain and had evolved through time. These had been passed down through Native oral histories from generation to generation and finally recorded by the Spaniards. They eventually became embedded in New Mexico's collective memory as the "Legend of Teguayo." This legend played a critical role in shaping the strategic thinking of eighteenth-century New Mexican authorities about unexplored areas to the north of the colony. A desire to test the veracity of the legend and to search for sources of mineable silver led Governor Vélez Cachupín to send out the Rivera expeditions. He made Rivera his personal emissary and provided him with explicit written instructions regarding his anticipated prospecting and explorations of the Colorado River and the even more distant Teguayo.[8]

In addition to a number of other general charges, Rivera received some very specific instructions. These included:

> When they get to the Río del Tizón, they [Rivera and his men] shall examine in very great detail which nations inhabit both sides of the river and whether the (nations) I mean information the Utes give us is true that there are large pueblos on the other side of the river and some type of white people with beards and dressed like Europeans. They shall inform themselves well and examine these circumstances."[9]

In his instructions the governor went on to state:

> Likewise, they shall inform themselves about whether the Río del Tizón originates in the great Lake Copala, which the Pueblo Indians call Taguayo, which is said to be its origin, and about how far this lake is from the capital [Santa Fe]. We must suppose the lake to be between north and northwest of here, surrounded, according to ancient and modern reports, by many large pueblos with a king or sovereign."[10]

Until the founding of *Alta* (Upper) California in 1769, New Mexico anchored the northern reaches of New Spain west of the Mississippi. Even at this late date old, persistent, and often mythical accounts suggested that golden *otro Perus* might still lie just beyond the horizon of New Mexico in the fabled provinces of both Teguayo and Quivira. The high rugged mountains of the Southern Rockies had not yet been explored, let alone breached, but were believed to separate these two large regions to the north of Santa Fe. These regions were generally indicated in the 1684 Peñalosa Map of New Mexico illustrated in Figure 27. This map fairly portrayed what little was then known about the location of Teguayo.[11]

The land of Quivira was also legendary and supposedly lay somewhere toward the Mississippi River far north and east of New Mexico. Its existence, however, was never verified. The legend of Quivira was thus perhaps all too readily discredited and, like Teguayo, was relegated to the status of myth. While Quivira was once probably a real place and/or Native socio-political unit (perhaps the old Cahokia paramount chiefdom? [Figures 1, 21) on the pre-Columbian landscape, scholars have yet to demonstrate that any elements of the legends surrounding it were factual. Some parts of it may, however, well have been true.[12]

Legendary Teguayo was clearly not an imaginary Native place or socio-political unit. Much to the contrary, it appears to have once been some manner of reality on the ancient Native landscape. The emergence story of the Tewa people of New Mexico indicated that it was the place from which they had migrated to New Mexico in prehistoric times. Hence, Teguayo may have had multiple meanings.

The open challenge for modern scholars has been to determine what it meant and exactly where it was located, just as Juan Rivera had been charged to do in 1765. Close evaluations of consistencies in accounts through time can often serve to demonstrate that things once misunderstood, underappreciated, and considered to be imaginary or mythical, could have been realities, just as was the case for the early criticisms of Lahontan's observations as discussed herein.[13]

The legend of Teguayo persisted far longer than that of Quivira. Explorations north and eastward across the buffalo plains (the central and southern Great Plains) toward Quivira had been comparatively easy for the Spaniards. Still, they always came up empty handed in terms of finding or at least recognizing and identifying it. Reaching the province of El Gran Teguayo was quite another matter! Some of the multiple sub-provinces that were said to make up the province appear to have been near Utah Lake and the Great Salt Lake. As the Spaniards then understood it in the 1760s, the very nearest part of the province lay some 500 difficult miles northwest of Santa Fe as the crow flies and nearly 700 or more miles by the sinuous trails that wound through the so rugged mountains and canyons of western Colorado.[14]

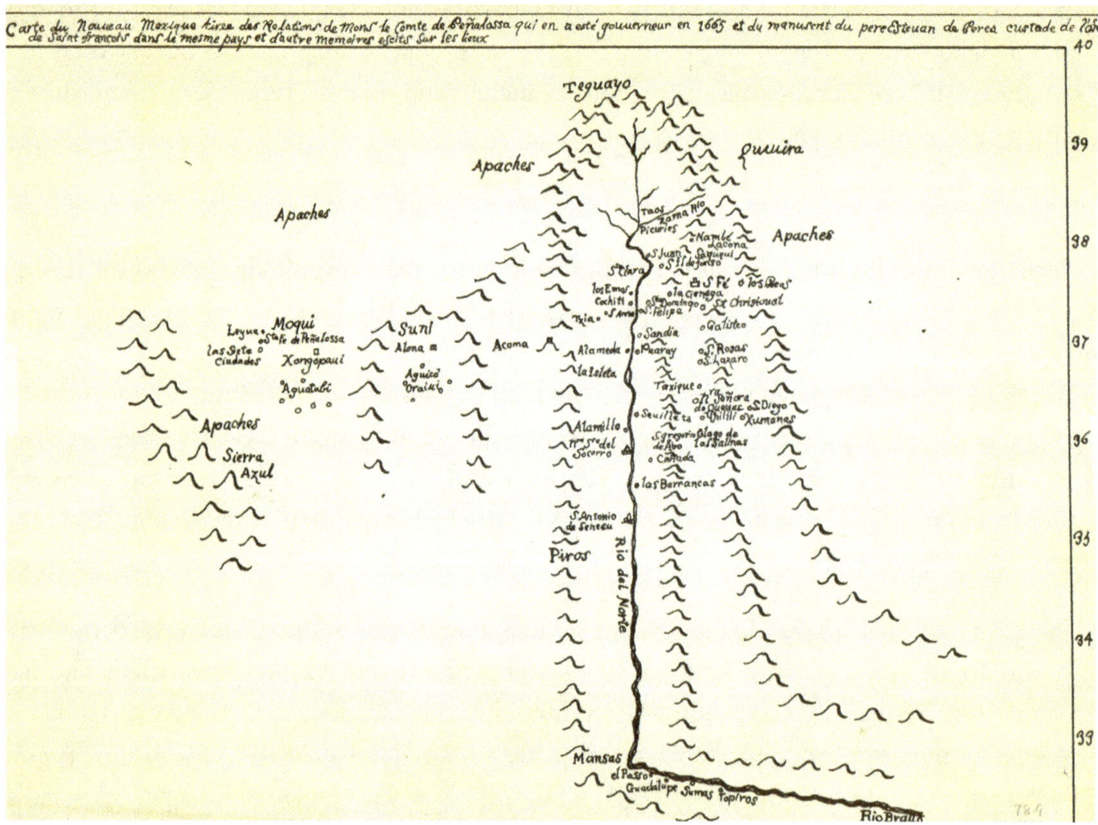

27. The ca. 1684 Peñalosa Map of New Mexico shows the generalized locations of Teguayo and Quivira as they were then only vaguely known to the Spaniards. The Colorado River/Rió Tizón is not shown since its upper reaches had not yet been explored, just as the Platte and other rivers of the central Plains were still unknown. This map is generally credited to Diego Dionisio de Peñalosa Briceño y Berdugo who was appointed governor of New Mexico in 1660, courtesy of Fray Angélico Chávez History Library, Palace of the Governors, Santa Fe.

The long distance just to reach its nearest border was only one obstacle to be overcome in exploring for Teguayo. Potentially hostile Ute-speaking Native people and their extensive and rugged western Colorado and eastern Utah mountain and canyon homeland further insulated the province from New Mexico. Even though Quivira was sought out early, the vast dominions of the Ute speakers effectively sheltered the mysteries of the Rió Tizón and the legendary Teguayo until late in the eighteenth century.[15]

Teguayo is believed to be a Tewa Native word. In Tewa it seems to be pronounced "*Tewayó*." Linguistic anthropologists think it means something like "the land of the Tewas." According to the earliest accounts in the Uto-Aztecan languages of Mexico, Teguayo may also have been known as "Copala," which is thought to have meant "a congregation of many different peoples and nations."[16]

The legend of Teguayo/Copala is obviously complex and is still only very imperfectly understood. It was certainly of indigenous origin, however, and had seemingly long persisted in the oral tradition of the Natives. The account was initially presented and added to through translations across time and multiple Native American languages, Spanish, French, and probably sign language or *lingua franca* as well. The picture that emerged from this process has thus not always been clear. Like most legends it likely included details from collective memories of an ancient past, as well as misunderstandings and embellishments added by Spaniards, that often related to the mythical presence of riches such as gold and silver. Much of what was known of Teguayo came from the first-hand account of a Jemez Native man named don Juanillo who had been a captive in Teguayo in the latter seventeenth century.[17]

Teguayo and Lake Copala, as well as the Río Tizón, were understood to lie far to the north and west beyond the San Juan River that extends along the border between present-day Colorado and New Mexico. The valley of the San Juan was by the mid-nineteenth century the southern territorial boundary area of the Ute-speaking Natives of western Colorado. The province of Quivira was said to spread from land far inland to the east and beyond the Great Plains thence westward toward the Rocky Mountains. Teguayo extended westward from these mountains and was once said to extend all the way to the Pacific Ocean. The two provinces were said to be near, if not touching one another, apparently in the Rocky Mountains, and wild cows (American bison) were supposed to be present in both.

Scholars have long suspected that Lake Copala, if it existed, was *Lake Timpanogos* of the Domínguez and Vélez de Escalante account. The veracity of this opinion of their equivalency has, however, never been well confirmed. That lake is the present-day Utah Lake, which is a substantial freshwater lake just a few miles south of the Great Salt Lake. From its north end Utah Lake drains into the Great Salt Lake by way of the Jordon River. These large closely neighboring lakes are still very notable features on the Utah landscape and the salt lake serves as a major topographical reference in following Lahontan's Long River narrative.[18]

Lahontan's descriptions of the lands and peoples of Mozeemlek, which he did not visit, are here compared with the direct observations of fathers Domínguez and Vélez de Escalante. They of course, in fulfilling Rivera's failed mission in 1776, entered the province they knew as Teguayo and left firsthand descriptions of its people. These descriptions were essentially identical to those the baron provided almost one-hundred years earlier. They help confirm that he was on the Platte River and, even with translation problems, did not fabricate when he tried to describe them. The Franciscans' cartographer, Bernardo de Miera y Pacheco, also left a painting of the bearded men of the province. (Figure 28)[19]

As demonstrated in the recent consideration of Rivera's travels, the account of these bearded Caucasian-looking men, no matter how or when it originated, factored mightily into both the expeditions of Juan Rivera and Fathers Domínguez and Vélez de Escalante. Some further factual information along these lines may also have come from the deposed and very controversial former governor of New Mexico, Peñalosa.[20]

No mention of a salt lake in the legend of Teguayo is yet known to predate the publication of Lahontan's widely circulated book. After the baron's account, there was no further mention of the salt lake in any known accounts until that of Fathers Domínguez and Vélez de Escalante in 1776. Even though the two Franciscans heard about the salt lake from the Natives and passed quite near it on their route via Utah Lake, they did not visit it.[21]

The general content of the old legend was reinforced by fray Carlos Delgado who was in residence at Isleta Pueblo in 1744. Father Delgado did not mention a salt lake or bearded men, in his document. He stated that the province was 200 leagues (roughly 500 to 600 miles) to the northwest of Santa Fe and made up of many different peoples all of whom were ruled by a dignified and ostentatious king. Because his severity was so great it was said that this monarch did not speak to or look at anyone, except momentarily. Fray Carlos reported that an unnamed priest had once visited the province and died there after he had catechized the king. In honor of this action, the priest's remains were said to have been kept in a box that Teguayo's inhabitants highly venerated. There is, unfortunately, no known documentary evidence to confirm or deny this lone fleeting account of this unnamed priest.[22]

The king of Spain had encouraged the exploration of Teguayo as early as 1678. Nearly a century went by, however, before New Mexican authorities finally made a meaningful effort to solve its mysteries by sending out Rivera's expeditions. They had been far too busy dealing with hostile Natives who surrounded the weak little colony, as well as threats from the French, to try to explore or settle any such far distant new lands.[23]

In1765 Governor Vélez Cachupín directed Juan Rivera to make his two expeditions from New Mexico toward the Gran Teguayo. Rivera was to try to locate the River Tizón, explore it, and learn about the people along its banks. He was very specifically instructed to gather information on the bearded white people who some accounts said dressed like Europeans and were at times referred to as the "Spaniards of the River Tizón." He was also to find out about Lake Copala in Teguayo, which reportedly had "many large pueblos with a king or sovereign." Such accounts appear to have contained information that Lahontan said he had gathered from the Mozeemleks because none of the Spanish accounts prior to his publication are known to have spoken of the bearded men.[24]

The account of the bearded men and the salt lake likely initially came from Lahontan through his book. It could well have been reinforced by later, undocumented oral accounts as well. In a mid-eighteenth-century account, a Navajo said he had met a bearded "Spaniard" on the Tizón and thus reinforced Lahontan's information. As it became available to the Spaniards, this published information from Lahontan, as well as whatever else he may have told them during his later exile, along with the Navajo's account, would have helped to fuel speculation of what was out in the far regions of the Gran Teguayo.[25]

Fathers Domínguez and Vélez de Escalante Travel to Teguayo

Fray Damián Martínez was assigned to serve Zuni Pueblo in the early 1770s. In 1774 Commandant Inspector Hugo O'Conor personally asked fray Damián to employ every means his intelligence and prudence might dictate to learn the truth of "the flying reports I have picked up on this frontier about the existence of a settlement of Europeans on the opposite bank of the river named Tizón, which is to the northwest of New Mexico."[26]

Before the Rivera account, there is no indication in the legend of Teguayo that the bearded men who lived there had clothing that, at least in its cut, was similar to that worn by Europeans or carried European style arms.[27] In April 1775 fray Damián responded by letter to O'Conor and addressed his questions regarding the purported settlement of Europeans on the far side of the Tizón. He attributed the account's origin to two sources; the independent account of the Navajo man who had been baptized and acquired some familiarity with the Spanish language, and an account attributed to unnamed Ute informants. Father Vélez de Escalante did not seem to give much credence to the Navajo's account.[28]

The Navajo must have related his account before 1765 because information about the unknown Spaniards is included in Vélez Cachupín's instructions to Rivera. In 1774 the Navajo who made the report was said to still be alive. His account must have incorporated the Spaniards' evolving notion into the legend of Teguayo. This idea and the associated description became memorialized in Vélez Cachupín's instructions to Rivera as well as in the later inquiry O'Conor made to fray Damián. This emphasizes the sort of imaginative vision the accounts may have been helping to shape in the minds of the New Mexico authorities by Rivera's time regarding unknown Spaniards or other Europeans on the Tizón.[29] At the time he wrote the Navajo was living in Belén in Bernabé Montaño's house. He was considered truthful, and on all the occasions he has told his story he had not varied it.[30]

Fathers Domínguez and Vélez de Escalante followed and traveled Rivera's footsteps toward the Tizón and beyond in their epic trek of 1776. The friars were not, however, as is almost universally believed by historian, just seeking an overland route from New Mexico to the newly founded Spanish missions in California. While that was originally the church's official goal and justification for ordering the padres to make the trip, the mysterious bearded white men of Teguayo also lured them, particularly Father Vélez de Escalante, so far northward into the interior. In Vélez de Escalante's mind, their trip was intended to complete Rivera's failed mission of finding out the truths about the mysterious bearded men.[31]

In large measure, the Franciscans were also responding to a further call from their government; a request for the church to assist in finding the truth about the legendary people of Teguayo. Hence there are very strong connections between the expeditions of Rivera, Lahontan and the Franciscan friars. These connections further demonstrate how seriously the colonial authorities were taking the rumors about the bearded men of Teguayo. These connections also illuminate the purposes behind both Spanish expeditions.[32]

By the time the friars were ready to leave on their trip in the summer of 1776, fray Francisco Hermenegildo Garcés had already demonstrated and reported on his discovery of a useable route from

California to New Mexico by way of Zuni. Despite fray Francisco's success, about which he was very well informed, Father Vélez de Escalante became obstinate on the matter and was not to be detered from taking what became a most unusual, roundabout northward trip. That trip ultimately took the Franciscan friars as much as five full degrees of latitude and perhaps 300 or more miles north of the direct route to Monterey from Santa Fe that Father Garcés pioneered. The fathers' route was also far north of the route to Monterrey that fray Silvestre had originally projected. It was also far north of the path which became the Spanish Trail between California and New Mexico in the nineteenth century. Further, it took them through some very rugged country of the American West. Though it took them directly to the bearded men, the fathers' route would have been a completely useless supply route from Santa Fe to California.[33]

Even though Vélez de Escalante initially seems to have been serious about exploring a direct route to California, he gave up on this mission once he learned of the reports of the bearded men of Teguayo. As early as the fall of 1775, nearly a year before Father Garcés demonstrated the open route by way of Zuni, Vélez de Escalante had already deemphasized his plan to seek a route to California. This is clearly spelled out in a most informative letter of October 28, 1775, from fray Silvestre to New Mexico's governor, Pedro Fermín de Mendinueta. This enlightening document outlined the Franciscan's plan for an expedition to the land of the bearded people. In keeping with the more recent report of the Navajo man, he referred to them as the "Spaniards" on the River Tizón. In this letter, he explained his plan to determine the nature of these unusual bearded men as well as his intention to abandon any plan to try to reach Monterey.[34]

That letter demonstrates that the expedition of Fathers Domínguez and Vélez de Escalante was, at least on fray Silvestre's part, intended to include a strategically directed ethnographic study, as was that of Juan Rivera, and not just an attempt to find a route to California. Father Domínguez had also been instructed to find a route to California before he departed Mexico City for the New Mexico mission field. He did not, however, arrive in New Mexico with his own set of instructions until fray Silvestre had already begun to question the wisdom of trying to reach Monterey from Santa Fe.[35] The father's letter of October 28, 1775, to Mendinueta explained how a trip to California was not really feasible and that a well organized and equipped expedition should instead try to reach Teguayo. He stated:

> I set forth to the fathers that the investigation [of the bearded "Spaniards" of the Tison] was unattainable by means of any pagan Indians and that supposing the Spaniards reffered to are on the other side of the large river which they call El Tison, if they exist in fact one could only learn who they are by an expedition...It must be forty years since reports of the said Spaniards were first had. It was printed in the diary of the journey of [17]51 which Father Fernando Consag made through California. Because the settlement of Monterrey is much more modern, it is inferred evidently that the Spaniards who have been seen on the other side of the great river of Tison cannot be from there. In circumstances wherein two nations so different as are the Californians and the Utes find themselves in accord, I myself, not having received further reports for so long a time, suppose that some shipwreck or other contingency threw upon the coasts of Monterrey

> some European people and that they, having penetrated inland, established themselves on the banks of the said river and that finally their descendants are those whom the Utes and the rest, perhaps because of the color and dress, call Spaniards [emphasis added]. Their discovery would be very useful to religion and the crown both to prevent any attack upon this kingdom, if they are foreigners, and to incorporate them with ourselves if they are, as they say, Spaniards.[36]

Father Domínguez was fray Silvestre's superior and had direct orders fom the church to go to California. When, toward the end of their monumental trip, the friars were debating the wisdom of trying to go on to California in the face of oncoming winter, fray Silvestre opposed doing so. He had already substituted an entirely different goal for their effort. It should be little wonder that these Franciscan friars then ended up casting lots to determine whether they should start back to Santa Fe, as they did, or continue on toward the Sierra Nevada and Monterey as initially ordered. Father Domínguez believed in discipline, order, and precision in fulfilling his duties on behalf of the church. At the apex of the expedition, the friars were already facing the harsh reality that even in October, winter snows were already capping the high peaks and filling the passes of the Sierra Nevada.[37]

Father Domínguez's orders have to date stood as the official justification for the expedition's travels to Teguayo. This is clearly outlined in the expedition journal Vélez de Escalante kept. The friars' route was at the very least a strange and perplexing one for finding a clear trail to California and took them directly to the region the Spaniards believed to be El Gran Teguayo. The Franciscans initially traveled toward Teguayo by exactly the same route directly pioneered in part and further reported on by Juan Rivera from information he garnered from the Utes. The friars also had personnel from Rivera's party with them, and they indicated that they carried a copy of Rivera's journal as well. Rivera had certainly not been looking for a route to California by traveling the primary trail to Teguayo. He was merely following his explicit orders from the governor to try to reach and explore the legendary province.[38]

By reaching Teguayo, the friars' historically famous trip was successful rather than the failure it is usually considered to have been because they did not reach California. They furthered the groundwork for meeting the colony's goals of securing its borders and hinterlands. In particular they completed Rivera's failed mission to explore Teguayo and learn the truths behind its legend. In this regard their trip was truly a resounding success! The Franciscan friars proved that elements of the legend of Teguayo were indeed true and, just as described by Lahontan nearly a century earlier, that there really were some very unusual bearded "savages" living there in the vicinity of the Great Salt Lake![39]

The legend of Teguayo essentially died away after the friars' trip and does not seem to have been added to or continued since. It vanished from the Spanish lore of New Mexico and its borderlands and only remaining quietly embedded in Tewa oral history and dusty Spainish archives. The church never attempted to develop a mission in Teguayo and the Spanish military never established the presidio there as Miera y Pacheco had recommended. The friars' stated search for a route to Monterey from Santa Fe has historically overshadowed their intentions of discovering the truths of Teguayo.

Just like the friars' important discovery was downplayed and overlooked within the contexts of historical scholarship, Native ethnology, and biological anthropology; so too was Lahontan's original description ofTeguayo/Mozeemlek. Once it acquired the territory from Spain, France never appears to have attempted to follow up on the matter prior to selling the region to the United States. Against this background it is now possible to compare the descriptions of the baron with those of the fathers and demonstrate that they were speaking of the same place and of the same people(s) and that the baron was on the Platte River when he recorded his observations. In chapter 11 the descriptions of the bearded men are explained from modern perspectives of biological anthropologists and their importance in terms of their contribution potential relative to the present understanding of the peopling of ancient North America.

Lahontan's Narrative of the People of Mozeemlek and Tahuglauk

The virtually identical descriptions of the heavily bearded men from near the Great Salt Lake, prepared by Fathers Domínguez and Vélez de Escalante in 1776 and the ones by Lahontan in 1689, testify to the veracity of the baron's so-harshly and unjustifiably criticized descriptions of them. Further, they provide extraordinarily rare early ethnographic documentation that may relate to ancestral and similarly Caucasian-appearing ancient Paleoamericans. These were atypical of most perceptions, both ancient and more modern, about the appearance of American Natives. Such people were certainly present on the landscape of the Desert West in Lahontan's time and well into the nineteenth century and perhaps even later as well as much earlier.

The learned Spanish priests and the educated young French marine officer who observed these people and wrote about them were not naïve newcomers unaccustomed to the New World landscape as it was dominated by American Natives. Readers must realize that they all had for years lived and worked among them. Accordingly, one must pay particularly close attention and accord credibility to what they are trying to tell us through translations from across the centuries. They were not making flippant comments on things that they were uninformed about.

If there were ever any such things as "typical" characteristics in the physical appearance of Native of Lahontan's New France or the fathers' New Mexico colony, they do not seem to have differed much, if at all, from those traditionally recognized by biological anthropologists of the twentieth century. The accounts of both the baron and the priests indicate that there were at least two highly contrasting and obvious physical characteristics evident among the Native populations (the "savages)" they encountered. One was seemingly consistent with the stereotypical visage of them given in physical anthropology textbooks in use when the present authors were still college students in the 1960s. These are not known to have changed much since that time. One example stated that "The basic traits American Indians have in common are yellow-brown to red-brown skin color; hair, black, straight, coarse, sometimes slightly wavy, very sparse on body and face, and usually entirely absent on the side of the face...."[40]

In Volume II of his *New Voyages to North America* Lahontan discussed the Natives as he had come to know them. He stated:

> In the mean time suffer me to acquaint you, that upon this Head I only speak of the Savages of Canada, excluding those that live beyond the River of Mississipi, of whose Manners and Customs I could not acquire a perfect Scheme, by reason that I was unacquainted with their Languages, not to mention that I had not time to make any long stay in their Country. In the Journal of my Voyage on the Long River, I acquainted you that they are a very polite People.[41]

Consistent with physical anthropology texts, the baron summarized his perception of the uniformity in the physical characteristics of the Canadian Natives that he was so familiar with: "Those who have represented the Savages to be as rough as bears, never had the opportunity of seeing them; for they have neither Beard nor Hair In any part of their Body, not so much as under their Arm-pits".[42]

However, seemingly not wanting to be credited with having personally checked too closely, he sarcastically added: "This is true of both Sexes, if I may credit those who ought to know better than I." [emphasis added][43]

Unlike the baron, however, the Spanish priests did not offer a final statement on the characteristic features of the Natives of the New Mexico colony. The closest they came was to imply a great difference in them, and to state that the heavily bearded men of Teguayo near the Great Salt Lake who had surprised them with their atypical appearance, "resemble the Spaniards in their physiognomy." The term "physiognomy" is truly a "big word" to find in a document from the eighteenth century. It is important in its indication that father Domínguez was indeed viewing the Natives from a critical learned perspective and why he was so surprised by the contrast presented between the heavily bearded men and the Natives he was otherwise familiar with.[44]

The information contained in the following discussion is drawn from and references to the lengthy quotation from the baron's narrative dated on or about January 26 when he was among the Gnasitare on the Platte River. The reader is referred to the numbered reference sections (such as **RS 1, 2, 3** etc.) ascribed to portions of that one quotation or to the baron's fully translated narrative for the entry.

At the time of the baron's visit the Gnacsitare were holding the four heavily bearded slaves from the far distant Mozeemlek people with whom they had for many years (**RS 3**) been engaged in an on-going war. The baron spoke of how he mistook these bearded "savages" for Spaniards and how his misunderstanding arose because of the great difference between the Gnacsitares and the Mozeemleks. (**RS 1**) He stated how the slaves wore clothing, such as long shirts, apparently made of animal hides, and had "thick bushy" beards. He noted that their hair was worn long, reaching to just below their ears and that their skin was swarthy or dark. The baron had a hard time believing that they were "savages" because of their "grave meen," or civil and submissive attitude, and their "engaging carraige" or manners. The baron did not, however, comment on the physical appearance of the Gnacsitares, seemingly because they fit the more stereotypical profile of the Native as he described him in the foregoing quote relative to their generally hairless nature. Despite the noteworthy attributes of the bearded Moozemleks, the baron was ultimately forced to conclude that they were only "savages." (**RS 2**)[45]

In his narrative the baron went on and described what else he learned, or thought he did, about the land of Mozeemlek, its people, and its location near the Great Salt Lake. His bearded Mozeemlek informants then told him about a neighboring people that they knew as the "Tahuglauk" who also lived near the salt lake. They specifically described these people as being very populous, stating that they were "as numerous as leaves of trees (such is the Expression that the Savages use for an Hyperbole)." (**RS 3**)[46]

The land and people of Teguayo known to the Spaniards are believed to have been one and the same with those of the Mozeemlek and/or Tahuglauk. In the fall of 1765, instead of referring to leaves on trees to describe the large population, Tabeguache Utes on the San Miguel River in western Colorado spoke about the people of Teguayo to Juan Rivera. As he reported in his journal on October 16, 1765; they stated that the people lived near a very large lake and that

those "who live there like rocks and more [plentiful] than rocks." This statement long puzzled the authors until they recalled the baron's account where the large quantities of tree leaves were similarly used to describe the substantial population.[47]

Both descriptions are in keeping with the 1689 account of Teguayo prepared from Native reports for the governor of New Mexico by fray Alsonso de Posada. For its time, which was exactly the same year when Lahontan met the Mozeemlek men, it was obviously a well populated region on the west side of Utah's Wasatch Front just as the baron described. In that account Posada stated:

> That there are many people and different nations in the kingdom of Teguayo is not only presumable, but it is certain since all of the nations of the North affirm it, especially one Indian...having been a captive for a period of two years in the provinces of Teguayo.[48]

The baron encouraged the Mozeemlek slaves to further describe the Tahuglauk who may have, along with the Mozeemlek, appear to have been people of Teguayo that the fathers would later encounter, describe, and which would be illustrated by the expedition cartographer, Miera y Pacheco, on his map of 1778. (Figure 28) With almost total precision the baron's description mirrored the men shown in close keeping with the painted image as well as a photo from 1871. (Figure 32)[49] The baron stated:

> I would fain have satisfied my Curiosity in being an eye-witness of the Manners and Customs of the *Tahuglauk*; but that being impracticable, I was forc'd to be instructed at second hand by these *Mezeemlek* Slaves; who assur'd me, upon the Faith of a Savage, that the *Tabuglauk* wear their Beards two Fingers breadth long; that their Garments reach down to their Knees; that they cover their Heads with a sharp-pointed Cap; that they always wear a long Stick or Cane in their hands, which is tipp'd, not unlike what we use in *Europe* [sic]; that they wear a sort of Boots upon their Legs which reach up to the Knee; that their Women never shew themselves, which perhaps proceeds from the same Principle that prevails in *Italy* and *Spain*; and, in fine, that this People are always at War with the puissant Nations that are seated in the Neighbourhood of the Lake; but withal, that they never disquiet the strowling Nations that fall in their way, by reason of their Weakness: An

admirable Lesson for some princes in the World who are so much intent upon the making use of the strongest hand.[50]

In keeping with the baron's foregoing description as provided by the men of Mozeemlek; the men of Teguayo in Figure 28 are not only sporting long hair and bushy beards, they also have buckskin shirts that hang down to their knees and some manner of little caps or bonnets. It is difficult to determine if they have high boots or just trouser-like leggings as described. They also carry the poles or cudgel-like staffs noted by the baron. The painting, from nearly a century after the baron wrote, conforms quite well with his 1689 description.[51]

28. Cartouche detail from the map of the territory traversed by Fathers Domínguez and Vélez de Escalante as prepared by Bernardo de Miera y Pacheco. (Adams, "Fray Silvester," 101) This map from 1777 is commonly known as the Miera y Pacheco Map and is published in Bolton, Pageant in the Wilderness, courtesy of the de Pagter Collection, Telluride, Colorado.

The so highly comparable information provided about the atypical, bearded men of Tahuglauk and Mozeemlek, by the baron and of Teguayo by the Spanish fathers, vindicates the baron from the charges of those of his critics who so strongly questioned his credibility in his descriptions of these people. The notion that they were both talking about the same or very closely related people is clinched since it is very clear that they were both from the near vicinity of the Great Salt Lake.[52]

Lahontan's book had been translated into multiple languages well before the middle of the eighteenth century. It would certainly have been known to the Spanish since the baron had communicated with the Spanish War Council as early as 1699 when he was seeking to spy for Spain. His Long River narrative would thus likely have helped to fuel speculation of what was out there in the distant region known as the Gran Teguayo.[53] Rivera reported as follows about the homeland of Teguayo from information he gathered from Ute Natives:

> Then one goes to the foot of a small sierra where there is a very large lake. There are people who live there like rocks and even more than rocks. From there one takes the route to the base of the sierra, and one goes to the Spaniards [this is the term by which Spaniards and Indians sometimes referred to the bearded men of Teguayo] who live on the bank of a small streamlet of ample water. This is their first settlement. They have houses like ours [presumably meaning brush wickiups or tipis as used by Utes or adobe pueblos like the Spanish?] and are Spaniards because they speak our language [Ute] like we do. They are very white with heavy beards, and they wear buckskin [as shown in Figure 28] because they do not have clothes like we have in our land.[54]

Eleven years after Rivera's trips Fathers Domínguez and Vélez de Escalante set out on their epic quest. They not only had personnel from Rivera's party with them, but they also had his diary and followed the route to Utah Lake about which Rivera had learned. Their journal has stood the test of time and become one of the most famous and best early travel narratives from the period of early western North American discovery.[55] Father Domínguez noted prior to the journey: "We are leaving this capital for the north-northwest with the aim of finding out, if possible, what nations in addition to the Yuta inhabit the regions between here and Monterey in the aforesaid direction, even though it may involve a roundabout route...."[56]

After arriving among what they referred to as the *Laguna*, or Lake People, who appear to have been the Tahuglauk, about Utah Lake near the Great Salt Lake in Teguayo, the Franciscans commented that "They possess good features, and most of them are fully bearded." They further stated that all the regions of the mountains to the southeast, south-southwest, and west were inhabited by many people of the "same [Ute speaking?] nation, language, and easy-going character as these Lagunas."[57] By the time they had reached the Sevier River to the west of Utah Lake the subject of beards had come to the forefront. The fathers reported here they came upon a very old Native of venerable countenance. He was alone in a tiny hut, and "he had a beard so full and long that he looked like one of the ancient hermits of Europe."[58]

As they met a group of twenty of the local Natives the fathers went on to state:

> Now these ones, more fully bearded than the Lagunas, have their nostril-cartilage pierced, and in the hole, by way of adornment, they wear a tiny polished bone…In their features they more resemble the Spaniards than they do all of the other Indians known in America up to now, from whom they differ in what has been said to exist on the other site of El Río del Tizón [Colorado River]. They employ the same language [Ute] as the Timpanogotzis [known to have been a Numic language]. From the river and site of Santa Isabel onward [Sevier River] begin these full-bearded Indians, who perhaps gave rise to the report about the Spaniards who were said to exist on the other side of El Río del Tizón.[59]

29. Late nineteenth-century Capuchin friars wearing the traditional barbas longas that the constitutions of their order mandated to be worn. It was to these kinds of beards that Fathers Domínguez and Vélez de Escalante were referring in their descriptions of the bearded Utes of Utah, courtesy of the Capuchin Provincial Archives, Detroit, Michigan, c/o Bro. Patrick McSherry, OFM Cap., Archivist.

As they passed beyond the Sevier River well to the south and west of the Great Salt Lake they met even more of the full-bearded and pierced-nose people. They stated that "The five of them who came first with their chief were so fully bearded that they looked like Capuchin padres or Bethlehemites."[60] The fathers had finally found the secrets of the Gran Teguayo and witnessed the people as first described by Lahontan and unsuccessfully sought in earnest by Juan Rivera in 1765. There was no cause for alarm! The bearded ones were not Europeans who had invaded Spanish territory. They were only Natives who looked remarkably different than most. In late November of 1776 Father Domínguez debriefed his superior about the discoveries made on the trip and emphasized the full bearded "*Yutas Barbónes*" as he called them. He stated:

> These Indians whom we discovered beyond the Lagunas generally have as dense a beard as the Spaniards. Most frequently they remove it, and some wear it so long that they look like Capuchin Fathers or Bethlehemites [Figures 28, 29]. In addition to this distinction from all the rest, the cartilage of their noses is pierced.[61]

For many years author Baker wondered just what the fathers were trying to describe when they said that at least some of the men they found in old Teguayo had beards as heavy as those worn by Capuchin or Bethlehemite friars. To better understand what the fathers were talking about in regard to these beards a Capuchin historian, Brother Patrick McSherry of Detroit, Michigan, was consulted. Father McSherry explained that after 1536 Capuchin friars were required to wear beards. The typical beard was called the "*barba longa*" or Long Beard. As late as 1940 the Capuchin Constitutions prohibited the friars from doing anything to take care of it "after the manner of seculars." The beard (Figure 29) was still considered to be part and parcel of Capuchin life until 1974.[62]

30. Heavily bearded Paiute men from the Las Vegas Valley of Nevada in 1873 as reproduced in Fowler and Fowler, Anthropology of the Numa, 74. J.K. Hillers photo "The Old Men" from the Powell Expeditions. Smithsonian Institution, National Anthropological Archives, Bureau of American Ethnology Collection, Washington, US public domain.

The individuals shown in Figure 30 are suspected to have been descendant members of the same atypical population of heavily bearded Natives noted by Fathers Domínguez and Vélez de Escalante in 1776. The man on the left has obviously trimmed his beard. In short, the fathers were talking about some truly huge beards being worn by male residents in and about old Teguayo. These were totally unlike any facial hair they had ever seen on a Native. Figure 29 illustrates some Capuchin friars who are sporting the traditional *"barbas longa"* with which the fathers were certainly referring to in describing the long beards. Although it was not just the heavy beards and long hair that so surprised both Lahontan and the fathers as well as other Natives, it was also other characteristics of, as Father Domínguez stated; their "physiognomy" (facial structure) that made them appear to look more like Europeans than those stereotypical Natives with which they were so familiar. The fact that they looked so much like Europeans is why Spaniards and others came to refer to them as the "Spaniards of the Rio Tizón."[63] Now that it is established that such atypical Natives as Lahontan described did exist, one must ask who they could have been. It was Vélez de Escalante who went to Teguayo on a quest to determine if these men were descendants of ship-wrecked European sailors who had made their way inland from the Pacific coast or if they were only unusual looking "savages."[64]

Upon completion of their trip, and in keeping with Rivera's original goal and their own instructions from the church, the two Franciscans used copious amounts of ink to brief their superiors about the physical attributes of the strange bearded men of Teguayo. They did so in surprisingly learned and scientifically couched language for the times. Yet, they said little about a potential route to California.[65] They noted how these people resembled bearded Europeans more than any other Natives they were familiar with. But in the end, in their eyes they proved only to be strange-looking Natives. Similarly atypical heavily bearded Natives were also encountered in the Desert West by fray Francisco Garcés in 1776 and others.[66]

In the friars' eyes they were not descendents of wandering shipwrecked Spaniards or other European interlopers encroaching on Spanish territory as Vélez de Escalante had posited. They posed no obvious threat to New Spain. Once these views were disclosed to their superiors, no further attention was given to this important ethnological discovery by either church or Crown, since it was no longer of potential strategic interest. These early accounts of the bearded Natives faded away into the mists of time and off the radar of virtually all older and more modern students of the American Native, including both ethnohistorians and archaeologists.

Over many years physical anthropologists have, just like Vélez de Escalante did, sought to learn more about the biological backgrounds of the American Native. Among them was an early one named George Birdsell whose work touched on heavily bearded Natives. Although he was not aware of these early accounts of them, he suggested that there was a di-hybrid origin behind them.[67] Utilizing an outmoded, and seemingly now invalid, model of the concept of "race" he suggested that the American Natives evidenced physical traits of both a "Caucasoid" and "Mongolian" nature.[68] He believed that some of the individuals he classed as "Caucasoid" were suggestive of an "Amurian" origin. As he used the term in the 1950's it enfolded the "Caucasoid Murrayians" and the closely related "Ainu" of Japan's Hokkaido and Sakhalin Islands in the Pacific.[69] Although the term has fallen from use by anthropologists, in the past these people were commonly referred to as the "hairy Ainu" because of their notably hirsute characteristics. These included heavy facial hair on males just as noted by the baron and the fathers.[70]

Birdsell noted that a Caucasoid strain, suggestive of an Amurian origin, was then in ca. 1951, still present in the contemporary Shoshone (a Numic language like Ute) speaking Cahuilla People of inland Southern California. In his view, a relatively luxurious beard seemed common among them. Birdsell further noted that "anthroposcopically," the bearded Cahuilla could pass as veritable Ainu! In 1873 John Wesley Powell's expedition photographed the heavily bearded Las Vegas Paiutes from Nevada. (Figure 30)[71] These individuals appear to be just the kind of atypical Native Americans noted by both the baron and the fathers and associated with the land of Teguayo. They are from the Great Basin to the west of Utah's Wasatch Front where the fathers first met the bearded men and to the east of the original territory in California of the bearded Cahuilla noted by Birdsell.

The historical accounts of the baron and the fathers certainly indicate that such bearded Natives were once a significant population in the old land of Teguayo. They have, however, today seemingly faded away from the ethnographic present and are not known to still exist unless some of their descendant populations survive in small remnant groups such as the Cahuilla.

Who were these so distinctive people noted by the early Spanish and French observers? Could they have descended from a very ancient portion of North America's prehistoric aboriginal population that might itself have sprung from multi-hybrid sources? One can only refer to Birdsell and on to the views of modern biological anthropologists discussed in chapter 11. As discussed, there appear to be some potential associations with the Ainu.

One thing is, however, a certainty compliments of the Baron Lahontan and the Fathers Domínguez and Vélez de Escalante. That certainty is that there was once a population of "savages," as they knew them, in the American West who were notably hairy. In addition to their hairiness, these people's overall physical appearance contrasted so sharply with most of the other "savages" of America that they were commonly mistaken for Europeans by bright and educated European explorers as well as other Natives. Figure 31 further illustrates how the bearded men described by the baron and the fathers may have appeared. The image shown in that figure is based on a formal forensic sculpture of the skeletal facial anatomy of one ancient individual from the American West that was prepared by biological anthropologists at the Smithsonian Institution.[72] This man shows how ancestors of the men observed by the baron and the fathers may well have appeared.

31. Eyewitness Spanish, French, and American historical accounts demonstrate that heavily bearded men with long hair who, like the individual shown here, in terms of their facial physiognomy looked more like Europeans than stereotypical American Natives, existed in or about the region once known as Teguayo, Moozemlek, and Tahuglauk. The base image for this derivative sketch was the forensic reconstruction sculpture of Kennewick Man with additional and unkempt hair added by artist Gail Carroll-Sargent of Centuries Research, Inc. The original sculpture is illustrated in the final report on Kennewick Man, Owsley and Jantz, Kennewick Man, permission to modify and utilize the image of the original sculpture courtesy of Dr. Douglas Owsley of the Smithsonian Institution, US public domain.

Native men who looked like the image in Figure 28 lived near the Great Salt Lake from at least as early as 1689, and likely much earlier, and remained in the Desert West until the 1870s or later. In 1775 Father Vélez de Escalante questioned whether these people were American Natives or s imply the descendants of Europeans who may have been shipwrecked and made their way inland. Modern biological anthropologists believe that there is a greater chance that these heavily bearded men derive from ancient Caucasian-looking Paleoamericans such as Kennewick Man, and their descendant populations known to have been present in North America thousands of years ago, than from shipwrecked Europeans. The descriptions and images provided here are apparently the only existent ethnographic links to some very ancient Paleoamerican occupants of North America.

Notes:

1. Baker, et al., *Juan Rivera's Colorado*, 13-34.

2. Swift, *Travels*.

3. Thwaites, "Introduction," xxxvii-xliii; This chapter is largely extracted from Baker et al., *Juan Rivera's Colorado,* 12-34.

4. Lahontan, *New Voyages*, 192-93.

5. Eccles, "La Mer de l'Ouest," 5.

6. Baker et al., *Juan Rivera's Colorado;* Crouse, *La Verendrye*, 80-81,191.

7. Baker et al., *Juan Rivera's Colorado* 14, 24-29.

8. The classic description of Teguayo/Copala was by Fray Alonso Posada. Thomas, *Alonso Posada Report*; Also see Zárate Salmeron, *Relaciones*; Sánchez, *Explorers, Traders. Spanish Search For*; Tyler, *Before Escalante, Myth of*; Tyler and Taylor, *Report of Fray Alonso de Posada*; Vélez Cachupín, "Instructions."

9. Vélez Cachupín, Instructions," as contained in the journal for Rivera's second trip of 1765. Rivera, "Journals;" Baker et al., *Juan Rivera's Colorado*, 298.

10. **Vélez Cachupín, "**Instructions," 298.

11. A copy of the 1684 "Peñalosa Map of New Mexico" (Figure 21) is available by that name in the Fray Angélico Chávez History Library, Palace of the Governors, Sante Fe. The historical context of the map is discussed by Weber, "A Map," 29-32 and Scholes, *Troublous Times*. Diego Dionisio de Peñalosa y Berdugo was appointed governor of New Mexico in 1660 and was in large measure responsible for promoting the legend of Teguayo and elevating it as a strategic interest for the Spanish crown.

12. For discussion of the lure that Teguayo and Quivira held through time, see Bolton, *Coronado;* Flint and Flint, *Coronado Expedition to, Coronado Expedition From*. Zárate Salmerón; *Relaciones;* Scholes, *Troublous Times;* Thomas, *Alonso Posado Report;* Weddle, *French Thorn*, 12-14, *Wreck of the Belle*, 85-96; Wagner, *Spanish Southwest*, 281-83; D. Weber, *Myth and the History;* M. Weber, "A Map."

13. Although it continues to be a popular subject among readers of Spanish colonial history as indicated by the many entries on the internet, remarkably few scholars have traced the evolution of the legend of Teguayo and Copala in any thorough detail. Its veracity has thus long remained in scholarly limbo. Noted Utah historian, Lyman Tyler, was one of the few to attempt to do so. He never accorded any credibility at all to the legend. He directly denounced it as nothing more than myth. Tyler, *Before Escalante; Myth of*. Tyler and Taylor, *Report of Fray Alonso de Posada;* Bancroft also referred to Copala as being part of the supposedly mythic northern geography of New Mexico. Bancroft, *History of Arizona*, 168-73; Richie, *Spanish Relations*, 130; Joseph Sánchez, *Explorers and Traders*, 11-12, 16, *Spanish Search*, 146-48. Sánchez has suggested that Teguayo also appeared to be a myth in official Spanish thinking well into the eighteenth century. There does not, however, appear to be any evidence at all that the Spanish officials

ever considered it a myth. Quite to the contrary, Teguayo figured prominently in the intrigues between France and Spain as they involved New Spain and was discussed in depth by Father Posada under a royal command (*cédula*) of the king of Spain in 1686 because of its suspected potential importance to the Crown and known threats then being made against both it and Quivira by the French. Thomas, *Alonso de Posada Report;* Tyler and Taylor, *Report of Fray Alonso de Posada*. Also see Scholes, *Troublous Times;* Wagner, *Spanish Southwest;* M. Weber, "A Map;" Weddle, *French Thorn, Wreck of the Belle.* This subject has recently been discussed in detail and the Legend of Teguayo proven to have been no myth by Baker et al., *Juan Rivera's Colorado, 13-34.* Juan Rivera's instructions from the governor of New Mexico and other documents prove that the Spanish government did not consider the legend to be a myth. VInstructions" as reprinted in Baker, et al., *Juan Rivera's Colorado*, 298.

14. Thomas, *Alonso de Posada Report,* 42-44; Hackett, *Revolt of the Pueblo,* (II)500-06; Tyler and Taylor, *Report of Fray Alonso de Posada,* 305-06.

15. Tyler discussed the early Spanish interest in Teguayo and the unsuccessful early attempts to locate the province. Tyler, "Before Escalante."

16. Vélez Cachupín, "Instructions." This information on the early content of the legend is to be found in Father Posada's report of 1686 in Thomas, *Alonso de Posada Report,* 42-44. Also see Chávez, "Pohé-Yemós Representative."

17. Thomas, *Alonso de Posada Report.*

18. From Letters of fray Carlos Delgado as are found in the Archivo General de la Nación, Historia, Mexico City, Tomo 25; e.g. Tyler, *Before Escalante*, 326-327; Sánchez, *Explorers, Traders*, 12, *Spanish Search For*.

19. Baker et al., *Juan Rivera's Colorado*, 13-21; Lahontan, *New Voyages*, 192-95; Miera y Pacheco, *Plano Geographico de la tierra;* Bolton, *Pageant in the Wilderness;* Chávez and Warner, *Domínguez Escalante Expedition.*

20. Baker et al., 13-21; Vélez Cachupín, "Instructions." In his discussion of Teguayo and Lake Copala, Sánchez, for example, stated that the legend included a salt lake. None of the early accounts mention a salt lake. They only mention a lake. Sánchez said: "That word was Teguayo, a large area near a great salt lake associated with the mythical origins of the people of Mexico." Sánchez, *Explorers, Traders*, 5; *Spanish Search for*. It has been suggested that the Posada reference to a large lake could be the first reference to the Great Salt Lake. Thomas, *Alonso de Posada Report*: 44. It might, however, be a reference to the nearby Utah Lake. The remarks of Domínguez and Vélez de Escalante regarding the Great Salt Lake were made on September 25, 1776. Bolton, *Pageant in the Wilderness*, 186; Chávez and Warner, *Domínguez Escalante Expedition*, 61. Lahontan's discussion of a large lake of salt is obviously the first known record of the existence of the Great Salt Lake. Lahontan, *New Voyages*, 194. There is some evidence that a scouting party sent out by Dulhut in 1680 may have reached the Great Salt Lake while searching for the Western Sea and may be responsible for its discovery. Kingston "Western Sea," 134.

21. Vélez Cachupín, "Instructions;" Sánchez, *Explorers, Traders*, 5; Thomas, *Alonso de Posada Report,* 44. The remarks of Fathers Domínguez and Vélez de Escalante regarding the Great Salt Lake were made

on September 25, 1776. Bolton, *Pageant in the Wilderness*, 186; Chávez and Warner, *Domínguez Escalante Expedition,* 61; e.g. Baker, et al., *Juan Rivera's Colorado*, 13-21.

22. Tyler, *Before Escalante*, 326-327; Sánchez, *Explorers and Traders*, 12.

23. Adams, "Fray Silvestre," 99-101; Bancroft, *History of Arizona*, 166; Tyler and Taylor, *Report of Fray Alonso de Posada*, 286-87.

24. Vélez Cachupín, *Instructions*; Baker et al., *Juan Rivera's Colorado*; Rivera, "Transcripcion of the original."

25. Adams, *Fray Silvestre*, 99-101; Adams attributes this communication to a letter of August 9, 1776 from Hugo O'Conor to Viceroy Bucareli in the Archive General de la Nación, Mexico, Historia, (52), exp. 9.

26. Adams, *Fray Silvestre*, 99-101; Vélez Cachupín, *Instructions*.

27. This reference to European style clothes seems to refer to the "cut" of the clothing including the jackets, pants, and boots made of animal hides (buckskins) that they wore and does not necessarily mean they had woven textile garments as the Spaniards may have surmised. Miera y Pacheco illustrated the cut of the clothing in Figure 22. Lahontan described the clothing of the Tahuglauk like that illustrated in Figure 26 also. Lahontan, *New Voyages*, 195-96; Miera y Pacheco, *Plano Geographica*.

28. Adams cites the letter of April 1, 1775 from fray José Damián Martínez to Hugo O'Conor in the Archivo General de la Nación, Mexico, Historia, (52), exp. 9. Adams, *Fray Silvestre*, 99-101.

29. Adams, *Fray Silvestre*, 99-101

30. Fray Damián Martínez's 1775 letter to Hugo O'Conor. In E. Adams, 99-101.

31. Baker et al., *Juan Rivera's Colorado*, 24-34.

32. Rivera's trail journal specifically refers to his goal of reaching Teguayo. Rivera, "Transcripción;" Vélez Cachupín (1765) "Instructions; Baker, et al., *Juan Rivera's Colorado*, 24-34.

33. Byrkit, *Regarding the Roads*.

34. Silvestre Vélez de Escalante to Governor Pedro Fermín de Mendinueta, Santa Fe, October 28, 1775. In Thomas, *Forgotten*, 150-158.

35. Adams, *Fray Silvestre*.

36. Vélez de Escalante to Mendinueta, October 28, 1775.'s Letter of October 28, 1775 to Governor Mendinueta. Thomas, *Forgotten Frontier*, 150-58.

37. The fathers cast lots to reach a decision about turning back or proceeding on to California on October 11, 1776. Chávez and Warner, *Domínguez Escalante Expedition,* 72-73; Warner gives background information on Fathers Domínguez and Vélez de Escalante. Warner, "Editor's Introduction," xii-xix; e.g. Adams, *Fray Silvestre;* Bolton, *Pageant in the Wilderness*, 9-11; Byrkit, "Regarding the Roads;" Thomas, *Forgotten Frontier*, 150-66.

38. Baker, et al., *Juan Rivera's Colorado*, 27-34.

39. Warner discusses the fathers' failure to achieve their goal of reaching California. Warner, "Editor's Introduction," xiv. The fathers themselves discussed this in their journal from October 5 through 11, 1776. Chávez and Warner, *Domínguez Escalante Expedition,* 68-73. At the completion of their trip, the fathers wrote letter report debriefings that carefully and knowingly discussed elements of the evolved legend of Teguayo. These are critical reading in any attempt to develop a comprehensive understanding of the subject. Adams and Chávez, *Missions of New Mexico,* 283-89, 302-08; Twitchell, *Spanish Archives*, (II), 278-79; Miera y Pacheco's report was reprinted by Bolton in *Pageant in the Wilderness,* 243-52; Thomas, *Forgotten Frontier*, 150-58.

40. Montagu, *Introduction to Physical*, 495.

41. Lahontan, *New Voyages*, (II), 414.

42. Lahontan, 414-15

43. Lahontan.

44. Adams and Chávez, *Missions*, 283-89, 302-08.

45. Lahontan, *New Voyages*, 192-93.

46. Lahontan, 194; Baker, et al. *Juan Rivera's Colorado*, 240, 303.

47. Baker, et al., 240, 303; Rivera, "Transcripcion."

48. Thomas, *Alonso de Posada Report*, 42-44; Baker et al., 18.

49. Miera y Pacheco, *Plano Geographico;* Baker et al., 23.

50. Lahontan, *New Voyages*, 195-96.

51. Lahontan, 196; Fouillade, "Translation."

52. Baker et al., *Juan Rivera's Colorado*,18-21.

53. Lahontan, "Mappa del Missisip;" Lahontan, *New Voyages*, (2), 718-31.

54. Baker et al., 303.

55. Bolton, *Pageant in the Wilderness;* Chávez and Warner, *Domínguez Escalante Expedition.*

56. Domínguez, *Missions;* Adams and Chávez, *Missions;* Baker et al., *Juan Rivera's Colorado*, 12-27.

57. Chávez and Warner, *Domínguez Escalante Expedition*, 60.

58. Chávez and Warner, 63.

59. Chávez and Warner, 64.

60. Chávez and Warner, 66.

61. Domínguez, *Missions*. Adams and Chávez, *Missions.*

62. A detailed, and tightly documented scholarly memorandum on the history and nature of Capuchin beards was kindly prepared as a personal e-mail communication to Steven Baker in October, 2004 by Bro. Patrick McSherry, OFM Cap., the archivist for the Capuchin Provincial Archives in Detroit, Michigan. That document is the basis of the summary statement given herein regarding the *barbas longas*. Fowler and Fowler illustrate the bearded Indians encountered by the Powell Expedition, *Anthropology of the Numa*, 53, 74; Sánchez discusses those encountered by Father Garcés. Sánchez, *Explorers and Traders*, 48.

63. Domínguez, *Missions*. Adams and Chávez, *Missions.*

64. Vélez de Escalante letter of October 28, 1775 to governor Mendinueta reprinted in Baker et al., *Juan Rivera's Colorado*, 26; Thomas, *Forgotten Frontiers*.

65. Chávez and Warner, *Domínguez Escalante Expedition,* 70-73; Warner, "Editor's Introduction;" xiv. Adams and Chávez, *Missions*, 283-289, 302-08.

66. Chávez and Warner, *Domínguez Escalante Expedition,* 70-73; Warner, xiv; Adams and Chávez, 283-289, 302-08.

67. Birdsell, *Problem*, 1-68.

68. Ishida, *Ancient People*, 52-56.

69. Fitzhugh and Dubreuil, *AINU*.

70. e.g.Ishida, *Ancient People*, 53. Ohnuki-Tierney, *Ainu*, 1-5.

71. Fowler and Fowler, *Anthropology of the Numa*, 74.

72. Owsley and Jantz, *Kennewick Man.*

11

• THE PEOPLE OF TEGUAYO AND MOZEEMLEK: POSSIBLE CONNECTIONS TO AN ANCIENT PALEOAMERICAN COASTAL POPULATION •

by

GEORGE W. GILL

This chapter considers the reality and importance of the early physical descriptions of the mysterious European-looking bearded men from the region known variously as Teguayo, Mozeemlek, and/or Tahuglauk. The most current evidence for suggesting possible connections between these documented peoples and ancient Paleoamerican populations from the western Great Plains of North America is discussed from the perspective of biological anthropologists.[1]

Recent research has established that in 1765 New Mexico governor, Tomás Vélez Cachupín, sent the two exploratory expeditions, previously discussed in chapter 10 and led by Juan Antonio María de Rivera, northward from Santa Fe into the then unexplored regions of what is now the western slope of Colorado.[2] The governor's main purpose in sending these was to search for the Colorado River and to learn what Native peoples were located beyond it.[3] More specifically, the peoples of primary interest were the ones living in the province—to that point unexplored—known to the Natives and Spaniards of New Mexico as "*El Gran Teguayo*" (The Great Teguayo). This was located (Figure 27) at least in part in present-day Utah. Rivera was also to determine the veracity of two specific things purportedly located within that unexplored part of the American west: 1) sources of minable silver and 2) unusually heavily bearded Native inhabitants of Teguayo. The interest in Teguayo centered on reports by Natives that some of its bearded male inhabitants looked more like Europeans than the Natives of New Mexico.[4]

Juan Rivera never reached Teguayo, but the legends of the bearded men that he heard about on his trips and retold in New Mexico apparently provided part of the justification for a subsequent trip northward by the Fanciscan Fathers Domínguez and Vélez de Escalante.[5] They reached Teguayo in 1776 and met and described the unusual bearded men living there.[6] In the late 1680s the baron Lahontan had added elements to the legend of Teguayo through his travels on the Long River.[7] In 1689 when he was on the Platte River with the Plains Apaches (Gnacsitares), the baron met and interviewed four heavily bearded Native captives they were holding.

These men had been captured, according to the Apaches, from a remote people living near a large salt lake far to the west of the Platte on the other side of a large mountain range. Their home in that region was known to them and the Apaches as the land of Mozeemlek. It was near another land known as Tahuglauk, also near the salt lake, where other heavily bearded men also lived. Puzzled by the bearded men, Silvestre Vélez de Escalante raised the question with his superiors whether these Natives could have been the descendants of Europeans and Natives.[8] Biological anthropologists and archaeologists are continuing to shed more and more light on this issue. The current consensus is that there is a greater likelihood the bearded Natives derive from Caucasian-looking Paleoamericans and their descendants known to have been present in North America thousands of years ago than from more recent intrusive populations, such as shipwrecked Europeans.[9]

Paleoamerican Skeletal Features: Comparisons and Contrasts

The skeletons of the earliest inhabitants of the Americas, known as Paleoindians or Paleoamericans, differ noticeably from most skeletons from later periods. Some of the first physical anthropologists to examine samples of early American skeletons noticed these contrasts. Spencer and Jennings have pointed out that J. B. Birdsell, the well-known physical anthropologist from the 1950s, 60s and 70s, referred to the overall pattern of Paleoindian traits as "vaguely Caucasoid." Steele and Powell reached the same conclusion in the early 1990s in their systematic study of available Paleoindian remains.[10]

Late Pleistocene populations of northwestern China (Upper Cave Zhoukoudian) also exhibit this same, vaguely Caucasoid pattern of skeletal traits as do existing cranial series of eastern Polynesians (and other remote Polynesians) and the Ainu of northern Japan.[11] Both the Ainu and the Polynesians are populations of continental Asiatic origin, but from coastal regions. They have largely escaped the most recent waves of population movement and gene flow out of interior East Asia.[12]

The craniofacial trait complex of most populations of late prehistoric and protohistoric American Natives, on the other hand, is clearly not Caucasoid-like, and in fact reflects clearly what skeletal biologists refer to as the "Mongoloid craniofacial trait complex." This trait complex consists of robust, shovel-shaped incisor teeth; heavy mandibles with blunt, median chins; wide cheekbones (flaring zygomatic arches) with angled zygomaticomaxillary sutures; short elliptic palates with straight palatine sutures; and reduced nasal bridges (low interorbital projection).[13] In the case of East Asians, this complex also includes a high-vaulted, brachycranic skull form. These dimensions produce the distinctive high, rounded, "globular" cranial form of most modern East Asians. This head form is not found in American Native populations. The cranial vault height in the case of most late period American Native populations is low, and the head shape tends more often to be medium (mesocranic).[14] American Natives (esp. males) also reveal much more frequently a distinctive concavo-convex nasal profile than do the East Asians, who more often show a concave nasal profile. The concave nasal profile is common within all Mongoloid populations; the concavo-convex occurs less often in most groups, at least in East Asia.

The soft tissue features that accompany these skeletal features consist of straight, black hair (thick, round cross-section), medium to light brown skin pigmentation, dark eyes, and varying degrees of an internal epicanthus (eye fold). The latter, the internal epicanthus, which produces the distinctive "almond eye" shape common to nearly all East Asian individuals (sometimes extreme in development) is less extreme and less common (sometimes totally lacking) within the American Native populations. Native males (unmixed) tend to lack facial hair, and body hair is not heavy.

The Caucasoid craniofacial trait complex differs significantly from the Mongoloid complex. Cheekbones are more modest, without the flaring, curved zygomatic arches of the Mongoloid peoples, and the zygomaticomaxillary sutures are curved not angled.[15] Palates are parabolic in form, not elliptic, and instead of a straight palatine suture almost always show a distinctive jagged palatine suture.[16] The parabolic palates of some whites are so narrow anteriorly as to be termed "triangular" in form by some researchers.[17] Mandibles are slender with a prominent, often bilateral chin.[18] Incisor teeth are rarely shovel-shaped (less than 10% among Europeans as opposed to 98% within American Native groups).

Most distinctive among whites (at least western Europeans and their relatives) is a high- bridged nose, often narrow with a quite sharp nasal sill, which is the lower margin of the nasal aperture. The overall interorbital projection is high.[19] This interorbital shape alone distinguishes 90% of whites from members of all other human populations.[20] Skulls are large with a high cranial vault and tend to be either long and narrow (dolichocranic) or medium (mesocranic) in overall form.[21]

The soft tissue characteristics that accompany the Caucasoid craniofacial skeletal trait complex are relatively fine hair (oval in cross-section) that is often wavy and light in pigmentation, well-developed male beards (sometimes heavy), and light skin pigmentation. Also, eye color is sometimes hazel or blue instead of brown.

Turning now to the skeletal traits of the Paleoamericans, as mentioned before, an important level of contrast is found between these most ancient Americans and their late prehistoric descendants. The Paleoindian pattern of craniofacial traits, described by Howells as "archaic," consists of a number of Caucasoid-like traits, a few common to the Mongoloid complex and some that are absent from both the modern Caucasoid and modern Mongoloid trait complexes.[22]

The Paleoamerican skeletal characteristics that persist, and therefore are also common to later American Native groups, are robust shovel-shaped incisor teeth and occasionally robust mandibles. Also, sometimes a slightly elliptic palate occurs on certain Paleoamerican skeletons rather than a parabolic one. Additionally, interorbital projection sometimes falls slightly into the "non-white" sector, as in the case of Kennewick Man.[23] Those Paleoindian traits that normally fall closer to the Europeans and US whites than to the late American Indians are high-vaulted skulls, long, narrow (dolichocranic) crania modest cheek bones and slender mandibles with prominent, bilateral chins.[24]

A characteristic that is very common to Paleoamericans and yet quite rare among late American Natives and almost totally lacking among whites is the dull (or "blurred") nasal sill. Whites nearly always reveal a quite sharp nasal sill, and late American Indians have a very medium one. The modern populations that show dull nasal sills in combination with fairly prominent nasal bridges and occasionally even prominent nasal spines, like the Paleoamericans, are the Polynesians and Ainu.[25] Most Polynesians and the Ainu also possess long, high-vaulted skulls like the Paleoindians and the whites. The closest modern populations in overall appearance, to Paleoamericans are Polynesians and the Ainu of northern Japan.[26]

A look at the soft tissue traits of the contact period Ainu and East Polynesians, such as the Easter Islanders, is particularly important to the central focus of this chapter, namely the possible origins of the Teguayo inhabitants. Early contact period accounts are more appropriate than later ones since they largely avoid the physical alterations brought about by genetic admixture with other groups after contact. Observations and photographs of the Ainu people (Figure 32) at the time of early contact show a people with Caucasian-like facial features, light skin, and wavy hair. Heavy male beards and body hair are likewise noted and amply illustrated in the early photographs. The earliest European explorers noted similar traits on Easter Island. Even though skin color was variable on Easter Island, many inhabitants had light skin and European-like facial features. Male Individuals showed full beards. These traits were quite surprising to explorers who had seen South American Natives and central Polynesians but had not yet observed the more Caucasian-like natives of Easter Island.

Temporal Continuity of Paleoamerican Skeletal Traits

It is pertinent to question just how long and how well Caucasoid-like traits of Paleoindians can be tracked within western North America. In one rather well-studied region, the northwestern Plains, clear evidence exists for a period of temporal continuity of thousands of years for these skeletal traits. Pertinent portions of the skeletal record within the northwestern Plains are presented to demonstrate the patterns of both continuity and change. The focus of this section is largely on this region of the west since co-author George Gill's bioarchaeological studies and many of his skeletal biology studies in North America have centered within that area of the Great Plains. As the biological anthropologist on this project, Gill's skeletal database from within the US is also drawn largely from that region. Figure 12 shows the location of the northwestern Plains area as relied upon by Gill and Weathermon.[27] This is essentially the same definition presented by Frison.[28]

32. 1871 photo of an Ainu man from the Japanese island of Hokkaido showing certain Caucasian-like facial features which, along with his dress and accoutrements, compare quite favorably with the men from Teguayo shown by Miera y Pacheco in Figure 28, courtesy C. A. Longfellow Papers, Longfellow House-Washington's Headquarters National Historic Site, Cambridge, US public domain.

Evidence presented here shows that by late prehistoric times within the Northwestern Plains area, the "archaic" skeletal traits disappear. None of the late populations seem to retain that full complex of skeletal traits so common among earlier populations.[29] At least no skeletal samples discovered so far from the late temporal periods of the northwestern Plains show these traits so common to the earlier periods. Utilizing much larger samples over a wide area of North America, Jantz and Owsley and others have found similar dramatic changes from skeletal populations spanning these time periods.[30] As stated over a decade ago, by Late Prehistoric times (300-1,500 BP) in the Northwestern Plains, there were no individuals remaining with the complex of skeletal traits exhibited by certain Paleoindians such as Spirit Cave Man of Nevada and Kennewick Man.[31] By that time, at least within the northwestern Plains area, these "ancient ones" with their Caucasoid looks, were completely replaced by people with low-vaulted, shorter skulls; heavy jaws with blunt rounded chins; and robust, forward projecting cheekbones. These "new people" also possessed (as do their modern East Asian cousins and contemporary American Native descendants), "short, often elliptic palates (with straight palatine sutures), widely divergent 'angled' zygomaticomaxillary suture lines, a complete lack of nasion depression (producing a smooth nasal root), medium nasal sills (and spines), and very robust shovel-shaped anterior teeth oriented with a more vertical edge-edge occlusion".[32]

A look at some specific northwestern Plains skeletal samples from that long period of time between the Paleoamericans and the late prehistoric populations provides important information regarding the slow and uneven pattern of change involved. First, very few specimens from the northwestern Plains currently exist from that all-important, earliest temporal zone, the Paleoindian period (7,500-12,000 BP). The Anzik site from Park County, Montana, is one. It consists of subadult human remains associated with Clovis projectile points and has been described by Owsley and Hunt and dated to 11,000 BP.[33] The Gordon Creek burial site is another. This site on the northern Colorado border, south of Laramie, Wyoming, contained the well-preserved remains of an adult female and is dated at 9,550 BP.[34] These two sites provide the only Paleoamerican skeletal samples to date from this vast region of the American west.

The Anzik site contains only fragmentary skeletal remains that, even though suggestive of a long-headed Paleoamerican morphology, contains insufficient material to be definitive as to overall appearance. The Gordon Creek female, however, is well preserved. This skeleton reveals a morphological pattern divergent from that exhibited by Spirit Cave Man and Kennewick Man, more in the direction of the trait patterns found in the Late Prehistoric and Protohistoric periods. A similar dichotomy is seen between certain Paleoamerican skeletons in the Great Basin area. Spirit Cave Man from western Nevada (9,400 BP) shows the Caucasoid-like trait pattern described above, and yet Wizard's Beach Man, also from western Nevada (9,200 BP), shows a craniofacial pattern of traits more like that found with the later groups (i.e. the basic Mongoloid craniofacial trait complex).

To explain these differences between Paleoamerican skeletons, some bioanthropology researchers postulate separate settlement routes by different early populations, one by sea along the Pacific coast and the other by land over the Bering land bridge.[35] Others favor a single, highly variable population entering the Americas over the land bridge, as postulated in the traditional settlement model.[36] The "two wave" hypothesis (both sea route and land bridge route) is gaining support among skeletal biologists based upon both craniometrics and analysis of forensic-style non-metric cranial trait complexes combined with mid-facial metrics as well as some DNA results. Recent archaeological findings supporting a very early connection between coastal California and coastal East Asia (Jomon/Japan) have likewise been reported.[37]

Additional northwestern Plains skeletal remains occur later in the Early Plains Archaic, at just over 7,200 BP. Fragmentary remains of adult females come from two sites: the Stud Horse Butte/J.

David Love site in southwestern Wyoming and the Smilden-Rostberg site in northern North Dakota.[38] Both are fragmentary and provide little for analysis regarding population traits. The Smilden-Rostberg remains, however, which consist of only an anterior maxillary fragment (with the nasal sill and several teeth) shows two important traits: a great amount of alveolar prognathism (projection of the mouth area) and a dull nasal sill. These are traits common to Paleoamericans and some later Plains Archaic skeletons. A well-preserved Early Plains Archaic male from the Dunlap-McMurry burial site is available but has never been fully described regarding population traits. A Middle Archaic skeleton from western Nebraska, the Sydney burial (3,910 BP) is fragmentary but reflects the Paleoamerican pattern of Spirit Cave Man and Kennewick Man.[39]

Many more burials are available from the Late Plains Archaic/Plains Woodland period (1,000-3,000 BP) than from these earlier periods. This is assumed to be due to increasing human numbers.[40] Scheiber lists 21 Late Plains Archaic burial sites from the northwestern Plains region with 25 individuals represented from them and 19 sites from the temporally overlapping Plains Woodland with 123 individuals represented. Most Plains Woodland sites contain multiple burials, occasionally in burial mounds, and even though some may contain over 30 individuals, as Scheiber pointed out, most contain fewer than 10.[41]

The largest Woodland mound discovered in Wyoming is at the Huntley site in the extreme southeastern corner of the state. This large mound, which contained from 19 to 30 individuals, was looted by souvenir hunters immediately following its discovery in 1963. Gill eventually described the few complete or nearly complete crania from that site that were salvaged for study, the Huntley remains and the Willson cranium. Radiocarbon dates were obtained for two well-preserved adults, the Huntley female (1,705 ± 50 BP) and the Willson male (2,090 ± 40 BP). The skeletons from this site are quite valuable due to the large number of Paleoamerican skeletal traits they exhibit.[42]

The Harlan County Lake skeleton from central Nebraska is another Archaic period skeleton from the region with many of the same Caucasoid-like characteristics common in Paleoamerican and Huntley/Willson specimens.[43] As mentioned before, "This well-preserved skeleton shows such strongly developed Caucasoid skeletal trait patterns that it was first thought to be a white fur trapper interred intrusively into more ancient deposits."[44]

A well-preserved Late Plains Archaic skeleton from southwest Wyoming, the Boar's Tusk male (2,480 ± 110 BP), does not show the Caucasoid-like trait pattern common to other Archaic skeletons and to Spirit Cave and Kennewick Man. Like the Wizard's Beach and Gordon Creek Paleoindians, the Boar's Tusk male reflects instead the Mongoloid craniofacial trait complex. Therefore, it is clear that in this region of the West the same physical diversity that can be documented among the earliest Americans continues at least through the Early, Middle and Late Plains Archaic. Another way to state this from the evidence presented here is that the same high level of expression of the Caucasoid-like trait complex documented among the Paleoamericans continues throughout the entire 6,000 years of the Plains Archaic, at least within the northwestern Plains area. In the nearby region known at the time of Spanish contact as Teguayo, perhaps just west of the northwestern Plains (in the great Salt Lake region) could this complex of traits have persisted as well, but lasted a few centuries longer?

Concluding Thoughts

The answer to the above question is, of course, yes. To state that question another way: Could a complex of ancient, archaic craniofacial characteristics, which includes several Caucasian-like features, that survived very well for at least 6,000 years after the Paleoindian period within the northwestern Plains, have survived another 1,200 years in a region just to the west? A more appropriate question might be: How did these traits not survive into late prehistory in the northwestern Plains and so many other areas of North America? This is especially true now that we know how widespread and long lasting the earlier trait pattern was during the Plains Archaic. This question has been pondered especially for the northwestern Plains area by Jantz regarding the changes in cranial vault height, by Gill and Deeds in reference to the dramatic changes in the nasal sill, and Gill regarding the sudden appearance of several other important morphological characteristics of the "Mongoloid skeletal trait complex."[45]

Although biological anthropologists have concluded that migration from more northerly latitudes occurred, with subsequent gene flow, some genetic swamping and perhaps even occasionally some total replacement, selection may have likewise played a role in this transformation. Scheiber's work supports the concept of new people arriving in the northwestern Plains in large numbers with a new way of life (probably bow and arrow technology) producing a dramatic increase in conflict.[46] This is evidenced by a significant increase in projectile point injuries to the skeleton, as well as a fifteen-year decrease in longevity from Archaic to Late Prehistoric times. Evidence for a shift in diet also exists, from a high frequency of dental caries in the Archaic (substantial carbohydrate level) to a lower frequency in the Late Prehistoric, suggesting an increase in the consumption of meat.[47]

The exact reasons for these sudden changes physically from Archaic to Late Prehistoric times are much less important here than the fact that they happened, and that could not be clearer from the skeletal record. Furthermore, these changes happened within such a brief span of time and within such a recent time frame that it leaves open the good possibility that certain places, like Teguayo, could have missed the changes entirely.

It must be said that nothing presented in this chapter rules out the possibility that shipwrecked European explorers mixing with an indigenous population(s) might account for the existence of the bearded men of Teguayo or Moozemlek. Yet, the evidence presented here does open wide the possibility that the bearded men of Teguayo represented, "descendants of the documented, very ancient American Natives of a Caucasian-looking strain like the highly publicized Kennewick Man."[48]

Notes:

1. Gill, "Northwestern Plains;" "Morphological Features;" "East Polynesian."

2. Baker et al., *Juan Rivera's Colorado*.

3. Cachupín, "Instructions."

4. Baker et al., *Juan Rivera's Colorado*, 14.

5. Baker et al.

6. Baker et al., 14; Bolton, *Pageant in the Wilderness;* Chávez and Warner, *Domínguez and Escalante Expedition*.

7. Lahontan, *New Voyages*.

8. Vélez de Escalante, Letter to Governor Mendinueta, Oct. 28, 1775. In Baker et al., 26, from Thomas, *Forgotten Frontiers*, 150-58.

9. Baker, et al., *Juan Rivera's Colorado*, 28, 34-48n.

10. Spencer and Jennings, *Native Americans;* Birdsell, "Problem of;" Steele and Powell, "Peopling."

11. Brace et. al., "Ainu and Jōmon;" Gill, "Basic Skeletal Morphology;" "Morphological Features;" "East Polynesian;" Jantz and Owsley, "Circumpacific Populations;" Jantz and Spradley, "Cranial morphometric evidence;" Brace et. al. "Ainu and Jōmon;" Gill, "Basic Skeletal Morphology;" "Morphological Features."

Gill, "Basic Skeletal Morphology;" "East Polynesian;" "Jantz and Spradley, "Cranial morphometric evidence;" Powell and Rose, "Report on the Osteological Assessment."

12. Gill, "Basic Skeletal Morphology;" "East Polynesian;" Jantz and Spradley, "Cranial morphometric evidence;" Powell and Rose, "Report on the Osteological Assessment."

13. Bass, *Human Osteology;* Byers, *Introduction to Forensic;* Gill, "Craniofacial Criteria;" Rhine, "Non-Metric Skull Racing;" White et. al., *Human Osteology.*

14. Gill, "Craniofacial Criteria."

15. Gill.

16. Gill.

17. Byers, *Introduction to Forensic;* Rhine, "Non-Metric Skull Racing."

18. Bass, *Human Osteology;* Gill, "Craniofacial Criteria;" Rhine, "Non-Metric Skull Racing."

19. Gill et al., "Racial Identification;" Gill and Gilbert, "Race Identification."

20. Bass, *Human Osteology;* Byers, *Introduction to Forensic;* Gill et al., "Racial Identification;" Gill, "Craniofacial Criteria."

21. Howells, *Cranial Variation;* Jantz and Owsley, "Circumpacific Populations."

22. Howells, "Crania from Wyoming."

23. Gill, "Morphological Features."

24. Jantz and Owsley. "Circumpacific Populations;" Gill, "Appearance;" "Morphological Features."

25. Gill, "Morphological Features;" "East Polynesian."

26. Brace et. al., "Ainu and Jōmon;" Gill, "Morphological Features;" "East Polynesian;" Jantz and Spradley, "Cranial morphometric."

27. Gill and Weathermon, *Skeletal Biology.*

28. Frison, *Prehistoric Hunters,* 1-2.

29. Gill, "Appearance of the;" Stuart and Gill, "Northwestern Plains Indian."

30. Jantz and Owsley, "Variation Among;" "Circumpacific Populations."

31. Gill, "Appearance," 263-65.

32. Gill, 264.

33. Owsley and Hunt, "Clovis and Early Archaic."

34. Breternitz et al., "An Early Burial."

35. Gill, "Basic Skeletal Morphology;" "East Polynesian;" Jantz and Owsley, "Variation Among;" Jantz and Spradley, "Cranial morphometric."

36. Powell and Rose, *"Report on the Osteological."*

37. Brace et al., "Ainu and Jōmon;" Jantz and Owsley, "Variation Among;" Jantz and Spradley, "Cranial morphometric;" Gill, "Basic Skeletal Morphology;" "Morphological Features;" "East Polynesian;" Perego et al., "Distinctive Paleo-Indian;" Erlandson, "From Coast to Coast."

38. Gill, "Appearance," 533.

39. Lovvorn et al., "Microevolution."

40. Gill, "Advances in Northwestern."

41. Scheiber, "Life and Death."

42. Gill, "Northwestern Plains."

43. Baker, "Osteological Analysis;" Gill, "Human Skeletal Remains."

44. Gill, "Northwestern Plains," 241.

45. Jantz, "Temporal and Geographic;" Gill and Deeds, "Temporal Changes;" Gill, "Appearance."

46. Scheiber and Gill, "Bioarchaeology of the;" Scheiber, "Life and Death."

47. Zitt, *Prehistoric and Early Historic*.

48. Baker et al., *Juan Rivera's Colorado*, 23.

12

•LILLIPUTIANS AND BROBDINGNAGIANS OR TYPICAL MISSISSIPPIAN BEHAVIORS? •

by

STEVEN G. BAKER AND W. RAYMOND WOOD

Doubts about the veracity of Lahontan's narrative were compounded by his critics' lack of knowledge about the North American Natives. They believed his descriptions of those he encountered were of unrealistic, exotic, fanciful, behaviors and physical appearances. Some critics believed these people were completely fictional, only conjured up by the baron, perhaps just to help him sell books. Some of the primary critics who voiced such observations included Adams, Parkman, Roy, Sayre, DeVoto, and Thwaites. Some equated the peoples about whom the baron wrote to have been "Byzantine" and the inspiration for the wholly fictional *Lilliputians* and *Brobdingnagians* invented by the Irish author, Jonathon Swift, in *Gulliver's Travels.*[1]

The complex Native cultures the baron observed and described contrasted sharply with those of the Canadian Natives. The Native peoples his critics were familiar with by the time they observed them and then wrote had changed and exhibited much less sophisticated profiles than those Lahontan met along the more distant waters he traveled. They were the only Native cultures they knew.[2] Those critics could neither begin to envision how highly developed some Native cultures had once been nor how much and how fast their post-contact experiences had altered them. Their alterations had led them into declines so severe that the connections between the mound-building Mississippian peoples and the Natives with which his critics were familiar were lost and only started being understood in the latter nineteenth century.[3] Lahontan's critics could, therefore, not believe that people whom they considered to be their racial inferiors could have been the mound builders. These peoples had essentially left their mounds over a large portion of the Mississippi drainage. For the most part, they collectively lumped all the things the baron described as "humbug."

The degrees to which core elements of Native cultures evolved in post-contact times ranged greatly. Key attributes of such cultures can include the preservation of many core cultural traditions and particularly the retention of past political and economic autonomy. Once these elements were lost, cultures withered and generally faded away until they no longer resembled what they once were. Thus, by the time most of them began writing in the nineteenth century, Lahontan's critics were only familiar with Natives who had been in post-contact modes for many generations or had even lost their core cultural traditions and autonomy. By that time their cultures bore little resemblance to those the baron had observed at first contact.[4]

Francis Parkman, who exemplified these Victorian era critics, stated that the baron's Natives of the Long River "are as real as the nations visited by Captain Gulliver." He offered no obvious justification for his opinion.[5] Adams, who, along with Sayres, wrote in the twentieth century still spoke only of the "curious tribes of Indians" Lahontan wrote about. Adams took his lead from the earlier writers and even questioned the baron's account of the Essanape leader.[6] Although he did not elaborate, Thwaites also compared Lahontan's "fantastic" Natives to Swift's characters: "May one not see in this an anticipation of Swift, in his more famous *Gulliver's Travels*, and recognize in Lahontan's fantastic Eokoros, Essanapes, etc., the predecessors if not the prototypes of Lilliputians and Brobdingnagians?"[7]

With the growth of modern ethnographic knowledge, such views are now obviously and totally groundless as reasons to distrust the baron's narrative. Before the rise of archaeological knowledge which settled the question of who the Moundbuilders had been, some of the baron's older critics might be excused from having relied upon such views as reason to doubt him. Today, any attempt to rely on such outdated views to justify condemnation of Lahontan's narrative, however, betrays an astounding lack of information about America's Natives. Almost everything the baron described relative to the peoples he met on the Long River is wholly in keeping with what ethnographers know was there or should anticipate having been present in his day.

More specifically, the behaviors the baron described are fundamental ones known to have been practiced by the leaders among Native peoples from those societies that were once part of or otherwise influenced by the prehistoric, theocratically focused Mississippian "chiefdoms." Chiefdoms were "ranked" societies characterized by ruling elite chiefs ("Suns") with great power over subordinate elements of their populaces. Native behaviors demonstrating strong elements of dominance and subordination were commonplace in Lahontan's narrative with evidence of respect for, deference to, and veneration of ranking nobility. The baron routinely and primarily interacted with the ruling elites of the people he met and described. The behaviors he witnessed were thus those of such highly ranked individuals or their subjects' behaviors toward them.

One of the most blatant, and only specifically noted, examples of the lack of elementary ethnographic knowledge by one of the baron's past critics, and one that completely negates that criticism, was provided in Percy G. Adams's *Travelers and Travel Liars*.[8] Adams disparagingly judged Lahontan's description of the Essanapes' custom of strewing leaves along the path ahead of their chieftain (a Sun ?) and at times having six subordinates carry him on a litter. Adams stated that "such practices, much more appropriate for an Eastern potentate, were of course unknown among the red men of America." Bernard DeVoto referred to these cultures as Byzantine.[9]

Adams obviously was not consulting with ethnographers and was totally unfamiliar with the prehistoric and early historic Mississippian societies of the Southeastern and Midwestern US. The Mississippians commonly carried their leaders (Suns) or other nobles, on litters.[10] The present authors are personally acquainted with at least six well-documented examples of such behaviors by American Natives. Smith and Halley list even more.[11] One of these from the early eighteenth century is an example from the Natchez people of the lower Mississippi Valley as illustrated in Figure 33. The man who left us the image was an early eyewitness who reported:

> On the feast-day the whole nation set out from their village at sunrising, leaving behind only the aged and infirm that are not about to travel, and a few warriors, who are to carry the Great Sun on a litter upon their shoulders. The seat of this litter is covered with several deer skins, and to its four sides are fastened four bars which cross each other, and are supported by eight men, at every hundred paces transfer their burden to eight other men, and thus successively transport it to the place where the feast is celebrated...[12]

Lahontan's description of the use of litters for carrying the Essanape chieftain stated:

> I cannot but acquaint you in this place, that the higher I went up the River, I met with more discretion from the Savages. But in the mean time I must not take leave of the last Village, without giving some account of it. 'Tis bigger than all the rest, and is the Residence of the Great Commander or Generalissimo, whose Apartment is built by it self towards the side of the Lake, and surrounded with fifty other Apartments, in which all his Relations are lodg'd. When he walks, his way is strow'd with the leaves of Trees: But commonly he is carry'd by six Slaves. His Royal Robes are of the same Magnificence with those of the Commander of the Okoros: For he is naked all over, excepting his lower parts, which are cover'd with a large Scarf made of the barks of Trees.[13]

33. Early eighteenth-century image of the Great Sun leader of the Natchez People of Louisiana, one of the best documented Mississippian chiefdoms, being ceremoniously carried on a litter, as was common, to the Harvest Feast. The Sun is wearing a feather crown while seated on a litter covered with deer skins with painted designs and with its back covered with leaves and flowers from Du Pratz, 1774, US public domain.

When the Spaniards began visiting the coast of the Carolinas in the 1500s they were in contact with Mississippian people from the province known as Duhare, which was ruled by a so-called tall "king" known as "Datha." The historian, Peter Martyr de Angherra, reported that early witnesses stated that Datha was carried about on a litter.[14] Another well-known example of such a custom is also from South Carolina and the Mississippian chiefdom known as "Cofitachique."[15] When the Soto entrada entered that province, it was met by a noble female emissary of the paramount "lady of Cofitachique." That emissary was carried on a litter when she went to greet the Spaniards, as were the principal chiefs of the Tascalusa and the Coosa of Alabama later in the Spaniards' travels.[16] Among anthropologists it is thus common knowledge that chieftains and other nobles were still being carried about on litters within the cultural sphere of the Mississippians during the early contact era.[17] Although the practice quickly died away in the post-contact era, in Mississippian ceremonials it was as a sign of deference to, and veneration of, nobility.

The baron was obviously intrigued about the sociopolitical structures and their associated ceremonial behaviors and rituals, particularly those related to highly ranked chieftains' greetings of guests. He devoted a considerable amount of space to the matter but was unable to come to any real conclusions about them, although he spoke of "chiefs, generalissimos, rulers, kings." Like the baron, many early explorers struggled to find the best words to describe persons of authority among the Natives and the structures of their authority. Lahontan's narrative is still filled with descriptors relating to comparative power, dominance, and authority as well as subservience, submissiveness, and veneration among the peoples he encountered on the Long River. This was particularly the case with respect to the way their leaders greeted their French guests or attended their own nobility within what are suggestive of ritualistic, though perhaps attenuated, Mississippian protocols.[18]

The ranked Mississippian-like societies on the Long River were complex and had likely evolved to become chiefdoms. Chiefdoms, including Cahokia, sometime evolved to become incipient states in various areas of the world and not just North America. It is believed useful to here summarize these societies, as well known to anthropologists, but not necessarily to all readers, such as obviously including most of Lahontan's past critics.[19]

The Prehistoric Mississippian Cultures and Chiefdoms

In anthropological terms, "Mississippian" refers to a widespread and sophisticated mound building Native American civilization that archeologists have traditionally dated from about 800 to 1600CE. This larger Mississippian culture sphere was composed of a series of many urban settlements with satellite villages linked by trade, religion, and a variety of other networks. The largest Mississippian city north of Mexico was Cahokia in the American Bottoms along the Mississippi River in Illinois near St. Louis, Missouri, opposite the mouth of the Missouri River. (Figure 21)

The Mississippian civilization flourished from the southern shores of the Great Lakes in western New York and western Pennsylvania and the present-day eastern Midwest. From there it extended to the south and southwest into the lower Mississippi Valley and then easterly around the southern portion of the Appalachian Mountains and through the Southeastern US, the region from where it is probably best known. It also spread westward and northwestward up the Missouri River and other tributaries of the Mississippi. The baron's narrative suggests that elements of it may even have still been present in 1688 among the Essanapes along the Platte River.[20]

Cahokia and the surrounding area contained many large mounds and is believed to have been a major sociopolitical and religious center with strong influences over a vast region.[21] Hernando de Soto explored much of the Mississippian cultural sphere when he traveled through the Southeastern US in 1539-43. Although he did not visit Cahokia, he found that many of the other Mississippian communities were by then either no longer functioning or were in decline.[22] Several obvious traits characterize Mississippian culture, including the construction of large, truncated, earthen, pyramidal or platform mounds, which commonly were the special locations of the houses of nobility/elites, temples, and ossuaries.

Mississippian civilization was rooted in intensive agriculture, which emphasized growing corn, beans, and squash. This helped to support large populations and craft specializations. The civilization had wide-ranging trade networks extending over much of North America. It was a ranked society with institutionalized social inequality and complexity that evolved to at least the chiefdom level and in cases perhaps even to that of incipient city states, as possibly existed at Cahokia. A combination of centralized political and religious power was invested in venerated noble theocratic individuals and kin groups who held high degrees of power and authority over most of the populations. There was a hierarchical settlement system within which there were obvious mounds if the settlements had been in existence long enough for them to have been constructed.[23] Such centers, through their ruling elites, exerted influence and/or control over smaller communities from which they are thought to have commonly extracted tribute, often through military might and/or religion.

Some of the chiefdoms became so large and took in so much area and so many people that they are referred to as "paramount chiefdoms." The Mississippians commonly practiced ancestor worship as a central part of their ideology and participated in the "Southeastern Ceremonial Complex"/ "SECC") or "Southern Cult" and made and used its elaborate artistic paraphernalia.[24] Chiefdom were not necessarily permanent socio-political structures. One, such as a paramount one, might at a point in time enfold several smaller polities organized at a localized smaller scale from a wide area but still individually structured as chiefdoms. Such entities might decide that they wished to depart from the larger structure and, unless the larger one could, by military action, or otherwise, entice them back into the fold, part of the larger structure might be lost. Thus, their size could wax and wane through time.

The Greater Chiefdom of Cofitachique survived long enough to be documented and was determined from multiple lines of evidence to have taken in people and territory from much of both North and South Carolina.[25] In the case of the paramount chiefdom or incipient state of Cahokia, as a great prehistoric urban center, it should have had a very wide-ranging influence, if not control, over diverse people and their cultures and territories. Since it was seemingly failing and somewhat depopulated prior to being historically documented, the maximum extent of its reach cannot be determined. Lahontan's Long River narrative suggests, but does not prove, that some of the peoples he encountered, such as the Essanapes, may once have been under the influence, if not control of Cahokia. The Essanapes might just have once been a remnant component of the larger chiefdom before its obvious collapse.

Mississippian societies were evolving toward the chiefdom stage of sociopolitical development after about 1000CE. They were politically centralized and could be composed of multiple polities. Within these polities there was an emphasis on social ranking of individuals, largely through kinship. The keys to understanding Mississippian chiefdoms include the following salient elements.[26] Communities within a chiefdom were under the control, generally believed to have been absolute, of a hierarchy of single leadership. A male usually stood at the apex of this hierarchy, although women are known to have also occupied that position. This individual was thought by his or her subjects to be semi-divine and typically believed to be a direct descendant of the Sun. They were, accordingly, referred to as "Suns" or even "great Suns."[27]

Belief in the divinity of the Sun was reinforced by a cult of ancestor worship. Within this the direct ancestors of the individual or other nobles were highly venerated, and in at least some cases their physical remains were preserved in special ossuaries. Elaborate sumptuary rules based on ancestry governed this aspect of the culture and separated the Suns from the rest of the chiefdom's populace.

The Sun and his kinsmen and their noble ranks were determined by genealogical proximity to the Sun's direct lineage. These people held superordinate rank and status over the commoners within a chiefdom.

Overt displays of submission and veneration were commonly directed toward the Suns and other nobility by lower ranking individuals. They in turn displayed symbols and actions demonstrating their power and authority. These most likely involved the highly developed and artistic paraphernalia common to the Southeastern Ceremonial Complex.[28] The administrative centers for many chiefdoms were towns with obvious earthen platform mounds. These structures held important if not critical roles in the political and religious aspects of the chiefdoms. The Suns at times even had some control over food surpluses and other wealth produced by their subjects and could redistribute them as they wished.

Lahontan's Descriptions of the Natives of Canada and the Long River: A Comparison

Lahontan's second volume of his *New Voyages...* was largely devoted to discourse on the Natives of North America.[29] Importantly, and in keeping with his practice of trying to maintain fidelity in his observations, he prefaced that discourse by stating how language problems prevented him from better understanding the Natives from beyond the Mississippi.[30]

The baron's narrative still, however, contains descriptions of Native behaviors that do not appear to be out of line with those known to have been practiced within ranked societies, such as the Mississippian chiefdoms. In such a context, the behaviors, particularly the greeting rituals involving native nobility and foreigners, which the baron most commonly witnessed and described, merit review. The context for this review is the last years of the Late Mississippian Period and just before the local prehistory and/or protohistory gave way to the full post-contact era, which Lahontan ushered in for the peoples he visited. His descriptions of the Long River peoples are notable in the way in which they contrast with the critical summary he gave about the Natives of Canada, particularly the Algonquin-speaking Ottawas.

Although he spoke little about structures of authority among the Canadian Natives and the many aspects of their culture that he had personally observed, he emphatically stated that they were strangers to "Superiority and Subordination; and live in a state of Equality pursuant to the Principal of Nature."[31] This comment on sociopolitical organization stood in stark contrast to the ones he made about the Long River peoples where there are many references to chiefly authority. The baron's notions of superiority, rank, submission, veneration, authority, and subordination are entirely missing from his description of the Canadian Natives. His descriptions hinted at the complexity of the polities he observed on the Long River, although he was unable to really understand them.

Among the Natives of Canada that Lahontan wrote about, he knew the Algonquian-speaking Ottawas best from his first days in New France. Much of what he described about Natives relates to them and perhaps to the closely related Ojibwas.[32] While his descriptions of the Long River peoples reflect elements of ranked societies, the baron's Canadian Natives are reflective of the more egalitarian nature of the cultures of the Algonquian speakers of Canada during the baron's time. These had evolved rapidly following the French colonization and the concomitant rise of the fur trade.[33] The Canadian Natives the baron described are also not fully reflective of the prehistoric or protohistoric cultures which would once have existed there. In the 1680s the Ottawas and others of Canada were long past the late prehistoric stage. The Canadian Natives' cultures and populations had already been greatly reduced by disease and warfare that attended their post-contact experience over many generations.

The Baron's Observations on Ranked Native Nations

Among the nations the baron encountered on the Long River, it was only the Eokoros and Essanapes for whom he gave enough description to suggest that they were perhaps ranked societies reflecting attributes of chiefdoms.

Observations on the Eokoros/Otoes

In describing these people Lahontan spoke of the "Great Governor," who was "a venerable Old Gentleman" and noted that "There seems to be something of Governance and Subordination among this People. [34]

Observations on the Essanapes/Pawnees

Lahontan's company would have entered Pawnee/Essanape territory along the Platte in east-central Nebraska where their historic villages have been well documented.[35] The baron spoke of his reception at the village where he first stopped by stating that: "as we stood upon the shore, all the Essanapes prostrated themselves three or four times before us, with their Hands upon their Foreheads; after which we were conveyed **[carried]** to the Village with such Acclamations of Joy, as perfectly stop'd us."[36]

Fouillade translated the phrase "we were carried and taken ceremoniously." He used the word "carried" rather than "led" or "accompanied" into the presence of the chief or governor. This statement is, however, not all that clear, and Lahontan may have been stating that he and his men were indeed physically "carried." That would not seem to have been all that unusual in Mississippian culture. The baron further noted that "after arriving at the Gate [to the village] our conductors stop'd us till the Governour, a Man of fifty years of Age marched out."

These passages suggest that relatively typical Mississippian greeting protocols were involved.[37] This chief then led the party into a special purpose building that was not a residence but was described as the "the Cottage of Peace **[Peace Lodge]**." There was, however, a misunderstanding with this Essanape leader. The baron's Native companions felt that the company had been disrespected since its hosts retained their weapons and they feared violence might break out.[38]

The baron's Essanape slaves then led him upriver toward their "Metropolitan" **[rural capital].** The baron resolved to go to that main village to complain to the ranking chief or generalissimo about the threats previously made against the company by the subordinate chief. This man, whom the baron also called the "Head General" **[high chief]** received them most kindly and told the baron that they should have kidnapped the other "Governour or leading officer" and brought him with them. The baron noted that when his Essanape slaves met this highest-ranking man, whom he then referred to as a "petty King," they made a show of respect or veneration for half an hour by "prostrating themselves several times before him." Such actions are again entirely in keeping with what is known about chiefdoms. The usual exchange of gifts was then made to everyone's satisfaction.[39]

This man's village where he, as the "head General/Generalissimo," lived was said to have been larger than all the others of the Essanapes. His house was built in a part of the settlement (though no mound was mentioned) that was set off from the rest of it and was surrounded by fifty other houses that all belonged to his relatives. This statement seems reasonable and compares well with what is known of chiefdoms wherein the ranking leaders and other nobles are typically related and are thought to have segregated themselves from the society's commoners. He also pointed out that the houses, constructed of reeds or sticks covered in mud, were shaped like large and tall ovens. This is a good description of the classic earthen lodges of the Pawnees and many other Native peoples of the Great Plains. (Figure 25)[40] The baron stated that the large extent of this Village might justly intitle it to the name of a "City."

The generalissimo readily accommodated the baron's request for the loan of four pirogues to replace his birchbark canoes. In keeping with Mississippian protocols for the greeting of strangers, he also offered to send two or three hundred men as an escort when the company left for the distant Gnacsitare territory.[41] The baron graciously accepted that offer. Lahontan then, as previously discussed, commented that the great leader of the Essanapes was carried about on a litter.[42]

About the People of the Long River

Lahontan was on a voyage of wide-ranging discovery, which, due to his interest in Natives and nature, included learning all he could about them, as well as seeking an inland passage and information on the Spaniards. Although there is a vast literature concerning early post-contact period Native cultures in North America, there are very few to compare with the baron's eye-witness account of the very first ephemeral contacts for what were still essentially prehistoric people.[43] Over a period of only a few weeks, the baron documented elements of what were essentially still prehistoric cultures of the Otoes, Pawnees, Plains Apache/Kiowas, Missouris, and some Numic-speaking Utes from the lands of Tahgulauk and Mozeemlek in present-day Utah, as well as what was known to the Spaniards as Teguayo.

In their post-contact eras, the peoples the baron documented quickly gave up many of their Mississippian ways and rapidly evolved into equestrian-focused cultures.[44] In the absence of early information such as the baron provided, these cultures, and ultimately the residues from their destruction, became the stereotypes by which they are best known historically. Although archaeologists have gained some perspective on the prehistoric and early historic cultures involved, their findings do not do much to help better understand the nature of their prehistoric sociopolitical structure(s).

In terms of geography, if they were long present where the baron found them, the peoples of the lower Missouri River, and perhaps even the Platte, could well have been at one time enfolded into the Mississippian chiefdoms by complex processes of "domination and ideology." Those were active within the paramount Chiefdom of Cahokia during its heyday, which archaeologists believe certainly were ending by ca. 1600CE.[45] If more recent arrivals in the locations where the baron found them, then they had apparently been acculturated to at least some of the "ways" of the Mississippians at other locations.

Lahontan's narrative of his interaction with the Otoes, is the first meaningful description of them, although Marquette first documented their existence in 1673. They were then occupying a region west of the Mississippi roughly in the area of the border between what is today Iowa and Minnesota. By 1714 they, or at least some of them, were apparently further to the west, near the mouth of the Platte River.[46] This would seem to put them in about the same approximate location where the baron found them.

The Otoes and Missouris were not better documented until well into the eighteenth century when they began serving as middlemen between French and Spanish traders and other tribes further up the Missouri River. Internecine warfare and disease, including smallpox, had almost destroyed them by the end of the eighteenth century when they were largely absorbed into other groups.[47] Since the paramount chiefdom of Cahokia died away before it could be documented, there is no information as to what, if any, extent the Otoes were involved in it. Like so many other Native peoples, the Otoes had become an equestrian people by the nineteenth century when Lewis and Clark encountered them living with Missouris on the south bank of the Platte near the Elkhorn River.[48]

Lahontan's narrative of his interaction with Pawnees from along the Platte in east-central Nebraska is also the first description of them. They may have been known as the Harahey as early as 1541 when Coronado sought Quivera on the central Plains, but this is only surmised from limited linguistic data. Like the Otoes, Marquette in 1673 and by La Salle in 1682 documented their existence, but no European other than Lahontan is believed to have traveled to their villages until the early eighteenth century.[49] The Pawnees became well known to the French and were their trading partners, apparently because Lahontan was the first to visit and befriend them.

By the end of the seventeenth century the Pawnees were critical players in the French and Spanish rivalry for trade and influence on the Plains. Pawnees and Otoes helped the French who massacred Pedro de Villasur's expedition from New Mexico in the Platte country in 1720. They remained closely aligned with the French for the early portion of the eighteenth century and then became significant players in the fur trade of Spanish Louisiana.[50] By the nineteenth century the Pawnees had become a largely equestrian people. They are known to have maintained a complex sociopolitical and religious structure that may well have had roots in former chiefdoms like Cahokia.[51]

Lahontan's Athabaskan-speaking Gnacsitares (Plains or Kiowa Apache) are not well documented from an early time in the Platte River region where the baron found them. His documentation is apparently the first for them at that location. They have typically been lumped by ethnologists into the Apachean designation as one of several similar peoples noted at various locations around the Great Plains, particularly by the early Spaniards. There is still disagreement among anthropologists as to their identity and origins.[52]

The identification of the Gnacsitares as Plains Apaches is based on the degree to which the late seventeenth- to early eighteenth-century Dismal River archaeological aspect or phase has been attributed to occupation by these people.[53] The Dismal River aspect is known from western Nebraska, western Kansas, eastern Colorado, and eastern Wyoming. Archaeological remains from this time frame in western Nebraska where the baron met the Gnacsitares are almost certainly derived from the Plains Apaches. Like other Plains dwellers, Plains Apaches developed highly equestrian cultures and entered the internecine wars of the Plains after giving up their homes in western Nebraska and commencing to range widely.

As previously noted, the baron reported that these people had taken up residence on islands in the Platte or in the Lake of the Apaches (Figures 16-19) to protect themselves from raids by the hostile Mozeemlek people.[54] It is also noteworthy that the baron's brief description suggests that these people may have had a ranked system of authority. This and considerably more archaeological study could possibly provide a far different view of their level of sociopolitical complexity than previously understood.[55]

Lahontan's Long River narrative adds an entirely new dimension to our understanding of the early ethnography of the lower Missouri and Platte rivers. It helps to better place the involved peoples on the landscape in space and time. It also assists in gaining some further perspective on the complexity of their sociopolitical structures and how they may have been influenced by or as directly part of the paramount chiefdom of Cahokia. Scholars of these peoples should not be surprised to find that they had been significantly influenced by Cahokian systems.[56] Collective memory of Native people still maintained Cahokia as an important place on the landscape when Lahontan met the Fox people. There he was told multiple times how the calumet would ensure his safety as far as the "plantation of the sun."[57]

Although they did not know the vanished chiefdom and its primary settlement as Cahokia, the Fox could have only been referring to it. As the largest and likely most influential Native city and power that ever existed in North America north of Mexico, it would once certainly have been known far and wide among generations of Native peoples. The fact that it was mentioned on multiple occasions as a major landmark for Lahontan to note cannot be overlooked and demonstrates that it was still present in the collective memory of the Fox who lived far to the north of Cahokia. The Native societies and behaviors, which Lahontan's critics wrongly denounced so stridently, can readily be equated with some which were typical of ranked Mississippian societies.

Notes:

1. The primary criticisms of the baron's narrative were generated and kept alive by a few scholarly critics such as these. Many other writers, however, accepted their opinions and reiterated them over and over. Adams, *Travelers,* 1, 56-60;Parkman, *France and England*, 1051; Roy, *Le Baron de Lahontan;* Thwaites, "Introduction," xl-xlii; Sayre, *Les Sauvages,* xvii, 41, 90-93; Swift, *Travels Into;* DeVoto, *Course of Empire*, 64.

2. Ethnologist Eleanor Leacock has offered a useful model of historic culture change that mirrors repetitive changes that occurred among the North American Native peoples. She stated that "Phase II commences [after the purely prehistoric phase] with early contacts, either directly with explorers, missionaries, and traders or indirectly with goods traded through neighboring tribes. The extent to which a reintegration of Indian institutions followed these first contacts has often been underestimated. It has been all too common for anthropologists to assume that the cultural information they were gathering from elders about lifestyles that stretched back to the beginning of the nineteenth century and even earlier represented pre-Columbian society." Leacock, "Introduction," 11; Lurie, "Contemporary," 423-34.

3. Squier and Davis, *Ancient Monuments;* Smith, "Introduction: Research;"Thomas, *Report of the Mound,* "Who Were the Moundbuilders;"Willey and Sabloff, *A History of*, 42-63; Williams, "Foreword."

4. Baker et al., "Protohistoric and Historic," 57; Leacock, "Introduction," viii-ix, 11; Lurie, "Contemporary," 423-25.

5. Parkman, *France and England*, 1051.

6. Adams, *Travelers*, 57; e.g. Sayre, *Les Sauvages.*

7. Thwaites, "Introduction," xlii.

8. Adams, *Travelers*, 58.

9. Lahontan, *New Voyages*, 88, December 14, 1688; DeVoto, *Course of Empire*, 64.

10. Hudson, *Knights of Spain*,17-26; Galloway and Jackson, "Natchez," 603-06; Le Page du Pratz, *History of Louisiana*, 73-83, 299-301, 311-25; Smith and Hally, "Chiefly Behavior," 100.

11. Smith and Hally, 100; Lorant, *New World*, 109.

12. du Pratz, *History of Louisiana*, 321.

13. Lahontan, *New Voyages*,188. ca. December 14, 1688.

14. Baker, "Cofitachique,"64; Hudson, *Southeastern Indians*, 34-35; MacNutt, *De Orbe Novo*, vol. II, 259.

15. Baker, "Cofitachique;" "Historic Catawba."

16. Baker, "Cofitachique," 91; DePratter, "Cofitachique;" Hudson, *Southeastern Indians*,110, 112, 205,

331-33; Lewis, "Narrative of," 174-76; e.g. Clayton, Moore, and Knight, *deSoto Chronicles.*

17. Smith and Hally, "Chiefly Behavior," 100.

18. Brown, "Calumet Ceremony;" Smith and Hally, 100.

19. Sahlins, *Tribesmen.*

20. Portions of the following discussion have been adapted by the authors from Baker, "Cofitachique;" Hudson, *Southeastern Indians; Knights of Spain.* https://en.wikipedia.org/wiki/Mississippian_culture accessed May 7, 2019 and other sources as cited. Lahontan, *New Voyages*, 184-89.

21. e.g. Hudson, *Knights of Spain*, 307-09; Mink, *Cahokia;* Pauketat, *Ancient Cahokia;* Pauketat and Emerson, *Cahokia; Domination.*

22. Hudson, *Knights of Spain.*

23. Some might question if a settlement might not have been 'Mississippian" because there is no evidence of the mounds that are so characteristic of most developed Mississippian settlements. It should be noted, however, that unless a settlement had been in existence long enough to organize the manpower through the substantial time it would take to build substantive mounds, there may be none even evident, although the settlement was still a product of Mississippians. A great many smaller mounds have also now been destroyed by agricultural activities and overbuilding by cities and towns.

24. Knight, "Ceremonialism;" Waring and Holder, "A Prehistoric Ceremonial."

25. Baker, "Cofitachique;" "Historic Catawba." DePratter, "Cofitachique;" *Late Prehistoric;* Ferguson, *South Appalachian Mississippian.*

26. There is a vast and growing literature on the Mississippians, and this is only a brief introductory summary. For those who might wish to learn more, the authors refer readers to the *Southeast* volume (No. 14) of the *Handbook of North American Indians* and the published works referenced in that large volume and the works of Charles Hudson and Timothy Pauketat as well as that of Bruce Smith and Le Page du Pratz: in particular. e.g. Hally and Mainfort, "Prehistory of the Eastern," 273-74, 284-85; Pauketet and Emerson, *Cahokia: Domination.* Smith, *Mississippian Emergence;* Smith and Hally, "Chiefly Behavior."

27. Hudson, *Knights of Spain*, 17-26; Galloway and Jackson, "Natchez, 603-06;" du Pratz, *History of Louisiana*, 73-83, 299-301, 311-25; e.g. Pauketat and Emerson, *Cahokia Domination;* Barker and Pauketat, "Lords of the Southeast;" Smith, *Mississippian Emergence;* Smith and Hally, "Chiefly Behavior."

28. Knight, "Ceremonialism;" Waring and Holder, "A Prehistoric Ceremonial."

29. Lahontan, *New Voyages*, (2):411-616.

30. Lahontan, (2):414.

31. Lahontan, (2), 454.

32. Feest and Feest, "Ottawa," 772-77; Jenness, *Indians of Canada*, 274-83.

33. Jenness, 119-26; Feest and Feest,772-777. Helm and Leacock, "Hunting Tribes," 350-56.

34. Lahontan, *New Voyages*, 181-82. ca. late November 1688.

35. e.g. Ludwickson, "Historic Indian Tribes,"136; Parks, "Pawnee," 515; Wedel, *Introduction to Pawnee Archeology*, 3-23.

36. Lahontan 1905:184 (ca. late November 1688); Brown, "Calumet Ceremony," 379-80.

37. Brown, 379-380; Smith and Halley, "Chiefly Behavior."

38. Lahontan, 184-87.

39. Lahontan, 186-88.

40. Ludwickson, "Historic Indian Tribes," 144; Parks, "Pawnee," 524; Roper and Pauls, *Plains Earthlodges*.

41. Smith and Halley, "Chiefly Behavior."

42. This description fits behaviors well-known to have been associated with America's Natives who participated in ritualized Mississippian behavioral patterns toward their leaders. Lahontan, *New Voyages*, 188, December 3, 1688.

43. Leacock and Lurie, *North American Indians;* Barlowe, "Barlowe's Narrative of the First Voyage." Good eyewitness accounts of first contact by Native peoples are rare. Thomas Barlowe's 1584 account of the first voyage made to the coast of Virginia was prepared for Sir Walter Raleigh who financed that expedition. Barlowe described the meetings that took place with Natives who had never before seen a white man and their reactions in doing so. Barlowe, "Captain Arthur Barlowe's [1584] Narrative;" Connolly and Anderson, *First Contacts*. Another source that compares to the baron considered the Highland people of New Guinea in the twentieth century. That volume by Bob Connolly and Robin Anderson described the first white contacts of the Highlanders, which Michael Leahy of Australia originally documented in the 1930s. With film and narrative, Leahy documented the reactions of the highlanders as their post-contact experience commenced the destruction of their traditional stone age culture. Connolly and Anderson went one step further and, at a much later time, interviewed Highlanders who remembered those early encounters and recorded how they recalled them.

44. Hanson, "Late High Plains;" Holder, *Horse and the Hoe*.

45. e.g. Mink, *Cahokia;* Pauketat and Emerson, *Cahokia: Domination*, 2.

46. Schweitzer, "Oto and Missouri," 447.

47. Schweitzer, 447-48.

48. Schweitzer.

49. Parks, "Pawnee," 515-17; Wedel, *Introduction to Pawnee Archeology*.

50. Parks, "Pawnee," 517-19; Wedel, *Introduction to Pawnee Archeology*, 3-23.

51. Parks, "Pawnee."

52. Foster and McCollough, "Plains Apache," 926-27.

53. Butler, "Some Thoughts;" Gunnerson and Gunnerson, *Ethnohistory;* Levy, "Kiowa;" Gunnerson, "Plains Village" 239, 242; *Archaeology of High Plains*, 113-20; Ludwickson, "Historic Indian Tribes," 135-45; Baker et. al., "Protohistoric and Historic," 88-92.

54. Lahontan, *New Voyages*, 187.

55. Foster and McCollough, "Plains Apache."

56. e.g. Emerson, "Cahokia Elite."

57. Lahontan, *New Voyages*, 177.

13

• LAHONTAN'S POST-LONG RIVER YEARS •

by

Steven G. Baker

It seems odd that Lahontan's first action after returning from the Long River would have been to sit down and prepare an account of his travels simply for the edification of his regular correspondent back in France. He already had his full journal and would have had ample future time to prepare such an extracted account before he could have even posted it to France and, when compared to his other letters, it was done so much more quickly. The baron was, however, as were all explorers, obligated by the Crown's orders to deliver a report to the authorities in Montreal immediately after making his exploratory trip.[1] As stated previously, it certainly appears that the narrative given in Lahontan's Letter XVI may have been first drafted as the required written diary for the governor and intendant as part of his debriefing. It should have served such a purpose quite well.

Since Lahontan's detachment and his Ottawa companions had journeyed with him to the Long River, and others from Michilimackinac would have known of his long absence from there, it would have been impossible for the baron to have kept his travels secret. To do so would defy all logic of any reasonable person! This would have particularly been the case since he departed Michilimackinac with his full detachment for such a long period under the very nose of the commandant and the residents there.

The fact that his letter contained a proposal for a massive and obviously hugely expensive additional expedition implies that he was intending for representatives of the Crown, or others of very substantial means and/or authority, to see it.[2] In such a case, it appears that someone high in authority turned a blind eye to the baron's long trip and did not give it much notice. As a junior military officer, unless he could draw the attention of the Crown through its representatives in Canada, his proposal would appear to have served no obvious purpose unless he was anticipating that his correspondent in France might help make it a reality. When he made his report, the governorship was changing from Denonville back to Frontenac. Since he made his report to Denonville, the information he imparted may simply have been overlooked in the shuffle of a shifting bureaucracy. Lahontan was certainly not, however, a stupid man and would have known that he could not have kept such a trip a secret. He had utilized the king's soldiers and resources, and likely those of local traders from Michilimackinac, for his trip and had set out for such a long period from there in full view. That act alone might well have officially been seen as a desertion if any of his superiors were even concerned about it.

Although Frontenac was no longer governor when Lahontan made his trip, his fur trading cartel was still a major economic and political force in the colony and in large measure dominated by his cohorts, many who had deep connections with Michilimackinac.[3] Frontenac may have been in France, but that would not necessarily have stopped his cartel's involvement. He had been the driving force behind the earlier searches for the inland passage by Marquette, Jolliet, and La Salle. They undertook their trips under his orders. He was the prime advocate for opening western lands to the fur trade and for establishing trading facilities within them.[4] Much to the chagrin of the other Montreal traders, by the time Frontenac was recalled from his first appointment, he and his cohorts had been rapidly establishing a trading empire in much of the Mississippi drainage.

If an inland passage to the Pacific could be found and controlled by them, Frontenac and/or his partners would have been in a wonderful position to exploit it and generate huge profits for themselves as well as the Crown. All the circumstances surrounding Lahontan's travels point to the distinct possibility that he may have been sent out or quietly underwritten by the Frontenac cartel to find the inland passage. Those men could have readily supplied the funding and trade goods Lahontan obviously needed and could even have cut him in for a share of the profits if he did some trading while on the trip. The amounts of his backloads from the trip certainly suggest that he was carrying substantial amounts of something back with him.[5] Furs were about the only thing he could have obtained on the trip.

Since the Crown had long been offering a reward to whomever could find an inland passage, it strains credibility to believe that the baron's long trip was solely an independent action. He had no money and it had to have been inspired by more than his simple curiosity and unlinked to any of the entrenched financial interests involved in the fur trade of New France or the Crown's promise.[6] It was, of course, at that time believed by the Crown that, in addition to making peace with the Iroquois, discovery of an inland passage to the Pacific was the most important task yet to be accomplished on behalf of New France.[7]

Within this context it is not surprising that the baron suggested that he be allowed to lead another very substantive and costly expedition to push on to the source of the Long River where everyone, including Frontenac, believed an inland passage would be found.[8] In his introduction to Marquette's 1673 journal of his and Jolliet's Mississippi River trip in the *Jesuit Records*, Dablon stressed that both Governor Frontenac and Talon, the intendant, recognized the importance of finding an inland passage.[9]

The Baron and Governor Frontenac

By the time the baron reached Quebec in the summer of 1689, Denonville had been recalled and was waiting to begin his trip back to France. The far more popular Frontenac (Figure 3) had been appointed to replace him and was soon due back in the colony. At this time the baron had once again been granted his desired leave to return to France that Denonville had been refusing him. Lahontan was respected by him and got along well with Frontenac so he was anticipating that the new governor would finally allow him to return. But he was again disappointed when Frontenac also refused to let him leave. His rare abilities and experience were once more needed in working to improve the troubled condition of the colony, particularly including its relations with the Iroquois. The governor, therefore, made him a personal counselor and his regular traveling companion. As compensation, the baron was made a member of his household and paid by the governor himself since by then Lahontan's only income appears to have been his sparse military pay.

The baron was finally able to return to France in the fall of 1690 when Frontenac tasked him with carrying good news to the French king and his court. The British had been threatening the colony with an armada standing off the capital under Admiral Sir William Phipps. The armada finally withdrew, and the baron sailed to France with the news and a personal letter of recommendation from Frontenac to Seignelay. This was the opportunity he had been waiting for; he not only had a written recommendation but also a powerful spokesman at court. He should finally get a leg up and be able to ask for favors and redress from the Crown! Unfortunately, by the time he returned to France his powerful protector, Seignelay, had died and the baron was left without his key voice before the Crown and court.[10]

Although he was not totally rebuffed in his entreaties, he did not meet with much success from Pontchartain, Seignaley's successor, even though he was in France for much of 1691. In recognition of the good news he had carried about the British armada, he was granted a small title and a promotion to captain but received no redress for his financial and other claims. Further, his wealthy uncle, the Abbé des Couttes, who may well have been his correspondent, did not feel obligated to assist the poor baron financially. Lahontan was only given a short time to try to resolve his troubled affairs and was ordered to return to New France in the fall. By then there was no way that he could have any chance of salvaging them. The time was too short, and matters were complicated and too far gone. He became even more embittered about what he saw as "venality and favoritism" at the French court. He was, however, still in the military and under orders to return to Quebec. He dutifully arrived back there on September 18,1691, and was readily welcomed back into Frontenac's household.

During the winter of 1691–1692, Lahontan came close to marrying Geneviève d'Amours, the governor's goddaughter. Had it taken place this marriage would have helped restore the baron to prosperity, but Lahontan was resolutely unwilling to trade his liberty for financial and social security. Frontenac did not take kindly to the baron's rejection of Geneviève's hand, and despite orders to the contrary, passed over the young captain when an opportunity to give him a larger command arose.

Despite this setback, Lahontan went to work preparing a plan for defending the upper country from the Iroquois who continued to harass the colony. Frontenac was so pleased with the plan that he ordered the baron to return to France and personally present it to the Ministry of the Marine. Lahontan sailed again from New France in the summer of 1692 on a frigate bearing not only his plan but also the governor's dispatches for the court. Stopping over in Plaisance (Placentia) in Newfoundland, his ship waited for the fishing fleet to arrive to fill out the convoy that would be relied on to protect the ships from British raiders. Just as the convoy was ready to sail, the garrison at the fort at Plaisance was surprised to learn that five English frigates were sailing up the bay toward it.

The garrison prepared to defend itself even though its fortifications were poor and ammunition scarce. The baron was dispatched with sixty local men to defend against any landing that British marines might attempt. He succeeded in preventing such a landing, and the British commander offered to negotiate. Lahontan and a companion went aboard one of the ships as the French representatives. These negotiations were unsuccessful, so the governor strengthened his defenses with such energy that the English ships finally withdrew but not until they had fired two thousand rounds into the fort and burned some nearby fishing villages. In helping to beat back the much larger and better supplied English force Lahontan had even better news to carry to the French court. With a remarkably fast passage of only seventeen days, the baron arrived at Saint Nazere on October 23,1692, and was quickly back before the court in Versailles.

He found that while it welcomed all his good news from New France, the court was not enthused in the least about providing the substantial funds the baron's plan would require for the defense of its remote colony. Although he was quickly dismissed, he was rewarded by being given command of an independent company of one hundred men and the high honor of being named Lieutenant of the King of Newfoundland and Acadia.[11] While the baron believed that simple chance was what led him to receive this honor, it was not overly enthusiastic about it. He would have been more pleased if the court had accepted his plan and sent him back to Canada to carry it out. He pointed out that he preferred the solitary life in the woods among the Natives over the prospect of living along the gloomy, storm-swept fjords of the Newfoundland coast, particularly since he would be under command of a governor known for his temper and bad habits. Lahontan discusses this period of his life in Letters XX-XXIV.[12]

His promotion to lieutenant proved to be a double-edged sword for the young officer. When he arrived back in Plaisance in 1693, Lahontan was not received by Governor De Brouillon with any enthusiasm. He believed the baron's presence might hinder the advancement of his own family's interests. The governor's bad temperament was well known, and an open feud soon developed between the two men. Locals appeared to side with Lahontan when he resisted the governor's attempts to make him an obedient underling. With his perpetually sarcastic and caustic wit, the baron publicly mocked his superior.[13]

De Brouillon sent dispatches to the court railing against the baron. The final straw for Lahontan occurred when the governor and some of his staff wearing masks broke into his home, smashed up his furniture, and damaged other belongings. The next day a group of these same men attacked some of the baron's staff and gave them "an unmerciful drubbing." This unfortunate set of circumstances led Lahontan to fear for his life. As consequence he deserted his official military post at Plaisance, thus bringing on his nearly complete downfall and forever sealing off any future chance to win favor with the Crown. Other than at the end of his Long River narrative there was never any mention of the baron's proposal to further explore the Missouri or otherwise seek an inland passage.

Into His Exile

Lahontan managed to hire the captain of a small fishing boat to help him escape from Plaisance and transport him to Europe where he finally landed in Portugal. As a deserter he could not return to France where he would endure even further disgrace and might even end up a prisoner in the Bastille. With his official pay now forfeit and his inheritances wiped away, all he could do was try to survive as best he could and, along with many others of his victims, patiently await the day that the wicked Pontchartrain "should either remove to Paradise or do Justice" to all the people he had wronged.[14] Lahontan discussed this period of his adventures in Letter XXV.

Holland was then a magnet for refugees, who, like the baron, were running from the evils of the French court. He ended up among them there. Lahontan then traveled on to Hamburg and from there sent what Thwaites believed to be a fraudulent letter intended to catch the notice of the French court.[15] This was purported to have been an account of La Salle's ill-fated expedition to the Gulf coast as had been related to the baron by survivors of that expedition. The baron claimed to have recently met these individuals in Hamburg, which may or may not have been true. He had, however, met some of them in the spring of 1688 back at Michilimackinac as he detailed in Letter XV.

According to Thwaites, the French court investigated and determined that Lahontan had invented the account simply to win favor. He certainly had, however, had opportunities to hear accounts of some survivors. It is reasonable that the baron, in trying to restore his good name, would have attempted to provide the court with an account of La Salle. Thwaites overlooked the fact that the baron met some and had heard their accounts. In this oversight Thwaites perhaps inappropriately believed it proved that Lahontan was capable of lying about things, including his Long River narrative, just to improve his financial condition.[16]

Failing to gain any favor with the court, Lahontan then went to Copenhagen and there obtained the favor of the French ambassador, De Bonrépaux. The ambassador attempted to assist him by sending letters on his behalf to the court. The intention of these communications was to secure a pardon for the baron and get him restored to the Crown's favor. The king, however, would not accept the justifications of one of his officers who had challenged his superior and deserted. Failing to gain reinstatement, the baron attempted to return to his native province of Béarn where his now-confiscated lands had been located. He was not welcomed there and an order for his arrest had been sent from the court. A fugitive from the French Crown, he escaped to Spain and prepared letters there at Zaragoza in October 1695.

Lahontan then wandered for some years in the Low Countries, Denmark, Britain, and ultimately Hanover, but his life in this period is barely documented. He was in Lisbon in 1699 and from there attempted to obtain the favor of the Spanish Court by offering his services as a spy. He also sent a copy of a map (Figure 24) he had prepared of the Mississippi and Long Rivers to the Duke of Jovenazo of the Spanish War Council.[17] He also offered him the journal of the Sieur Cavelier's trip back to Canada from the mouth of the Mississippi.[18] The outcome of Lahontan's overtures is unclear, but he did not end up in Spain.

Lahontan seems to have been in Holland in about 1703 when his book was first published there. Its publication was certainly an attempt by the bankrupt Baron, who was still a fugitive, to cash in on the rising popularity of travel accounts. He then went to Britain where he apparently oversaw the translation and publication of the first English edition of his book in 1703. While there he also prepared a plan that he offered to the British by which they might have been able to expel the French from Acadia by capturing Port Royal and establishing trade relations with the Natives in the Lake Huron and Ontario Region. The British did not accept his plan.[19] Lahontan was then in desperate straits and attempting to find a secure place to settle by making himself useful to some country other than France. These included both Britain and Spain.

In addition to his 1689 plan for further exploring the Long River outlined in his narrative, the baron produced at least three other grand plans in hopes of finding such a place. In about 1692, while assisting Frontenac as an advisor, he developed a plan for the defense of New France's upper country against the Iroquois. The governor thought so highly of the plan that he again dispatched the baron to carry it to the court in Versailles. In addition to the plan, he also carried news of the withdrawal of the British fleet that had been threatening the colony. Although the French court welcomed the news, the baron's plan was not implemented. He also had ideas about increasing the colony's population through the addition of French Huguenots. Sometime between about 1710 and 1713 he is believed to have authored a plan for the regulation of trade between New England and New France, which was also never put into practice. In that document the baron twice referred to his previous voyages and to his publication of the journal of that trip. While the financially strapped man was trying to sell his services to almost any country that might pay for them, there is some suggestion that he may also have fostered a plan to spy for Spain after he escaped arrest in France and fled the country. In 1703 Lahontan developed another plan by which he felt that Britian could wrest Acadia and the fur trade from the French. He unsuccessfully tried to obtain British interest in it.[20]

By 1710 Lahontan was at the court of the Elector of Hanover where he was "recognized as an accomplished man beset by ill fortune."[21] He was apparently supported in Hanover by Leibnitz, the famed savant philosopher and mathematician, and was writing more things he intended to publish. His health had, however, deteriorated, and according to the records of Hanover's Church of Saint-Clement, he died there on April 21, 1716, at age forty-nine just before he had received communion at Easter as he had been intending.[22] Leibnitz is said to have published some of the baron's works after his death.[23] The fact that two of the greatest minds in Europe, Leibnitz and the famous physician and naturalist, Sir Hans Sloan, fellow and president of the Royal Society, would take him into their folds and admire and befriend the baron reinforces the notion that they considered him an extremely bright fellow, perhaps even on their own level of savant. It is little wonder that as an early writer of the Enlightenment he brought the New World to the Old.[24] Hayne spoke as follows about the baron and his words seem an appropriate way to close the great man's biography:

In our own century, Lahontan's works are no longer widely read, and he himself has become a shadowy figure. There is no extant portrait of him, and we know only that he was tall, lean, and pale [sic]. Proud and independent, impulsive and inconstant, he chafed under the restraints of military discipline and never accepted those of marriage. He loved the open-air life of the forests of New France, where he could please himself, spending one day with his Native hunters and the next with Anacreon or Petronius: "a solitary Life is most grateful to me, and the manners of the Savages are perfectly agreeable to my Palate." In Europe he led of necessity a more sociable existence: "He is witty and has a Gascon vivaciousness about him that puts him on good terms with everyone he meets," wrote Bonrepaus, "the most responsible people open their homes to him and are delighted to have his company." Among his admirers were two of the greatest minds of his time. Indeed, the pendulum of Lahontan's life had more than once swung between solitude and society, between Europe and North America. As a youthful subject of Louis XIV, he had left the Old World for the New; as an early writer of the Enlightenment, he brought the New World to the Old.[25]

NOTES:

1. Heindenreich, "Early French Exploration," 67; Talon to the King, "his Majesty's Intentions," (9)64.

2. Lahontan, *New Voyages*, 210-15.

3. Eccles, "Conte de Frontenac," *Frontenac*, 78-92, 98.

4. Eccles.

5. Lahontan, *New Voyages*, 207. On that trip the baron reported that he had to hire 400 Illinois Indians to transport his canoes and baggage over a long 13 league (36 mile) portage. This entry was checked to see if it could have been misprinted whereby "40" persons instead of "400" had originally been so employed. The baron spelled it out as "four hundred men." It was apparently not, therefore, a misprint. It thus seems that the baron must have had a large cargo of furs with him on his back trip through the Illinois county.

6. Heidenreich, "Early French Exploration," 126; Colbert to Talon, "His Majesty's Intentions," (9) 89; Eccles, "Conte de Frontenac."

7. Heidenreich, "Early French Exploration,"126; Colbert to Talon, "His Majesty's Intentions." (9) 89.

8. Lahontan, *New Voyages*, 210-15.

9. Dablon, "*On the Departure*," 87.

10. It has not yet been possible to determine just what, if anything, the relationship between Seignelay and the baron was based on other than the fact that they were in the same department and the baron had recommendations from Frontenac. Thwaites' *Introduction*, xxi-xxvi; does not seem to clarify this. Thwaites, however, refers to Seignelay as the baron's "protector." As minister of the Ministry of the Marine, he was certainly in a powerful position with the court to assist the baron in pursuing his claims. Whatever the relationship was based on, the baron sought Seignelay's assistance by means of a letter he prepared for him while at Michilimackinac in the spring of 1688 after he had left Fort Saint Joseph.

When he arrived back at Michilimackinac he learned that his financial affairs in France were in poor condition and thus composed his letter of entreaty. In it he recited the services his father had rendered to the Crown and summarized the injustices that had been done to his rights of inheritance since his father's death and his own absence from France. He attributes these injustices to the fact that he was not present in France to defend his rights. The baron discusses the circumstances and reprints his letter in *Letter XIV.* Lahontan, *New Voyages*, 135-51.

11. Thwaites, "Introduction," xxx.

12. Lahontan, *New Voyages.*

13. Thwaites, "Introduction," xxxi.

14. Thwaites, xxxii.

15. Thwaites, xxxii.

16. Thwaites, xli; Weddle, *The French Thorn*, 124, discusses these men.

17. See Figure 39. Lahontan, "*Mappa del Missisip.*"

18. Delanglez, *Journal;* Hayne, "Lom D'Arce;" Lahontan, "*Mappa del Missisip.*"

19. Lahontan, "Brief Discourses," ms.

20. Lahontan, "Brief Discours qui;" "Concerning the Regulation of the Limits...," 215, 224; Haney, "Lom D'Arce de;" Towle and Rawlyk, "A new Baron De Lahontan Memoir...".

21. Thwaites, *"Introduction,"* xxxiii.

22. Ouellet, "Baron of Lahontan," 4.

23. Thwaites, "Introduction," xxxiii.

24. Hayne, "Lom D'Arce De Lahontan."

25. Hayne, 1.

14

LAHONTAN'S LONG RIVER LEGACIES

by

Steven G. Baker and W. Raymond Wood

This detailed reappraisal of Lahontan's Long River narrative is believed to have resolved those various questions and issues discussed in chapter one supported by high levels of evidence and thus confidence. These of course were those then misunderstood issues that led to his critics' various condemnations of it over the many years. Most notably, the baron's Long River has unequivocally been shown to have been the Platte in combination with the lower Missouri/Pekistanouï River as discovered by Marquette and Jolliet who believed it could lead to an inland passage. After extensive testing it has proven that all those other condemnations of the baron's narrative, other than his mapping of the Long River's location, have no merit and that it appears to be an authentic seventeenth-century accounting of an actual voyage of discovery in search of an inland passage. There is no evidence of any kind to support suggestions that the baron's narrative was a work of fiction.

Summary of This Reappraisal

The most glaring negative critiques have had to do with the baron's incorrect mapping of the location of the Long River. As discussed in chapter 15, this, a back story to the narrative, appears to have been an intentional act by him intended to serve as a feint to mislead any others who may have wished to retrace his route and discover an inland passage ahead of him, and thereby claim the large reward promised by the King of France. It also may have had something to do with his seeming armed intrusion into what were Spanish lands, rather than French ones. The fact that he misled his readers with his incorrect location of the river, does not indicate he did not make the trip.

Over time the host of other condemnations were rooted in the anthropological barrenness, lack of knowledge of Native Americans, and the geography of the central Plains and Platte, as well as the ethnocentrism of Lahontan's critics. They were also tainted by prevalent, then typically racially biased views of Europeans toward the American Natives. These issues form another of the significant backstories behind the denunciations of his account. The baron's observations were way ahead of the popular perceptions of his own times and as they later came to hallmark those of the Enlightenment.

The narrative is a first description of the greatest rivers of the central Plains and some of their Native peoples, in particular the Pawnee, Plains Apache and Otoe. It is also the earliest known report of Caucasian-looking Natives, the Mozeemleks from near the Great Salt Lake, who might descend from ancestral Paleoamericans who may well have had ancient connections to the Ainu People of Japan. This information helps to widen an entirely new avenue of investigation into the physical anthropology of the American Natives and their occupation of North America.

The sequencing and dating of all the baron's letters conform well to his known whereabouts in 1688–1689, and within the appropriate historical contexts of events in and about New France. There is no apparent reason to doubt that he prepared them for and sent them on to his correspondent in France. There are also no indications that the letters, and particularly number XVI with its Long River narrative, were fictional literary devices intended only to help him sell books as some have implied.[1] Lahontan presented his work as that of an honest and attentive observer.

The baron also did not focus his narrative on his personal actions or glorify his own role with descriptions of any daring deeds or spell binding, narrow brushes with disasters that might be expected if he wanted just to build himself up to stoke his own ego or capture readers' attention. This is believed to be a notable attribute of his story. To the contrary, he admits to his fears of being attacked, captured, and possibly tortured by Native enemies. He tells when discretion indicated it was time to prepare for or retreat from danger. His narrative is a straight-forward, though quite unique for its early time, scholarly description of travels among new lands and unknown Native peoples. It is truly a very rare type of work intended by its extremely bright author to inform his readers about the wonders of new lands that he had been so eager to explore even before arriving in New France.

Following his return to Michilimackinac from the Long River and preparation of his narrative late in May of 1689, Lahontan next wrote to his correspondent from Quebec on September 28 in Letter XVII. In that he described his trip back down to Montreal and how he nearly lost his life in the Lachine Rapids. He also told how, immediately after arriving in Montreal, he met with the colony's governor and intendant and provided them with the required report of his voyages. This quite likely included much the same written narrative he provided in his letter as he eventually published it.[2]

To reach the Platte by canoe Lahontan had to have traveled south down the Mississippi, just as he had been planning when he left Michilimackinac for the southern countries.[3] That portion of the trip then required him to travel hundreds of miles up the Missouri River to the Platte as there was no other way to reach it by water. This fact proved that his Long River was indeed the lower Missouri and the Platte and that he could not have traveled north on the Mississippi to reach it. Thus, it was finally determined where he traveled and how he could have gotten there. All of his time was spent to the south of the Wisconsin River and not to the north as he initially misled his readers to believe. This is another major point which his critics overlooked in their haste to follow his trail northward on the Mississippi. Another major question concerned why he traveled up the Platte rather than following the Missouri on northward beyond it toward its source as had been his original plan?

The Platte ran westward toward the Pacific and was also a bigger river than the Missouri at their confluence. It is not surprising that when the baron encountered it, he chose to follow the larger river. When that route failed to lead him to the Pacific, Lahontan was running out of time and had to get back to Michilimackinac. He then, however, still hoped to follow the Missouri to the north beyond the Platte and proposed another, even larger expedition apparently to follow it to its source, still with the hope of finding an inland passage.

34. A portion of the Segesser hide painting depicting the battle of the Spanish Villasur Expedition against a combined force of Pawnee, Otoe, and French in 1720 in the vicinity of the Platte River. Note the palisaded Pawnee (?) village and the Spanish horses with leather armor and riders fighting with lances and what appear to be war dogs against warriors with only bows and arrows, courtesy of the Palace of the Governors Photo Archives Santa Fe, 149798.

The baron's Long River trip took place in what historian Conrad Heidenreich referred to as Period 3 (ca. 1665–1700) of the major periods of French Canadian exploration. This commenced after the administration of New France had been completely reorganized and thereafter governed by the Crown instead of the *Compagnie de la Nouvelle-France*. During this period exploration was encouraged and, to be successful in major part, depended on the capabilities of explorers in dealing with America's Natives. This was critical to such endeavors since Natives were able to provide geographical information, serve as guides, hunters, business partners, interpreters, promoters of alliances, and protectors.[4]

The baron was obviously highly successful in mastering the fundamental skill sets necessary in so dealing with Natives. This is a fact that is fully in keeping with everything that is known about him and the reason that he remained so important to the colony in the wars with the Iroquois. He relied upon this mastery in capably completing his Long River travels. His trip is thus notable relative to the baron's respect for and diplomacy accorded to the Natives he encountered. His travels proceeded relatively smoothly even when they could have quickly soured if he had not played his hand smartly. Overall, there were only limited threats or violence involved in his travels.

The baron's narrative brims with myriad small and large realistic details of encounters with Natives who had never before seen a European. This is particularly the case for the baron's descriptions of the Natives' reactions to meeting him and their behaviors as ranked and still functioning Mississippian-like societies. These well-fit the templates of our knowledge about ranked Mississippian peoples and their cultures.

Lahontan's narrative portrays an essentially prehistoric composure of the ethnographic landscapes of Lahontan's time. This was prior to the time that these groups of the Long River had begun to be appreciably altered by European contact and before the evolution of the famous equestrian Native cultures of the Great Plains which only evolved after his visit.[5] The baron's narrative is thus not only the first meaningful account of some of these peoples. It also records the reactions of these Stone Age Natives to the first Europeans they met. It well demonstrates how the French became established in the Platte country so early and how they came to rival the Spaniards of New Mexico for trade hegemony in the Trans-Mississippi West.

The baron appears to have begun the diplomacy that allowed the peoples from the Platte to assume an important historical role in that region and emerge as a French-friendly barrier to Spanish influence. Soon after his visit, French traders were beginning to travel to the Platte country and were seemingly welcomed by its peoples. This encroachment on Spanish territory and trade competition from New France became an ongoing concern for New Mexican authorities. All this led to the ill-fated Villasur expedition of 1720 when a combined French, Pawnee and Otoe force near the Platte nearly annihilated the substantial Spanish and Native army sent against it from New Mexico.[6] (Figures 34, 35) The baron literally opened the portal to the region for the French. After his visit they were quick to begin trading into it.[7]

35. A portion of the Segesser hide painting depicting the defeat of the Spanish Villasur Expedition (in battle square at image center) by a combined force of Pawnee, Otoe, and French in 1720, courtesy of the Palace of the Governors Photo Archives Santa Fe, 158345.

The Baron's Cartographic Legacy

Historian Bernard DeVoto was among the many distinguished writers who have judged the Baron Lahontan's Long River narrative in terms ranging from "imaginary" and "fanciful" to outright lies. One widely shared representative dismissal by DeVoto related to the baron's negative cartographic legacy. He emphasized how the one single chapter led him to befog a large area of North America's geography for half a century as well as create a big lake of salt water in the interior West, which was a fact, and discover on its shores "an Indian culture as ornate as the Byzantine."[8]

Erroneous conclusions such as that of DeVoto and so many others would indeed be merited by a casual and ethnologically uninformed reading of Lahontan's narrative, as well as a quick look at his mapping, by anyone steeped only in the literature of the Great Lakes region. As previously explained, however, the recent recognition of critical Spanish documents provides the first independent confirmation of any part of his narrative since the time it was written. This was particularly the case for the actual presence of the Great Salt Lake and the bearded men of Teguayo, Mozeemlek and Tahuglauk who are now known to have been living near it in Lahontan's time, exactly as he described.[9] When he made his trip the upper Great Lakes were only just beginning to be mapped and the only available and reasonably accurate map of the Mississippi was that prepared by Father Marquette and later published in slightly modified form by Thévenot.[10] (Figure 5)

There were apparently no additional maps of the Mississippi after that of Marquette's until those produced by Thévenot in 1681 and Father Hennepin in 1683 and 1698.[11] Other than for Marquette, the Jesuits do not appear to have mapped the Mississippi in their early cartographic efforts about the Great Lakes.[12] Thévenot's map closely mirrors Marquette's original unembellished one and shows the location of the Long River, although it is not named that. Hennepin's maps are not generally considered to be particularly accurate, and he did not personally travel the entire length of the Mississippi. The Thévenot map does reflect the discoveries made by Marquette and Jolliet. These include the location of the Long River, which was obviously the Missouri, which they ultimately named the "Pekitanouï," even though it was not denoted as such or otherwise named on the Marquette map. (Figure 5)

Although he published various maps of Canada in his book, the baron's Long River trip resulted in the production of only two maps in the first English edition. These include his *General Map of New France...* (Figures 2, 7) on which he incorrectly showed the location of the Long River. The second is his detailed *Map of the Long River* where he again illustrated the incorrect location of the river. On this one he combined his own detailed map of the river with his redrawn version of the map originally prepared for him on a deer hide (Figures 18, 19) by the Natives along the Platte. This map showed the Long River and the distant lands of Mozeemlek and Gnactsitare in relation to it and the Rocky Mountains. It first appeared in the 1703 French edition.

The base maps that Lahontan used for showing New France, the Great Lakes, the Mississippi River, and the erroneous location of the Long River (Figures 2, 18) are suspected to have been prepared by the baron himself at some point following his trip and prior to the first publication of his book. They could not have been included in the original unpublished version of Letter XVI from 1689. They could only have been prepared and engraved specifically to illustrate his book many years after he wrote his letter. These maps are very similar, although text and imagery varies a bit between the initial English and French versions.

The noted cartographic historian, Carl Wheat, attributed these two slightly different versions of what seems to be only one base map to the baron's hand, which seems to be the case. Despite a concerted search for other pre-1703 maps the baron may have copied or adapted for his purposes, no maps were found that conform at all closely with his base map.[13] The baron's base map of New France (Figure 7) appears to be acceptably executed for its time, despite the incorrect placement of the Long River. When the baron testified to the accuracy of his maps, his comment seems appropriate in terms of the base map in particular and the detail of the Long River itself, but not the river's placement on them.[14] As discussed in chapter 7, these two maps show his Long River joining with the Mississippi from the west well above the mouth of the Wisconsin River. (Figure 18)

The baron prepared one other very important map, but it was not included in his book and has not been commonly reproduced or referenced. This is the manuscript map dated 1699 (Figure 24), which is preserved in the Spanish archives in Seville.[15] This manuscript map is better crafted, but it still misplaces the Long River by showing it entering the Mississippi between the Wisconsin and Missouri Rivers. As with his other maps, it would not have been offered with this error if the baron intended for it to faithfully illustrate his travels. It is, however, still important in that it supports his descriptions and more clearly details some of the points raised in his narrative of his time on the Platte. As discussed previously, it is obvious that the baron never intended for his mapping to faithfully illustrate his travels. The evidence suggests quite the opposite and that they were never so intended.

If the baron did adapt his base map (s) from information contained in someone else's, then he most likely used those derived from Jean-Baptiste-Louis Franquelin. In 1686 Franquelin was made *Hydrographe du Roy* at Quebec and held that post until 1697. In this post he was responsible for making sure that all maps of New France were up to date for the Crown. From 1684 until ca. 1700 he was the major "compiler and disseminator" of cartographic information on New France for all the leading mapmakers of the time, including Coronelli, Jailot, Mortier, and DeLisle.[16] Between 1684 and 1688 Franquelin produced a series of maps of New France that depicted the Great Lakes similarly and somewhat realistically.

After taking a few years break from mapping, he began again in 1697 when he began updating his maps of New France. What has been termed his masterpiece was produced in 1699.[17] This was a very large map produced in four sections that became his base map for later versions published after Lahontan's of 1703.[18] Wheat discussed Franquelin's maps and along with Heidenreich indicated how complex a subject it really is. Determining where the baron's base maps or the information in them originated is well beyond the scope of this study. Suffice to say that the baron may well have developed them himself, likely with assistance from any of the maps of Franquelin that may have been available to him.[19]

The baron at times carried his astrolabe with him and was hoping to determine the latitudes of locations where he might end up while on his military expeditions to the Great Lakes.[20] This is an important point because it suggests that the baron may have had a much bigger role in the evolution of North American cartography than previously realized. Instead of just being held responsible for "befogging" so many subsequent maps with his deceptive placement of the Long River, he may well have been the source of some information that was useful to Franquelin in the production of his maps.

As with his English version of 1703, as well as all subsequent editions, the baron's maps for the Long River all show it inaccurately entering the Mississippi above the mouth of the Wisconsin River and far above that of the Missouri. (Figures 2, 7) This configuration appeared on many later maps by other cartographers, including Moll's, where many elements might be viewed as having been derived from the baron's maps. No maps are known to have shown the Long River as denoted as such prior to the publication of Lahontan's book in 1703.[21]

Lahontan's 1699 manuscript map (Figure 24) in the Spanish archives offers new information seemingly not available to earlier writers. This map shows the Mississippi River and its tributaries from its upper reaches to the Gulf of Mexico. On it the baron placed the Missouri River, which he calls the "Tamoroa," correctly below the mouth of the Illinois. He correctly depicts the Tamoroas living near its mouth, while the Missouris are further upstream, as indeed they were.[22] At this time the Missouris lived near the mouth of the Grand River, probably at least in part at Utz, a well-known site they are believed to have occupied until about 1712, and the adjoining region until about 1794.[23]

The engravers cannot be blamed for a misinterpretation with regard to the erroneous placement of the Long River on the 1703 maps. Lahontan also shows it incorrectly on his 1699 manuscript chart.[24] There, the Long River became the "Masotanta River." Its source was now the Lake of the Apaches, which the baron discussed in his narrative relative to his Gnacsitares. The stream is still shown emptying into the Mississippi above the Missouri but below the Wisconsin.[25]

As detailed in chapter 5, some geologists have recently come to believe that there was a series of substantial ancient ephemeral lakes or perhaps dammed up/cut off braided river channels at locations on the upper Platte River which created lakes, just as indicated in the 1699 map.[26] What was taken to be a lake may well have been nothing more than an old dammed up braided channel of the Platte. Thus, the Lake of the Apaches on the 1699 map may well have been a "lake-like" body of water present during Lahontan's time and may well be accurately shown.

Additionally, Lahontan spoke of the Essanape leader's "Capital Canton" as being seated "upon a sort of a lake" that was full of bullrushes.[27] In keeping with that comment, the principal village of the Essanapes could well have been on the shore of a cut off old, braided channel of the Platte, or just a slow moving "lake-like" section of the wide Platte. (Figure 14) Details of the 1699 map certainly help to further illuminate the geographic and ethnographic landscape of the Platte region at an early time.

The source of the 1699 map is unclear. Given its date, it is thought to have been made after Lahontan had become estranged from the Jesuits and the French Court and was living in exile in Spain. It was dedicated to the "Most Excellent Lord Duke of Jovenazo," a member of the Spanish War Council. The map places the Long River more nearly in Spanish territory, but it is still in error. The Mississippi River shows some features that hint that they may in part derive from Louis Hennepin's map published in 1698.[28] As with Lahontan's other maps, this misplacement of the Platte as part of the Long River is not something the baron would have done were he attempting to construct a map that was intended to be truly illustrative of his travels. It of course does not seem to have ever been so intended. The baron was fully capable of producing accurate maps if he so wished. Placing the Long River as he did certainly concealed its real location to the south and down the Mississippi from the Wisconsin. The location he showed firmly placed it in French rather than in Spanish territory. In any event, his 1699 map by itself does nothing to substantiate Lahontan's narrative relative to the Long River's location. It simply moved it downstream to another erroneous location.

Lahontan's books were not only best sellers, but his maps influenced those of a number of subsequent mapmakers besides Moll. Unfortunately, they contributed to degrading the imagery of the Great Lakes area because they incorporated the incorrect location of Lahontan's Long River into them.[29] In 1703 Guillaume DeLisle was one of the first to be taken in by Lahontan's misrepresentation.

His map was soon followed by another in 1710 made by John Senex which also included information from Lahontan, including the inaccurate location of the Long River.[30]

Hermann Moll's maps of 1712 and 1720 continued to follow Lahontan in a retrograde rendition of the Great Lakes and included his Long River. Moll also engraved Lahontan's map in English for his own London edition map of 1735. Maps by Bénard de La Harpe in about 1720, Guillaume Delisle in 1703, Henry Popple in 1730 and Daniel Coxe in 1741 are other examples of Lahontan's influence. By the mid-eighteenth-century cartographers were beginning to catch up with exploration and Lahontan's influence began to disappear from regional cartography.[31]

In addition to seemingly having some cartographic skills, the baron was also a bit of an artist in that he was probably responsible for all the sketches of the flora and fauna, as well as the Natives and their accoutrements, which so well graced the pages of his books. Although he does not appear to speak to any such role, someone well familiar with the pictured topics had to have been the source behind these engravings made by the printers. They had to have seen them and have a skilled hand such as the baron likely did.

The Authors' Concluding Thoughts

The French historian, Villiers du Terrage, regarded Lahontan's narrative as legend: "it never took place." Du Terrage went on to inaccurately assert that the fame of La Salle's 1682 expedition inspired H. Bossu, Mathieu Sagan (a contemporary of Bourgmont's son), and Baron Lahontan to elaborate their narratives.[32] He asserts that Lahontan certainly had knowledge of the *Relation* of Sagan, and that it gave him wild ideas to add to his narrative. Du Terrage also states, without explanation, that Lahontan equally "taxed" the *Relation* of Marquette.[33] Thus, by the mid-1700s, stories of white, bearded, and supposedly civilized Natives living in the west, which we now know were true, were filtering across Louisiana as well as among the Spaniards of New Mexico.[34] They were not just "stories," but actual early, rudimentary, primitive, ethnological accounts recounted via poorly informed speculative gossip.

Lahontan's fascinating tale of travels in western America was published at a time when little was known, and speculation abounded, about the region west of the Great Lakes and the Mississippi River. The supposedly fictional journeys of *Moncahat-ape*, told I n 1758 by Le Page du Pratz, echoing Lahontan's account, told of a tribe of short white Natives in the far west with long beards that lived near the Pacific Ocean, or just possibly the Great Salt Lake instead, and had firearms.[35] This element in Moncahat-ape's elaborate and incredible tale may well have been borrowed or inspired from the baron's account, which, despite the then-perceived curious nature of the bearded men, were true as explained herein. It also speaks to geography which is also quite suggestive of the valley of the Platte and possibly the Great Salt Lake as well.

Certainly, other curious tales were being told in the 1700s of residents of the far west: among them were stories of a nation of dwarfs no more than three feet tall. La Vérendrye carried such a tale back to New France. It was said that they lived on the banks of the Missouri.[36] Such lore of little people with large heads was recorded by later explorers, among them Lewis and Clark.[37] Dwarfism is known among peoples throughout the world. The presence of a few noted by explorers among some Native populations does not mean they were fictional or made up an entire sociopolitical entity or were some distinctive "race." It only suggests that someone met some, such as one family group perhaps with specific genetics, of these so afflicted folks somewhere.

But Bossu, Sagan, and Le Page du Pratz were writing well after Lahontan's book was published. The baron had just been the first to write of such western marvels. Questions, thus, arose very early about the baron's Long River narrative, for it was then supported by no other sources as it now has been herein. In 1714 François (or Jacques-Joseph?) Le Maire wrote that "In this country we regard what the Baron de La Hontan wrote of this western district of Louisiana as an account written to please rather than to inform the reader."[38] Le Maire's 1716 manuscript map shows the Missouri River in simple form as far as the Pawnees on the Platte River.[39]

Despite Lahontan's broader contributions to the early literature of French Canada, as his book also included his Long River narrative, there are no monuments to him and even his name has largely been forgotten by both Canadians and Americans.[40] His writings are no longer widely read, except by students of early Canadian History and ancient French literature.[41] As discussed by Stephen Leacock, despite his notable contributions, the baron has become a shadowy figure. He is still a historically important individual who has unfortunately been dropped into the deep mists of time from the heritage and past glory of French Canada.[42]

The baron left no known heirs in New France and the name *"Lahontan"* is not readily found to exist in the populaces of either the US or Canada. No significant place names are known to be derived from his name in either Canada or the areas of the US, such as Minnesota, where he has by some been thought to have explored. He has certainly not yet had any in Nebraska where he seemingly did explore and claim for France. Only a small community near North Bay in Ontario and an insignificant street in Montreal are known to bear his name today.[43]

The baron was, however, not neglected by the US geologists who explored the American West in the years before and after the American Civil War. Pleistocene Lake Bonneville, that shrank to become today's Great Salt Lake, inspired long quotations from Lahontan when Captain Howard Stansbury of the United States Topographical Engineers surveyed the lake between 1849 and 1850. The fact that the baron was seemingly the first to mention the Great Salt Lake in print was clearly not lost by Stansbury.[44]

Matters went a step further in 1867 when Clarence King, director of the War Department's Geological Exploration of the Fortieth Parallel, explored Carson Sink in western Nevada. There he discovered that Pyramid Lake and its neighbor to the east were but dwarfed remnants of a giant Pleistocene body of water that once covered 8,500 square miles. He named it Lake Lahontan so that, despite all critics, the baron has a geographic monument, albeit an all-but-dead lakebed.[45] Today one will note uses of Lahontan's name in Nevada and California where numerous businesses and organizations are named after him. There are also a Lahontan Cutthroat Trout, a Lahontan Valley and its Recreation Area in Nevada. While his name lives on, it is not, unfortunately, because of any positive legacy deriving from his Long River or any other of his explorations and experiences he undertook on behalf of his king and country.

A Lahontan Denouement

Stephen Butler Leacock (1869–1944) was a Canadian who became one of his country's most internationally successful writers. Although he held a PhD in economics and political science from the University of Chicago, he was perhaps the best-known English-speaking humorist in the world between 1915 and 1925. He also taught economics and political science for many years at McGill University in Montreal where he chaired that department. He was also a serious scholar of Canadian history. Leacock studied the Baron Lahontan and his Long River narrative and spoke about and edited a collection of essays on the subject.[46]

The authors here turn again to Leacock since he was one of the only significant historians who ever defended Lahontan and his Long River narrative after thoughtful study of the subjects. Unfortunately, like everyone else this scholar also tumbled headlong into the baron's "great deception" about the location of the river and attempted an explanation that took him northward up the Mississippi and then up the Minnesota River. Despite this huge misstep, his prose is quite compelling as he discussed the young baron and how he managed to, as he put it, "get off on the wrong foot." In so doing he had one of his own (or one of the) most notable accomplishments in New France wind up on the scrap heap of historical literature. Although he did not realize the nature of the baron's deception, the following quotes are from the address he gave before the Minnesota Historical Society on October 18, 1933.[47] Leacock's so well-chosen words should help readers ease into better understandings of the baron and the context within which he wrote about the Long River. Due to his fine yet relaxed writing style, his words are thought to be a fitting way to close this revisit of his Long River narrative.

> One would look in vain in the honor roll of the explorers and discoverers of the Great Lakes and the Mississippi Valley for the name of the Baron de Lahontan. Not a single monument has been erected in his memory, not a single tablet inscribed in his honor. Yet, if the forgotten baron had his deserts, his name would stand beside those of Marquette and Jolliet and La Salle in the history of the Father of Waters. In particular the state of Minnesota would recall his memory as the man who was the first to push his way into the north central part of that state [sic] and to approach the great northern divide over a century before it became known to the world. French Canada, where the name of the baron is either utterly forgotten or utterly despised, ought to honor him as one of the most gallant, most talented, and most devoted of the nobles of France who spent the best of their years in the service of New France. But it was the fate of the baron to "get in wrong." He went to Canada in 1683 as an officer in the army. He was at that time a boy of seventeen. In the letters which he wrote home, and which he printed twenty years later as his Voyages, he was silly enough to repeat the barrack room stories he had heard about the class of women that the king of France had sent out to Canada twenty years before to be the brides of a disbanded regiment of his soldiers. The merry young baron "made his mouth warm over it," as the French have it, without realizing the falsity and the reach of the insult. As a matter of fact, it has reached down the centuries until today, and those of the people of Quebec who have ever heard of the name of Lahontan know it, therefore, as that of the man who slandered "the mothers of French

Canada." In the light of that, all else that the baron did went for nothing. But the unhappy young nobleman "got in" even worse. In his same letters of travel he expressed his opinion very frankly about the priests of New France and told how they tried, as he saw it, to tyrannize over the life of the colonists; worse than that, he was ill-advised enough to put into his travels and memoirs a lot of the skepticism already coming into fashion in his day. His dialogue on Christianity, carried on with an imaginary [sic] Indian, would have been enough to damn him even without the unlucky references to the women and the priests. As a consequence the real achievements of Lahontan were belittled and his voyage of discovery into present-day Minnesota [sic] was laughed at as a fabrication. A few people in France tried to defend the story, but they lacked facts. The legend of Lahontan as a liar grew and solidified. It was presently accepted as a fact without further examination. Even the honest and industrious Francis Parkman compares the story to Gulliver. For once Parkman seems to prefer popular approval to the search after historic truth and accepts without proper investigation the current story. Finally, Mr. J.E. Roy, in a paper-admirable but erroneous-presented to the Royal Society of Canada in 1894, covers the whole career of Lahontan and rules him out of court as an infidel and a liar. Since then oblivion has fallen on the baron. In the latest edition of the Encyclopedia Britannica there is no article on Lahontan and no reference to his name. The singular charm of Lahontan's writing, as fascinating today as it was two hundred years ago, appealed to thousands of people who would have yawned over the pages of the Jesuit Relations or the history of Charlevoix. Even today no one disputes the wonderful accuracy of Lahontan's account of war and peace in New France. But when the book came out, Lahontan was already in disgrace. A quarrel with his senior, the governor of Newfoundland,-a quarrel of youth with age, of wit with stupidity, of efficiency with ineptitude-had led to his banishment from France. He lived and died (1713) [sic] in exile. His banishment further helped to discredit, most unjustly, his reputation. Now when the young Baron de Lahontan, still well under thirty, was in command at Michilimackinac, it occurred to him that he might use the enforced leisure of an interval of temporary peace in a voyage of exploration. His own curiosity was always insatiable, and at the moment the curiosity of all the world was turned toward the Mississippi...Now begins the controversial matter. Lahontan, like a chess player, has got beyond the moves in the book. He cannot copy. What he says is that he found here a long, long river.[48]

Leacock ended his address by stating as follows about the baron's Long River narrative:

The whole matter resolves itself into giving a dog a bad name and then hanging him. It remains for some Minnesota scholar on the spot to follow up the track, measure the distances, locate the islands or the marshes, and vindicate a courageous name from historic slander."[49]

This book is intended to be a vigorous and strongly supported and modern scholarly response to Leacock's unanswered call from 1933 to rescue and redeem the reputation of a great early

French explorer of the New World. In doing so this study is believed to have added an important new chapter to the baseline ethnography of the Natives of the central Plains, and particularly of Nebraska, as well as to the heritage of French Canada and North American discovery. It is now up to the readers of this book to render their own judgments. All that remains to be said is "Vive Lahontan!"[50] Baron, now finally come, come, and assume your rightful place among the other giants of North American exploration at that "great table of the discoverers."

NOTES:

1. Thwaites, Introduction," xl-xli.

2. Lahontan, *New Voyages,* 216-20. It is presumed that the baron would have made some changes in his narrative before publishing it.

3. Lahontan, 164, 176.

4. Heidenreich, "Early French Exploration," 68-69, 118.

5. Hanson, "Late High Plains;" Holder, *Hoe and Horse;* Ludwickson, "Historic Indian Tribes."

6. Chávez, "Segesser Hide;" Parks, "Pawnee" 517-18; Jones, *Pueblo Warriors;* Swagerty, "History of the U. S," 264; Thomas, *After Coronado*. Figures 34 and 35 well depict that battle (s), Figure 34 in particular, show (s) how a presumed Pawnee village was palisaded and how the Villasur Spanish force had horses and seemingly war dogs and was fighting in part with lances. Figure 35 shows how the seemingly nearly defeated Spanish infantry has, as a last defensive effort, against nearly hopeless odds, been formed into a fighting square for its best protection. An infantry square, also known as a hollow square, was a historic close order combat formation used by infantry usually when threatened with cavalry attack. To deploy its weapons effectively, a traditional infantry unit would generally form a line. By arranging the unit so that there was no undefended rear or flank, an infantry commander could organize an effective defense against cavalry attack. With the development of modern firearms and the demise of cavalry, the square formation is now obsolete. https://en.wikipedia.org/wiki/Infantry_square accessed 5/23/24.

7. Nasatir, *Before Lewis and Clark*, 1-10.

8. Parkman, *France and England*, 110; Thwaites, "Introduction," xxxiii; DeVoto, *Course of Empire*, 64.

9. Baker, et al., *Juan Rivera's Colorado*.

10. Thévenot's map was published in his book which existing copies bear a publication date of 1682 in Paris. Crouse, however, references it to 1681. Crouse, *In Quest of the Western Ocean* 110-13; Marquette, "Map of the New Discovery;" Kupfer and Buisseret, "Seventeenth-Century Jesuit."

11. Hennepin, *Description de la. A New Discovery;* Heidenreich, "Seventeenth-Century Maps." 96; Parkman, *France and England*, 883-911; Rioux, "Hennepin." *Recueil de Voyages*.

12. Kupfer and Buisseret, "Seventeenth-Century Jesuit."

13. Wheat, *Mapping the*, 69.

14. Lahontan, *New Voyages*, 10.

15. Lahontan, "Mappa del."

16. Heidenreich, "Seventeenth Century Maps," 96.

17. Franquelin, *Partie / De L'Amerique*.

18. Heidenreich, "Seventeenth Century Maps," 96-97.

19. Wheat, *Mapping the,* 51-52; Heidenreich, "Seventeenth Century Maps,"

20. Lahontan, *New Voyages*, 133.

21. Karpinski, *An Historical Atlas*, 49; Wheat, *Mapping the,* 61-62.

22. Lahontan, "Mappa del."

23. Bray, "Utz Site," 9.

24. Lahontan, "Mappa del."

25. Lahontan, *New Voyages*, 188-91.

26. Loope et at., "Dune-dammed paleovalleys," "Thinking Like a Dune;" Muhs et al.

"Geochemical Evidence."

27. Lahontan, *New Voyages*, 186, 188.

28. Hennepin, *New Discovery*

29. Karpinski, *An Historical Atlas,* 49.

30. Wheat, *Mapping the,* 61-62.

31. Karpinski, *An Historical Atlas;* Wheat, 60-62.

32. Bossu, *Nouveaux Voyages aux Indes,* 167-69; References to Sagan are in Nasatir, *Before Lewis and Clark*, vol.1: 5n.

33. Villiers du Terrage, *La decouverte du Missouri,* 28.

34. Baker et al., *Juan Rivera's Colorado*.

35. du Pratz, *History of Louisiana*, 288; Davis, *Journey of*. 1883.

36. Smith, *Explorations of the La.* 20.

37. Moulton, *Journals of,* (2), 504-05.

38. Nasatir, *Before Lewis and Clarke*, (I), 5n quote.

39. M. Wedel, *Deer Creek Site,* 8.

40. Hayne, "Lom D'Arce de;" Lahontan, *New Voyages;* Neave, "Lahontan and the;" Ouellet, "Baron of Lahontan."

41. Ouellet, "Baron of Lahontan."

42. Leacock, *Lahontan's Voyages*, "Lahontan in Minnesota;" Hayne, "Lom D'Arce de;"

43. Ouellet, "Baron of Lahontan."

44. Stansbury, *Exploration of the*, 151; Lahontan, *New Voyages*, 194.

45. King, *Systematic Geology*, 13; Stansbury, 151.

46. Leacock, *Lahontan's Voyages,* "Lahontan in Minnesota;" Biographical detail on Stephen Leacock is found in: McGill University, "Leacock." Canadian Economic Association, "Stephen Butler Leacock;" Wikipedia, "Stephen Leacock."

47. Leacock, "Lahontan in Minnesota."

48. Leacock.

49. Leacock.

50. Portions of this chapter were read by W. Raymond Wood before the 64th Annual Plains Anthropological Conference in Topeka, Kansas in November of 2006 as the second of two papers in a symposium entitled "Reconsidering the Authenticity of the Baron Lahontan's Account of His Longue (Platte) River Journey of 1688-1689." Wood published his part of the symposium online late in 2006 at: http://www.academia.edu/5172780/A_Review_of_Past_Criticisms_and_the_Baron_LaHontans_Mapping_of_His_Long_River, accessed July 21, 2009. Baker, "Spanish Documentary Confirmation;" Wood, "Review of Past Criticisms."

15

• UNDERSTANDING LAHONTAN'S GREAT LONG RIVER DECEPTION •

by

Steven G. Baker

Although all lines of evidence indicate that Lahontan intentionally misled his readers as to the location of his Long River, it is believed to have herein been indisputably demonstrated to have been a combination of the lower Missouri and, particularly, the Platte Rivers. This, the only detectible deception in his narrative, was the root cause of his critics deeming it fraudulent and was in large measure what ruined his reputation. That act appears to have been a classic feint intended to mislead anyone who might wish to duplicate his journey and perhaps find an inland passage before he could. Since he had already been there, he is suspected to have then been one of the few, if not the only, Frenchman who really knew anything about the Missouri as the most likely way to such a passage and had some remaining potential to further seek it. Any reasonable person in such a circumstance, and with the kind of financial needs the baron had, would endeavor to protect that potential by carefully guarding what he knew.

The place where Lahontan claimed he ended his travels would have been on the Platte River in western Nebraska; far from the deceptive one he mapped for it relative to the Wisconsin, Mississippi, and other rivers.[1] As indicated in his locational maps (Figures 2,18) he showed the river as being to the north above the Wisconsin and southward below the Minnesota. At the start of his trip Lahontan appears to have known about where the Long River and the Eokoro (Otoe) people were then located and the approximate latitude of its mouth on the Mississippi as well. Even before he reached the Mississippi he discussed these matters with the Fox headman who also knew something about the river.[2]

Lahontan's Feint: The Northward Interpretation

Lahontan's deception commenced with this erroneous mapping of the Long River's location and his words, though contrary to most everything else in his narrative that indicate he traveled southward, he artfully molded around it to bolster its credibility. There was never a river such as the baron described at or anywhere near that location he published. He then attested that his mapping was very accurate. It is not possible to attribute this gross error to a simple mistake by the printers who obviously engraved the two maps showing the river's incorrect location. The rudimentary maps of the Platte portion of the Long River itself (Figures 18, 19) are correctly done; they are, however, primitive and simplified; having been made at small scale from the perspective of only traveling on the river. Since he published them at least twice, and seemingly sequentially in both the French and English editions of his book, the baron had obviously reviewed the final versions of each and thus had opportunity to correct them before stating:

> I have likewise corrected almost [emphasis added] all the Cuts of the Holland Impression, for the Dutch Gravers had murder'd 'em,by not understanding their Explications which were all in French. They have grav'd Women for Men, and Men for Women; naked persons for those that are cloath'd and è Contra. As for the Maps, the Reader will find them very exact [emphasis added]; And I have taken care to have the Tracts of my Voyages more nicely delineated, than in the Original [meaning the first French version of 1703].[3]

Lahontan obviously allowed his deception to be repeated in the new edition after inspecting the incorrect map engravings in the original. This further indicates it was his intent to continue to mislead rather than making corrections. It was also not just Lahontan's reprinting of the maps which demonstrates the intentional deception rather than doing the cuts over. This, in addition to the inaccurate latitude he recorded, further misled Lahontan's critics. He went even further to mislead by use of a single important term after he gained the Mississippi. In the original English version of his narrative, which many of his critics relied on, the baron stated that on "The 2nd of November we made the Mouth of the Long River, having first stem'd [emphasis added] several rapid Currents of that River [the Mississippi], though 'twas then at lowest Ebb."[4]

According to every one of several English dictionaries consulted, in standard parlance the terms "stem," "stemmed," or "stemming" relative to marine navigation has always meant to fight upriver or otherwise against a tide or current. Fouillade's and Wilson's translations of the 1703 French text are consistent with the original English translation.[5] They indicate that the baron said that he stemmed upriver against the current by his use of the words *"refoule plusieurs courants de ce Fleuve"* or "stemmed several currents of this river." There is no other possible explanation for his use of the term other than to mislead and indicate that he traveled northward up the Mississippi as his mapping indicated. Even though he very seldom again used the term in his book, he confirmed its definition in his "Table explaining some Terms made use of in both Volumes." In that he states: "Stem a Tide or the Current of a River, ie: to sail against the Current, or to steer for the place from whence the Tides or Currents come." [6]

In keeping with his own definition, the baron's 1703 English text states he reached the Long River after *"having first stem'd several rapid Currents of that River* [the Mississippi]. "It thus seems reasonable that his critics, against all this evidence, would have no justification upon only cursory inspection of the entire narrative to doubt that he traveled upriver to the north.[7] Though overlooked by virtually all of his critics, there is the considerably more information within his narrative that demonstrates that the baron certainly traveled southward from the Wisconsin via the Mississippi to the Missouri. (Figures 1, 4) This is opposed to a view that he might have gone northward to the Minnesota River as so many have surmised if they believed he even made the trip.[8] The Minnesota is a substantial westerly tributary of the upper Mississippi that it joins well north of the Wisconsin by no more than about two hundred miles at present-day Minneapolis. This was the region then occupied by the Sioux. It is to be noted that the baron stated that he was planning to travel to the source of the Long/ Pekistanouï River.[9] It was only the Missouri and clearly not the Mississippi which he wanted to travel to its source. It is truly unbelievable how any thoughtful critics of the baron's narrative could have overlooked this critical point and even suggested that he traveled northward to the Minnesota River.

By relying solely on the foregoing evidence, virtually all of the baron's critics also completely ignored the contradictory statement he made just prior to his departure when he stated that he was going to travel to the "southern countries."[10] In short, his locational maps are incorrect, his related prose is similarly deceptive and supportive of his maps, and then he emphatically attested to the accuracy of his mapping. It is apparent that Lahontan was being quite creative in trying to convince his readers that he had traveled northward from the Wisconsin rather than southward, particularly when so much other evidence indicates he traveled southward.

There are also other reasons that would have precluded the baron from traveling northward to the Minnesota River. The first is that he told the Fox chieftain with whom he was talking that he was going to seek the source of the Long River which was obviously not the Mississippi. He could only reach it by traveling southward down the Mississippi once he reached it by way of the Wisconsin River. He certainly could not reach the Missouri by canoe by traveling northward. He told this same man that he was going to stay far away from the Sioux who lived upriver from the Wisconsin and were dire enemies of the Fox. He, thus, could not have taken his small contingent of Fox men, as loaned by their leader, northward on the Mississippi into Sioux territory.[11] Further, fall and winter would soon be at hand and the Minnesota and other northern rivers then freeze solid. All the waterfowl, which the baron found so plentiful on the Long River, then fly south to congregate along the Platte or other warmer waters. (Figure 17)

The baron also encountered crocodiles in his travels and they are certainly not known to have occupied the northern waters of Minnesota in any season.[12] Further, he discussed travels on the Missouri, the Osage, and the Wabash Rivers which certainly do indicate that he had gone far south from the Wisconsin. The baron also turned homeward by way of the Illinois River in order to reach Lake Michigan. Since the Illinois enters the Mississippi to the south of the Wisconsin, that fact alone further demonstrates that he had traveled southward. Those who have not noted these contradictions in the baron's narrative either failed to see them or intentionally overlooked them in order to justify their suggestions that he was either a liar or may have gone northward. They only looked at his mapping and did not closely study or honestly evaluate his narrative before condemning him.

This may in part have also been due to the ease with which they were led to rely on the intentionally misplaced latitude of the Long River on some of Lahontan's maps, including his *General Map of New France...* and a small part of his *Map of the Long River....* (Figures 2, 18) On them he indicated the river was about 48 degrees north.[13] North Platte, Nebraska, about where he terminated his travels, sits at only 41.14 degrees. He thus misrepresented the river's location by a good five or six degrees too far north. This misplacement was surely intentional given that he claimed he understood and knew how to determine latitude.[14]

Moreover, the baron likely had seen the 1681 Thévenot copy of Marquette's 1673 map of the Mississippi. (Figure 5) Both the original attributed to Marquette and the Thévenot copy show the latitude of the confluence of the Missouri and Mississippi Rivers at about 37 degrees North, which is closer to it true location today at about 38 degrees and 49 minutes.[15] Thévenot's map was published in his 1682 book. which Crouse dated to 1681.[16] How Thévenot came by this map is not clear. His published version should, however, have been available to Lahontan in France prior to his sailing to New France in 1683. It certainly showed the location of the mouth of his targeted river.[17]

The baron also possessed an astrolabe, just as Father Marquette seems to have, and from early on was planning to determine the latitudes of the places where he was posted.[18] He said he also knew how to roughly gauge his latitude even without such an instrument by the positions of the stars. This information was conveyed in a small text box inset into his detailed *Map of the Long River*. (Figure 18)[19]

Finally, an understandable reason for Lahontan's deception becomes obvious at the end of his Letter XVI where he proposed, seemingly initially for his superiors, such as the governor and intendant, the requirements for another major expedition that he implied he would most happily lead.[20] This major expedition Lahontan proposed was to seemingly continue all the way to the source of the Long River/Missouri. There would have been no point for him to try to revisit the Platte. He had already gained good information about its source which rose in high mountains to the west. It was obviously not going to lead to an inland passage.

The expedition he described was far better suited to a very substantial river such as the upper Missouri rather than the notoriously shallow and sandbar-ridden Platte. This is apparent since he stated that the river could handle substantial sloops, which the Platte certainly could not.[21] It would seem that Lahontan could not have failed to observe the major confluence of the Platte and the Missouri but then Bourgmont did, as earlier stated, later note that the Missouri at that point was noticeably smaller than the Platte.[22] The baron did not mention this important confluence though he proposed following what could only have been the Missouri on northward.

Lahontan was certainly still hoping to explore to the source of the Missouri because it was so commonly still believed to be the way to an inland passage. In his proposal he could only have been targeting the source of the upper Missouri River far northward beyond where it joined the Platte. From the outset, the baron's goal had been to follow the Long River all the way to its source.[23] As originally described by Natives at the time Marquette and Jolliet discovered it in 1673, the Missouri, which they called the Pekistanouï was known to be a river of "Considerable size, coming from the Northwest, from a great Distance; and it discharges into the Missisipi."Thus the appellation "the Long River" described it over all others in the region. In his journal Father Marquette had added that "There are many Villages of savages along this river, and I hope by its means to discover the vermillion or California sea."[24]

In 1674 Governor Frontenac had written the king's minister, Colbert, and commented on Jolliet's memories of his trip down the Mississippi with Marquette and how both believed the Missouri tributary might lead to a passage to the Western Sea.[25] In completing his Long River expedition the baron became the one man who was leading on the trail to discover such a passage. Because he was hoping to further explore the river to find one, the baron appears to have intentionally embedded this deception into his narrative as a well-designed and complex feint.[26] This covered his tracks by obscuring the true identity and location of the river he searched.

Southward Travel

From the earliest days of New France many individuals hoped to discover inland or northwest passages. To be successful, such explorations of discovery through the history of mankind have required gathering intelligence on one's target, learning what competitors might already have accomplished, and anticipating what they might be planning, and then sometimes working to throw them off course. There were times when overt deception was critical and relied upon to guard secrets of past discoveries and future plans.[27] The baron was certainly aware that there was a strong possibility for potential competition. He might even have believed it might even come from his superiors or the church who might be waiting for an opportunity to discover the great prize, particularly if he divulged all he knew about finding a passage.

It is noteworthy and little wonder that Lahontan, trained to be a French military officer, would have been very familiar with the concepts of deception and feints in competitive circumstances. When Lahontan finally published the narrative so many years had passed that the deception's original purpose was no longer of concern to him. He could neither return to Canada nor again count on the Crown's resources to help him mount another expedition.

Another famous explorer provided an excellent example of a feint when he used a similar deception to throw competitors off his track when, through exploration, he hoped to make an important discovery. This was Percy Fawcett, a British explorer, who provided misleading latitude and longitude for his basecamp from whence he started his various treks into the Amazon jungle in search of the lost city of Z.[28] Unbeknownst to his rivals as they tried to follow his trails from that location and beat him to the discovery, Fawcett had intentionally mislocated his camp by a hundred miles to throw them off his routings. Such deceptions certainly occurred through the efforts of both nations and individuals through time in all kinds of competitions, including military actions where it is an old and often successful strategy.[29]

Raymond Wood always believed that Lahontan may also have placed the river at the incorrect location to try to demonstrate that it was clearly in French rather than Spanish territory and thus embolden France's claim to it.[30] Since the geography of the region was not then known and mapped, and although he would not remain an ardent supporter of the French Crown, that seems to be a possible additional motivation for the baron's deception. He had invaded Spanish territory with armed French troops. Since Spain was then on the cusp of going to war with France this might have been considered a hostile act. Relative to the competition between the two countries, the baron was also spying by actively seeking information about the Spaniards of New Mexico and/or the Gulf coast from Natives he encountered.[31] Wood always correctly emphasized that Lahontan's mapping of the Long River's location was obviously not done to accurately illustrate where he had traveled.[32] Clearly, Lahontan was not even attempting to make his mapping accurate as to the location of the Long River. His mapping of the Platte River portion of his travels in Figure 18 was, however, relatively well done and attempted to accurately illustrate his travels just as Wood believed it should have.

With few exceptions, such as Cecil Alter and Louis Houck, who, quite inexplicably completely overlooked the Platte River as a likely explanation, no one seems to have ever suggested that the baron was initially on or writing about the lower Missouri region.[33] Additionally, no one who has dealt with Lahontan's narrative could have been aware of the Spanish documentation that helps demonstrate that he ascended the Platte where he met the heavily bearded Native men from the vicinity of the Great Salt Lake in present-day Utah which was directly, yet far, west of his location there. (Figures 18, 20)

The Missouri joins the Mississippi at Saint Louis about 450 river miles south of the Wisconsin. One must thus ask if that distance could be covered on the Mississippi in birch bark canoes in only nine or fourteen days? In the 1703 English translation Lahontan reported that he left the vicinity of the Wisconsin River on October 24 and reached the mouth of his Long River on November 2nd and entered it on the 3rd. His first French edition concurs with this statement.[34] His revised French edition of 1705, however, states that he reached the Long River on November 7.[35] Why this change was made is unknown. It thus took him no less than nine days and perhaps as many as 14 to travel by canoe down the Mississippi to his Long River. While it has herein been shown that Lahontan ended up on the Platte, and regardless of the exact timing, he could only have accessed it by water from the Missouri.[36]

To reach the Missouri in the time he states, the baron's canoes would have had to average about fifty miles per day, or approximately thirty-two miles per day if it took a full fourteen days. The Mississippi commonly runs at a rate of two or three mile per hour downriver from its headwaters.[37] In a twelve- or fifteen-hour day of paddling or sailing with the current, as was not uncommon, fifty miles per day seems a reasonable time for Lahontan to have traveled to the Missouri. Birchbark canoes like the baron used are notably light and comparatively fast relative to other watercraft, and on calm water an experienced crew could average four to six miles per hour.[38] By paddling or sailing with the current the company may well have traveled at a rate even faster. Thus, when he stated that he entered the Long River on November 3, he would have entered the Missouri, and the time frame he states (up to around thirty or more miles per day) would have been more than sufficient for him to have traveled downriver from the Wisconsin. After reaching the Missouri, Lahontan's company would still have had to stem upriver approximately another 630 river miles to access the Platte.[39]

In comparison to the fast birchbark canoes the French first used there, with the coming of steamboats to the Mississippi and Missouri, men could move boats upriver against a strong current at a rate of only about fifteen miles per day. This was the speed assigned for bateaus, flatboats, and keelboats as used much later than the baron's time. This could be accomplished by a combination of poling, paddling, towing, and sailing. [40]

After entering the Missouri, the company traveled hard and steadily from at least November 3 to the 27th by paddling and sailing for long stretches when winds were favorable and at times long into the night as on November 21. During these periods it traveled hard and briefly met and described many Eokoro/Otoe people along the river before finally encountering the Essanape or Pawnee people, presumably on the lower Platte by November 27. The Pawnees had by then been shown as the *"Paniassa"* on the unnamed river that was obviously the Pekistanouï /Missouri River on Marquette's1673 map (Figure 5) the version of which Shea published in 1852.[41] Bourgmont noted that the *"Pani"*/Pawnee lived in ten villages about 90 miles up the Platte from its confluence with the Missouri.[42] This places their villages in the drainage of the Lower Loup River about the vicinity of Columbus, Nebraska. This is in the same locations where scholars have long understood they were then living.[43]

Lahontan had to canoe thirty miles or more per day to travel the seven hundred or so miles between the Mississippi and the lower Pawnee villages on the Platte in the time indicated. The baron mentions daily mileages of this length and in one case when the company was delayed by fatigue, he lamented that it was only able to move upriver twenty-four miles in two days.[44] Bourgmont in his expedition of 1714 also covered the same distance in birchbark canoes but only went to the mouth of the Platte and required about eighty days to make his trip.[45] This was a distance of only about 625 miles, but he traveled neither hard nor long and reported surprisingly short daily mileages, as well as stopping for weekend layovers and side trips. He thus averaged somewhat fewer than ten miles a day on his way upriver. Lahontan's company made two to three times Bourgmont's rate by pushing hard. Lahontan never mentions his departure from the Missouri onto the Platte, so exactly how long it took him to travel to the Platte is unknown.

Why the baron did not push on north up the Missouri from the Platte is also unclear, but he was likely running out of time and needed to get back to Michilimackinac and resume his duties as an officer in the marines. He also may have decided to heed the Fox headman's warning not to venture too far up the Long River "by reason of the multitudes of People that I would find there, though they have no stomach for War: He mean'd, that some numerous party might surprise me in the Night-time." [46] It is little wonder that when Lahontan proposed his second expedition, he recommended taking a large contingent of soldiers as well as portable leather defensive structures that could turn away arrows.[47]

Summary

For the past three hundred or so years Lahontan's critics have ignored a lot of evidence and taken him in entirely the wrong direction on the Mississippi. They also underappreciated the depths of his information and intellectual preparation for his trip. They have also been unaware of the ethnography of the Native peoples of the Plains and the Platte River, as well as even more westerly regions. Other than for the baron's account, these subjects would not even be witnessed, let alone be written about, until much later. That included the recently recognized information in the Spanish source materials and the extensive writing by modern scholars on Mississippian culture. Among these uninformed critics were Adams, De Voto, Parkman, Roy, Thwaites, and many others.[48]

These noted writers were unable to interpret Lahontan's Long River narrative because of his deception. There was no way they, or anyone else, could make sense of the narrative in the context of an unlikely northward trip up the Mississippi unless they were willing to really study the narrative. In addition to his deception, his critics lacked crucial ethnographic and geographical knowledge. Rather than admitting they could not solve the puzzle of the narrative, they simply declared the baron a liar and branded his account fraudulent. His critics did, however, emphasize the fact that the Long River could not have been where Lahontan's map seemed to indicate it was. They also failed to seek any alternate explanations, namely that he traveled southward down the Mississippi precisely as he said he was going to do.

Notes:

1. Baker and Wood, "Reconsidering the Authenticity;" Lahontan, *New Voyages*, 156, 285.

2. Lahontan, 176.

3. Lahontan, 9-10.

4. Lahontan, 178, e.g. 65, 161.

5. Fouillade, "Translation;" Wilson, "Translation."

6. Lahontan, *New Voyages*,. (2), 407. The baron's intentional use of the term "stem-d" and its implications for understanding the contradictions in his narrative was considered to be highly relevant to this discussion. Claude Fouillade went to significant pains to understand it in regard to his use of the term while the baron traveled the Mississippi. There was a great need to know if there was any realistic potential that he could have meant to say or imply something different. Fouillade was unable to find any French dictionary that included the term "*refouler*" earlier than 1762, well after Lahontan's days. In his view, however, the very authoritative Féraud's 1787 *Dictionaire Critique De La Langue Francaise* confirmed the baron's meanings of refouler: "*En terme de Marine, refouler la marée, aler contre le cours de la marée. Et neutralement: la marée refoule, descend*." Fouillade's English translation of the above definition is: "Stemming..." which in naval terms, means "to stem the tide," or to go against the flow of the tide. And neutrally: the tide "stems," or goes down. Fouillade's investigation demonstrated that the baron's use of the term could only have been meant to indicate that he was saying that he had traveled upriver against

the current, which he could not have done. Claude Fouillade, personal e-mail communication with Steven Baker, March 2017. Féraud, *Dictionaire Critique.*

7. Thwaites, "Introduction," xxiv.

8. Adams, *Travelers;* Leacock, *Lahontan's Voyages,* "Lahontan in Minnesota;" Thwaites, "Introduction," xxi-xxxix.

9. Lahontan 176. He told the leader of the Outagamis that he wished to travel to the source of the Long River.

10. Lahontan, 164.

11. Lahontan, 176.

12. Lahontan, 204, 346-47.

13. Lahontan, *New Voyages,* 157, 285.

14. Lahontan, 133, 284, caption Figure 14 herein.

15. Crouse, *Contributions of the Canadian Jesuits,* 113; Thévenot, *Recueil de Voyages;* Marquette, "Map of the New Discovery."

16. Thévenot, *Recueil de Voyages;* Crouse, *Contributions of the Canadian Jesuits,* 110-13.

17. Crouse, *Contributions of the Canadian Jesuits.*

18. Lahontan, *New Voyages,* 133.

19. Lahontan, 285.

20. In Chapter 6 the probable reasons for Lahontan's preparation of Letter XVI and its Long River narrative are discussed. Since he prepared it immediately upon his return to Michilimackinac and just before his formal debriefing of the governor and intendant, it appears probable that it served as his required written diary of his explorations long prior to its publication in *New Voyages.*

21. Lahontan, *New Voyages,* 211. All dictionaries define a sloop as the Dutch term "*sloep*," in turn from French "*chaloupe.*" They are sailing boats with a single mast and a fore-and-aft rig. A sloop has only one headsail. A vessel with two or more headsails is referred to as a "cutter." https://en.wikipedia.org/wiki/Sloop, accessed 2/24/2004.

22. Norall, *Bourgmont,* 123.

23. On only one occasion did the baron specifically mention the river he was intending to explore in the "Southern Countries." This was in Letter XVI after he had already left Michilimackinac and was speaking with a Fox chief on October 13, 1688. Lahontan, *New Voyages,* 175-76. Near the end of the English translation of Letter XVI, however, he only refers to how boldly one could "go to all the Countries that

lye to the West of Canada, without any apprehension of danger..." and proposed that he was the man qualified to undertake such a task.

24. Dablon, "Discovery of the Mississippi." (58), 108; Marquette, "Departure of the Father," (LIX)139-41.

25. Frontenac to Colbert, "General Memorandum," (ix), 16. November 14, 1674.

26. Lahontan, *New Voyages*, 176.

27. Sun Tzu, *Art of War*, 8, art. 18.

28. Grann, *Lost City*, 102.

29. Heidenrich, "Early French Exploration," 126; Colbert to Talon, "His Majesty's Intentions...," (9), 89; Sun Tzu, *Art of War*, 8, art18.

30. Wood, "Review of Past Criticisms."

31. Lahontan, *New Voyages*, 192, 202, 04.

32. Wood, "Review of Past Criticisms."

33. Alter, "Some Useful Early Utah," 27; Houck, *A History*, I-239.

34. Lahontan, *Nouveaux Voyages.*

35. Lahontan, *Voyages du Baron.*

36. American historian, Peter Wood, has published a strange alternate pedestrian routing for the baron's travels from the Wisconsin to his Long River. Peter Wood, *A Venture to the Plantation*. Rather than taking Lahontan northward on the Mississippi into present Minnesota by canoe as others have—or even southward to the Missouri as done herein—he proposed that the baron directly crossed the Mississippi into northern Iowa from the Wisconsin. From there he hypothesized that over the next nine days the baron stripped his company of all its cargos (which he clearly did not do) and then portaged his canoes and some very limited supplies 300 miles completely across present Iowa on the old forest path known as the "*Chemin des Voyageurs*" to the Missouri. After striking the Missouri he further hypothesized that Lahontan then canoed northward upriver and spent time among the Natives, such as the Mandan. The trek Peter Wood proposed would seemingly have made it the longest single canoe portage in Canadian history. e.g. *Wikipedia*, "Grand Portage National." This would have required a sustained speed of more than 33 miles per day for the baron's company. Such speed approaches that of the U.S. Cavalry in the nineteenth century, which might in a push make 40 miles or thereabouts in a day. Rickey, *Forty Miles A Day*. In comparison the baron noted that his first substantive land-carriage of a bit over two miles to the Wisconsin River took his original company two days to complete. Lahontan, *New Voyages*, 177. On his return trip while among the Illinois people he stated "...to lessen the drudgery of a great Land-carriage of twelve great Leagues [36 miles], ingag'd four hundred Men to transport our Baggage...." Lahontan, 207. Even with all the extra help this portage to the Chicago River still required four days to accomplish.

37. U.S. National Park Service, *Mississippi River Facts.*

38. Johnson, *Pre-Steamboat Navigation*, 18; Nute, *Voyageur,* 27.

39. Moulton, *Journals*, (2), 406—09.

40. US Department of State, *An Account of Louisiana*, 5.

41. Shea, *Discovery and Exploration;* Thévenot, *Recueil de Voyages;* Marquette, "Map of the New Discovery;" e.g. Wedel, *Introduction to Pawnee Archeology*, Map 3.

42. Norall, *Bourgmont*, 123.

43. Hyde, *Pawnee*, 11-21; Ludwickson, "Historic Indian Tribes," 136-37; Parks, "Pawnee," 515; Wedel, *Introduction to Pawnee Archeology*, 12-13, Map 3.

44. Lahontan, *New Voyages*, 183

45. Norall, *Bourgmont*, 113-23.

46. Lahontan, *New Voyages*, 176, October 11, 1688.

47. Lahontan, 209-15.

48. Adams, *Travelers and Travel Liars;* De Voto, *Course of Empire;* Ouellet, *Oeuvres Complétes;* Parkman, *France and England*, 1051; Roy, *Le Baron de Lahontan;* Thwaites, "Introduction."

•REFERENCES•

Adams, Eleanor B. "Fray Silvestre and the Obstinate Hopi." *New Mexico Historical Review* 38, no. 2 (1963): 96-138.

Adams, Eleanor B., and Fray Angélico Chávez. *The Missions of New Mexico 1776; A Description by Fray Francisco Atanasio Domínguez with other Contemporary Documents*. Santa Fe: New Edition, Sunstone Press, 2012.

Adams, Percy G. *Travelers and Travel Liars, 1660–1800*. Berkeley and Los Angeles: University of California Press, 1962.U

Alexander, Thomas G. "The Rivera Expedition." Utah.Gov/History to Go, https://historytogo.utah.gov/rivera-expedition/ (accessed September 12, 2012).

Allan, Peter. "The Baron Lahontan." Master's thesis. University of British Columbia, Vancouver, 1966.

Allen, John Logan. Ed. "French Exploration." In *A Continent Defined*, Vol. 2, *North American Exploration,* 144-520. Lincoln: University of Nebraska Press.

Allin, Lawrence C. "A Mile Wide and an Inch Deep: Attempts to Navigate the Platte River." *Nebraska History* 63 (1982): 1-15.

Alter, J. Cecil. “Some Useful Early Utah Indian References.” *Utah Historical Quarterly* 1, no. 1 (1928): 26-32.

Amaud, Balvay. “Amérindiens et soldats des troupes de la marine en Louisiane et au Pays d’en Haut (1683–1763).” PhD diss. Université Laval, 2004.

Ambrose, Stephen E. *Nothing Like It in The World: The Men Who Built the Transcontinental Railroad, 1863–1869*. New York: Touchstone, 2000.

______. *Undaunted Courage: Meriwether Lewis, Thomas Jefferson, and the Opening of the American West*. New York: Simon and Schuster, 1996.

Auerbach, Herbert S. “Father Escalante’s Journal, 1776-77: Newly Translated with Related Documents and Original Maps.” *Utah Historical Quarterly* 11, nos. 1-4 (1943):1-211.

Baker, Scott J. “Osteological Analysis.” In *Archaeological and Osteological Analysis of Two Burial Sites Along Harland County Lake, Nebraska: Chronological and Evolutionary Implications*, edited by W. L. Tibesar. Report to the U.S. Army Corps of Engineers, Kansas City District, prepared by Larson-Tibesar Associates, Laramie (1989): 69-87.

Baker, Steven G. “Cofitachique: Fair Province of Carolina.” Master’s thesis. Dept. of History, University of South Carolina, 1974.

______. “The Historic Catawba Peoples: Exploratory Perspectives in Ethnohistory and Archaeology.” Department of History and Division of Advanced Studies and Research, University of South Carolina, 1975. Unpublished manuscript in author’s possession and University of South Carolina Libraries.

______. “Historical Archaeology Exploration and Assessment of the 2nd Los Pinos Indian Agency,” Vol. 1, Uncompahgre Valley Ute Project, Report Series, No. 5, Montrose, Centuries Research, Inc., 2004. Unpublished manuscript at History Colorado.

______. "Ethnographic Evidence of a Di-Hybrid Origin for the Aboriginal Inhabitants of the Western U.S.: A Missive to Modern Anthropologists from 17th and 18th Century Spanish and French Observers." Abstract. Paper read at the 2005 Bi-Annual Meeting of the Rocky Mountain Anthropological Conference, Provo, Utah, 2005. Unpublished manuscript in author's possession.

______. "Historical Archaeological Assessment of the 1870's Reservation Period Ute/Mexican Component at the Chief Ouray Ranch (5MN847), Montrose County, Colorado." Uncompahgre Valley Ute Project, Report Series, No. 11, Centuries Research, Inc., Montrose, 2005. Unpublished manuscript in author's possession at History Colorado.

______. "Spanish Documentary Confirmation of Lahontan's Observations Regarding the Great Salt Lake and the Atypical Bearded 'Ainu-Like' Indians of Utah's Gran Teguayo." Part I in The Symposium: "Reconsidering the Authenticity of the Baron Lahontan's Account of His Longue (Platte) River Journey of 1688–1689" by Steven G. Baker and W. Raymond Wood. Abstract. Paper read at the 64th Annual Meeting of the Great Plains Anthropological Conference, Topeka, 2006. Unpublished manuscript in author's possession.

______. "Ethnographic Evidence of a Di-Hybrid Origin for the Aboriginal Inhabitants of the Western U.S.: A Missive to Modern Anthropologists from 17th- and 18th- Century Spanish and French Observers." Abstract. Paper read at the 30th Bi-Annual Great Basin Anthropological Conference, Las Vegas, 2006. Unpublished manuscript in author's possession.

______. "The Bearded Utes Recorded by the Baron Lahontan in 1688 and Domínguez and Escalante in 1776." Abstract. Paper read at the 2006 Annual Meeting of the Colorado Council of Professional Archaeologists, Estes Park, 2006. Unpublished manuscript in author's possession.

______. "The Baron Lahontan's 1688–89 Ethnographic Observations on the Dismal River and Other Peoples of the Platte River in Nebraska Part I: The History and Authenticity of the Baron Lahontan's Long River Narrative." Abstract. Paper read at the symposium: "In with the New and ...Out with the Old? New Directions in Dismal River Aspect Research," 71st Plains Anthropological Conference, Loveland, 2013. Unpublished manuscript in author's possession.

______. "The Baron Lahontan's 1688–89 Ethnographic Observations on the Dismal River and Other Peoples of the Platte River in Nebraska Part II: The Baron Lahontan's Ethnographic Observations on the Essanape/Pawnee and Gnacsitare/Plains Apache." Abstract. Paper read at the symposium: "In with the New and…Out with the Old? New Directions in Dismal River Aspect Research," 71st Plains Anthropological Conference, Loveland, Colorado, 2013. Unpublished manuscript in author's possession.

______. Cofitachique. Hudson, Southeastern Indians. Knights of Spain. https://en.wikipedia.org/wiki/Mississippian_culture, Voyages, 184-89 (accessed May 7, 2019).

Baker, Steven G., Richard F. Carrillo, and Carl D. Späth. "Protohistoric and Historic Native Americans." In *Colorado History: A Context for Historical Archaeology*, edited by E. Steven Cassells, 29-107. Denver: Colorado Council of Professional Archaeologists, 2007.

Baker, Steven G., Rick Hendricks (translator and foreword), and Gail Carroll Sargent (illustrator). *Juan Rivera's Colorado, 1765: The First Spaniards Among the Ute and Paiute Indians on the Trails to Teguayo*. Lake City, Colorado: Western Reflections Publishing, 2015.

Baker, Steven G., and W. Raymond Wood. "Reconsidering the Authenticity of the Baron Lahontan's Account of His Longue (Platte) River Journey of 1688–1689." Abstract. Paper read in two parts at the 64th Annual Meeting of the Great Plains Anthropological Conference Topeka, 2006. Unpublished manuscript in author's possession.

Baldwin, Leland D. *The Keelboat Age on Western Rivers*. Pittsburg: University of Pittsburg Press, 1941.

Bancroft, Hubert Howe. *History of the Pacific States of North America. In The North American States, 1531–1800*, vol. 1 of 10. San Francisco: A. L. Bancroft, 1883.

______. *The Works of Hubert Howe Bancroft,* vol. 14: *History of Mexico*, vol. 6: 1861–1887. San Francisco: The History Company Publishers, 1888.

______. *The Works of Hubert Howe Bancroft*, vol. 26, *History of Utah, 1540–1886*. San Francisco: The History Company Publishers, 1889.

______. *History of Arizona and New Mexico, 1530–1888*. Facsimile of the 1889 edition. Albuquerque: Horn and Wallace, 1962.

Barker, Alex W., and Timothy R. Pauketate, eds. "Lords of the Southeast: Social Inequality and the Native Elites of Southeastern North America." *Archeological Papers of the American Anthropological Association*, 3. Washington, DC, 1992.

Barlowe, Arthur. "Captain Arthur Barlowe's [1584] Narrative of the First Voyage Made to the Coasts of America by Two Ships..." In *The New World: The First Pictures of America*, edited and annotated by Stefan Lorant, 125-33. New York: Duell, Sloan, and Pearce, 1946.

Bass, William M. *Human Osteology: A Laboratory and Field Manual.* Special Publication No. 2. Columbia: Missouri Archaeological Society, 2005.

Bellin, Jacques Nicolas. *Parte occidentale de la Nouvelle France ou du Canada*. Nürnberg: Horman Erben, 1755.

Benson, Maxine, ed. *From Pittsburgh to the Rocky Mountains: Major Stephen Long's Expedition, 1819–1820*. Golden, Colorado: Fulcrum, 1988.

Berkhofer, Robert F., Jr. "White Conceptions of Indians." In *History of Indian-White Relations*, edited by Wilcomb E. Washburn, 522-47. *Handbook of North American Indians*, vol. 4. Washington, DC: Smithsonian Institution, 1988.

Birdsell, Joseph B. "The Problem of the Early Peopling of the Americas as Viewed from Asia." In *Papers on the Physical Anthropology of the American Indian*, edited by William S. Laughlin, 1-68. New York: The Viking Fund, Inc., 1951.

Blakeslee, Donald. "The Origin and Spread of the Calumet Ceremony." *American Antiquity* 46, no. 4 (1981): 759-68.

Bleed, A., and C. Flowerday, eds. "An Atlas of the Sand Hills." *Resource Atlas 5A*. Lincoln: University of Nebraska, 1990.

Bolton, Herbert E. *Pageant in the Wilderness: The Story of the Escalante Expedition to the Interior Basin, 1776*. Salt Lake City: Utah Historical Society, 1950.

Bolton, Herbert Eugene. *Coronado: Knight of Pueblo and Plains*. New York: Whittlesey House/McGraw-Hill, 1949. Reprint with foreword by John L. Kessell. Albuquerque: University of New Mexico Press, 1991.

Boss, Richard C. "Keelboat, Pirogue, and Canoe: Vessels Used by the Lewis and Clark Corps of Discovery." *Nautical Research Journal,* 29(2) 1993.

Bossu, H. *Nouveaux Voyages aux Indes Occidentales*, 2 vols. Paris: Chex La Jay Library, 1768.

Bozell, John R. "Late Precontact Village Farmers: An Agricultural Revolution." In *The Cellars of Time, NEBRASKAland Magazine* 72, no. 1 (1994): 121-31, Lincoln: Nebraska Game and Parks Commission.

Brace, C. L., N. Seguchi, A. R. Neslon, P. Qifeng, H. Umeda, A. Wilson, and M. L. Brace. "The Ainu and Jōmon Connection." In *Kennewick Man: The Scientific Investigation of an Ancient American Skeleton*, edited by D. W. Owsley and R. L. Jantz, 463-71. College Station: Texas A&M Press, 2014.

Brandão, José. "Introduction." In *Edge of Empire, 1671–1716: Documents of Michilimackinac*, edited by Joseph L. Peyser and José Brandão, xxxiii-xlii. Kalamazoo: Michigan State University Press/Mackinac Island State Park Commission, 2008.

Brandão, José António. *"Your Fyre shall burn no more," Iroquois Policy towards New France and Its Native Allies to 1701*. Lincoln: University of Nebraska Press, 1997.

______. *Mémoires of Michilimackinac and the Pays d'en Haut*. East Lansing: Michigan State University Press, 2019.

Brandão, José António, and K. Janet Ritch. *Nation Iroquois: A Seventeenth-Century Ethnography of the Iroquois*. Lincoln: University of Nebraska Press, 2003.

Brandão, José António, and William A. Starna. "The Treaties of 1701: The Triumph of Iroquois Diplomacy." *Ethnohistory* 43, no. 2 (1996): 209-44.

Bray, Robert T. "The Utz Site: An Oneota Village in Central Missouri." *The Missouri Archaeologist* 52 (1991): 1-146.

Breternitz, David A., Alan C. Swedlund, and Duane Anderson. "An Early Burial from Gordon Creek, Colorado." *American Antiquity* 36, no. 2 (1971): 170-82.

Brewerton, George Douglas. *Overland with Kit Carson: A Narrative of the Old Spanish Trail in '48*. Lincoln: University of Nebraska Press, 1993.

Brown, Ian. "The Calumet Ceremony in the Southeast As Observed Archaeologically." In *Powhatan's Mantle: Indians in the Colonial Southeast*, edited by P. H. Wood, G. A. Waselkov, and M. T. Hatley, 371-420. Lincoln: University of Nebraska Press, 2006.

Brugge, David M. "El Gran Teguayo and Trans-Great Basin Trade. Threads, Tints, and Edification: *Papers in Honor of Glenna Dean*," edited by Emily J. Brown, Karen Armstrong, David M. Brugge, and Carol J. Condie. *Papers of the Archaeological Society of New Mexico* 36. (2010): 33-8.

Burpee, Lawrence, J. *The Search for the Western Sea: The Story of the Exploration of North-Western America*. Toronto: Musson Book Co., 1908.

Butler, William B. "Some Thoughts on the Dismal River Aspect." *Southwestern Lore* 86, no. 92 (2020): 30-46.

Byers, Steven N. *Introduction to Forensic Anthropology*. Boston: Pearson/Prentice Hall, 2011.

Byrkit, Jim. "Regarding the Roads Not Taken: The 1775 and 1776 Letters of Fr. Silvestre Vélez de Escalante and Fr. Francisco Garcés." *Canyon Legacy* 53 (2005): 13-20.

Callaway, Donald C., Joel Janetski, and Omer C. Stewart. "Ute." In *Great Basin*, edited by Warren L. D'Azevedo, 336-67. *Handbook of North American Indians*, vol. 11. William C. Sturtevant, series editor. Washington, DC: Smithsonian Institution, 1986.

Canada, *Statistics Canada*, "Early French settlements (1605 to 1691)."

Canadian Economics Association. "Stephen Butler Leacock (1869–1944)." *Canadian Journal of Economics and Political Science* 10, no. 2, (1944): 216-30.

Canadian Museum of History. The Virtual Museum of New France, https://www.historymuseum.ca/virtual-museum-of-new-france/the-explorers/louis-aarmand-de-lom-darce-baron-lahontan-1684–1689 (accessed November 14, 2020).

______. "Louis-Armand de Lom d'Arce, Baron Lahontan 1684–1689." The Virtual Museum of New France. "The Explorers." Gatineau, QC, https://www.historymuseum.ca/virtual-museum-of-new-france/the-explorers/louis-armand-de-lom-darce-baron-lahontan-1684 (accessed March 4, 2021).

Cassells, E. Steve. *The Archaeology of Colorado*. Boulder: Johnson Books, 1997.

______, ed. *Colorado History: A Context for Historical Archaeology*. Denver: Colorado Council of Professional Archaeologists, 2007.

Cavelier, Jean. *The Journal of Jean Cavelier: The Account of a Survivor of La Salle's Texas Expedition, 1684–1699*, translated and edited by Jean Delanglez. Chicago: Institute of Jesuit History Publications, 1938.

Cavelier, John. "Relation of M. Cavelier (1684)." In *Early Voyages Up and Down the Mississippi, by Cavelier, St. Cosme, Le Sueur, Gravier, and Guignas*. Introduction, notes, and index by John Gilmary Shea, 13-42. Albany, New York: Joel Munsell, 1861.

Chappell, Phil E. "A History of the Missouri River." *Kansas State Historical Transaction* 9 (1906): 237-97. State Printing Office, Topeka: Nabu Public Domain Reprints.

Chardon, Roland. "The Linear League in North America." *Annals of the Association of American Geographers* 70, no. 2 (1980): 129-53.

Charlevoix, Pierre-François-Xavier de. *History and General Description of New France*. Translated by John Gilmary Shea. Vol. 1. New York: John Gilmary Shea, 1866.

Chartrand, René. Various personal email and telephone communications, between Chartrand, a French Canadian military historian from Muséoplume, Gatineau, Quebec, with Steven G. Baker, Centuries Research, Inc., Montrose, Colorado, 2008.

Chávez, Fray Angélico. "Pohé-Yemó's Representative and the Revolt of 1680." *New Mexico Historical Review* 42, no. 2 (1967):120-22.

Chávez, Fray Angélico, trans. and Ted J. Warner, ed. *The Domínguez-Escalante Journal: Their Expedition Through Colorado, Utah, Arizona, and New Mexico in 1776*. Provo: Brigham Young University Press, 1976.

Chávez, Thomas E. "The Segesser Hide Paintings: History, Discovery, Art." *Great Plains Quarterly* 413 (1990), http://digitalcommons.unl.edu/greatplainsquarterly/413 (accessed January 2, 2019).

Clayton, Lawrence A., Vernon J., Moore, and Edward C. Moore. *The DeSoto Chronicles : The Expedition of Hernando de Soto to North America in 1539–1543*. University of Alabama Press, Tuscaloosa, 1993.

Colbert, M. to M. Talon. "His Majesty's Intentions…" June 4, 1672. CDNY, (9):89.

Connolly, Bob, and Robin Anderson. *First Contact: New Guinea's Highlanders Encounter the Outside World*. New York: Viking Penguin, 1987.

Couture, Patrick. n.d. "History of Québec and French North America. Nouvelle-France 1524 á 1763," https://www.republiquelibre.org/cousture/NVFR2.HTM (accessed March 15, 2021).

Crane, Vernor W. *The Southern Frontier, 1670–1732*. Durham, N. C.: Duke University Press, 1928. Reprint. Ann Arbor: University of Michigan Press, 1964.

Crompton, F. C. B. *Glimpses of Early Canadians: Lahontan*. Toronto: Thomas Nelson & Sons, Limited, 1925.

Crouse, Nellis M. *La Verendrye: Fur Trader and Explore*r. Port Washington, New York: Kennikat Press, 1956.

______. *In Quest of the Western Ocean*. New York: William Morrow, 1928.

______. "Contributions of the Canadian Jesuits to the Geographical Knowledge of New France, 1632–1635. PhD diss. Cornell University, 1924. Reprint. New Delhi, India: Isha Books, 1971.

Cumming, William P. *The Southeast in Early Maps*. Chapel Hill: The University of North Carolina Press, 1962.

______, ed. *The Discoveries of John Lederer*. Charlottesville: University of Virginia Press, 1958.

Cutter, Donald C., trans."Translation of the 1765 Diaries of Juan María Antonio de Rivera." 1968. Unpublished manuscript in author's and Steven G. Baker's possession.

______. "Prelude to a Pageant in the Wilderness." Abstract. Presidential Address before the Sixteenth Annual Conference of the Western History Association, Denver, October 13-16, 1976. Unpublished manuscript in author's possession and Steven G. Baker's possession.

______. "Prelude to a Pageant in the Wilderness." *The Western Historical Quarterly* 8, no.1 (1977): 5-14.

______. "Cross on the Cottonwood." Unpublished manuscript in the author" and Steven G. Baker's possession possession, 2002.

______ "Forerunners of the Old Spanish Trail? I'll give you six!" *Spanish Traces* 10, no. 3 (2004): 10-15.

D'Azevedo, Warren L., ed. *Great Basin. Handbook of North American Indians*, vol. 11. William C. Sturtevant, general editor. Washington, DC: Smithsonian Institution, 1986.

______. "Introduction." In *Great Basin. Handbook of North American Indians*, vol. 11. William C. Sturtevant, general editor. Washington, DC: Smithsonian Institution, 1986.

Dablon, Claude. "Discovery of the Mississippi." *JR* 58, 108.

Dablon, Claude, ed. *Relation de la descouverte de plusieurs pays situez au midi de la Nouvelle-France, faite en 1673*. Quebec: Claude Dablon, 1674.

______. "On the Departure of the Father from the Illinaois; of the Painted Monsters Which He Saw Upon the Great River Mississippi; of the River Pekitanoui. Continuation of' the Voyage," edited by Father Claude Dablon. Travels and Explorations of the Jesuit Missionaries in New France 16-10-1791. *JR and Allied Documents*, edited by Rueben Gold Thwaites. vol. 59, 137-41 Cleveland: Burrows Brothers, 1899. Moses.creighton.edu/kripke/jesuitrelations/relations_59.html#_edn20 (accessed February 16, 2021).

Davis, Andrew McFarland. "The Journey of Moncahat-ape." *Journal of the American Antiquarian Society* (1883): 321-48.

Delanglez, Jean. "Franquelin, Mapmaker." *Mid-America* 25, no. 1 (1943): 29-74.

______. translation. and annotation. *The Journal of Jean Cavelier: The Account of a Survivor of La Salle's Texas Expedition, 1684–1688*. Chicago: Institute of Jesuit History, 1938.

Delisle, Guillaume. "Carte du Mexique et de la Florida." In *The Southeast in Early Maps*, by William P. Cumming, Plate 43. 1703. Reprint. Chapel Hill: University of North Carolina Press, 1962.

DeMallie, Raymond J., ed. *Plains. Handbook of North American Indians*. William C. Sturtevant, general editor. vol. 13, pt. 2. Washington, DC: Smithsonian Institution, 2001.

DePratter, Chester B. "Cofitachique: Ethnohistorical and Archaeological Evidence." In *Studies in South Carolina Archaeology: Essays in Honor of Robert L. Stephenson*, edited by Albert C. Goodyear III and Glen T. Hansen. Anthropological Studies 9. Columbia: South Carolina Institute of Archaeology and Anthropology, 1989, 133-56.

______. *Late Prehistoric and Early Historic Chiefdoms in the Southeastern United States*. New York: Garland, 1991.

DeVoto, Bernard. *The Course of Empire*. Boston: Houghton Mifflin, 1952. Reprint. New York: Mariner Books/Harper Collins, 1998.

Dickason, Olive P. *The Myth of the Savage and the Beginnings of French Colonialism in the Americas, 1984*. Reprint 1970. Edmonton: University of Alberta Press.

Dickey, Michael. *The People of the River's Mouth: In Search of the Missouri Indians*. Columbia: University of Missouri Press, 2011.

Domínguez, Francisco Atanasio. *The Missions of New Mexico, 1776: A Description*, translated and edited by

Eleanor B. Adams and Fray Angélico Chávez. Santa Fe: New Edition, Sunstone Press, 2012.

Dort, Wakefield, and J. K. Jones, Jr., eds. *Pleistocene and Recent Environments of the Central Great Plains*. Lawrence: University Press of Kansas, 1970.

Du Pratz, Antoine Simon Le Page. *The History of Louisiana*. London: T. Becket, 1774.

Dunn, James Taylor. "Du Luth's Birthplace: A Footnote to History." *Minnesota History* 46, no. 6 (Summer 1979): 228-32.

Dupré, Céline. "Cavelier de la Salle, René-Robert." In *Dictionary of Canadian Biography*, vol. 1. University of Toronto/Université Laval, 2003, http://www.biographi.ca/en/bio/cavelier_de_la_salle_rene_robert_1E.html (accessed May 1, 2021),

Eccles, W. J. *The Canadian Frontier, 1534–1760*. New York: Holt, Rinehart and Winston, 1969.

______. "La Mer de l'Ouest: Outpost of Empire." In *Rendezvous: Selected Papers of the Fourth North American Fur Trade Conference, 1981*, edited by Thomas C. Buckley, 1-34. St. Paul: The North American Fur Trade Conference, 1984.

______. "The Fur Trade in the Colonial Northeast." In *History of Indian-White Relations*, edited by Wilcomb E. Washburn, 324-34. *Handbook of North American Indians* William C. Sturtevant, general editor. vol. 4. Washington, DC: Smithsonian Institution, 1988.

______. "French Exploration in North America, 1700–1800." In *A Continent Defined,* edited by John Logan Allen, 149-202. *North American Exploration*, vol. 2. Lincoln: University of Nebraska Press, 1997.

______, *Frontenac: The Courtier Governor*. Lincoln, University of Nebraska Press. 2003.

———. "Brisay de Denonville, Jacques-René de, Marquis de Denonville." In *Dictionary of Canadian Biography*, vol. 2, University of Toronto/Université Laval, 2003, http://www.biographi.ca/en/bio/brisay_de_denonville_jacques_rene_de_2E.html (accessed August 16, 2020).

———. "Comte de Frontenac et de Palluau." In *Dictionary of Canadian Biography*, vol. 1, University of Toronto/Université Laval, 2003, http://www.biographi.ca/en/bio/buade_de_frontenac_et_de_palluau_louis_de_1E (accessed December 24, 2018).

Emerson, Thomas E. "Cahokia Elite Ideology and the Mississippian Cosmos." In *Cahokia, Domination and Ideology in the Mississippian World*, edited by Timothy R. Pauketat and Thomas E. Emerson, 190-228. Lincoln: University of Nebraska Press, 1997.

Erlandson, J. "From Coast to Coast: New Insights into the First Peopling of Americas." Annual Lecture at the George C. Frison Institute of Archaeology and Anthropology, University of Wyoming, 2014.

Eschner, Thomas R., Richard F. Hadley, and Kevin D. Crowley. "Hydrologic and Morphologic Changes in Channels of the Platte River Basin in Colorado, Wyoming, and Nebraska: A Historical Perspective." *U.S. Geological Survey Professional Paper 1277-A*. Washington, DC: GPO, 1983.

Feest, Johanna, and Christian F. Feest. "Ottawa." In *Northeast*, edited by Bruce G. Trigger, 772-91. *Handbook of North American Indians*, vol. 15. Washington, DC: Smithsonian Institution, 1978.

Féraud, Jean Francois. *Dictionaire Critique de la Langue Francaise*, 1787–88, https://feraud.atilf.fr/ (accessed April, 28, 2024).

Ferguson, Leland G. "South Appalachian Mississippian." PhD diss., Dept. of Anthropology, University of North Carolina, Chapel Hill, 1971.

Fernández Duro, Cesareo. *Don Diego de Peñalosa y su descubrimiento del Reino de Quivera*. Madrid: Noticias de Expediciones, 1884.

Fitzhugh, William W., and Chisato O. Dubreuil, eds. *AINU: Spirit of a Northern People*. Arctic Studies Center, National Museum of Natural History, Smithsonian Institution/University of Washington Press, 1999.

Flint, Richard, and Shirley Cushing Flint. *The Coronado Expedition from the Distance of 460 Years*. Albuquerque: University of New Mexico Press, 2003.

______. "Diego Dionisio de Penalosa Briceno y Berdugo." New Mexico Office of the State Historian. 2004-2009b *(http://www.newmexicohistory.org/filedetails.php?fildID=473* accessed September 8, 2009).

______, eds. *The Coronado Expedition to Tierra Nueva: The 1540–1542 Route Across the Southwest*. Boulder: University Press of Colorado, 1997.

Fogelson, Raymond D. *Southeast*. *Handbook of North American Indians*, edited by Raymond D. Fogelson and Warren L. D'Azevedo, William C. Sturtevant, series editor, vol. 14. Washington, DC: Smithsonian Institution, 2004.

Fontana, Bernard L. "On the Meaning of Historic Sites Archaeology." *American Antiquity* 31, no. 1 (1965): 61-64.

Fortier, John. "Juchereau de Saint-Denys, Charles." In Dictionary of Canadian Biography, vol. 2. University of Toronto/Université Laval, 2003, http://www.biographi.ca/en/bio/juchereau_de_saint_denys_charles_2E.html (accessed April 30, 2021),

Foster, Morris W., and Marth McCollough. "Plains Apache." In *Plains*, edited by Raymond J. DeMallie, 926-40. *Handbook of North American Indians*, William C. Sturtevant, series editor. vol. 13, pt. 2. Washington, DC: Smithsonian Institution, 2001.

http://www.biographi.ca/en/bio/juchereau_de_saint_denys_charles_2E.html.

Fournier, Marcel. *Les Officiers Des Troupes De La Marine In Canada 1683–1760*. Quebec City: Bibliothèque et Archives National du Quebec, 2017.

Fouillade, Claude. Unpublished French to English Translation of Portions of Lahontan's Letter XVI and Related Letters. 2020.

Fowler, Don D., and Catherine S. Fowler, eds. *Anthropology of the Numa: John Wesley Powell's Manuscripts on the Numic Peoples of Western North America 1868–1880*. Smithsonian Contributions to Anthropology, no. 14. Washington, DC: Smithsonian Institution Press, 1971.

Fowler, Melvin L. "Cahokia and the American Bottom: Settlement Archeology." In *Mississippian Settlement Patterns*, edited by Bruce D. Smith, 455-75. New York: Academic Press, 1978.

Franquelin, Jean-Baptiste-Louis. Partie/De L'Amerique/Septentrionale/....1699. Service historique de la Marine, Bibliothèque, 4040B, no. 12 a-d. Paris, 1699.

Fremont, John. *A Report on an Exploration of the Country Lying Between the Missouri River and the Rocky Mountains; on the Line of the Kansas and Great Platte Rivers*. United States Senate, Washington, 1843.

Freshfield, Douglas W., and Captain W. J. L. Wharton, eds. *Hints to Travelers Scientific and General*. London: The Royal Geographical Society, 1893.

Frison, George C. *Prehistoric Hunters of the High Plains*. 2nd edition. New York: Academic Press, 1991.

Frontenac to Colbert. "General Memorandum on the State of the Colony." CDNY, vol 9, no. 16, November 14, 1674.

Gagnon, Francois-Marc, ed., with translation by Nancy Senior and modernization by Réal Ouellet, n.d. *The Codex Canadensis and the Writings of Louis Nicolas: The Natural History of the New World*. Tulsa: Gilcrease Museum/McGill-Queen's University Press, 2011.

_______. "Introduction." In *The Codex Canadensis and the Writings of Louis Nicolas: The Natural History of the New World*, edited by Francois-Marc Gagnon, 3-91. Tulsa: Gilcrease Museum/McGill-Queen's University Press, 2011.

Galloway, Patricia, ed. *The Hernando de Soto Expedition: History, Historiography, and "Discovery" in the Southeast*. Lincoln: University of Nebraska Press, 1997.

Galloway, Patricia, and Jason Baird Jackson. "Natchez and Neighboring Groups." In *Southeast*, edited by Raymond D. Fogelson. 598-615. *Handbook of North American Indians*, William C. Sturtevant, series editor. vol. 14. Washington, DC: Smithsonian Institution, 2004.

Gill, George W. "Human Skeletal Remains of the Northwestern Plains." In *Prehistoric Hunters of the High Plains*, edited by George C. Frison, 431-47. 2nd edition. New York: Academic Press, 1991.

______. "Craniofacial Criteria in Forensic Race Identification." In *Forensic Osteology: Advances in the Identification of Human Remains*, edited by K. J. Reichs, 293-317. 2nd edition. Springfield, Illinois: Charles C. Thomas, 1998.

______. "Basic Skeletal Morphology of Easter Island and East Polynesia, with PaleoIndian Parallels and Contrasts." In *Pacific 2000: Proceedings of the Fifth International Conference on Easter Island and the Pacific*, edited by Christopher M. Sevenson, Georgia Lee, and F. J. Morin, 447-56. Los Osos, Calif.: The Easter Island Foundation, 2001.

______. "Appearance of the 'Mongoloid Skeletal Trait Complex' in the Northwestern Great Plains: Migrations, Selection, or Both?" In *PaleoAmerican Origins: Beyond Clovis*, edited by Robson Bonnichsen, Bradles T. Lepper, Dennis Standford, and Michael R. Waters, 257-66. College Station, Texas: Texas A&M University, Center for the Study of the First Americans, 2005.

______. "Northwestern Plains Archaic Skeletons with PaleoAmerican Characteristics." In *Skeletal Biology and Bioarchaeology of the Northwestern Plains*, edited by G. W. Gill and R. L. Weatherman, 257-61. Salt Lake City: University of Utah Press, 2008.

______. "Advances in Northwestern Plains and Rocky Mountain Bioarchaeology and Skeletal Biology." In *Prehistoric Hunter-Gatherers of the High Plains and Rockies*, edited by M. Kornfeld, G. C. Frison, and M. L. Larson, 531-52. 3rd edition. Walnut Creek, Calif.: Left Coast Press, 2010.

______. "Morphological Features that Reflect Population Affinities." In *Kennewick Man: The Scientific Investigation of an Ancient American Skeleton*, edited by D. W. Owsley and R. L. Jantz, 503-18. College Station: Texas A&M University Press, 2014.

______. "East Polynesian and Paleoindian Parallels and Contrasts in Skeletal Morphology." In *Skeletal Biology of the Ancient Rapanui (Easter Islanders)*, edited by V. H. Stefan and G. W. Gill, 269-85. Cambridge: Cambridge University Press, 2016.

Gill, George W., and B. Miles Gilbert. "Race Identification from the Midfacial Skeleton: American Blacks and Whites." In *Skeletal Attribution of Race: Methods for Forensic Anthropology*, edited by G. W. Gill and S. Rhine. *Anthropological Papers No. 4*. Maxwell Museum of Anthropology, Albuquerque, New Mexico (1990): 47-53.

Gill, George W., and Carlos J. Jimenez. "Paleoamerican Skeletal Features Surviving into the Late Plains Archaic." In *New Perspectives on the First Americans*, edited by Bradley T. Lepper and Robson Bonnichsen, 137-42. College Station: Texas A&M University, Center for the Study of the First Americans, 2004.

______. "PaleoAmerican Skeletal Features Surviving into the Late Plains Archaic." In *New Perspectives on the First Americans*, edited by Bradley T. Lepper and Robson Bonnichsen, 137-41. College Station: Texas A&M University, Center for the Study of the First Americans, 2004.

Gill, George W., and Cresta Valentine Deeds. "Temporal Changes in Nasal Sill Development Within the Northwestern Plains Region." In *Skeletal Biology and Bioarchaeology of the Northwestern Plains*, edited by G. W. Gill and R. L. Weathermon, 263-70. Salt Lake City: University of Utah Press, 2008.

Gill, George W., and Rick L. Weathermon, eds. *Skeletal Biology and Bioarchaeology of the Northwestern Plains*. Salt Lake City: The University of Utah Press, 2008.

Gill, George W., Susan S. Hughes, Suzanne M. Bennett, and B. Miles Gilbert. "Racial Identification from the Midfacial Skeleton with Special Reference to American Indians and Whites." *Journal of Forensic Sciences* 33, no. 1 (1988): 92-99.

Gillespie, Michael. *Wild River, Wooden Boats: True Stories of Steamboating and the Missouri River*. Stoddard, Wisconsin: Heritage Press, 2000.

Goddard, Ives. "The Languages of the Plains." In *Plains*, edited by Raymond J. DeMallie, 61-7. *Handbook of North American Indians*, vol. 13, pt. 2. Washington, DC: Smithsonian Institution, 2001.

Goetzmann, William H. *Exploration and Empire: The Explorer and the Scientist in the Winning of the American West*. New York: Alfred A. Knopf, 1971.

Grann, David. *The Lost City of Z: A Tale of Deadly Obsession in the Amazon*. New York: Vintage Books, 2010.

Greenly, A. H. "Lahontan: An Essay and Bibliography." *Papers of the Biographical Society of America* 48, no. 4 (1954): 324-88.

Gregg, Kate L. "The Missouri Readers: Explorers in the Valley." *Missouri Historical Review* 39, no. 3 (April 1945): 354-88.

Green, William, and Roland L. Rodell. "The Mississippian Presence and Cahokia Interaction at Trempealeau, Wisconsin." *American Antiquity* (1994): 334-59.

Gunnerson, James H. "An Introduction to Plains Apache Archaeology: The Dismal River Aspect." *Bureau of American Ethnology Bulletin* 173, no. 58 (1960): 131-260.

______. "Plains Apache Archaeology: A Review." *Plains Anthropologist* 13, no 41 (1968):167-88.

______. *Archaeology of the High Plains*. Cultural Resource Series, 18. Denver: Colorado Bureau of Land Management, 1987.

______. "Plains Village Tradition: Western Periphery." In *Plains*, edited by Raymond J. DeMallie, 234-

44. *Handbook of North American Indians*, William C. Sturtevant, series editor. vol. 13, pt. 1 Washington, DC: Smithsonian Institution, 2001.

Gunnerson, James H., and Dolores A. Gunnerson. *Ethnohistory of the High Plains*. Cultural Resource Series, 26. Denver: Colorado Bureau of Land Management, 1988.

Hackett, Charles Wilson. *Revolt of the Pueblo Indians of New Mexico and Otermín's Attempted Reconquest, 1680–1682*. Albuquerque: University of New Mexico Press, 1942.

Hafen, LeRoy R., and Ann W. Hafen. *To the Rockies and Oregon, 1839–1842: With Diaries and Accounts*. Glendale, Calif.: Arthur H. Clark, 1955.

Hally, David J., and Robert C. Mainfort, Jr. "Prehistory of the Eastern Interior after 500 B.C." In *Southeast*, edited by Raymond D. Fogelson, William C. Sturtevant, series editor. 265-85. *Handbook of North American Indians*, vol. 14. Washington, DC: Smithsonian Institution, 2004.

Hanson, Jeffery R. "The Late High Plains Hunters." In *Archaeology on the Great Plains*, edited by W. Raymond Wood, 456-80. Lawrence: University Press of Kansas, 1998.

Harrington, John Peabody. "The Ethnogeography of the Tewa Indians." *Extract from The Twenty-Ninth Annual Report of the Bureau of American Ethnology*. Washington, DC: GPO, 1916.

Harris, Marvin. *The Rise of Anthropological Theory: A History of Theories of Culture*. London: Routledge and Kegan Paul, 1972.

Harvey, David Allen. "The Noble Savage and the Savage Noble: Philosophy and Ethnography in the Voyages of the Baron Lahontan." *French Colonial History* 11 (2010): 161-91.

Hayne, David M. "Lom D'Arce de Lahontan, Louis-Armand de, Baron de Lahontan." In *Dictionary of Canadian Biography*, vol. 2, University of Toronto/Université Laval, 2003, http://www.biographi.ca/en/bio/lom_d_arce_de_lahontan_louis_armand_de_2E.h (accessed November 5, 2018

Hayne, David M. "Charlevoix, Pierre-Francois-Xavier De." In *Dictionary of Canadian Biography*, vol. 3, University of Toronto/Université Laval, 2003, http://www.biographi.ca/en/bio/charlevoix_perre_francois_xavier_de_3E.html (accessed July 5, 2022).

Heap, Gwinn Harris. *Central Route to the Pacific, from the Valley of the Mississippi to California: Journal of the Expedition of E. F. Beale...and Gwinn Harris Heap, from the Missouri to California in 1853*. Philadelphia: Lippincott, Grambo, and Co., 1854 (undated reprint by the Michigan Historical Reprint Series. University of Michigan, University Library).

Hébert, Yves. "Roy, Joseph-Edmond." In *Dictionary of Canadian Biography*, vol. 14, University of Toronto/Université Laval, 2003, http://www.biographi.ca/en/bio/roy_joseph_edmond_14E.html (accessed March 11, 2021).

Heindenreich, Conrad E. "Seventeenth-Century Maps of the Great Lakes: An Overview and Procedures for Analysis." *Archivaria* 6 (1978): 83-98.

_______. "Early French Exploration in the North American Interior." In *A Continent Defined*, edited by John Logan Allen, 65-148. Vol. 2 of *North American Exploration*. Lincoln: University of Nebraska Press, 1997.

Helm, June. "Essays on the Problem of Tribe." *Proceedings of the 1967 Annual Spring Meeting of the American Ethnological Society*. Seattle: University of Washington, 1968.

Helm, June, and Eleanor Burke Leacock. "The Hunting Tribes of Subarctic Canada." In *North American Indians in Historical Perspective*, edited by Eleanor Burke Leacock and Nancy Oestreich Lurie, 343-74. New York: Random House, 1971.

Hennepin, Father Louis. *A New Discovery of a Vast Country in America*, 2 vols. Introduction, notes, and index by Reuben Gold Thwaites. 1698. Reprint. Chicago: A. C. McClurg, 1903.

Hennepin, Louis. "Louis Hennepin." In EN:UNDEF:public_citation_publication, vol. 2. University of Toronto/Université Laval, 2003, http://www.biographi.ca/en/bio/hennepin_louis_2E.html. 1969 (accessed January 13, 2019).

______. *Description de la Louisiane, nouvellement découverte*. Paris: Chez la Veuve de Sebastien Huré, 1683.

______. *Nouvelle Découverte d'un trés grand Pays situé dans Amérique*. Utrecht: Guillaume Broedelet, 1697.

Henning, Dale R. "Plains Village Tradition: Eastern Periphery and Oneota Tradition." In *Plains*, edited by Raymond J. DeMallie, William C. Sturtevant, series editor. 222-33. *Handbook of North American Indians*, vol. 14, pt. 1. Washington, DC: Smithsonian Institution, 2001.

Hilger, M. Inez. *Together with the Ainu: A Vanishing People*. Norman: University of Oklahoma Press, 1971.

Hill, Mathew E., Jr., and Sarah Trabert. "Reconsidering the Dismal River Aspect: A Review of the Current Evidence for an Apachean (Ndne) Cultural Affiliation." *Plains Anthropologist* 247 (2018): 198-222.

Hodge, Frederick Webb. *Handbook of North American Indians North of Mexico*, 2 *vols. Bureau of American Ethnology Bulletin 30*. Washington, DC: GPO, 1906.

Holder, Preston. *The Hoe & the Horse on the Plains: A Study of Cultural Development Among North American Indians*. Lincoln: University of Nebraska Press, 1970.

Houck, Louis. *A History of Missouri from the Earliest Explorations and Settlements Until the Admission of the State into the Union*. 3 vols., Arno Press/*The New York Times*. 1908. Facsimile reprint. Chicago: R. R. Donnelley & Sons, 1971.

Howe, Daniel Walker. "Victorian Culture in America." In *Victorian America*, edited by Daniel Walker Howe, 3-28. Philadelphia: University of Pennsylvania Press, 1976.

Howells, W. W. "Crania from Wyoming Resembling 'Minnesota Man'." *American Antiquity* 3, no. 4 (1938): 318-26.

______. *Cranial Variation in Man: A Study of Multivariate Analysis of Patterns of Differences Among Recent Human Populations*. Cambridge: Harvard University Press, 1973.

Hudson, Charles. *Southeastern Indians*. Knoxville: University of Tennessee Press, 1976.

______. *The Juan Pardo Expeditions: Exploration of the Carolinas and Tennessee, 1566–1568*. Washington, DC: Smithsonian Institution Press, 1990.

Hudson, Charles, and Robbie Ethridge. *Knights of Spain and Warriors of the Sun: Hernando de Soto and the South's Ancient Chiefdoms*. Athens: The University of Georgia Press, 1997.

Hyde, George E. *Pawnee Indians*. Denver: University of Denver Press, 1951. Reprint. Norman: University of Oklahoma Press, 1974.

Irving, Washington. *Three Western Narratives: A Tour on the Prairies (1835), Astoria (1836), The Adventures of Captain Bonneville (1837).* New York: G. K. Hall, 2004.

Ishida, Hajime. "Ancient People of the North Rim: Ainu Biological Relationships with their Neighbors." In *AINU: Spirit of a Northern People*, edited by William W. Fitzhugh and Chisato O. Dubreuil, 52-56. Arctic Studies Center, National Museum of Natural History, Smithsonian Institution/University of Seattle: Washington Press, 1999.

Janetski, Joel C. *The Ute of Utah Lake. University of Utah Anthropological Papers No. 116*. Salt Lake City: University of Utah Press, 1991.

Jantz, R. L., and Douglas W. Owsley. "Pathology, Taphonomy, and Cranial Morphometrics of the Spirit Cave Mummy." *Nevada Historical Quarterly* 40, no. 1 (1997): 62-84.

______. "Variation Among Early North American Crania." *American Journal of Physical Anthropology*, 114, no. 2 (2001): 146-55.

______. "Circumpacific Populations and the Peopling of the New World: Evidence from Cranial Morphometrics." In *Paleoamerican Origins: Beyond Clovis*, edited by R. Bonnichsen, B. T. Lepper, D. Stanford, and M. R. Waters, 267-75. College Station: Texas A&M University Press, 2005.

Jantz, Richard L. "Temporal and Geographic Variation in Vault Height in the Great Plains, Great Basin, and Northwestern Plains." In *Skeletal Biology and Bioarchaeology of the Northwestern Plains*, edited by G. W. Gill and R. L. Weathermon, 271-79. Salt Lake City: The University of Utah Press, 2008.

Jantz, Richard, and M. Katherine Spradley. "Cranial Morphometric Evidence for Early Holocene Relationships and Population Structure." In *Kennewick Man: The Scientific Investigation of an Ancient American Skeleton*, edited by D. W. Owsley and R. L. Jantz, 472-91. College Station: Texas A&M Press, 2014.

Jefferson, Thomas. *Notes on the State of Virginia*. 1954. Reprint edited by William Peden. Chapel Hill: The University of North Carolina Press, 1787.

Jenness, Diamond. *The Indians of Canada*. Toronto: University of Toronto Press, 1977.

Johnsgard, Paul A. *The Platte: Channels in Time*. Revised edition. Lincoln: University of Nebraska Press, 2008.

______. *Wings Over the Great Plains: Bird Migrations in the Central Flyway*. Lincoln: Zea Books, 2012.

Johnson, John Amos. "Pre-Steamboat Navigation on the Lower Mississippi River." PhD diss. Louisiana State University, 1963, http://digitalcommons.lsu.edu/gradschool/892 (accessed May 25, 2017).

Jolliet, Louis and Jacques Marquette. *Map of the New Discovery Made by the Jesuit Fathers in and Continued by Father Jacques Marquette, from the Same Group, Accompanied by a Few Frenchmen in the Year 1673, Named "Manitounie"*. [Place of Publication Not Identified: Publisher Not Identified, 1673] Map. https://www.loc.gov/item/2021668635/. US Library of Congress, control number 2021668635.

Jones, Daniel W. *Forty Years Among the Indians: A True Yet Thrilling Narrative of the Author's Experiences Among the Natives*. Los Angeles: Westernlore, 1960.

Jones, Oakah, Jr. *Pueblo Warriors and Spanish Conquest*. Norman: University of Oklahoma Press, 1966.

Jones, Stephen R. *The Last Prairie: A Sandhills Journal*. Lincoln: University of Nebraska Press, 2000.

Joutel, Henri. *A Journal of La Salle's Last Voyage*. New York: Corinth Books, 1962.

Karpinski, Louis C. *An Historical Atlas of the Great Lakes and Michigan*. Lansing: Michigan Historical Commission, 1931. Reprinted as *Maps of Famous Cartographers Depicting North America*. Amsterdam: Meridian, 1977.

Kavanagh, Thomas W. "Comanche." In *Plains*, edited by Raymond J. DeMallie, William C. Sturtevant, series editor. 886-906. *Handbook of North American Indians*, vol. 13, pt. 2. Washington, DC: Smithsonian Institution, 2001.

Kay, Marvin. "The Great Plains Setting." In *Archaeology on the Great Plains*, edited by W. Raymond Wood, 16-47. Lawrence: University Press of Kansas, 1998.

Kellogg, Louise P., ed. "The Mississippi Voyage of Jolliet and Marquette." In *Early Narratives of the Northwest, 1634–1699*, 223-57. New York: Charles Scribner's Sons, 1917.

Kellogg, Louise Phelps. *The French Régime in Wisconsin and the North-west*. Madison: State Historical Society of Wisconsin, 1925.

Kent, Timothy J. *Rendezvous at the Straits,* vol.1. Ossineke, Michigan: Silver Fox Enterprises, 2004.

______. *Birchbark Canoes of the Fur Trade*, vols. 1 and 2. Ossineke, Michigan: Silver Fox Enterprises, 1997.

Kessell, John L. *Kiva, Cross, and Crown: The Pecos Indians and New Mexico, 1540–1840*. Albuquerque: University of New Mexico Press, 1987.

_______. *Miera y Pacheco: A Renaissance Spaniard in Eighteenth-Century New Mexico*. Norman: University of Oklahoma Press, 2013.

King, Clarence. *Systematic Geology*. Professional Papers of the Engineer Department, U.S. Army, No. 18. Washington, DC: U.S. Army, 1878.

Kingston, C. S. "The Western Sea in the Jesuit Relations." *The Oregon Historical Quarterly* 28 (1927): 133-46.

Klinkenberg, Dean. "American Icon: The Mighty Mississippi." *Smithsonian* 51, no. 5 (2020): 9-11.

Knight, Vernon James. "Ceremonialism Until 1500." In *Southeast*, edited by Raymond D. Fogelson, William C. Sturtevant, series editor 734-41. *Handbook of North American Indians*, vol. 14. Washington, DC: Smithsonian Institution, 2004.

Kono, Motomichi, and William W. Fitzhugh. "Ainu and Northwest Coast Peoples: A Comparison." In *AINU: Spirit of a Northern People*, edited by William W. Fitzhugh and Chisato O. Dubreuil, 116-23. Arctic Studies Center, National Museum of Natural History, Smithsonian Institution/Seattle: University of Washington Press, 1999.

Kuper, Carl and David Buisseret. "Seventeenth-Century Jesuit Explorer's Maps of the Great Lakes and Their Influence on Subsequent Cartography of the Region." *Journal of Jesuit Studies* 6, no. 1 (2019): 57-70.

Lahontan, Louis Armand. *New Voyages to North-America, 1703*. 1970 facsimile edition of the 1905 facsimile edition, edited by Reuben Gold Thwaites, vol. 1 of 2. New York: Burt Franklin, 1970.

______. "Brief Discours qui montre en substance Combien il seroit important de russir dan deux enterprise proposes et continues enc ce memoir," 12. Clements Library, University of Michigan, ca. 1702–1704. http://www.clements, umich.edu/Webguides/Arlenes/L.Lanontan.html (accessed April 12, 2005).

______. *Nouveaux Voyages de Mr. Le Baron de La Hontan, dans l'Amerique Septentrionale*, 3 vols. La Haye, Chez les Freres l'Honore, Marchands Libraires, 1703a.

______. *New Voyages to North America: An Account of the Several Nations of that Vast Continent*, 3 vols. London: H. Bonwicke, T. Goodwin, M. Wotton, B. Tooke, and S. Manship, 1703b.

______. *Brief Discours qui montre en substance Combien il seroît important de réussir dans deux entreprises proposes et continues en ce mèmoire*. MS, William L. Clements Library, University of Michigan, 1703. http://www.clements.umich.edu/Webguides/Arlenes/L/Lahontan.html (accessed April 12, 2005).

______. *Voyages du Baron de La Hontan dans l'Amerique Septentrionale*, 3 vols. La Haye: Chez Jonas l'Honoré, et Compagnie, 1705.

______. *Voyages Du Baron De La Hontan Dans L'améique Septentrionale: Qui Contiennent Une Rélation Des Différens Peuples Qui Y Habitent; La Nature De Leur Gouvernement, Leur Commerce, L Coûtumes, Leur Religion, & Leur Maniére De Faire La Guerre; L'intérêDes Francois & Des Anglois Dans Le Commerce Qu'Ils Font Avec Ces Nations; L'Avantage Que L'Angleterre Peut d'Arce. Retirer De Ce Païs, Etant En Guerre Avec La Franc. 2nd éd. Revue, corr. & augm. Ed.* Amerstdam, F. L'Honorê, 1974.

______. "Concerning the Regulation of the Limits Between New-England and New-France and the New York In the Lakes of North America." In *A New Baron De Lahontan Memoir on New York and the Great Laker Basin.*, edited by Edward L. Towle and George A. Rawlyk, 218-28. N.p: n.p., 1965.

Lamontagne, Léopold. "Troyes, Pierre De, Chevalier de Troyes." In *Dictionary of Canadian Biography*, vol. 1, University of Toronto/Université Laval, 2003, http://www.biographi.ca/en/bio/troyes_pierre_de_1E.html (accessed August 16, 2020).

Lavender, David. *The Way to the Western Sea: Lewis and Clark Across the Continent*. New York: Harper & Row, 1988.

Leacock, Eleanor B. "Introduction." In *North American Indians in Historical Perspective*, edited by Eleanor B. Leacock and Nancy O. Lurie, 3-28. New York: Random House, 1971.

Leacock, Eleanor B., and Nancy O. Lurie, eds. *North American Indians in Historical Perspective*. New York: Random House, 1971.

Leacock, Stephen, ed. *Lahontan's Voyages*. Ottawa: Graphic Publishers Limited, 1932.

______. "Lahontan in Minnesota." Address delivered to the Minnesota Historical Society, St. Paul, October 18, 1933. *Minnesota History* 14, no 4 (1983): 367-37.

Lederer, John. *The Discoveries of John Lederer in Three Several Marches from Virginia to the West of Carolina and Other Parts of the Continent*. London: Printed by J. C. for Samuel Hryick, 1672.

Levy, Jerrold E. "Kiowa." In *Plains*, edited by Raymond J. DeMallie, William C. Sturtevant, series editor. 907-25. *Handbook of North American Indians*, vol. 13, pt. 2. Washington, DC: Smithsonian Institution, 2001.

Lewis, Theodore H., trans. "The Narrative of the Expedition of Hernando De Soto." By the Gentleman of Elvas. In *Spanish Explorers in the Southern United States, 1528–1543*, edited by Franklin Jameson, 128-272. New York: Charles Scribner and Sons, 1907.

Long, Major Stephen H. *Account of An Expedition from Pittsburg to the Rocky Mountains, Performed in the Years 1819 and '20*, compiled by Edwin James. Philadelphia: H. C. Carey and I. Lea, 1823. Reprint. 1988, edited with an introduction by Maxine Benson, Golden, Colorado: Fulcrum, 1988.

Loope, David B., and James B. Swinehart. "Thinking Like a Dune Field: Geologic History in the Nebraska Sand Hills." *Great Plains Research* 10 (2000): 5-35.

Loope, David B., James B. Swinehart, and Jon P. Mason. "Dune-dammed paleovalleys of the Nebraska Sand Hills: Intrinsic versus climatic controls on the accumulation of lake and marsh sediments." *GSA Bulletin* 107, no. 4 (1995): 396-406.

Lorant, Stefan. *The New World, the First Pictures of America*. New York: Duell, Sloan and Pearce, 1946.

Lovis, William A. and Randolph E. Donahue. "Space, Information, and knowledge: Ethnocartography and North American Boreal Forest Hunter-Gathers." In *Information and its Role in Hunter-Gatherer Bands*, edited by Robert Whallon, William A. Lovis, and Robert Hitchcock, 59-84. Los Angeles: The Cotsen Institute of Archaeology Press, 2011. https://www.academia.edu/18864714/Space_Information_and_Knowledge_Ethnocartography_and_North_American_Boreal_Forest_Hunter_Gatherers?email_work_card=thumbnail (accessed July 11, 2021),

Lovvorn, Marjorie B., George W. Gill, G. F. Carlson, J. R. Bozell, and T. L. Steinacher. "Microevolution and the Skeletal Traits of a Middle Archaic Burial: Metric and Multivariate Comparison to Paleoindians and Modern Amerindians. *American Antiquity* 64, no. 3 (1999): 527-45.

Ludwickson, John. "Historic Indian Tribes: Ethnohistory and Archaeology." In "The Cellars of Time," *NEBRASKAland Magazine* 72, no. 1 (1994): 125-45. Lincoln: Nebraska Game and Parks Commission.

Lurie, Nancy O. "The Contemporary American Indian Scene." In *North American Indians in Historical Perspective*, edited by Eleanor B. Leacock and Nancy O. Lurie, 418-80. New York: Random House, 1971.

MacNutt, Francis Augustus, trans. and ed. *De Orbe Novo: The Eight Decades of Peter Martr De'Anghera*, 2 vols. New York: G. P. Putnam's Sons, 1912.

Malakoff, David. "The Story of Kennewick Man." *American Archaeology* 18, no. 4 (2015): 19-25.

_______. "Searching for Etzanoa." *American Archaeology*, 20, no. 1 (2016): 26-31.

Mapp, Paul W. *The Elusive West and the Contest for Empire, 1713–1763*. Chapel Hill: University of North Carolina Press, 2011.

Marcy, R. B., Colonel. *A Hand-Book for Overland Expeditions*. New York: Harper and Brothers, 1859.

_______. *Thirty Years of Army Life on the Border*. New York: Haynes Brothers, 1866.

Margry, Pierre, ed., *Découvertes et établissements des Francais dans L'Amèrique septentrionale, 1614–1754*. 6 vols. Paris: D. Jouaust, 1876–86.

_______. *Memoires et documents...dècouvertes et etablissements des Francais dans l'ouest et dans le sud de l'Amérique Septentrionale*. 6 vols., 1614–1754. Paris: D. Jouaust, 1878–88.

Marquette, Father Jacques. *Father Marquette's Journal*. Lansing: Michigan Historical Center, 1998.

Marquette, Jacques. "Map of the New Discovery Made by the Jesuit Fathers in 1672 and Continued by Father Jacques Marquette, from the Same Group, accompanied by a Few Frenchmen in the Year 1673, Named "Manitounie." National Archives of France, 1673. https://www.wdl.org/en/item/15487/, accessed February 17, 2021. JR, (LIX) 108.

_______. "Voyages of Marquette in the Jesuit Relations," 59, with French and English text. March of America facsimile series, Ann Arbor: University Microfilms, 1966.

_______. "Departure of the Father From the Ilinois; of the Painted Monsters Which He Saw Upon the Great River Missisipi; Of the River Pekitanoui. Continuation of the Voyage." In *Travels and Explorations of the Jesuit Missionaries in New France 16-10-1791*, edited by Claude Dablon, 137-41. In *JR and Allied Documents*, edited by Rueben Gold Thwaites, vol. 49. Cleveland: The Burrows Brothers Publishers, 1899. Moses.creighton.edu/kripke/jesuitrelations/relations_59.html#_edn20 (accessed February 16, 2021).

Marquette, Jacques, and Claude Dablon. "Of the First Voyage made by Father Marquette toward New Mexico, and How the Idea Thereof was Conceived." *JR, Document* 28, vol. 59, 139-41, 1674.

______. "Voyages of Marquette, Description of the Calumet." *JR,* vol. 59, 129, 1674.

Marquette, Jacques, and Claude Dablon. "Of the First Voyage made by Father Marquette toward New Mexico, and How the Idea Thereof was Conceived." *JR, Document* 28, vol. 59, 139-41, 1674.

______. "Voyages of Marquette, Description of the Calumet." *JR,* vol. 59, 129, Date?.

Mattes, Merrill J. *The Great Platte River Road: The Covered Wagon Mainline Via Fort Kearny to Fort Laramie*. Publications, 25. Lincoln: Nebraska State Historical Society, 1969.

McGill University. "About McGill, Stephen Leacock." https://www.mcgill.ca (accessed April 25, 2021).

Miera y Pacheco, Bernardo. "Miera's Report to the King of Spain, 1777." In Herbert E. Bolton, *Pageant in the Wilderness*, 243-50. Salt Lake City: Utah State Historical Society, 1950.

______. Plano Geographico de la tierra descubierta nuebamente á los Rumbos Norte, Noroested, y Oeste, del Nuebo México, demarcada por mi Don Bernardo de Miera y Pacheco, á que entro á hacer descubrimiento en compañía de los RR.s PP.s Fr. Francisco Atanaskio Doming.s y Fr. Silbestre Velez ssegun consta en el Diario y Derrotero que se hizo y se remitió á S.Md por mano de su Virrei, con otro Plano á las letra…1778 [map]. Reproduced as inserted map in Bolton, *Pageant in the Wilderness*, 243-50. Salt Lake City: Utah State Historical Society, 1950.

Miller, David E. "The Fur Trade and the Mountain Men." In *Utah's History*, edited by Richard D. Poll, 53-70. Provo: Brigham Young University Press, 1978.

Miller, Wick R. "Numic Languages." In *Great Basin*, edited by Warren L. D'Azevedo, William C. Sturtevant, series editor. 98-106. *Handbook of North American Indians*, vol. 11. Washington, DC: Smithsonian Institution, 1986.

Mink, Claudia Gellman. *Cahokia, City of the Sun: Prehistoric Urban Center in the American Bottom* edited by William Iseminger. Revised edition. Collinsville, Illinois: Cahokia Mounds Museum Society, 1999.

Montagu, M. F. Ashley. *Introduction to Physical Anthropology*. 3rd edition. Springfield, Illinois: Charles C. Thomas, 1960.

Moore, Christopher. "Colonization and Conflict." In *The Illustrated History of Canada*, edited by Craig Brown, 105-88. Toronto: Lester and Orpen Dennys, 1987.

Moulton, Gary E., ed. *The Journals of the Lewis and Clark Expedition*, vol. 2. Lincoln: University of Nebraska Press, 1986.

______. *The Journals of the Lewis and Clark Expedition*, vol. 8. Lincoln: University of Nebraska Press, 1993.

______. *The Journals of the Lewis and Clark Expedition*, vol. 9. Lincoln: University of Nebraska Press, 1995.

Muhs, Daniel, and Vance T. Holiday. "Evidence of Active Dune Sand on the Great Plains in the 19th Century from Accounts of Early Explorers." *Quaternary Research* 43, no. 2 (March 1995): 198–208.

Muhs, Daniel R., James B. Swinehart, David B. Loope, with Josh Been, Shannon A. Mahan, and Charles A. Bush. "Geochemical Evidence for an Eolian Sand Dam Across the North and South Platter Rivers in Nebraska." *Quaternary Research* 53 (2000): 214-99.

National Park Service. "Mississippi River Facts." https:/www.nps.gov/miss/riverfacts.htm; http:/idealibrary.com (accessed May 24, 2017).

NEBRASKAland Magazine, "The Cellars of Time." *NEBRASKAland Magazine* 72, no. 1 (1994). Lincoln: Nebraska Game and Parks Commission.

Nabakov, Peter. *Indian Running*. Santa Barbara: Capra Press, 1981.

Nasatir, A. P., ed. *Before Lewis and Clark: Documents Illustrating the History of the Missouri, 1785–1804*, vol. 1. Lincoln: University of Nebraska Press, 1990.

Neave, Judith Chamberlain. "Lahontan and the Long River Controversy." *Revue de l'Université d'Ottawa* 48 (1978): 124-47.

______. "A Study of Historical Veracity in the Works of the Baron de Lahontan." PhD Diss. University of Toronto, 1979.

Necomb, William W. "Wichita." In *Plains*, edited by Raymond J. DeMallie, William C. Sturtevant, series editor. 548-66. *Handbook of North American Indians*, vol. 13, pt. 1. Washington, DC: Smithsonian Institution, 2001.

Neely, Paula. "Prehistoric Canoe Discovered in Louisiana." *American Archaeology* 21, no. 3 (2017): 9.

Newton, Cody. "Using Euro-American Hunting Data to Assess Western Great Plains Biogeography; 1803–1835." *Great Plains Research* 21 (2011): 17-26.

______. "Native Place, Environment, and the Trade Fort Concentration on the South Platte River, 1835–45." *Ethnohistory* 59, no. 2 (2012): 239-60.

Norall, Frank. *Bourgmont, Explorer of the Missouri, 1698–1725*. Lincoln: University of Nebraska Press, 1988.

Norris, Lola Orellano, ed. and trans. *General Alonso de León's Expeditions into Texas, 1686–1690*. College Station: Texas A&M University Press, 2017.

Nute, Grace Lee. *The Voyageur*. Saint Paul: Minnesota Historical Society Press, 1987.

O'Brien, Michael J., and W. Raymond Wood. *The Prehistory of Missouri*. Columbia: University of Missouri Press, 1998.

Ohnuki-Tierney, Emiko. *The Ainu of the Northwest Coast of Southern Sakhalin*. Prospect Hills, Illinois: Waveland Press, 1974.

Opler, Morris. "The Apachean Culture Pattern and Its Origins." In *Southwest*, edited by Alfonso Ortiz, William C. Sturtevant, series editor. 368-92. *Handbook of North American Indians*, vol. 10. Washington, DC: Smithsonian Institution, 1983.

Ortman, Scott G. "Genes, Language, and Culture in Tewa Ethnogenesis, A.D. 1150–1400." PhD diss. Arizona State University 2009, http://village.anth.wsu.edu/publications/theses (accessed March 13, 2009).

_______. *Winds From the North: Tewa Origins and Historical Anthropology*. Salt Lake City: University of Utah Press, 2012.

Osler, E. B. "Tonty, Henri." In *Dictionary of Canadian Biography*, 2, University of Toronto/Universitė Laval, 2003, http://www.biographi.ca/en/bio/tonty_henri_2E.html (accessed May 1, 2021).

Ouellet, Réal, "Baron of Lahontan," Encyclopedia of French Cultural Heritage in North America, 2007, http://www.ameriquefrancaise.org/en/article-471/Baron_of_Lahontan.html (accessed January 2, 2019).

_______, ed. *Oeuvres Complétes Lahontan: [The complete works of Lahontan]. Edition critique par Réal Ouellet avec la collaboration d'Alain Beaulieu*. Montréal: Presses de l'Université de Montréal, 1990.

Owsley, Douglas W., and David R. Hunt. "Clovis and Early Archaic Crania from the Anzick Site (24PA506)." *Plains Anthropologist* 46, no. 176 (2001): 115-24.

Owsley, Douglas W., and Richard L. Jantz, eds. *Kennewick Man: The Scientific Investigation of an Ancient American Skeleton*. College Station: Texas A&M University Press, 2014.

Paltsits, Victor Hugo. "Lahontan Bibliography." In *New Voyages to North-America*, edited by Rueben Gold Thwaites, li-xciii. New York: Burt Franklin, 1905. Reprint. New York, Lenox Hill, 1970.

Parkman, Francis. *The California and Oregon Trail: Being Sketches of Prairie and Rocky Mountain Life*. George G. Putnam. Republished as *The Oregon Trail*, Penguin Classics, 1985, New York, 1849.

______. *France and England in North America*, vol. 3. Boston: Little, Brown, 1931.

______. "La Salle and the Discovery of the Great West." 1869. Reprint with notes and chronology by David Levin. 1: 713-1055. New York: Library Classics of the United States of America, 1983.

______. *Count Frontenac and New France under Louis*. Boston: Beacon Press, 1966.

Parks, Douglas R. "Enigmatic Groups." In *Plains*, edited by Raymond J. DeMallie, 965-73 *Handbook of North American Indians*, William C. Sturtevant, series editor. vol. 13. Washington, DC: Smithsonian Institution, 2001.

______. "Pawnee." In *Plains*, edited by Raymond J. DeMallie, 965-73 *Handbook of North American Indians*, vol. 13. William C. Sturtevant, series editor. Washington, DC: Smithsonian Institution, 2001.

Patterson, Carol. "Ute Indian Rock Art Maps and Game Drives in Western Colorado: A Preliminary Study of Ute Rock Art Maps in Gunnison Gorge National Conservation Area and Dominguez-Escalante National Conservation Area." In *American Indian Rock Art*, vol. 40, edited by Peggy Whitehead and Mavis Greer, 1195–1214. Ancient Hands Around the World, International Federation of Rock Art Organizations 2013 Proceedings. American Rock Art Research Association, Glendale, Arizona, 2013.

Pauketat, Timothy R. *Ancient Cahokia and the Mississippians*. Cambridge: Cambridge University Press, 2004.

Pauketat, Timothy R., and Thomas E. Emerson. "Introduction: Domination and Ideology in the Mississippian World." In *Cahokia: Domination and Ideology in the Mississippian World*, edited by Timothy R. Pauketat and Thomas E. Emerson, 1-29. Lincoln: University of Nebraska Press, 1997.

Pauketat, Timothy R., and Thomas E. Emerson, eds. *Cahokia: Domination and Ideology in the Mississippian World*. Lincoln: University of Nebraska Press, 1997.

Peabody Museum of Archaeology and Ethnology. "Against the Winds: American Indian Running Traditions." On-Line Exhibition. 1999, http://www.peabody.harvard.edu/menh_running/ (accessed on January 18, 2008).

Perego, U.A., A. Achilli, N. Angerhofer, M. Accetturo, M. Pala, A. Olivieri, B. H. Kashani, et al. "Distinctive Paleo-Indian Migration Routes from Beringia Marked by Two Rare mtDNA Haplogroups." *Current Biology* 19 (2009): 1-8.

Perkins, J. R. *Trails, Rails and War: The Life of General G. M. Dodge*. Indianapolis: Bobbs-Merrill, 1929. Reprint. New York: Arno Press, 1981.

Peyser, Joseph L., and José Brandáo, eds. *Edge of Empire, 1671–1716: Documents of Michilimackinac*. Kalamazoo: Michigan State University Press/Mackinac Island State Park Commission, 2008.

Phillips, Paul Criliser. *The Fur Trade*. Norman: University of Oklahoma Press, 1967.

Pike, Zebulon M. *Exploratory Travels Through the Western Territories of North America*. Denver: W. H. Lawrence, 1889.

Poling, Jim Sr. *The Canoe: An Illustrated History*. Woodstock: The Countryman Press, 2000.

Poll, Richard D., ed. *Utah's History*. Provo: Brigham Young University Press, 1978.

Powell, Joseph F., and Jerome C. Rose. "Report on the Osteological Assessment of the 'Kennewick Man' Skeleton." CENWW.97. Kennewick. In "Report on the Non-destructive Examination, Description and Analysis of the Human Remains from Columbia Park, Kennewick, Washington" [October 1999], National Park Service. http://www.nps.gov/archeology/kennewick/powell_rose.htm (accessed May 5, 2006).

______. "Report on the Osteological Assessment of the 'Kennewick Man' Skeleton." National Park Service Kennewick Man Scientific Investigation. National Park Service Archaeology and Ethnography Program. NPS Center for Cultural Resources. NPS AEP: Kennewick Man Web Page. 1997, http://www.nps.gov/archeology/kennewick/powell_rose.htm (accessed May 5, 2006 and October 10, 2012).

Preuss, Charles. "Topographical Map of the Road from Missouri to Oregon, Commencing at the Mouth of the Kansas in the Missouri River and Ending at the Mouth of the Wallah Wallah in the Columbia" in 7 sections, Section 2, Baltimore: E. Weber & Company, 1846.

Reide, Felix. "Steps Towards Operationalizing and Evolutionary Archaeological Definition of Culture." In *Investigating Archeological Cultures: Material Culture, Variability, and Transmission*, edited by Benjamin W. Roberts and Marc Vaner Linden, 245-70. New York: Springer Science and Business Media, 2011.

Reinhartz, Dennis. "Herman Moll, Geographer: An Early Eighteenth-Century European View of the American Southwest." In *The Mapping of the American Southwest*, edited by Dennis Reinhartz and Charles C. Colley, 18-36. College Station: Texas A&M University Press, 1987.

Reinhartz, Dennis, and Charles C. Colley, eds. *The Mapping of the American Southwest*. Texas A&M College Station: Texas A&M University Press, 1987.

Rhine, Stanley. "Non-Metric Skull Racing." In *Skeletal Attribution of Race: Methods for Forensic Anthropology*, edited by G. W. Gill and S. Rhine, 9-20. Anthropological Papers, 4. Albuquerque: Maxwell Museum of Anthropology, 1990.

Richie, Eleanor Louise. "Spanish Relations with the Yuta Indians, 1680–1822." Master's thesis. University of Denver, 1932.

Rickey, Don, Jr. *Forty Miles a Day on Beans and Hay*. Norman: University of Oklahoma Press, 1963.

Rights, Douglas L., and William P. Cumming. *The Discoveries of John Lederer*, edited by William P. Cumming. Charlottesville: University of Virginia Press, 1958.

Rioux, Jean Roch "Hennepin, Louis." in *Dictionary of Canadian Biography*, vol. 2, University of Toronto/Université Laval, 2003, http://www.biographi.ca/en/bio/hennepin_louis_2E.html (accessed July 3, 2021).

Roch Rioux, Jean "Hennepin, Louis." In *Dictionary of Canadian Biography*, vol. 2, University of Toronto/Université Laval, 2003, http://www.biographi.ca/en/bio/hennepin_louis_2E.html (accessed July 3, 2021),

Ritterbush, Lauren W. "Late Prehistoric Oneota in the Central Plains." In *Kansas Archaeology*, edited by Robert J. Hoard and William E. Bank, 151-64. Lawrence: University Press of Kansas, 2006.

Rolingson, Martha Ann. "Prehistory of the Central Mississippi Valley and Ozarks After 500 B.C." In *Southeast*, edited by Raymond E. Fogelson, 534-44. *Handbook of North American Indians*, William C. Sturtevant, series editor. vol. 14. Washington, DC: Smithsonian Institution, 2004.

Roper, Donna. "The Pawnee in Kansas, Ethnohistory and Archaeology." In *Kansas Archaeology*, edited by Robert J. Hoard and William E. Banks, 233-37. Lawrence: University Press of Kansas, 2006.

Roper, Donna, and Elizabeth P. Pauls, eds. *Plains Earthlodges: Ethnographic and Archaeological Perspectives*. Tuscaloosa: University of Alabama Press, 2005.

Roy, J. Edmond. Le Baron de Lahontan. *Proceeding and Transactions of the Royal Society of Canada for 1894*, section I (1894): 109-65.

Sahlins, Marshall. *Tribesmen*. Prentice-Hall, Englewood Cliffs, New Jersey, 1968.

Sánchez, Joseph P. *Explorers, Traders, and Slavers: Forging the Old Spanish Trail*. Salt Lake City: University of Utah Press, 1997.

______. "The Spanish Search for Teguayo: New Mexico and the Yuta Country, 1678–1778." *Colonial Latin American Historical Review* 14, no. 2 (2005): 135-51.

Sando, Joe S. "The Pueblo Revolt." In *Southwest*, edited by Alfonso Ortiz, 194-97. *Handbook of North American Indians*, William C. Sturtevant, series editor. vol. 9. Washington, DC: Smithsonian Institution, 1979.

Sayre, Gordon M. *Les Sauvages Américains: Representations of Native Americans in French and English Colonial Literature*. Chapel Hill and London: University of North Carolina Press, 1997.

Scheiber, Laura L. "The Late Prehistoric Oneota in the Central Plains." In *Kansas Archaeology*, edited by Robert J. Hoard and William E. Banks., 133-50. Lawrence: University Press of Kansas, 2006.

______. "Life and Death on the Northwestern Plains: Mortuary Practices and Cultural Transformations." In *Skeletal Biology and Bioarchaeology of the Northwestern Plains*, edited by G. W. Gill and R. L. Weathermon, 22-41. Salt Lake City: University of Utah Press, 2008.

Scheiber, Laura L., and George W. Gill. "Bioarchaeology of the Northwestern Plains." In *Archaeological and Bioarchaeological Resources of the Northern Plains*, edited by George C. Frison and Robert C. Mainfort, 91-119. Fayetteville: Arkansas Archaeological Survey, 1996.

Scholes, Francis V. *Troublous Times in New Mexico, 1659–1670*. Albuquerque: Historical Society of New Mexico, 1942.

Schroeder, Albert H., and Omer C. Stewart. "Indian Servitude in the Southwest." In *History of Indian-White Relations*, edited by Wilcomb E. Washburn, William C. Sturtevant series editor. 19-46. *Handbook of North American Indians*, vol. 4. Washington, DC: Smithsonian Institution, 1988.

Schweitzer, Margorie M. "Otoe and Missouria." In *Plains*, edited by Raymond J. DeMallie, William C. Sturtevant series editor. 447-61. *Handbook of North American Indians*, vol 13, pt. 1. Washington, DC: Smithsonian Institution, 2001.

Secoy, Frank Raymond. *Changing Military Patterns on the Great Plains: 17th Century through Early 18th Century*. New York: J. J. Augustin, 1953.

Senior, Nancy. "Translators' Preface." In *The Codex Canadensis and the Writings of Louis Nicolas: The Natural History of the New World*, edited by Francois-Marc Gagnon, 259-65. Tulsa, Montreal, London and Ithaca: Gilcrease Museum and McGill-Queen's University Press, 2011.

Shaffer, James L., and John T. Tigges. *The Mississippi River: Father of Waters*. Chicago: Arcadia, 2000.

Shea, John. G. *Discovery and Exploration of the Mississippi Valley, with the Original Narratives of Marquette, Allouez, Membré, Hennepin, and Anastase Douay*. Redfield, New York: ClintonHall, 1852.

Shoumatoff, Alex. "Flight Club." *Smithsonian* (March 2015): 54-67.

Simmons, Marc. *The Last Conquistador: Juan de Oñate and the Settling of the Far Southwest*. Norman: University of Oklahoma Press, 1991.

Skinner, Claiborne A. *The Upper Country: French Enterprise in the Colonial Great Lakes*. Baltimore: The Johns Hopkins University Press, 2008.

Skotheim, Robert Allen. *The Historian and the Climate of Opinion*. New York: Garland Publishing, Inc., 1985.

Smith, Bruce D. "Introduction: Research on the Origins of Mississippian Chiefdoms in Eastern North America." In *The Mississippi Emergence*, edited by Bruce D. Smith, 1-8. Washington, DC: Smithsonian Institution Press, 1990.

______. *The Mississippian Emergence.* Washington, DC: Smithsonian Institution Press, 1990.

Smith, G. Hubert. *The Explorations of the La Vérendryes in the Northern Plains, 1738–43*, edited by W. Raymond Wood. Lincoln: University of Nebraska Press, 1980.

Smith, Marvin T., and David J. Hally. "Chiefly Behavior: Evidence from Sixteenth Century Spanish Accounts." In *Lords of the Southeast: Social Inequality and the Native Elites of Southeastern North America*, edited by Alex W. Barker and Timothy R. Pauketat, 99-100. Washington, DC: American Anthropological Association, 1992.

Spencer, R. F., and J. D. Jennings. *The Native Americans.* New York: Harper and Row, 1977.

Squier, E. G., and E. H. Davis. *Ancient Monuments of the Mississippi Valley.* Washington, DC: Smithsonian Institution, 1848.

Staley, E. O., and W. J. Wayne. "Epeirogenic and Climatic Controls of Early Pleistocene Fluvial Sediment Dispersal in Nebraska." *Geological Society of America Bulletin* 83 (1972): 3675-90.

Stansbury, Howard. "Exploration of the Valley of the Great Salt Lake of Utah." 32nd Congress, special session, Senate Executive Document, No. 3. Washington, DC, 1853.

Steele, D. Gentry, and Joseph F. Powell. "The Peopling of the Americas: The Paleobiological Evidence." *Human Biology* 64, no. 3 (1992): 303-36.

Steinacher, Terry L., and Gayle F. Carlson. "The Central Plains Tradition." In *Archaeology of the Great Plains*, edited by W. Raymond Wood, 235-68. Lawrence: University Press of Kansas, 1998.

Steward, Julian H. *Basin-Plateau Aboriginal Sociopolitical Groups. Bulletin 120.* Washington, DC: Smithsonian Institution, Bureau of American Ethnology, 1938.

Stewart, T. D. *The People of America.* New York: Charles Scribner's Sons, 1973.

Strong, William Duncan. *An Introduction to Nebraska Archaeology*. Smithsonian Miscellaneous Collections, 93, no. 10. Washington, DC: Smithsonian Institution, 1935.

Stuart, L. Jaimeson, and George W. Gill. "Northwestern Plains Indian Skeletal Remains: Metric Analysis." In *Skeletal Biology and Bioarchaeology of the Northwestern Plains*, edited by G. W. Gill and R. L. Weathermon, 160-176. Salt Lake City: University of Utah Press, 2008.

Sun Tzu. *The Art of War*. Pittsburg: Dorrance Publishing, 2014

Swagerty, William R. "Indian Trade in the Trans-Mississippi West to 1870." In *History of Indian-White Relations*, edited by Wilcomb E. Washburn, William C. Sturtevant series editor. 351-75. *Handbook of North American Indians*, vol. 4. Washington, DC: Smithsonian Institution, 1988.

_______. "History of the United States Plains to 1850." In *Plains*, edited by Raymond J. DeMallie, William C. Sturtevant series editor. 256-79. *Handbook of North American Indians*, vol. 13, pt. 1. Washington, DC: Smithsonian Institution, 2001.

Swanton, John R. The Indian Tribes of North America. *Bureau of American Ethnology, Bulletin* 145. Washington, DC: Smithsonian Institution, 1952.

Swedlund, Alan, and Duane Anderson. "Gordon Creek Woman meets Kennewick Man: New Interpretations and Protocols Regarding the Peopling of the Americas." *American Antiquity* 64, no. 4 (1999): 569-76.

Swift, Johnathon. *Travels Into Several Remote Nations of the World by Lemuel Gulliver*. London: Benjamin Motte, 1726.

Talbot, William, translator and collector. *The Discoveries of John Lederer in Three Several Marches from Virginia to the West of Carolina*. London: Samuel Heyrick, 1672.

Talon, Jean to the King,"Extracts…," CDNY, (1670): 9:64, 189.

Temple, Wayne C. Atlas: Indian Villages of the Illinois Country, *Illinois State Museum Scientific Papers*, 2, no. 1 (1975): supplement.

Thévenot, Melchisedech. *Recueil de Voyages de Mr. Thevenot*. Paris: Estienne Michallet, 1682.

Thevenot, Melchisédec. *Recuel de Voyages de Mr. Thevenot*. Paris: Chez Estienne Michallet ruë S. Jaques à l'image S Paul, 1681.

Thomas, Alfred Barnaby. *Forgotten Frontiers: A Study of the Spanish Indian Policy of Don Juan Bautista de Anza Governor of New Mexico, 1777–1787*. Norman: University of Oklahoma Press, 1932.

______, trans. and ed. *After Coronado: Spanish Exploration Northeast of New Mexico, 1696–1727*. Norman: University of Oklahoma Press, 1935.

______. *Alonso de Posada Report, 1686: A Description of the Area of the Present Southern United States in the Late Seventeenth Century*. Pensacola: The Perdido Bay Press, 1982.

Thomas, Cyrus. "Report on the Mound Explorations of the Bureau of Ethnology," In *12th Annual Report of the Bureau of Ethnology to the Secretary of the Smithsonian Institution*, edited by J. W Powell, 3-720, Washington, DC: Smithsonian Institution, 1894.

______. "Who Were the Moundbuilders?" *American Antiquarian and Oriental Journal* 2 (1885): 65-74, Chicago.

______. "Report on the Mound Explorations of the Bureau of Ethnology." Classics of Smithsonian, Anthropology. 1894. Reprint. Washington, DC: Smithsonian Institution, 1985.

Thornbury, William D. *Regional Geomorphology of the United States*. New York: John Wiley and Sons, 1965.

Thwaites, Reuben Gold. *How George Rogers Clark Won the Northwest and Other Essays in Western History*. Chicago: A. C. McClurg & Co., 1903. Reprint. Freeport, New York: Books for Libraries Press, 1970.

______. "Introduction." In *New Voyages to North-America, by the Baron Lahontan*. 1905. Reprint of the 1905 facsimile edition of the original 1703 English edition. 2 vols., 1: ix-xlix. New York: Burt Franklin, 1970.

Towle, Edward L. and George A. Rawlyk, eds. "A New Baron de Lahontan Memoir on New York and the Great Lakes Basin." *New York History*, 46, no. 3 (July 1965): 212-29.

Twitchell, Ralph Emerson. *The Spanish Archives of New Mexico*, vol. 2. Cedar Rapids: The Torch Press, 1914.

Tyler, S. Lyman. "Before Escalante: An Early History of the Yuta Indians and the Area North of New Mexico." PhD diss. Dept. oof History, University of Utah, 1951.

______. "The Myth of the Lake of Copala and Land of Teguayo." *Utah Historical Quarterly* 20, no. 4 (1952): 313-29.

Tyler, S. Lyman, and H. Darrel Taylor. "The Report of Fray Alonso de Posada in Relation to Quivera and Teguayo." *New Mexico Historical Review* 33, no. 4 (1958): 285-314.

Tzu, Sun. *The Art of War*. Translated by Lionel Giles, Pax Librorum. First Published 1910. Toronto: Magoria Books, 2009.

U.S. Geological Survey. *Map of the Region Occupied by the Ancient Ruins in Southern Colorado, Utah, and Northern New Mexico and Arizona* U.S. Geological and Geographical Survey of the Territories, 10th Annual Report. Washington, DC: U.S. Geological Survey, 1878.

U.S. National Park Service. *Draft National Historic Trail Feasibility Study and Environmental Assessment: Old Spanish Trail: New Mexico, Colorado, Utah, Arizona, Nevada, California*. Denver: National Park Service, 2000.

U.S. National Parks Service. Mississippi River Facts.

United States Department of State. *An Account of Louisiana Being an Abstract of Documents in the Office of the Departments of State and of the Treasury*. Philadelphia: William Duane, 1803.

Villaescusa, Julián. *Monograíia de las aguas y banos minerals de Alange*. Madrid: Tip. De D. Saavedra y Compañía, Madrid, 1923. Reprint. New York: Nabu Press, 2012.

Verner, Coolie, and Basil Stuart-Stubbs. *The Northpart of America*. Don Mills, Ontario: Academic Press, 1979.

Villiers du Terrage, Marc de. *La decouverte du Missouri et l'histoire du Fort d'Orleans (1673–1728)*. Paris: Librairie Ancienne Honoré Champion, 1925.

_______. *The Discovery of the Missouri and the History of Fort Orleans, 1673–1728*, translated by Harriet Hopkins. N.P.: n.p., n.d. (copy in the library of the Missouri State Historical Society, Columbia).

Wagner, Henry Raup. *The Spanish Southwest, 1542–1794*.Albuuerque: Quivera Society, 1937. Reprint. New York: Arno Press, 1967.

Walthall, John A., and Thomas E. Emerson, editors. *Calumet and Fleur-de-Lys: Archaeology of Indian and French Contact in the Midcontinent*. Washington, D.C: Smithsonian Institution Press, 1992.

Warhus, Mark. *Another America, Native American Maps and the History of Our Land*. New York: St. Martin's Press, 1997.

Waring, Antonio J., Jr., and Preston Holder. "The Southeastern Ceremonial Complex In The Southeastern United States." In *The Waring Papers: The Collected Works of Antonio J. Waring, Jr.* edited by Stephen Williams,.9-30. The Peabody Museum, Harvard University and University of Georgia Press, 1965.

Warner, Ted J., ed. "Editor's Introduction." In *The Domínguez-Escalante Journal*, translated by Fray Angélico Chávez and edited by Ted J. Warner, xii-xix. Provo: Young University Press, 1976.

Waselkov, Gregory A. "Indian Maps of the Colonial Southeast." *In Powhatan's Mantle: Indians in the Colonial Southeast*, edited by P. H. Wood, G. A. Waselkov, and M. T. Hatley, 292–343. Lincoln: University of Nebraska Press, 2006.

Waselkow, Gregory A., Peter H. Wood, and Tom Hatley, eds. and introduction. *Powhatan's Mantle: Indians in the Colonial Southeast*. Lincoln: University of Nebraska Press, 2006.

Weber, Michael. "A Map to Bait the French." *El Palacio* 76, no. 1. (1969): 29-32.

Weddle, Robert S. *The French Thorn: Rival Explorers in the Spanish Sea*. College Station: Texas A&M University Press, 1991.

______. *The Wreck of the Belle: The Ruin of LaSalle*. College Station: Texas A&M University Press, 2001.

Wedel, Mildred M. *The Wichita Indians, 1541–1750: Ethnological Essays*. Reprints in Anthropology 38. Lincoln: J&L Reprint Company, 1988.

Wedel, Mildred Mott. *The Deer Creek Site, Oklahoma: A Wichita Village Sometimes Called Ferdinandia*. Oklahoma City: Oklahoma Historical Society, 1981.

______. "Iowa." In *Plains*, edited by Raymond J. DeMallie, William C. Sturtevant series editor. 432-47. *Handbook of North American Indians*, vol. 1. Washington, DC: Smithsonian Institution, Bureau of American Ethnology, 2001.

Wedel, Waldo R. *An Introduction to Pawnee Archeology*. Bulletin 112, Smithsonian Institution. Washington. 1936.

______. "Coronado's Route to Quivera, 1541." *Plains Anthropologist* 15, (49) (1970): 161-68.

Weilbrenner, Bernard. "Morel de la Durantaye, Olivier." In *Dictionary of Canadian Biography*, vol. 2. University of Toronto/Université Laval, 2003, http://www.biographi.ca/en/bio/morel_de_la_durantaye_olivier_2E.html (accessed March 4, 2021).

Wheat, Carl I. *Mapping the Transmississippi West, 1540–1861*, vol. 1. San Francisco: Institute of Historical Cartography, 1957.

White, Richard. *The Middle Ground: Indians, Empires and Republics in the Great Lakes Region, 1650–1815*. New York: Cambridge University Press, 2011.

White, T. D., M. T. Black, and P. A. Folkens. *Human Osteology*. Boston: Elsevier Academic Press, 2012.

Wikipedia. "Sloop." https://en.wikipedia.org/wiki/Sloop (accessed June 22, 2017).

______. "Great Plains." https://en.wikipedia.org/wiki/Great_Plains#Paleontology (accessed July 20, 2017).

______. "Mississippian Culture." https://en.wikipedia.org/wiki/Mississippian_culture (accessed March 18, 2019).

______. "Platte River." https://en.wikipedia.org/wiki/Platte_River (accessed September 14, 2020).

______. "Grand Portage National Monument." https://www.npw.gov/grpo/index.htm (accessed November 10, 2020).

______. "The Villasur Expedition." https://en.wiki/Villasur_expedition (accessed November 27, 2020).

______. "Moundbuilders." https://en.wikipedia.org/wiki/Mound_Builders (accessed January 29, 2021).

______. "Tanoan Languages." https://en.wikipedia.org/wiki/Tanoan_languages (accessed January 30, 2021).

______. "King William's War." https://en.wikipedia.org/wiki/King_William%27s_War (accessed March 15, 2021).

______. "Stephen Leacock." https://en.wikipedia.org/wiki/Stephen_Leacock (accessed April 25, 2021).

Willey, Gordon R., and Jeremy A. Sabloff. *A History of American Archaeology*. San Francisco: W. H. Freeman and Company, 1974.

Williams, Gwyn A. *MADOC The Making of a Myth*. Eyre Methuen, England, 1979.

Williams, Joseph. "Narrative of a Tour from the State of Indiana to the Oregon Territory, in the Years 1841-42." In *To the Rockies and Oregon, 1839–1842; With diaries and accounts by Sidney Smith, Amos Cook, Joseph Holman, E. Willard Smith, Francis Fletcher, Joseph Wiliiams...and the Rockies historical series 1820–1875*, edited by LeRoy R. Hafen and Ann W. Hafen, pp 34-39. Glendale, Calif.: Arthur H. Clark, 1955.

Williams, Stephen. "Foreword." In *The Mississippian Emergence*, edited by Bruce D. Smith, xv-xvii. Washington, DC: Smithsonian Institution Press, 1990.

Windsor, Justin. "Baron La Hontan, a bibliographical and critical note by the editor." In *Narrative and Critical History of Americ*a, vol. 4, by Justin Windsor, 257-62. Cambridge: The Riverside Press, 1884.

Wood, Peter H. "A Venture to the Plantation of the Sun: Lahontan's 1688 Journey Across Iowa and Beyond." *Journal of the Iowa Archaeological Society* 62 (2015): 1-12.

Wood, W. Raymond, ed. *Archaeology on the Great Plains*. Lawrence: Kansas University Press, 1998.

______. *Prologue to Lewis & Clark: The Mackay and Evans Expedition*. Norman: University of Oklahoma Press, 2003.

______. "A Review of Past Criticisms and the Baron Lahontan's Mapping of His Long River." Abstract. Part 2 in the two-part symposium: Reconsidering the Authenticity of the Baron Lahontan's Account of His Longue (Platte) River Journey of 1688–1689, by Steven G. Baker and W. Raymond Wood. Paper read at the 64th Annual Meeting of the Great Plains Anthropological Conference Topeka, 2006, http://www.academia.edu/5172780/A (accessed December 3, 2016). Unpublished manuscript in author's possession.

______. *A White-Bearded Plainsman: The Memoirs of Archaeologist W. Raymond Wood*. Salt Lake City: University of Utah Press, 2011.

______. W. Raymond Wood, 1931–2020. *The Columbia Daily Tribune*. October 5, 2020. https://www.columbiatribune.com/obituaries/story-obituaries-2020-10-06-w-raymond-wood-1931-2020-114226164 (accessed March 9, 2021).

______. "Ethnohistory and Euro-American Contact in Missouri." *Missouri Archaeologist* 74 (December 2013): 7-35. Table 3, 43

Young, Gloria A., and Michael P. Hoffman. *The Expedition of Hernando de Soto West of the Mississippi, 1541–1543*. Fayetteville: University of Arkansas Press, 1993.

Zárate Salmerón, fray Gerónimo de. *Relaciones*, translated by Alicia Ronstadt Milich. Albuquerque: Horn and Wallace Publishers, 1966.

Zitt, Jennifer O. "Prehistoric and Early Historic Subsistence Patterns and Dental Pathology on the Northwestern Plains." Master's thesis. University of Wyoming, Laramie, 1992.

ABOUT THE AUTHORS AND TRANSLATOR

Steven G. Baker (1945–2024) was a native Kansan who earned his BA in anthropology from the University of Kansas and his MA in American History from the University of South Carolina. Baker is an independent, locally focused Colorado scholar who has worked as an archaeologist (Registered Professional #10537) and ethnohistorian for nearly 60 years. He worked in Canada for Parks Canada in the 1960s and gained experience in French Canadian colonial history and archaeology. He is the founder and president of Centuries Research, Inc. of Montrose, Colorado, one of the first cultural resource management firms established in the United States. Early in his career he conducted much trail research—including that for John Lederer, John Lawson, and Hernando DeSoto—and is credited for having been the first to correctly plat the Native landscape of South Carolina, including the location of the paramount chiefdom of Cofitachique from the DeSoto expedition. His most recent significant contributions within a long bibliography extending back to 1967 are *Juan Rivera's Colorado, 1765: The First Spaniards Among the Ute and Paiute Indians on the Trails to Teguayo* (Western Reflections Publishing 2015, and Finalist for Colorado Book Award in history, 2017) and "Protohistoric and Historic Native Americans," In *Colorado History: A Context for Historical Archaeology* (Colorado Council of Professional Archaeologists, 2007) and *My Name Is Pacomio, Colorado's Sheep Herder Artist*, (Western Reflections Publishing, 2017; new edition, Sunstone Press, 2024). His special interests and skill sets lie in historical archaeology, trail research, American Culture of the Victorian Era, and the early post-contact period of the American Indian, especially the Catawba People of South Carolina and the Utes of Colorado.

George W. Gill (1941–) is a native Kansan who earned his BA with Honors in zoology from the University of Kansas. After which he entered military service as a U.S. Army Combat Ranger from which he received an honorable discharge as a captain. He earned his PhD in anthropology with a fellowship from the University of Kansas in 1971 and joined the anthropology faculty at the University of Wyoming where he taught physical anthropology and researched until his recent retirement and award of emeritus status. Dr. Gill has excavated and studied several hundred human skeletons from tropical west Mexico, Easter Island, and the northern Great plains of North America. He is as a Fellow of the American Academy of Forensic Sciences and has served as a director on the national certification board for forensic anthropologists. In the late 1980s, partly in response to demands from American forensic anthropology to scrutinize methods of racial identification in order to ensure accuracy in legal cases, Gill tested, supported, and developed craniofacial anthropometric and other means of estimating the racial origins of skeletal remains. He found that the employment of multiple criteria can yield very high rates of accuracy, and even that individual methods can be accurate more than 80 percent of the time. His many publications include: "Paleoamerican Skeletal Features Surviving into the Late Plains Archaic." In *New Perspectives on the First Americans* (Center for the Study of the First Americans, 2004).

W. Raymond Wood (1931–2020) was a native of Nebraska. He earned his BA and MA in anthropology at the University of Nebraska and his PhD in anthropology from the University of Oregon in 1960. He taught anthropology at the University of Missouri from 1963 to 2001 and then retired as a member of the Emeritus Faculty. After his retirement he remained deeply involved in archaeological and ethnohistorical research in Missouri and in each of the states that touch the Missouri River. He became a renowned ethnohistorian and powerful and highly respected voice in the archaeology of the Great Plains. Wood specialized in Lewis and Clark and their predecessor expeditions; the explorations of Prince Maximilian and the products of his artist-companion, Karl Bodmer; early mapping of the Missouri River; and studies of the Native Americans that lived along the Missouri, especially the Mandans and Hidatsas in present North Dakota. During the course of his career he produced an immense and truly legendary volume of salient literature and received many awards. These included the Lifetime Achievement Award from the Society for American Archaeology, and the Distinguished Service Award from the State Historical Society of Missouri and the Plains Anthropological Society; as well as honors from major states in which he worked and from Indian Tribes, such as the Mandan. Among Woods' many books are *Prologue to Lewis and Clark* (University of Oklahoma Press, 2002), *Karl Bodmer's Studio Art* (University of Illinois Press, 2003), and *The Memoirs of Archaeologist W. Raymond Wood* (University of Utah Press, 2011). Wood died in Columbia, Missouri in 2020.

Rick Hendricks (BA, PhD), Author of Foreword, was the New Mexico state historian and now is the Director of the State Records Center and Archives. He is a professional historian, editor, and Spanish translator trained in history and Ibero American Studies. For many years he was an editor of the Vargas Project at the University of New Mexico. His many published works on the history of the American Southwest and Mexico include co-authoring the award-winning book, *The Witches of Abiquiu, 1750–1766,* published by University of New Mexico Press in 2006.

Claude J. Fouillade (1946–2020), **Translator,** was a native of Paris, France. He was first educated at the Sorbonne and then served as an officer and English instructor in the French Air Force before completing his PhD in Romance Languages (Medieval French Literature) at the University of New

Mexico. Fouillade taught language studies at the University level for over fifty years, including the last thirty-five years at New Mexico State University, where he served for some years as Chair of the Language Department and taught thousands of students French, Spanish, Latin, and French culture. He retired from NMSU in 2018 as Professor Emeritus. Beyond the classroom, Claude was immensely passionate in his research and writing on Francophone cultures in the Americas, medieval literature, interdisciplinary studies on 19th century France, creative writing (short story, poetry and film script), and translation about which he published numerous works. He died in Las Cruces, New Mexico in 2020.

INDEX

www.ingramcontent.com/pod-product-compliance
Lightning Source LLC
LaVergne TN
LVHW081250100826
845148LV00009B/1186